SOCIAL WORK PRACTICE FOR PROMOTING HEALTH AND WELLBEING

Promoting health and wellbeing is an essential part of all effective social work – not just for practice in healthcare settings. In fact, the IFSW holds that 'social workers in all settings are engaged in health work' and physical and mental resilience can make a major difference to all service users' lives.

Drawing on international literature and research, the authors collected here encourage thinking about the social, political, cultural, emotional, spiritual, economic and spatial aspects of health and wellbeing, and how they impact on the unique strengths and challenges of working with particular populations and communities. Divided into three parts, the first section outlines the major theoretical paradigms and critical debates around social work and ideas of wellbeing, globalization, risk and vulnerability, and the natural environment. The second part goes on to explore how diverse understandings of culture, identity, spirituality and health require different strategies for meeting health and wellbeing needs. The final part presents a variety of examples of social work research in relation to health and wellbeing with specific populations, including mental health.

Exploring how structural inequality, oppression and stigma can impact upon people, and drawing upon a social model of health, this book is an important read for all practitioners and researchers interested in social work, public health and social inclusion.

Liz Beddoe is Associate Professor of Social Work at the University of Auckland, New Zealand. Her teaching and research interests include critical perspectives on social work education, professional supervision, the professionalization project of social work, interprofessional learning and media framing of social problems.

Jane Maidment is Senior Lecturer in the Department of Human Services and Social Work at the University of Canterbury, New Zealand. She has been a practitioner in the health sector and has researched and written extensively in the areas of field education, aged care and craft as a vehicle for social connectedness. She currently coordinates field education and teaches practice skills, field integration and theory for practice.

SOCIAL WORK PRACTICE FOR PROMOTING HEALTH AND WELLBEING

Critical issues

Edited by
Liz Beddoe and Jane Maidment

Routledge
Taylor & Francis Group

LONDON AND NEW YORK

First published 2014
by Routledge
2 Park Square, Milton Park, Abingdon, Oxon, OX14 4RN

and by Routledge
711 Third Avenue, New York, NY 10017

Routledge is an imprint of the Taylor & Francis Group, an informa business

British Library Cataloguing-in-Publication Data
A catalogue record for this book is available from the British Library

Library of Congress Cataloging-in-Publication Data

Social work practice for promoting health and wellbeing : critical issues /
   [edited by] Liz Beddoe, Jane Maidment. — 1st Edition.
      pages cm
   1. Social service.   I. Beddoe, Liz, 1956– editor of compilation.
II. Maidment, Jane, editor of compilation.
HV40.S61953   2014
361.3'2—dc23   2013026253

ISBN: 978-0-415-53520-5 (hbk)
ISBN: 978-0-415-53521-2 (pbk)
ISBN: 978-0-203-11281-6 (ebk)

Typeset in Bembo
by Apex CoVantage, LLC

Printed and bound in the United States of America by
Edwards Brothers Malloy

CONTENTS

FIGURES

TABLES

NOTES ON CONTRIBUTORS

The editors

Liz Beddoe is Associate Professor of Social Work at the University of Auckland, New Zealand. Her teaching and research interests include critical perspectives on social work education, professional supervision, the professionalization project of social work, interprofessional learning and media framing of social problems. Liz has published articles on supervision and professional issues in New Zealand and international journals and co-authored *Best Practice in Professional Supervision: A Guide for the Helping Professions* (Jessica Kingsley, 2010) with Allyson Davys and *Mapping Knowledge for Social Work Practice: Critical Intersections*, with Jane Maidment (Cengage, 2009), and co-edited *Promoting Health and Well-being in Social Work Education* with Beth Crisp (Routledge, 2013).

Jane Maidment is Senior Lecturer in the Department of Human Services and Social Work at the University of Canterbury, New Zealand. She has been a practitioner in the health sector and has researched and written extensively in the areas of field education, aged care and craft as a vehicle for social connectedness. She co-authored with Liz Beddoe *Mapping Knowledge for Social Work: Critical Intersections* (Cengage, 2009); co-edited with Ronnie Egan *Practice Skills for Social Work and Welfare* (Allen & Unwin, 2009), and co-edited with Uschi Bay *Social Work in Rural Australia* (Allen & Unwin, 2013). Jane currently coordinates field education and teaches practice skills, field integration and theory for practice.

The contributors

Carole Adamson is Senior Lecturer in Social Work at the University of Auckland, New Zealand where her research and teaching focus on mental health, trauma, resilience and stress. She has research interests in developing resilient practitioners and in social work curriculum for disaster preparation and response. She has been a mental health social worker and also has experience in community development and residential social work. Carole sees as a major focal point in her work the articulation of theoretical perspectives and frameworks for social work practice that can integrate current, contextually-aware best practice and which can effectively be applied in practice settings.

Jim Anglem was Senior Lecturer in the Department of Human Services and Social Work at the University of Canterbury, New Zealand between the years of 2000 and 2011. He taught biculturalism and multiculturalism and writes on matters related to racism. Jim is Ngai Tahu Māori. He is currently Senior Lecturer in Research and Innovation and is a member of the Māori Research advisory group. He is also Kaumatua and board member for the Aotearoa New Zealand Association of Social Workers.

Uschi Bay is Senior Lecturer in the Department of Social Work at Monash University, Australia and a researcher with the Department's Gender, Leadership and Social Sustainability (GLASS) Research unit. Her research focuses on social and ecological sustainability, social movements, rural and remote communities, gender relations, transformative leadership and the role of practice theory in framing processes of critical reflexivity for students, allied health practitioners and community based organizations. Uschi is currently working with the Transition Town Movement in Australia, exploring its governance, gender relations and carbon emission reduction strategies.

Paul Bywaters is Professor of Social Work at Coventry University and Honorary Professor at the University of Warwick, England. He co-founded and was the first convenor of the Social Work and Health Inequalities Network in 2004, and led the writing of the International Federation of Social Workers policy on health (with Lindsey Napier). He has been researching and writing about social work and health for over 25 years. Publications include the co-authored *Social Work Health and Equality* (2000) and the co-edited *Social Work and Global Health Inequalities* (2009).

Michelle Courtney is Senior Lecturer in Occupational Science and Therapy at Deakin University, Australia. Prior to taking up this role in 2003, Michelle worked in a range of occupational therapy clinical, management and consultancy positions. She has published on professional issues (competence, mentoring and student transition to practice) and wellbeing for women participating in craft. More recently, Michelle has focused her research activities on the occupational perspective of contemporary pilgrimage and the experience of wellbeing.

Phil Crane is Senior Lecturer in Youth Services in the School of Public Health and Social Work at Queensland University of Technology, Australia. Over the past twenty years he has undertaken a wide range of community and place based research and consultancy projects related to young people and public space, many using action research and participatory approaches.

Viviene E. Cree is Professor of Social Work at the University of Edinburgh, Scotland. She has published extensively in social work-related fields over the last 20 years. Her main research focus is on qualitative research which aims to improve social work services, and hence, the lives of those who use the services. Viviene has specialised in research on social work history, feminism and gender in social work, and on HIV and children and young people affected by parental illness. Current research includes a cross-UK, inter-disciplinary Research Seminar Series investigating twenty-first century moral panics and a Knowledge Exchange in Scotland. Both are sponsored by the Economic & Social Research Council (ESRC).

Yvonne Crichton-Hill is Lecturer in the Department of Human Services and Social Work at the University of Canterbury, New Zealand. She has experience in social work practice with families and Pacific communities. Her areas of research and practice interest are culturally responsive social work practice, particularly in the areas of intimate partner violence and child welfare. She is a past Chair and current board member of Pacific Trust Canterbury, a Pacific health and social service provider based in Christchurch. Yvonne is of Samoan descent.

Christa Fouché is Associate Professor of Social Work at the University of Auckland, New Zealand. She has held positions as practitioner, educator, manager and researcher in the fields of chronic illness, HIV/AIDS and aged care. Her teaching and research expertise centres on capacity building in the social services workforce, including inter-disciplinary and collaborative initiatives. Christa has published in local and international journals and presented at various international conferences. Her chapter is informed by a funded, inter-disciplinary and inter-university research project on health professionals' competencies in the field of chronic illness.

Linda Haultain has provided professional leadership for social workers in a large New Zealand health service for over seven years. During this period of her career Linda undertook doctoral research exploring 'what is effective social work in an acute hospital context?' She has a passion for supporting health social workers to make the most effective contribution they can, in a context which historically has proven challenging for the profession. Linda's response continues to be focused on cultivating the profession's ability to articulate and demonstrate excellence in health social work practice.

Jay Marlowe is Senior Lecturer in the School of Counselling, Human Services and Social Work at the University of Auckland, New Zealand. Formerly a visiting fellow with the Refugee Studies Centre at the University of Oxford, he has published numerous papers on resettlement issues related to people's sense of wellbeing, identit(ies) and how their experiences relate to the wider society living around them. He is the lead editor of a forthcoming book entitled *South Sudanese Diaspora in Australia and New Zealand* and is currently leading a project on refugee background community responses to the Christchurch earthquakes.

Tanya McCall works part-time as the Manager of the Health in all Policies Team at Community and Public Health, New Zealand. Prior to this role, she worked as a litigation solicitor. Tanya holds a Bachelor of Arts degree and a Bachelor of Laws degree. She is currently undertaking study towards a postgraduate Diploma in Public Health. Tanya is of Samoan and Cook Island descent. She is the Chair of the Pacific Reference Group, Deputy Chair of Pacific Trust Canterbury and a member of the Pegasus Community Board.

Judith L. M. McCoyd is Associate Professor at Rutgers University's School of Social Work, New Jersey. Her research lies at the intersection of perinatal health care, medical technologies, decision-making and bereavement. Judith's research is also used to develop theory about social work practice, decision making and normative culture, and qualitative methodology. She is a licensed clinical social worker (Pennsylvania) who maintains a small clinical practice and serves in leadership roles with the National Association of Perinatal Social Workers.

Selma Macfarlane is Lecturer in Social Work at Deakin University, Australia. Her PhD from RMIT University explored the experience of support and recovery in a therapeutic community. Her interests include mental health, women's experiences across the lifespan, and social work theory and practice. She is also interested in the role of higher education more generally and the knowledge systems that underpin research in the postgraduate area. Selma is currently co-authoring an introductory textbook on critical social work.

Helen Meekosha is Associate Professor in the School of Social Sciences at the University of New South Wales, Australia. Her major research areas are situated in Critical Disability Studies and cover gender issues, the global South, the indigenous experiences of disability, welfare/workfare and the politics of care. Her work in Critical Disability Studies has broken new ground in setting disability in a context of neo-liberalism and globalization, in particular arguing the case for an examination of global North/South relations that affect the incidence and production of disability.

Lorraine Muller is Indigenous Australian, born on Kalkadoon country, raised in the Torres Strait and living on Girramay country in Australia. Her research interests include Indigenous knowledge, theory, practice and spirituality; decolonization; non-Indigenous mainstream Australian culture and intergenerational communication. Lorraine is a qualified social worker and her first PhD documented Indigenous Australian social-health theory, the theory that informs Indigenous Australians in the helping profession, and her second doctoral study shifts the research lens to explore non-Indigenous mainstream Australian culture.

Hong-Jae Park is Lecturer in the School of Counselling, Human Services and Social Work at the University of Auckland, New Zealand. He is also a registered social worker. As a native of South Korea, he has extensive experience in practice and research in the human services field. His areas of research interest include migration, ethics and justice, and ageing. He is particularly active in gerontological research in the areas of filial piety and elder abuse among different ethnic groups. He has a committed and passionate approach to synthesizing social values and practices across Eastern and Western cultures.

Joy Phillips is currently undertaking her PhD at Deakin University, Australia. Her study explores the experiences of same-sex attracted women and lesbians in the residential aged care context in Australia and she has published articles in this area. She has worked in diverse fields of practice and with people who are vulnerable and marginalized. She is currently working in aged care.

Karen Soldatic is a researcher in the School of Social Sciences at the University of New South Wales, Australia. Her main area of research traverses critical issues of social categorization and practices of value-oriented identity formation, attempting to capture the structural and agential mechanisms in their ambiguity, fragility and opacity and the ways in which social actors collectively mobilize to resist, confront and transform these processes and mechanisms. Hence, her research is always concerned with social movement mobilisation, policy dynamism and transformation for a just society.

Andrew Thompson teaches at the University of Auckland and is a social worker with the Consult Liaison Psychiatry Team at Starship Children's Hospital in Auckland, New Zealand. His work involves consulting with children, their families and staff across the hospital on issues relating to trauma adjustment, coping and adapting to treatment, and grief. Andrew was a founding member of the Paediatric Palliative Care team and established the first Bereavement Service at Starship. He continues to provide education and training in these fields of practice. Andrew has over 30 years of social work experience and is a Trustee of the Auckland Grief Centre.

Genevieve Togiaso currently works at Christchurch Polytechnic Institute of Technology in the Department of Nursing and Human Services, New Zealand. She has a wealth of experience in delivering in the health sector for close to 20 years as a nurse and more recently as a senior service manager for Pacific Trust Canterbury. Genevieve is a member of the Aniva Whitireia Pacific Nursing Leaders Fellowship. She was honoured by the Christchurch City Council with an award in recognition of "Heroism and Service" during and following the Christchurch earthquakes. Genevieve is of Samoan descent.

1

SOCIAL WORK PRACTICE FOR PROMOTING HEALTH AND WELLBEING

Liz Beddoe and Jane Maidment

Introduction: social work and health

Health is intrinsically part of being human – we experience our lives with our bodies and minds. The quality of our lives is inextricably bound up with our health and wellbeing which, in turn, incorporates physical, psychological, emotional, cultural, social and spiritual dimensions. Since the inception of the World Health Organisation (WHO), health has been conceptualised as broadly encompassing these dimensions and thus as much more than the absence of disease (WHO, 1948).

Social work involvement in healthcare, through government, not-for-profits and private sector services is a significant field of practice for our profession. Large numbers of social workers in New Zealand and Australia (as well as the United States, Canada and South Africa) are engaged in a broad range of health-related settings. Health spans not only clinical/medical settings but also community-based mental health and healthcare environments, drug and alcohol services, aged care services, end-of-life care and health and development services for children and families. Social workers are confronted with health-related issues across all fields of practice, including the criminal justice system, working with young people, migrant and refugee services, grief and loss issues, disability services, reproductive health and the health of older adults. Social workers' understanding of health and wellbeing fits comfortably with those wider descriptions offered by such seminal definitions as those offered by the influential Ottawa Charter for Health Promotion. This charter outlined an agenda which positioned health as a valuable resource, and recognised the contributions needed beyond the health sector in the promotion of health and wellbeing:

> Health promotion is the process of enabling people to increase control over, and to improve, their health. To reach a state of complete physical, mental and social wellbeing, an individual or group must be able to identify and to

realize aspirations, to satisfy needs, and to change or cope with the environment. Health is, therefore, seen as a resource for everyday life, not the objective of living. Health is a positive concept emphasizing social and personal resources, as well as physical capacities. Therefore, health promotion is not just the responsibility of the health sector, but goes beyond healthy life-styles to well-being. (WHO, 1986)

In 2008 the profession approved the IFSW Policy Statement on Health, which declares health to be an international social work issue. This important document states that health 'is an issue of fundamental human rights and social justice and binds social work to apply these principles in policy, education, research and practice' (2008, p. 1). Globally, recent research has identified the complexity of the interaction between socioeconomic status and social participation and the overall health and wellbeing of people, families and communities (Rose and Hatzenbuehler, 2009). The mission of social work to work towards improving the lives of all people through a reduction of inequalities brings health into the heart of social work. Bywaters, McLeod and Napier have significantly argued that 'Social work in all settings is concerned with the impact on people's lives of the social forces which determine health chances and health experience. . . . all social work has health impacts' (2009, p. 11). Bywaters and Napier emphatically suggest that:

> Social work is health work. . . . [s]ocial workers in all settings engage every day with children, men and women struggling to realize their basic rights to health. It is not only social workers in health settings such as hospitals or clinics who must be concerned with health issues. (Bywaters and Napier, 2009, p. 453)

Social workers are constantly challenged to integrate 'health thinking' into their work; Pockett and Beddoe (in press) have suggested that one approach is to include such thinking throughout the social work assessment process and the documentation of practice. For example, a social worker working in child welfare may acknowledge that inequitable access to healthcare for rural children with serious illness may lead to severe family hardship. Support and financial assistance needs are perceived as both a family problem requiring response but also as an indicator of a larger health inequity. Giles (2009) suggests that social workers develop a 'health equality imagination'. Practitioners can foreground the cumulative impact of health inequalities in the daily lives of children and families often obscured by a focus on neglect or abuse.

Generally, the engagement of social work in health has been focussed around hospital and home-based intervention related to illness and disability, but there is great potential for social work to reconceptualise health's significance in all social services work. Current trends towards strengthening primary health care underscore the need for social workers to have a broad understanding of health and wellbeing incorporating physical, social, emotional, cultural, spiritual, environmental and economic dimensions. This focus supports an understanding of the unique strengths and challenges of working with particular populations and communities. If the centrality of health in people's lives provides a strong rationale for seeing health as a central dimension of social work, then a second and equally important element is that 'health is primarily a product of social determinants such as food, water, income, housing, a safe environment and education' (Bywaters and Napier, 2009, p. 453).

The purpose and scope of this book

We are New Zealand social work educators and researchers who have practised in health settings with lifelong interests in health and wellbeing. Our aim was to deliver an internationally relevant book to support the dissemination of new research and thinking about health, wellbeing, and the social, political, cultural, emotional, spiritual and spatial aspects of health. *Social Work Practice for Promoting Health and Wellbeing* addresses this broad commitment to educating social workers about health, beyond the traditional text-book approach which has been to focus on sickness and medical treatment. We wanted to avoid chapters which referred to particular illnesses and to shift attention to a broad conceptualisation of health as a social good while acknowledging the focus of social work practitioners and researchers on issues of everyday lived experience of individuals, families and communities struggling with illness, trauma, disabling environments, poverty and environmental determinants. We were also moved to action by the growing awareness of health issues in the international social work arena, namely the International Federation of Social Workers (IFSW) Global Agenda for Social Work and the IFSW Policy Statement on Health (IFSW, 2008). These two key documents underpinned a starting point for us that awareness of health is central to human wellbeing and this has been underscored in many of the contributions to this book.

At the heart of our book is a framework drawing on notions of resilience, connectedness and relationship using progressive ideas and contemporary theory. We have encouraged our contributing authors to strike a balance between issues of structural inequality, oppression and stigma and the impact of these on the wellbeing of citizens while drawing upon a holistic, multifaceted and intrinsically social model of health. As such we asked authors to consider the emotional and interpersonal impact of health changes in peoples' lives within cultural, political and economic contexts. We asked each author to address two or three of the following themes: theory for health practice; critical perspectives on health including stigma, risk and vulnerability; culture, spirituality and diversity; issues of space and place; sustainability and resilience for individuals, families and communities; and collaborative practices.

Organisation of Social work practice for promoting health and wellbeing

The book is organised into three sections. The first, 'Current themes and critical issues' explores the major theoretical paradigms and critical debates in health.

We asked authors to ensure their material was grounded in current debates and evidence-based where this was appropriate. These chapters intend to provoke debate, and refer to the most contemporary understandings of health and wellbeing while acknowledging milestone knowledge development.

There are myriad ways of understanding and defining health and wellbeing. Jane Maidment's chapter discusses concepts of health and wellbeing within Western and other cultural contexts. She examines the relationship between spirituality, religion, health and wellbeing and the relevance of these for social work in health. The characteristics of salutogenesis and its relevance in this model for promoting public health are considered. Paul Bywaters explores key global health issues and their implications for social work and outlines some possibilities for practice informed by an analysis of globalisation. He provides examples from practice across the globe. Turning to the profession itself, Linda Haultain explores the perennial challenges and emerging themes social workers face in contemporary health care environments and revisits the core functions and roles of the profession based on research carried out in a large New Zealand teaching hospital. Haultain advocates for professional strategies that will help strengthen and sustain the profession's role in a health environment. Liz Beddoe examines how the social construction of risk permeates contemporary social care and health discourses including the creation of vulnerable populations in contemporary health and social policy. Risk and vulnerability constructs are critically interrogated with regard to their dual impact on the social work profession and service users.

Using the very current experience of civil defence emergencies and natural disasters as a focus, Carole Adamson employs an ecological lens to construct a relational understanding of resilience for social work practice. Ecological and constructivist approaches to social work are offered for exploration and critique and readers are challenged to develop perspectives on stress and resilience that incorporate and resonate with social work knowledge and principles. Vivienne E. Cree revisits the idea of stigma as part of a transformative agenda for change in social work and health. She argues that stigma remains a crucial core concept in aiding social workers to understand the impact of illness on identity and inclusion. The chapter draws on her experience as a practitioner and researcher studying the impact of HIV (parental and own) on Scottish children and families. Finally in this section, Uschi Bay starts with the consideration that people and nature are never separate; thus the wellbeing of both the natural environment and people needs to be fostered through understanding the need for respectful interdependence. Bay contends that the natural environment can be a source of 'distress and dis-ease' and promotes a rethinking of wellbeing that recognises the interdependence of people and nature in social work practice.

The second section, 'Diverse communities: culture, identity, spirituality and health', was designed to explore diverse forms of knowledge that inform our many understandings of health and wellbeing. This section intends to promote critical thinking and awareness of varied worldviews through inviting readers to consider alternative ways of knowing, doing and being that may often be marginalised by dominant discourses and structural inequalities. In doing this, authors were asked to describe diverse understandings of culture, identity, spirituality and health and related strategies for meeting health and wellbeing needs. A key role of social workers is to challenge the discriminatory environments endemic in the health arena in many countries.

Given the generally unequal health status of minority and indigenous peoples globally we believed it was essential for this book to carry non-Western voices and experiences of health and wellbeing. Lorraine Muller is an Indigenous Australian researcher whose chapter describes a journey to the restoration of Indigenous knowledge to assist in the healing and reclaiming of wellbeing. Muller discusses the process of colonisation and its negative effects on the wellbeing of Indigenous people. She describes decolonisation as a framework for research that is relevant to both the colonised and coloniser communities, for both are afflicted by the ideology of colonisation. Taking an historical perspective, Jim Anglem explores racism as an insidious and debilitating phenomenon affecting the health of the Māori population of New Zealand, producing health inequalities suffered by many Indigenous peoples.

Yvonne Crichton-Hill, Tanya McCall and Genevieve Togiaso are Pacific researchers who here explore concerns over the comparatively poor health status of Pacific peoples in New Zealand. The range of conceptual models presented will contribute to an understanding of how health interventions with Pacific communities might best be delivered.

Other minority groups can experience health inequalities and the adverse effects of stigma and social exclusion. Joy Phillips argues for a more just and inclusive society that recognises difference and diversity including the lived experience of GLBT people in sickness, health and wellbeing. Significant health and wellbeing disparities impact on GLBT people and raise issues of access and equity in health care. Phillips notes that older lesbians and gay men are often silenced by policy and practice which actively exclude and marginalise their needs and voices as they encounter the challenges of ageing. Helen Meekosha and Karen Soldatic explore the often troubled relationship social work has had with disabled people who were historically pigeonholed by their deficiencies. They note that practical intervention was often more traditionally focused on the family and/or carers of the disabled person. Meekosha and Soldatic argue for considerable improvement of the position of disability studies in the social work education curriculum so that social workers can play a critical role in facilitating the highest levels of health and wellbeing for disabled people.

The third section aims to capture examples of current research relating to health and wellbeing in specific populations where social work may make a difference. Our aim was to provide some key findings from research, but also have authors document any unique methodological issues encountered in conducting that research with a participant group. As such, each chapter addresses the dual objectives of documenting current research on specific issues, while strengthening research knowledge and culture for social work practitioners. The research studies that inform these chapters have many themes in common and, of particular note, is the recurring importance of these concepts in social work: collaborative practice and research, critical thinking about trauma and change, resilience and salutogenesis.

Andrew Thompson and Carole Adamson discuss the importance of collaborative practice in family-centred care in child health. The chapter draws on Thompson's research on families' experiences of family meetings and focuses our attention on the ethical and methodological challenges related to such practice-focused research, including concern about potential re-traumatisation for service-users and the intricacies of gaining consent from families and medical professionals for recording often painful, but crucial, meetings. Resolution of these challenges was achieved by attention to ethical and collaborative processes. Phil Crane considers 'space and place' in an examination of the contribution of public spaces to the wellbeing of young people. Using a case study he explores how participatory action research can be used as a process tool for contextually responsive, collaborative, iterative and multi-method, community-level practice. Crane argues that the addition of a spatial frame to practice can open up unexpected alliances and opportunities for enhancing the wellbeing of young people.

Hong-Jae Park acknowledges that older migrants face a range of challenges as they move to another culture late in life. At the same time, Park suggests that classifying older migrants as just a fragile or at-risk group does little to help us understand how people rise above adversity. Drawing on a study of the experiences of older Korean people in New Zealand, this chapter seeks to identify the factors that allow older people to achieve and maintain resilience under adverse circumstances. Addressing similar themes, Jay Marlowe notes that refugees make important contributions to their new host society. Drawing on a research project with resettled Sudanese men living in Australia, this chapter illustrates how being labelled a refugee can easily have pathologising inclinations informed through experiences of trauma and thus contribute to othering discourses in settlement contexts. Marlowe provides further insight into understandings of trauma and what it means to look beyond, to maintain a salutogenic focus towards health and wellbeing.

Critically reflective social work requires willingness to question assumptions and value diverse sources of knowledge. Our everyday behaviour – including language and interpersonal interactions – as practitioners can contribute to personal and social change. Drawing on research in a mental health setting, Selma Macfarlane presents alternative constructions of professionalism from voices that are not always heard and invites consideration of the assumptions underpinning our role as professionals. Economic, social and political changes over the past century have led to improved standards of living and related greater longevity. Christa Fouché explores the global challenge of sustaining resilience in the growing context of chronic illness. Drawing on a descriptive study of health professionals' views of core competencies in the context of chronic care, partnering is suggested as a core competency to address this challenge.

Jane Maidment, Uschi Bay and Michelle Courtney draw on findings from a qualitative study to argue that community-building processes naturally occurring amongst craft group participants can actively address issues of social isolation and loneliness. The authors note that craft groups cultivate a milieu of social inclusion, providing opportunities for meaningful community participation, peer support, friendship, continuing learning and development for older adults. Finally, Judith L. M. McCoyd notes that the creation of a new family is both culturally defined and medically mediated. In countries with high technology use, many decisions occur at the intersection of health, gender, socio-political context, risk interpretation and stigma. McCoyd discusses the challenges and rewards of undertaking research with women regarding reproductive health care. In a context often invisible in mainstream social work discourse, McCoyd explores the socio-political, family, emotional and medical issues women experience as they traverse the medical trajectory from identification of risk for foetal anomalies through to the aftermath of a pregnancy termination for anomaly.

Clearly the topics covered by contributors to this collection offer a diverse range of perspectives on health and wellbeing that serve to prompt examination of both the complexity and changing landscape of health social work. This professional milieu presents exciting opportunities and challenges for social work in the coming decade that will require practitioners to draw upon their personal stores of courage, creativity and tenacity to both defend social justice imperatives and promote health on a local, national and global scale.

Social work in health: opportunity and challenge

There are multiple areas where social workers are challenged to meet complex needs of diverse client groups and communities, and most of these challenges involve addressing some aspect of health and wellbeing. Out of these challenges however, arise opportunities for social work as a discipline to strengthen its advocacy and social justice agenda while responding in relevant and culturally appropriate ways. Two areas of professional challenge deserve particular attention in this regard. The first is how to work within a political context strongly influenced by the neoliberal discourse and growing poverty in an age of austerity, and the second requires consideration of how social work can respond effectively as a discipline to the global ageing population cohort.

Since the 1990s the strident principles underpinning neo-liberalism such as market-driven imperatives including privatisation of service provision, increased competition and individualism, have secured a stronghold in shaping welfare policy and delivery. Within this milieu the practice and profession of social work has increasingly occurred within a regulatory environment. Cost containment has resulted in services being cut; criteria for client eligibility for services have tightened; vulnerable people are now more dependent on family or charitable organisations for financial support; many welfare organisations are now being managed by personnel with no qualifications in social work (Dominelli, 2009; Wallace and Pease, 2011). Obviously these economic determinants have created social conditions where the disparity in health status between those with and without financial and social resources has become marked (Wilkinson and Pickett, 2009), and where stigma associated with being a welfare beneficiary is ever-present (Broussard *et al.*, 2012). There is no disputing the health and wellbeing impacts of living in poverty (Rose and Hatzenbuehler, 2009).

Within the neoliberal project there is a devaluing of social-work-specific knowledge and skill in preference to generic technocratic responses, a shift in focus that compromises professional identity and a sense of moral authority (Dominelli, 1999, cited in Wallace and Pease, 2011, p. 135). Clearly these conditions pose a significant challenge to social work and practitioner morale and professional vision can be severely impacted (Baines, 2006). Even so, there are still opportunities within this neoliberal context to practise ways that will still make a significant difference in clients' lives. In order to do so, social workers need to resist working in professional or organisational silos, partnering instead with diverse disciplines, sectors and organisations.

Following recent intense discussion of the prevalence and impact of child poverty in New Zealand (see, for example, the Child Poverty Action Group, 2013) the government has supported a recent collaboration between community and industry. The Kickstart Breakfast programme is delivered as part of a collaboration between schools, Fonterra (a dairy producer) and Sanitarium (a cereal manufacturer), to provide breakfasts in schools in low-income areas (Kickstart Breakfast, 2013). While this does not remove the necessity for political change to reduce the income disparities which produce child poverty, this programme highlights how partnership arrangements can benefit vulnerable client populations. Although Kickstart Breakfast has run for five years, the New Zealand government has only just promised financial support (due to increased media attention and voter concern about child poverty). This particular partnership and others of a similar ilk have been spurred through heightened awareness of the impact of poverty on child health, development and safety (Wynd, 2013).

Many social workers actively support the work of advocacy groups. Cross-sector collaboration demonstrates how social workers can be active in addressing the effects of structural inequalities and suggests practice approaches for bridging social capital between sectors and across disciplines to access practical resources and advocate for people in need. Social workers can also use their national professional associations to provide a further avenue to advocate for clients without fear of employer backlash. Independent of government funding, professional associations can speak on behalf of members and raise concerns with ministers about conditions that practitioners see having deleterious effects on clients. These strategies require social workers to be politically proactive, shifting their gaze from the immediate demands of the next allocation to consider ways in which the neoliberal project can be interrupted, stymied and called to account. In so doing, practitioners will create opportunities for the health and welfare of many, not just a few, to be significantly improved.

The second area of both challenge and opportunity for health social work is that of ageing. Global ageing is a demographic reality. Decreasing fertility rates mean the proportion of persons aged 60 and over is expected to double globally between 2007 and 2050 (United Nations, 2013). In response to this major demographic transition, in 2002 the United Nations developed the Madrid International Plan of Action on Ageing. This plan focuses on three priority areas for addressing ageing: older persons and development; advancing health and wellbeing into old age; and ensuring enabling and supportive environments (United Nations, 2002). Each of these priority areas is of particular relevance in contemporary social work education, service delivery and research. But persistent evidence suggests that students least prefer to work with older people (Richards *et al.*, 2013); ageist attitudes are cited as barriers to recruiting and training social workers for practice in this field (Wang and Chonody, 2013). Prevailing negative attitudes regarding this work, discussed in both Chapters 12 and 16 of this publication, present a serious professional challenge that social work as a discipline must address in order to competently and compassionately respond to the needs of the ageing population.

A recent published literature review of empirical studies on social work student and practitioner engagement with older adults provides reasons for a lack of interest in this field of practice (Wang and Chonody, 2013). A perceived lack of status in gerontological work; limited experience with, and exposure to, older persons; perceptions that older people cannot change, are depressed and lonely; and that work with older people is not challenging or rewarding, were explanations cited for students in particular not wishing to work in aged care (Wang and Chonody, 2013, p. 150). These attitudes reflect untested assumptions and stereotypical thinking that educational opportunities, including exposure to experiential learning and work with older people, would address. One consistent finding in the empirical literature was that practical experience of work with older adults was one of the strongest predictors for future engagement in gerontological work (Wang and Chonody, 2013, p. 151). Herein lies both the challenge and opportunity for social work, with recent research on social work education indicating 'widespread neglect in teaching content and practice learning' in programmes on social work with older people (Richards *et al.*, 2013, p. 1).

It is now urgent that our discipline addresses this educational neglect to ensure future cohorts of practitioners build knowledge and skills to work with older people, and have access to placement and research opportunities to create a more informed practitioner workforce. In this regard Hughes and Heycox (2010) examine in depth the complexities and nuances of social work with older people and encourage readers to move beyond an administrative response to this work, including, instead, interventions that help build meaningful social connections, promote civic activism to tackle pervasive ageism and other forms of discrimination experienced by older people, engage in community development and offer competent counselling services. These approaches for aged care social work are a far cry from the 'fix it' formula of arranging meals-on-wheels, day care and home-help. Instead they reflect a social justice agenda, and go some way to realising the priorities set down in the Ageing Action Plan developed by the United Nations (2002). Looking for ways to promote competent emancipatory aged care practice must be a priority for the profession, education providers and industry to prepare and future-proof the workforce to respond humanely and effectively in an ageing society.

Conclusion

Crisp and Beddoe (2013, p. 162) noted that health is often an optional extra, an elective, and rarely central to the social work curriculum. They asserted that there was a 'challenge for social work educators to question whether the ways in which we define social work may result in students concluding that consideration of health and wellbeing is an optional extra to some other more pressing or real tasks'. Clearly if social work is to take a more active role in promoting the IFSW's vision of health, then health must be more central to all aspects of the profession – in social work education, policy, research and practice.

In this publication we have attempted to capture a range of perspectives on health and wellbeing of relevance to contemporary social work practice. Inevitably there are topics that have not been explored in depth. While the cultural dimensions of health and wellbeing have been a strong theme throughout, we have not specifically focused on gender in relation to men's, women's or transgender health issues, although there is reference to these in Chapters 12 and 21. The impact and use of technology in health care, education and service delivery is a second theme that could have featured here. Finally, a greater presence of social work in primary health warrants specific attention. Despite these omissions we believe this publication will offer students and practitioners diverse, well-informed examinations of health and wellbeing across a wide practice spectrum.

We believe the collection offers a selection of well-linked, thematic chapters that address many of the pressing challenges to the enjoyment of healthy, satisfying lives. We are delighted our authors have produced such varied and yet theoretically coherent chapters, many of which showcase cutting-edge social work research that addresses core issues. While we explore many skills and concepts for work with particular populations we feel we have avoided producing another 'how-to' book for teaching practice skills in medical settings.

References

Baines, D. (2006) '"If you could change one thing": Social services workers and restructuring', *Social Work*, vol. 59, no. 1, 20–34.

Broussard, C., Joseph, A. & Thompson, M. (2012) 'Stressors and coping strategies used by single mothers living in poverty', *Affilia*, vol. 27, no. 2, pp. 190–204.

Bywaters, P., McLeod, E. & Napier, L. (eds) (2009) *Social Work and Global Health Inequalities*, The Policy Press, Bristol, UK.

Bywaters, P. & Napier, L. (2009) 'Revising social work's international policy statement on health: Process, outcomes and implications', *International Social Work*, vol. 52, no. 4, pp. 447–457.

Child Poverty Action Group (2013) CPAG's Budget Review 2013: An analysis of the New Zealand Government's 2013 Budget, CPAG, Auckland [online]. Available at: http://www.cpag.org.nz/

Crisp, B.R. & Beddoe, L. (2013) 'Conclusion: Developing an agenda to promote health and well-being in social work education', in *Promoting Health and Well-being in Social Work Education*, B.R. Crisp & L. Beddoe (eds) Routledge, London, pp. 157–162.

Dominelli, L. (2009) 'Repositioning social work', in *Social Work. Themes, Issues and Critical Debates*, 3rd edn. R. Adams, L. Dominelli & M. Payne (eds), Palgrave Macmillan, Basingstoke, UK, pp. 13–25.

Giles, R. (2009) 'Developing a health equality imagination: Hospital practice challenges for social work priorities', *International Social Work*, vol. 52, no. 4, pp. 525–537.

Hughes, M. & Heycox., K. (2010) *Older People, Ageing and Social Work*, Allen and Unwin, Crow's Nest, Sydney, Australia.

International Federation of Social Workers (IFSW). (2008) *International Policy on Health* [online]. Available at: http://www.ifsw.org/en/p38000081.html

Kickstart Breakfast (2013) Available at: https://kickstartbreakfast.co.nz/

Pockett, R. & Beddoe, L. (in press) 'Social work in health care: An international perspective', in *Socialt arbete I hälso-och sjukvård. Villkor, innehåll och utmaningar [Social Work in Health Care: Conditions, Content and Challenges]*, B. Blom, A. Lalos, S. Morén & M. Olsson (eds), Natur & Kultur, Stockholm, Sweden.

Richards, S., Sullivan, M.P., Tanner, D., Beech, C., Milne, A., Ray, M., . . . & Lloyd, L. (2013) 'On the edge of a new frontier: Is gerontological social work in the UK ready to meet twenty-first-century challenges?' *British Journal of Social Work*. doi: 10.1093/bjsw/bct082

Rose, S.M. & Hatzenbuehler, S. (2009) 'Embodying social class: The link between poverty, income inequality and health', *International Social Work*, vol. 52, no. 4, pp. 459–471.

United Nations (2002) *Political Declaration and Madrid International Action Plan on Ageing* [online]. Available at: http://social.un.org/index/Portals/0/ageing/documents/Fulltext-E.pdf

United Nations (2013) *Ageing* [online]. Available at: http://www.un.org/en/globalissues/ageing/index.shtml

Wallace, J. & Pease, B. (2011) 'Neoliberalism and Australian social work: Accommodation or resistance?', *Journal of Social Work*, vol. 11, no. 2, pp. 132–142.

Wang, D. & Chonody, J. (2013) 'Social workers' attitudes toward older adults: A review of the literature', *Journal of Social Work Education*, vol. 49, no. 1, pp. 150–172.

Wilkinson, R. & Pickett, K. (2009) *The Spirit Level: Why Equality is Better for Everyone*, Penguin, London.

World Health Organisation (WHO) (1948) *Constitution*, Author, Geneva.

World Health Organisation (WHO) (1986) *The Ottawa Charter for Health Promotion* [online]. Available at: http://www.who.int/healthpromotion/conferences/previous/ottawa/en/

Wynd, D. (2013) *Child Abuse: What Role Does Poverty Play?* Child Poverty Action Group, Auckland [online]. Available at: http://www.cpag.org.nz/assets/Publications

PART I

Current themes and critical issues in health and wellbeing

2

EXPLORING INTERPRETATIONS OF HEALTH AND WELLBEING FOR SOCIAL WORK

Jane Maidment

CHAPTER OBJECTIVES

1. *To discuss the concepts of health and wellbeing within Western cultural contexts;*
2. *To identify the characteristics of salutogenesis and discuss the relevance of this model for promoting public health;*
3. *To examine the relationship between spirituality, religion, health and wellbeing;*
4. *To raise awareness of environmental social work and the interrelationship between environmental factors and health.*

Introduction

There are countless ways of understanding and defining health and wellbeing. Exploring the essence of these concepts has occupied the minds of scholars, mothers, explorers, shamans, researchers and many others since the beginning of humanity, with statements being made about health long ago that are as true today as they were then . . .

> Health is the greatest gift, contentment the greatest wealth, faithfulness the best relationship.
>
> Buddha (563–483 BC)

> The part can never be well unless the whole is well.
>
> Plato (429–347 BC)

Both of these statements made centuries ago reflect the contemporary ideas on health and wellness that will be discussed as part of this chapter.

Much of what the general public knows about health is derived from repeated one- to two-minute media news bites focusing on stories that capture popular attention. These stories commonly illustrate tragic circumstances of suicide or accidental death (Thom *et al.*, 2012); moral panic related to issues such as obesity and diabetes (Saguy and Gruys, 2010); or extraordinary medical breakthroughs and/or cures for major diseases (Collins, 2013). Rarely do the social dimensions of gaining and sustaining good health seize the headlines. Yet, when compared to medical technologies, social remedies are accessible, simple and low-cost interventions that can significantly impact upon, and improve, wellbeing (Cattan *et al.*, 2011; Maidment and Macfarlane, 2008). In New Zealand, with just 4.5% of the total health budget dedicated to public health compared to 95.5% spent in secondary health and disability services (Ministry of Health, 2013) health promotion is virtually a fringe activity.

Social work practitioners across all fields of practice have an opportunity to promote a discourse of health and wellbeing. Understanding how to promote health literacy and awareness in everyday life and community functioning is central to integrating this approach in practice. In this chapter I attempt to distil the central principles about health promoting practice through examination of the concepts of wellbeing and salutogenesis, and the influence of spirituality and cross-cultural interpretations of health and living well. Not surprisingly, some key components, such as 'meaningful relationships and activity' can be located in all of the conceptual frameworks discussed. Simply doing meaningful things with others is at the heart of most social remedies.

Wellbeing: what is it?

A wealth of recent writing and research has recently emerged about the topic of wellbeing. In this chapter, wellbeing is discussed within the context of positive psychology, in relationship to environmental change, and from a macro-policy perspective.

The work of positive psychologist Martin Seligman has been particularly influential in conceptualising the notion of wellbeing (Seligman, 2011). Seligman contends that no single measure can explain wellbeing but it is a complex and dynamic concept made up five elements. These elements include *positive emotion* which essentially relates to the subjective sense of happiness and life satisfaction; *engagement*, a second subjective element denoting the state of 'flow' where the mind is completely and pleasantly occupied by the task at hand; *meaning,* which pertains to having connections to other people, or a sense of belonging and serving others in ways that give meaning to life; *accomplishment*, having capacity to successfully achieve meaningful goals including learning, developing, creating, and for some people, winning; and *positive relationships*, acknowledging the fact that we are social beings, where very little that is positive occurs as a solitary activity (Seligman, 2011, pp. 16–20).

This conceptualisation of wellbeing has been operationalised into 'Five ways to wellbeing' proven to advance mental health as outlined by the New Economics Foundation (2008). These five ways include connecting with others; being active; taking notice (as in engaging with nature; being aware of the world around, and demonstrating curiosity); and keeping on learning and giving (New Economics Foundation, 2008). Understanding wellbeing and its application to social work strongly resonates with the application of both critical social theory and ecological systems theory. From a critical perspective, social work practice pays attention to notions of difference and social justice in order to address issues of power and oppression (Burke and Dalrymple, 2009). Using this critical lens, the wellbeing of children who arrive at school hungry, unable to concentrate or muster the energy for robust play is addressed as a matter of poverty and economic oppression. The experiences of mothers and children living with violence, who are fearful, without choices or agency, and with diminished wellbeing as a consequence, reflect dominant gender politics resulting from misuse of power.

From an ecological systems perspective, the interrelatedness between people and their environment at micro, meso and macro levels strongly influences wellbeing. Within the micro and meso spheres, the quality of everyday relationships that people have with neighbours, friends and family, and accessibility to transport, employment, education, housing and leisure activities all significantly impact on individual, family and community quality of life. From a macro perspective, global policy initiatives influence domestic legislation and policy. For example, the United Nations Convention on the Rights of the Child (UNCRC), to which New Zealand is a signatory, was influential in the government action to repeal Section 59 of the Crimes Act in 2007. This change in legislation effectively ensures children's right to protection from all forms of physical and mental violence, prohibiting the use of physical punishment by parents to correct their children (Smith, 2009, p. 7).

Other macro-level activities that address health and wellbeing include the work of international and regional environmental policy coalitions that tackle environmental degradation. These coalitions of like-minded sectors including governments, international organisations, non-government organisations and corporations work together to regulate international action on environmental concerns that impact on population health and the wellbeing of whole nations (Downie, 2011). Stratospheric ozone climate change, global biodiversity, trade in endangered species, wetlands protection, ocean dumping and hazardous waste disposal are just a sample of the many global environmental problems that have been addressed by international policy, and brokered through diverse coalitions (Downie, 2011, p. 74). Simultaneously the environmental social work movement has emerged out of concern for the effects of climate change, the systematic destruction of renewable and non-renewable resources and consequent negative impact on all living species (Gray *et al.*, 2013).

Environmental social work

Social work as a discipline has been slow to engage with a broad definition of environment beyond the notion of the social. In this regard Coates (2004) argues that social work as a profession has generally ignored the physical environment, locating itself as a discipline within the context of modernity, where notions of individualism, materialism, consumerism and anthropocentrism prevail. Even so, actively engaging with civic environmentalism is increasingly being used as an intervention strategy with a range of groups identified with health vulnerabilities to promote and strengthen wellbeing (Townsend, 2006).

Research indicates that, while all populations are affected by changing environmental conditions, the most marginalised are disproportionally disadvantaged, including those who live in rural areas, Indigenous populations, people living in poverty and older people (Hetherington and Boddy, 2013, p. 50). These populations have compromised mobility and unequal access to resources such as finance, safe housing, food and water. The interconnected nature of the health and wellbeing of whole populations and environmental factors is well established (Wilkinson and Marmot, 2003), with a call going out to the profession to engage in eco-social work. This type of practice involves social workers challenging policy, legislation, actions and beliefs that are environmentally unsustainable (Hetherington and Boddy, 2013, p. 55), working instead to achieve global environmental justice and preservation. These notions are related to the just allocation of natural resources and promotion of environmental sustainability. Integral to this approach is the understanding that 'human wellbeing is only possible in the context of the wellbeing of all life – a healthy and thriving Earth' (Gray *et al.*, 2013, p. 8). In Chapter 8 (this volume), a more detailed analysis of the impact of the natural environment on wellbeing is provided.

Students and practitioners of social work are often very well versed on how to work with individual clients, groups and families at the micro level to achieve some measure of wellbeing. Efforts that demonstrate macro-level social work intervention in shaping policy and changing oppressive structural conditions are less evident. The lack of social work visibility in macro intervention has led to recent questioning as to whether 'social workers as individuals and through their organizations, have the political will to engage in social change efforts that could transform outcomes for the most vulnerable populations?' (Gamble, 2012, p. 674). Gamble supports the argument made above that the 'person in environment' construct used so readily in social work has rarely acknowledged transactions with natural resources and the biosphere. Citing the IFSW Statement of Principles (2004) Gamble goes on to urge social workers to proactively address all aspects of negative discrimination, violence, conditions of poverty and environmental sustainability – linking the social justice agenda of social work with fundamental aspects of wellbeing. In this regard Gamble also challenges practitioners to engage in practice research that will help define, integrate and measure notions of wellbeing in order to more fully synthesise the relationship of wellbeing with the broad social justice agenda of social work in meaningful ways (Gamble, 2012, p. 681).

Scholars from positive psychology, eco-social work and social work more generally, all agree that accounting for national GDP and conditions of abundance are not effective measures of wellbeing (Coates, 2004; Gamble, 2012; Seligman, 2011). As such, it is useful for social workers to engage with a range of diverse ways to interpret and understand health. Public health practice and research offer a number of models and theoretical frameworks to interpret and investigate health-promoting behaviour and environmental influences. One of the most influential of these is salutogenesis.

Salutogenesis

Salutogenesis is a theory developed by American-Israeli medical sociologist Aaron Antonovsky after conducting research about menopause with a group of women who survived living in concentration camps during World War II (Lindstrom and Eriksson, 2006). Antonovsky found that, despite the traumatic history that all of the women shared of having lived in the camps, there was a sub-group who had sustained good health and led meaningful lives. From this research he theorised that chaos and stress were part of life for all people, but that individual responses to these conditions differed. This particular research led Antonovsky to consider what causes health and its continued maintenance and promotion (salutogenesis), rather than the reasons for disease (pathogenesis) (Lindstrom and Eriksson, 2006, p. 241).

Salutogenesis includes examining the interrelationship between three key concepts. These concepts include a 'sense of coherence' (SOC); generalised resistance resources (GRRs), those elements that serve to avoid or combat stressors; and the existence of a *health ease/disease* (HE–DE) continuum (Wiesmann and Hannich, 2010, p. 350).

Sense of coherence is characterised by *comprehensibility* of one's world and one's place within it, *manageability* of life's stressors using available resources and *meaningfulness* in terms of the extent to which an 'individual feels life challenges are worth engaging with' (Almedom, 2005, p. 259). The level at which a person achieves a sense of coherence will determine where they sit on the health–disease continuum. In essence, a sense of coherence is the ability to make sense of one's life, experiencing a degree of control over life circumstances while utilising constructive coping strategies (Henry, 2013).

Antonovsky identified four domains within which the GRRs are located. These include physical and biochemical characteristics (the biological domain); cognitive and emotional characteristics (the psychological domain); valuative-attitudinal characteristics and relational characteristics (interpersonal domain); and artefactual-material characteristics and macro-sociocultural characteristics (sociocultural domain) (Taylor, 2004, p. 637). Resources within each of these domains are used to manage stress and the effects of environmental demands. From this summary it is possible to see that Antonovsky's theory of salutogenesis acknowledged the influence of how personal and structural characteristics such as genetics, identity, financial security, educational status, social ties, values and beliefs contribute to creating resilience and health.

This theory for understanding the creation of health, resilience and wellbeing was radical when first proposed, challenging as it did the dominant medical discourse of the pathogenic paradigm. The dominance of the medical paradigm has supported research focused on identifying risk factors for entering into ill-health (Levin, 2003), rather than strengthening health-promoting conditions.

Salutogenesis as a theory for examining and promoting health has strong synergies with both strengths-based practice and ecological models of social work. The four dimensions of salutogenesis outlined above can help guide the practitioner and client to identify and mobilise resources (GRRs) to ultimately strengthen an individual's sense of coherence.

As a theory salutogenesis has been used to inform health-related research and practice in diverse fields including gerontology, child protection, mental health, women-centred work; couples and parents in therapy, and nursing practice (Griffiths, 2009; Henry, 2013; Olsson *et al.*, 2006; Taylor, 2004). At the same time, a range of other diverse factors that establish and maintain good health have been explored in research and practice.

Relationship between religion, spirituality and health

While attention to the notion of spirituality has flourished in both health and social care literature and education during the past decade (Crisp, 2010; Timmins, 2011), religious practice as such no longer strongly features as it once did during the early to mid-20th century in terms of prescribing norms, values and belief systems within the New Zealand context. Falling church attendance is testament to changing societal views in this country on the place of religion in family life (Larson, 2005; Liefting, 2010). Even so, while there is a decline in religious affiliation to the four major denominations in New Zealand (Anglicans, Catholics, Presbyterians and Methodists), growing religious diversity in this country is evident. Spurred by global migration, a new plurality of faiths and traditions are emergent in New Zealand society (Hoverd and Sibley, 2010, p. 61).

Concomitantly there is much more civic engagement with the broader notion of spirituality. Spirituality can be understood as 'the sense of sacred companionship, of connection and meaning that comes from beyond oneself' (Milner, 2006). Religious people will link spirituality to some form of institutionalised God, 'to an organised system of beliefs, rituals and ways of worship' (Moxey *et al.*, 2011, p. 82); 'non-religious will recognize it as relational interconnectedness, the interaction and reliance that exists within and between people and the world in which they live. Māori [and other Indigenous peoples] add to this the dimension of the living and the dead, and the connection across generations, the past present and future' (Milner, 2006, p. 64). Either way, engagement with spirituality tends to be a journey unique to the individual or collective group, shaped by cultural and societal dimensions.

Social epidemiologist Jeff Levin has examined in some depth the relationship between engagement with religion and health (Levin, 2003). From his research Levin presents a strong case for incorporating religion into the dimensions of sense of coherence, found in salutogenesis (Levin, 2003). Levin's work on this subject has been inclusive of minority cultures and non-Western religious traditions, as well as Judaism and Christianity (van Ness, 2002). Specifically, Levin identifies key aspects of behaviour, religious practice and faith that positively influence wellbeing and strengthen protective health factors. These factors include engagement with socially supportive networks within spiritual communities that also provide a context for coping with suffering; having access to a belief system that helps in managing uncertainty; discouraging unhealthy behaviours (such as smoking, over-use of alcohol and drug taking); participating in worship activities such as prayer that engender positive emotions (such as contentment, catharsis, love); and where religious beliefs and practice in and of themselves promote 'optimism and hopeful expectation' (Levin, 2003, pp. 51–52). These same characteristics intersect with the notion of 'religious social capital' which conceptualises religiosity as one of the social determinants of health, with the presence of religious institutions in a community being linked to positive behavioural and social outcomes (Maselko *et al.*, 2011). Religious social capital refers to the resources found to be available to individuals and groups within the religious community including shared values, levels of trust and opportunities for incorporating both bonding and bridging social capital between members of one community, and between religious communities more broadly (Maselko *et al.*, 2011, pp. 760–761).

Outside of the religious domain, engagement with spirituality is considered an integral part of the lived experience, that is, part of everyday life (Crisp, 2010). Within this context, a person's connectedness with relationships, creativity, work activity; achievement of life course milestones, personal health and wellbeing are processes of 'being and becoming' where spirituality is the lens used for creating meaning and connection, tackling life's struggles and experiencing a sense of transcendence (Crisp, 2010; Tse *et al.*, 2005).

From an environmental perspective, Coates argues that the transition 'toward a holistic conception of the relationship of people and nature toward a world view in which humans and the rest of nature are seen as interdependent and intimately connected is of such significance that it can be, at its roots, a spiritual transformation' (Coates, 2004, p. 3). Transformation of this order involves a connectedness to others, nature and a larger presence, being strongly associated with characteristics such as creativity, compassion, trust, reverence, faith and a sense of oneness (Staude, 2005, cited in Crisp, 2010).

A systematic review of research in this field has revealed a strong correlation between good health and wellbeing with holding religious-spiritual beliefs (Koenig *et al.*, 2012). This correlation is put down to engaging in healthier lifestyles; having ample opportunities to socialise with others in both public and private domains; experiencing greater life satisfaction in relation to personal self-esteem, purpose and meaning; and enhanced coping strategies resulting in less mental ill-ness (Koenig *et al.*, 2012). These dimensions reflect robust protective measures in terms of sustaining health. From a practitioner perspective acknowledgement of religion–spirituality in work with clients demonstrates a holistic understanding of the relationship between people and their environment.

In some cultural contexts, the spiritual dimension is considered central to shaping the health and wellbeing of individuals, families and whole communities (Ng and Chan, 2009; Tse *et al.*, 2005). Long overdue recognition of the systemic oppression of Indigenous populations in colonised countries, alongside increasing rates of global migration requires social workers to respond to cultural imperatives appropriately. In order to provide relevant interventions practitioners need to learn about how to integrate cultural knowledges into their work with diverse client populations.

Culture and health

Culture has been defined as an 'integrated pattern of human behaviour, which includes, but is not limited to, thought, communication, language, beliefs, values, practices, customs, courtesies, rituals, manner of interacting, roles, relationships and expected behaviours of a racial, ethnic, religious, social or political group' (The National Centre for Cultural Competence, cited in Rowe and Paterson, 2010, p. 335). Using this definition the topic of culture includes examining the intersec-tions between diverse social groups through the lens of health. For the purposes of this chapter, ethnicity and disability will be briefly considered.

There are multiple examples where people from diverse cultural groups have been marginalised within the health and social service sector system (Maidment *et al.*, 2011; Sapey, 2009), making it imperative for practitioners to gain a better understanding of ways to improve accessibility and the consumer experience of service delivery. In terms of understanding the influence of culture on health, it is important practitioners remember that perceptions of health and illness vary between cultures; with culture influencing help-seeking behaviours; and care pro-viders from culturally and linguistically diverse populations being underrepresented in the health care system (Rowe and Paterson, 2010, p. 336).

In New Zealand and Australia, the dominant views of health are very much influenced by a Eurocentric biomedical model. Both countries share a history of European colonisation during the 1800s that has had traumatic long-term effects on the health and wellbeing of Māori and Aboriginal people (Durie, 2008; Muller, 2010). The contemporary health status of both populations, including mental health, cannot be separated out from the effects of on-going oppression, racism, environmental circumstances, stress and grief (Swan and Raphael, 1995, cited in Tse *et al.*, 2005, p. 183). More detailed analysis on the impact of colonisation on the health status of Māori and Aboriginal populations can be found in Chapters 11 and 12 of this publication.

While this history of colonisation provides the foundation for understanding the health disparities of these two populations when compared with Europeans living in both countries, there are other factors to consider when working with Aboriginal and Māori people. The concept of health is not considered as simply an individual issue focusing on physical wellbeing, but instead relates to the social, emotional, cultural and spiritual wellbeing of the whole community. Both Indigenous populations relate as collective societies, where the individual health of one reflects in the state of the whole, and vice versa (Tse *et al.*, 2005). Other belief systems shared by both cultures, and referred to in the discussion on spirituality is the connectedness between past, present and future, where time has no boundary; the interconnected nature of all aspects of life, including acknowledgment of sacred features found in the environment being related to a spiritual life-force; and the use of rituals and herbal remedies to foster healing.

New Zealand and Australia both have large immigrant populations from China. For Chinese, the concept of health is strongly influenced by Chinese philosophy and religion, using the principles of yin and yang to represent negative and positive energies. The interconnectedness of mind, body and spirit is integral to this belief system, where the aim is to foster a balance between these dimensions within, and between the person and their social and natural environment (Ng and Chan, 2009). From this perspective, body work enables the client to gain a sense of control. This type of work includes using qigong, tai chi, massage of meridian points, therapeutic touch, breathing and meditation in conjunction with addressing aspects of mind and spirit. The spiritual domain includes those factors discussed earlier in this chapter related to finding meaning in life, experiencing harmony with nature, personal transcendence and expressing compassion. The domain of the mind relates to accessing social support, feeling appreciation, letting go of unwanted or unhelpful feelings and beliefs, affirming and enabling emotional expression (Ng and Chan, 2009, p. 274). While some of these dimensions are not new to Western social work practice, the idea of paying attention to body work, incorporating the notion of balance within and with the environment, has not been well recognised or supported in current social work education.

Working with disability is a second area where social work education could be strengthened. While the impact of discrimination on the wellbeing of diverse populations, including those with disabilities has been well documented in the social work literature (Thompson, 2006), Sapey questions the role of social work in the lives of people with disabilities when he writes, 'by its very nature social work assumes that disabled people need to be "cared for"' (Sapey, 2009, p. 336). This notion of 'care' represents a form of social control. Even when delivered with the best of intentions, Sapey argues that traditional social work practice in this area has been based on a process of 'othering' (Sapey, 2009). From this perspective the category of disability has been social constructed and culturally enforced and defined within the helping professions and beyond (Harrison and Kahn, 2004).

Critical social work practice approaches are needed to challenge the notion of care, deconstruct the disability identity and reconstruct practice from the standpoint of health and wellbeing. Paying attention to use of language is important in this regard contributing as it does to shaping identity and the social construction of disability. Recent Australian research in this field sought to discover how a prosocial discourse of wellness was adopted by allied health staff in disability services across four large organisations (Breen *et al.*, 2011). Findings from this work point to a continuum on which each of the four organisations sat, from one organisation having no inclusion or understanding of a wellness discourse in service delivery, through to one organisation having a completely integrated health/wellness approach to their work in this sector. Wellness and its application in this field of practice appeared to be organisationally determined and not universally applied (Breen *et al.*, 2011). Herein lies a challenge for social work: to change the culture in disability services toward a focus on health promoting practice in its widest sense. This approach entails promoting access for people with disabilities to mainstream services while politicising issues and events that generate and maintain oppression for people with disabilities.

In this regard the election in 2011 of New Zealand's first deaf member of parliament, Mojo Mathers, has raised politicians' and public awareness of reasonable accommodations and issues of accessibility for people with disabilities (Convention Coalition Monitoring Group, 2012, p. 20). Although there have been other people in parliament who have identified as having a disability, Ms Mathers has been the first requiring technology to follow debates, with her initial denial of access thereto attracting strident media attention. The circumstances surrounding Mojo Mathers' entry into parliamentary debate exemplifies how constructs of difference challenge the dominant cultural context of inclusion in public affairs. More detailed analysis addressing the intersection between health and disability can be found in Chapter 19.

Conclusion

In this chapter a range of perspectives on health and wellbeing have been discussed with the view to examining how these may help broaden the way we both view the notion of health and canvass possibilities for social work intervention. A holistic interpretation of health and wellbeing has been used to include expressions of a political, spiritual, cultural and environmental order. In this regard a focus on providing balance between micro and macro health considerations has been deliberate throughout the chapter, with particular encouragement being given to shift the practitioner gaze from private troubles to public issues.

Learning how to use the lens of health and wellbeing to generate positive social and structural change is complex. This approach requires conscientious engagement with holism, to consider ways in which culture, politics, history and socially constructed meaning influences the way we work to generate hope, optimism, good health and ongoing sustainability.

QUESTIONS FOR REFLECTION

1. How might you generate the discourse of 'meaningful activity' within an organisation that has a demoralised workforce?
2. How can you personally get involved in a global initiative to improve the health of population groups or the environment? What's stopping you?
3. What activities might generate a 'sense of coherence' for clients, as conceptualised in salutogenesis?
4. Why do you think there has been an upsurge of interest in spirituality amongst the general public?

References

Almedom, A. (2005) 'Resilience, hardiness, sense of coherence, and posttraumatic growth: All paths leading to "Light at the end of the tunnel"', *Journal of Loss and Trauma*, vol. 10, no. 3, pp. 253–265.

Breen, L., Wildy, H., Saggers, S., Millsteed, J. & Raghavendra, P. (2011) 'In search of wellness: Allied health professionals' understanding of wellness in childhood disability services', *Disability and Rehabilitation*, vol. 33, no. 10, pp. 862–871.

Burke, B. & Dalrymple, J. (2009) 'Critical intervention and empowerment', in *Social Work. Themes, Issues and Critical Debates*, 3rd edn. R. Adams, L. Dominelli & M. Payne (eds), Palgrave Macmillan, London, pp. 261–269.

Cattan, M., Kime, N. & Bagnall, A. (2011) 'The use of telephone befriending in low level support for socially isolated older people – an evaluation', *Health and Social Care in the Community*, vol. 19, no. 2, pp. 198–206.

Coates, J. (2004) 'From ecology to spirituality and social justice', *Currents: New Scholarship in Human Services*, vol. 3, no. 1, pp. 1–10.

Collins, N. (2013) 'Stem-cell breakthrough', *The New Zealand Herald*, May 17th, p. A27.

Convention Coalition Monitoring Group (2012) *Disability Rights in Aotearoa New Zealand 2012*. A report on the Human Rights of Disabled People in Aotearoa New Zealand, Crown Copyright.

Crisp, B. (2010) *Spirituality and Social Work*, Ashgate Publishing, Farnham.

Downie, D. (2011) 'Global environmental policy: Governance by regimes', in *The Global Environment*, 3rd edn. R. Axelrod, S. van Deveer & D. Downie (eds), CQ Press; Sage Publications, Washington, D.C.

Durie, M. (2008) *Mauri Ora: The Dynamics of Maori Health*, Oxford University Press, South Melbourne, Australia.

Gamble, D. (2012) 'Well-being in a globalized world: Does social work know how to make it happen?', *Journal of Social Work Education*, vol. 48, no. 4, pp. 669–689.

Gray, M., Coates, J. & Hetherington, T. (eds) (2013) *Environmental Social Work*, Routledge, London.

Griffiths, C. (2009) 'Sense of coherence and mental health rehabilitation', *Clinical Rehabilitation*, vol. 23, no. 1, pp. 72–78.

Harrison, T. & Kahn, D. (2004) 'Disability rites: The cultural shift following impairment', *Family and Community Health*, vol. 27, no. 1, pp. 86–93.

Heatherington, T. & Boddy, J. (2013) 'Ecosocial work with marginalised populations', in *Environmental Social Work*, M. Gray, J. Coates & T. Hetherington (eds), Routledge, London, pp. 46–61.

Henry, H. (2013) 'An asset-based approach to creating health', *Nursing Times*, vol. 109, no. 4, pp. 19–21.

Hoverd, W. & Sibley, C. (2010) 'Religious and denominational diversity in New Zealand 2009', *New Zealand Sociology*, vol. 25, no. 2, pp. 59–87.

International Federation of Social Workers & International Association of Schools of Social Work (IFSW) (2004) *Ethics in Social Work, Statement and Principles* [online]. Available at: http://ifsw.org/policies/statement-of-ethical-principles/

Koenig, H., King, D. & Carson, V. (2012) *Handbook of Religion and Health*, Oxford University Press, New York.

Larson, V. (2005) 'The end of family life – as we knew it', *North and South*, April 2005, no. 299, pp. 36–42, 45–48.

Levin, J. (2003) 'Spiritual determinants of health and healing: An epidemiologic perspective on salutogenic mechanisms', *Alternative Therapies in Health and Medicine*, vol. 9, no. 6, pp. 48–57.

Liefting, A. (2010) 'Religious belief is declining on good faith', *The Press*, 27/05/2010, p. GL2.

Lindstrom, B. & Eriksson, M. (2005) 'Salutogenesis', *Journal of Epidemiology & Community Health*, vol. 59, no. 6, pp. 440–442.

Lindstrom, B. & Eriksson, M. (2006) 'Contextualising salutogenesis and Antonovsky in public health development', *Health Promotion International*, vol. 21, no. 3, pp. 238–244.

Maidment, J., Egan, R. & Wexler, J. (2011) 'Social work with older people from culturally and linguistically diverse backgrounds: Using research to inform practice', *Aotearoa New Zealand Social Work*, vol. 23, no. 3, pp. 3–15.

Maidment, J. & Macfarlane, S. (2008) 'Craft groups: Sites of friendship, empowerment, belonging and learning for older women', *Groupwork*, vol. 19, no. 1, pp. 10–25.

Maselko, J., Hughes, C. & Cheney, R. (2011) 'Religious social capital: Its measurement and utility in the study of the social determinants of health', *Social Science and Medicine*, vol. 73, no. 5, pp. 759–767.

Milner, V. (2006) 'Uncommonly sensible social work practice: Using depths of conventional wisdom and spirituality to match what we know with what we sense', *Social Work Review*, vol. 18, no. 3, pp. 61–68.

Ministry of Health (2013) *Health Workforce Development* [online]. Available at: http://www.publichealthworkforce.org.nz/public-health-funding_146.aspx

Moxey, A., McEvoy, M., Bowe, S. & Attia, J. (2011) 'Spirituality, religion, social support and health among older Australians', *Australian Journal on Ageing*, vol. 30, no. 2, pp. 82–88.

Muller, L. (2010) *Indigenous Australian social-health theory*. Doctoral Thesis, James Cook University, Australia.

New Economics Foundation (2008) *Five Ways to Wellbeing*, London, NHS Confederation [online]. Available at: http://www.Tinyurl.com/NEF-5-ways

Ng, S. & Chan, C. (2009) 'Alternative intervention: A Chinese body-mind-spirit perspective', in *Social Work: Themes, Issues and Critical Debates*, 3rd edn. R. Adams, L. Dominelli & M. Payne (eds), Palgrave Macmillan, Basingstoke, UK, pp. 271–280.

Olsson, M., Hansson, K., Lundblad, A. & Cederblad, M. (2006) 'Sense of coherence: Definition and explanation', *International Journal of Social Welfare*, vol. 15, no.3, pp. 219–229.

Rowe, J. & Paterson, J. (2010) 'Culturally competent communication with refugees', *Home Health Care Management Practice*, vol. 22, no. 5, pp. 334–338.

Saguy, A. & Gruys, K. (2010) 'Morality and health: News media constructions of overweight and eating disorders', *Social Problems*, vol. 57, no. 2, pp. 231–250.

Sapey, B. (2009) 'Physical disability', in *Social Work. Themes, Issues and Critical Debates*, 3rd edn. R. Adams, L. Dominelli & M. Payne (eds), Palgrave Macmillan, Basingstoke, UK, pp. 336–345.

Seligman, M. (2011) *Flourish*, Random House, North Sydney, Australia.

Smith, A. (2009) *Implementing the UNCRC in New Zealand: How Are We Doing in Early Childhood?* Keynote address to NZARE ECE Hui 30 November [online]. Available at: http://www.nzare.org.nz/pdfs/ece/Anne-Smith-keynote.pdf

Taylor, J. (2004) 'Salutogenesis as a framework for child protection: Literature review', *Journal of Advanced Nursing*, vol. 45, no. 6, pp. 633–643.

Thom, K., McKenna, B., Edwards, G., O'Brien, A. & Nakarada-Kordic, I. (2012) 'Reporting of suicide by the New Zealand media', *Crisis*, vol. 33, no. 4, pp. 199–207.

Thompson, N. (2006) *Anti-discriminatory Practice*, 4th edn. Palgrave Macmillan, Basingstoke, UK.

Timmins, F. (2011) *Spirituality in Nursing: The Challenges of Complexity*, Springer Publishing Company, New York.

Townsend, M. (2006) 'Feel blue? Touch green! Participation in forest/woodland management as treatment for depression', *Urban Forestry & Urban Greening*, vol. 5, no. 3, pp. 111–120.

Tse, A., Llyod, C., Petchkovsky, L. & Manaia, W. (2005) 'Exploration of Australian and New Zealand indigenous people's spirituality and mental health', *Australian Occupational Therapy Journal*, vol. 52, no. 3, pp. 181–187.

van Ness, P. (2002) 'Book reviews: God, faith and health', *The Journal of Religion*, vol. 82, no. 3, pp. 520–521.

Wiesmann, U. & Hannich, H-J. (2010) 'A salutogenic analysis of healthy aging in active elderly persons', *Research on Aging*, vol. 32, no. 3, pp. 349–371.

Wilkinson, R. & Marmot, M. (2003) *Social Determinants of Health: The Solid Facts*, World Health Organisation, Copenhagen, Denmark.

3

GLOBALISATION, SOCIAL WORK AND HEALTH

Paul Bywaters

CHAPTER OBJECTIVES

1. *To explore different understandings of globalisation;*
2. *To discuss key global health issues and their implications for social work;*
3. *To outline some possibilities for practice informed by an analysis of glo-balisation.*

Introduction

> Social justice is a matter of life and death. It affects the way people live, their consequent chance of illness, and their risk of premature death. We watch in wonder as life expectancy and good health continue to increase in parts of the world and in alarm as they fail to improve in others. A girl born today can expect to live for more than 80 years if she is born in some countries – but less than 45 years if she is born in others. ... These inequities in health, avoid-able health inequalities, arise because of the circumstances in which people grow, live, work and age, and the systems put in place to deal with illness. The conditions in which people live and die are, in turn, shaped by political, social and economic forces. (Commission on the Social Determinants of Health (CSDH), 2008, Preface)

The essence of this chapter can be found in this statement. Health is a global issue. Profound injustice is apparent in differences in health and life expectancy between (and within) countries. Health should be a central concern for social workers because it is an issue of social justice, affecting the way people live It is also a central social work concern because it is primarily social factors – the social determinants – which shape people's health and their life chances generally. The disadvantaged social conditions in which most social work service users live and the discrimination they often face are reflected in their common experiences of poor mental and physical health. Their poor health, in turn, further undermines their opportunities for securing the resources they need for happy, successful and healthy lives. The political, social and economic forces which shape these social conditions are partly locally created and maintained but they are increasingly subject to global forces which transcend national boundaries and to globalisation (Bywaters, 2009). Therefore, I will be arguing that social workers have to engage with the global dimension in order to make sense of the lives of the people with whom they work, to understand how their health is influenced by globalisation and to act coherently with others at local, national and international levels to enhance social justice and secure human rights.

This abstract argument may feel remote from the everyday tasks of social workers across the world. Most social workers don't wake up and go to work thinking about globalisation! But during the day, some of the service users they see may be refugees or asylum seekers, perhaps unaccompanied children, some may be unemployed and in poverty in an area where industry has collapsed or production moved to another country, some may not be able to access health services because of a decision by a distant transnational health care or health insurance company, some may be receiving social care from a cheap, barely trained, exploited migrant labour force. Globalisation touches all our lives – services users and service providers – every day, in multiple ways with particular consequences for our health.

Why think globalisation?

Health and illness feel like deeply personal issues, affecting our sense of who we are, our understanding of our bodies and our relationships with our family, friends, work and surroundings. But it is not difficult to see a multiplicity of ways in which health can also be seen as connecting us globally. The social determinants of health, the conditions of daily life, are forged within global political and economic systems and their environmental accompaniments (World Health Organization (WHO), 2011a). Although the evidence is complex, the global financial crisis of 2008 and subsequently (Suhrcke and Stuckler, 2012) and the policy responses in countries like Greece (Kentikelenis *et al.*, 2012) are clearly having a substantial worldwide impact on population health, and most immediately, mental health. Major illnesses, especially infectious or communicable diseases, cross national boundaries or are the common experience of peoples in different countries. Philanthropists, NGOs and international institutions now look to eradicate communicable and non-communicable diseases through global programmes (Gulland, 2010). Health care policy-makers look at other countries for ideas about how to create efficient and effective systems and health care providers. Pharmaceutical companies and health insurance providers are amongst the largest transnational companies with billions of customers. In 2010, three of the top ten highest paid CEOs in the world were running health care companies (Sherter, 2011).

Health policy within countries is subject to international rules on trade and other dimensions of economic policy, so that, most starkly through the 1990s, it has been suggested that the World Bank had more influence over international health policy than the WHO (Elmendorf, 2010). The 2010 bailout deals which Greece, Ireland and Portugal were forced to sign with the International Monetary Fund, the European Central Bank and the European Commission involved detailed pre-scriptions for their health policies, including fixed limits on health spending as a proportion of GDP, already relatively low in Greece and Portugal, the restructuring of health care systems and measures to open up their health economies to private, market-based solutions (Fahy, 2012).

This reflects the reality that the context of national, health-related social, eco-nomic and environmental policies is not just global but ideological. It is not simply that actions taken in one country have impacts in others, that we are connected to one another because we share the planet. Rather, it is that the holders of political, economic and military power mainly propound a particular approach to globalisa-tion which helps to maintain their positions of power: neo-liberalism (Labonte and Schrecker, 2007a, 2007b, 2007c). That is why the focus of this chapter is not just on global health but on globalised health.

Applied to health, neo-liberal globalisation is the belief that free markets create the best circumstances for economic development and, therefore, of securing and distributing the social conditions which underpin good population health. It is also argued that the economic success of free markets enable health *care* to be funded and create the most efficient ways of providing health care and of distributing health care across populations. By deregulating economies, it is suggested, mini-mising taxes on business and individuals, and reducing the size and influence of governments, competition is promoted between private health care and insurance companies with benefits for investors seeking to maximise returns on their wealth. This leads, it is argued, to low costs by comparison with publicly provided services. Such competition is said to promote innovation in treatment and care by offering high rewards to the commercially successful.

This approach to health and health care is, of course, profoundly contested (Berwick and Hackbarth, 2012; Lister, 2011). The evidence indicates that, on the contrary, private health care is highly inefficient and ineffective, with high admin-istrative costs (estimated at between 21% and 47% of total health costs in the USA) accompanying high risks for the quality of care as the expertise and quantity of front line and support staffing is driven down by low wages. Specialist staff are also attracted from countries where levels of health need are much greater. The search for profit results in the selling of unnecessary health care tests, procedures and treat-ments and the creation of spurious health needs, exemplified by the commercial cosmetic surgery business. The profoundly unequal societies created by neo-liberal economic policies are inimical to high levels of population health (Wilkinson and Pickett, 2009). For example, in the USA total health expenditure was 16.2% of gross domestic product in 2009, almost twice the European Union average (http://data.worldbank.org/indicator/SH.XPD.TOTL.ZS). However, average life expectancy at birth in the USA at 78 years, was below the 79 years of Costa Rica, Chile or Cuba, countries spending around 10% of greatly smaller GDPs (http://data.worldbank.org/indicator/SP.DYN.LE00.IN) or New Zealand (80 years) where total health care spending was around a third per head of that in the USA (Anderson and Markovitch, 2011). Despite this evidence, the grip that neo-liberal ideas have over political thought and power in developed countries is exemplified by the recent marketisation of the NHS in England (Lees and Player, 2011), one of the most efficient and effective health services in the world, with the highest level of popular support (Thomson *et al.*, 2011).

Social work internationally has similarly experienced the impact of neo-liberal policies with large numbers of jobs being lost in both health care and other settings, public services privatised and contracted out, and payment-by-results approaches introduced (Sulman *et al.*, 2001). Such changes are at odds with the profession's belief that health and social care are human rights.

Three significant developments may shift the current hegemonic grip of neo-liberal thinking on globalised policy making. The first is the challenge set out by the WHO Commission on the Social Determinants of Health (2008). The Commission's approach emphasises the importance of structural social, economic, environmental and political factors rather than medical intervention or individual behaviour as the source of good health. It makes reducing inequalities in health a central recommendation and policy goal, recognising that an emphasis on social determinants alone could result in increased inequity. Its analysis is in direct opposition to the dominant economic orthodoxy. Endorsed by the full WHO, the CSDH report was subsequently reinforced by an international conference supported by well over 100 countries in Rio Di Janeiro in 2011. Although criticised by the People's Health Movement amongst others for not going far enough, the Rio Declaration proposed five key actions, urging nations and global bodies to:

1. Adopt better governance for health and development;
2. Promote participation in policy-making and implementation;
3. Further reorient the health sector towards reducing health inequalities;
4. Strengthen global governance and collaboration;
5. Monitor progress and increase accountability. (WHO, 2011b)

Many local, national and regional bodies have conducted health policy reviews inspired and informed by the CSDH analysis although, as in England, it is possible for the language of 'social determinants' to be co-opted by politicians whose actions are increasing inequalities (Department of Health, 2010).

The second challenge comes from the emerging strategic interventions by the BRICS[1] countries (Global Health Strategies Initiatives (GHSI), 2011). As the GHSI Report (funded by the Bill and Melinda Gates Foundation) suggests, the BRICS are now creating a significant alternative power bloc to the Western powers which have dominated since the Second World War. They are seeking to present an alternative approach to health and development based on their own experiences. In some cases this may be positive. For example, Brazil's action to improve health by reducing poverty through the Bolsa Familia programme has been seen as having a significant impact. But as yet it is unclear to what extent the BRICS emergent power is producing a genuinely new approach to international health policy rather than a challenge to Western domination based on similar goals, ideologies and outcomes.

However, perhaps the most significant immediate threat to neo-liberal policy making comes from the continuing global financial crisis and the increasingly powerful democratic opposition which is building across Europe, in particular, at the time of writing in May 2012. It is by no means clear that the proposed solution to the crisis, the classic neo-liberal combination of reduced public expenditure, lower taxation and deregulated financial and labour markets can succeed in its own terms by reducing national deficits, because of the negative impact of austerity measures on growth, let alone maintain democratic support. The neo-liberal project looks increasingly unlikely to be able to solve some of the major global social and economic problems such as food security, migration or environmental sustainability and that is creating greater political instability and fuelling violent conflicts.

Social work action in the context of globalisation

Even if you accept that this globalised context is relevant to all social work practice and to service users' health, it can be hard to see how to respond in practice. How do you apply an understanding of globalisation to everyday practice? Here I am going to suggest three key dimensions: downstream, with individuals and families; midstream, with populations; and upstream, at a policy level.

Downstream action

An analysis of globalisation can inform social workers' assessment of the work situations they face whether that is the circumstances of service users or their own work context and practices. As I have suggested already, globalisation is affecting the social determinants of health on a daily basis. Current UK policies typify many Western economies in undermining ordinary families' opportunities for good quality housing, incomes, education and health and social care. House building has been at historically low levels while housing benefits are capped and cut so that families are being forced into deeper poverty. Welfare benefits generally are also being cut with an increasing emphasis on forcing claimants to find work, coupled with a draconian approach to claims on grounds of illness or disability, even though there are twenty people seeking work for every vacancy. State schools are being forced to become independent of local government to create a market-driven education system while so-called free schools run by private corporations and individuals are being preferentially subsidised. Health care is being privatised, while expenditure on social care (mainly privately provided) is increasingly squeezed. Meanwhile the over 700,000 reduction in public sector jobs means that more people are unemployed, further driving down wages. Some parents who are struggling with this perfect storm of social disadvantage will find it too hard to manage their caring responsibilities because of ill-health, particularly mental illness, drug and alcohol misuse or simple lack of money. An analysis which foregrounds the social determinants of health and wellbeing should inform social workers' assessments, their judgements about service users' lives and capacities, and their interventions, with workers seeking at all times to share their understanding of the wider context and their power with service users.

For example, in England the Marmot Review (2010) recommended that the highest priority for reducing health inequalities was to focus on the early years, before the school entry age of five. The main policy mechanism for this is the Children's Centre programme instituted some ten years ago. Although Children's Centres vary considerably in content, at their best these programmes provide wide-ranging support for parents from before birth to school entry, with an emphasis on the first two years. Usually a small local service, with strong parental involvement in governance arrangements, the key focus is intervention in three respects: children's cognitive development, communication and language, social and emotional development and physical health; parenting, the interactions between parent and child; and parental resources, including their mental wellbeing, their income and their support networks (Bowers and Strelitz, 2012). Children's Centres can combine support to individual families and children through a mixture of educative and self-help group activities such as baby massage, music-based groups or parenting programmes such as Triple P, with financial and debt advice and help to enable parents to gain skills relevant to employment. Provided by a partnership of social work, health, education and other agencies, Children's Centres work on the basis of progressive universalism. That is, they are open to all but greater proportions of service are provided to those who have greatest need. (In the absence of this, greater take-up by more affluent parents could make inequalities even wider.) This can be achieved by maximising access to basic services, for example, by combining focused outreach with running open-door drop-in sessions to ease participation by parents who may lack confidence or fear being stigmatised as bad parents. This enables staff to get alongside and steer those who have most to gain towards groups for which numbers are restricted. At the same time many parents are helped to move from being recipients of help to volunteers supporting others. Although a mixture of staff skills are valuable, the role of social workers is vital, their generic training enabling them to build relationships with individuals, see families' health needs in a broad social context and to establish a culture of safeguarding children designed to reduce the need for formal child-protection interventions.

Social workers, too, should analyse their own increasingly difficult working conditions as they find themselves in the front line of cutting expenditure by removing or refusing services to people with high levels of need. It is important that social workers recognise the globalised context of the eligibility criteria and the managerial systems they are operating within. Social workers could act collectively to defend services, building trade union and/or professional body support and on occasions taking the risk of refusing to collude with practice which is contrary to the UN Declaration of Human Rights. Article 25 asserts the right to:

> a standard of living adequate for health and well-being of self and of family, including food, clothing, housing and medical care and necessary social services, and the right to security in the event of unemployment, sickness, disability, widowhood, old age or other lack of livelihood in circumstances beyond his control.

Legal redress for service users, under human rights legislation may be a further avenue for individual or class action.

Midstream action

Midstream action on health can take a number of forms including population-based interventions; policy responses and activism. One of the key features of published examples of social work action on health inequalities in Bywaters *et al.* (2009) is that frequently social workers move from an individual case to a response to a population of similar cases. For example, Quinn and Knifton (2009) showed how mental health stigma which was preventing members of ethnic minority populations in Scotland from accessing needed services was reduced by engaging in structured conversations with the community as a whole. Heinonen *et al.* (2009) reported that a survey of women's health in a rural community in Inner Mongolia found many cases of severe difficulty and led to group-based training to promote health and other activities, empowering very disadvantaged women to act collaboratively and secure additional resources for their villages.

Such population-based action can often provide the evidence for mid-range policy change. Lethborg and Posenelli (2009) describe how social work services for cancer patients as a whole were transformed in a Melbourne hospital when the social work team focused on providing equal access to their services for all cancer patients, with priority given to those in greatest need. Creating new evidence-based protocols, screening tools and procedures also enabled the social work team to enhance its credibility with the wider hospital community. Such midstream policy action can include advocating for state or national level change. Sinclair *et al.* (2011) describe the development of a user-led First Nations suicide prevention programme for young people in Manitoba, Canada. They comment, amongst other things, on the range of skills required to build, establish and maintain the programme, skills which 'go beyond training and capacity building to include: policy analysis, government relations, advocacy, research projects, and membership of numerous national and provincial committees' (p. 34).

The recent international 'Occupy' movements are only one example of what is arguably a growing direct action response to the consequences of globalisation.

Social workers individually and collectively have to decide whether allying them-selves with such direct action is either an appropriate form of professional practice or an intervention to be taken up outside work. However, building alliances with service user groups and activists locally and nationally, as well as with like-minded professionals in other disciplines, are less controversial forms of action.

Upstream action

Hong and Song (2010) argue that a strategic social work response to globalisation – upstream action – could be based on three key transformations: the creation of globalised civil society movements, the establishment of globalised social policy making and the creation of a set of minimum standards in social welfare to which all countries would sign up. These transformations are best represented in social work by the Global Agenda for Social Work and Social Development[2] presented to the UN and national governments in March 2012 (http://www.globalsocialag enda.org/). It commits the profession to join other worldwide social movements to secure human rights and states that:

- the full range of human rights are available to only a minority of the world's population;
- unjust and poorly regulated economic systems . . . have damaged the health and wellbeing of people and communities causing poverty and growing inequality;
- cultural diversity and the right to self-expression . . . are in danger due to aspects of globalisation which standardise and marginalise peoples, with espe-cially damaging consequences for indigenous and first nations peoples;
- people live in communities and thrive in the context of supportive relation-ships, which are being eroded by dominant economic, political and social forces;
- people's health and wellbeing suffer as a result of inequalities and unsustainable environments related to climate change, pollutants, war, natural disasters and violence to which there are inadequate international responses.

Consequently, we feel compelled to advocate for a new world order which makes a reality of respect for human rights and dignity and a different structure of human relationships.'

Such a new world order would include a set of common welfare policies which, if implemented, would create a minimum level of social security and social ser-vices which all employers and all governments would be required to implement. This would place a limit on the capacity of the market to drive down wages and working conditions. This idea is most clearly expressed in the Social Protection Floor initiative of the International Labour Organization. Endorsed by the United Nations Chief Executives Board and by the Heads of State and Government in the 2010 Millennium Development Summit, it proposes an integrated set of policies designed to guarantee income security and access to essential social services for all, paying particular attention to vulnerable groups and protecting and empowering people across the life cycle. It includes guarantees of:

- basic income security;
- universal access to essential affordable social services in the areas of health, water and sanitation, education, food security, housing, and others defined according to national priorities (see http://www.ilo.org/public/english/pro tection/spfag/socialfloor/index.htm).

Social workers can support such upstream action by participating in the national and international social work representative organisations that support the Global Agenda and also by engaging directly with wider social movements, such as the People's Health Movement and the World Social Forum.

Conclusion

A globalised world requires that social work extends its thinking, skills and range of responses if it is to maximise its contribution to service users' health and to population health. Population and individual health is fundamentally a product of the social determinants of health. The unjust distribution of social, economic, environmental and political conditions results in unequal health outcomes which breach human rights. We are currently living through a historical period in which a particular form of ideology – neo-liberalism – dominates global policy making, commerce and international relations. This ideology has many health-damaging economic, environmental and political consequences and undermines the develop-ment or maintenance of universal health and social services. However, in the reac-tions of worldwide social movements, in the profound stresses in the international economy and in the shift in the balance of power to the BRICS countries and their allies, it is possible to see the seeds of neo-liberalism's self-destruction. In the mean-time, social work practice can be enhanced if social workers' analysis of their own work situation and the lives of service users are informed by an understanding of globalisation. Such an analysis calls for imaginative responses targeting downstream, midstream and upstream issues.

QUESTIONS FOR REFLECTION

1. How do you understand globalisation? How does it affect the social determinants of health and health inequalities?
2. How does globalisation impact on the health of service users and the work of social workers?
3. How can health-related social work practice be extended to respond to a context which is no longer just local, but global?

Notes

1. The BRICS countries are Brazil, Russia, India, China and South Africa. The terms BRIC was coined in 2001 by Jim O'Neil, then Head of Global Economic Research at Goldman Sachs to describe what he thought of as a four fastest growing emerging economies. The BRIC countries first met to coordinate policy in 2006 and in 2010 South Africa was invited to join.
2. The Global Agenda on Social Work and Social Development (http://www.globalsoci alagenda.org/) was formulated by the three large international organisations representing social work: the International Federation of Social Workers, International Association of Schools of Social Work and the International Council for Social Welfare.

References

Anderson, G.F. & Markovitch, P. (2011) *Multinational Comparisons of Health Systems Data, 2010.* Available at: http://www.commonwealthfund.org/~/media/Files/Publications/Issue%20Brief/2011/Jul/PDF_1533_Anderson_multinational_comparisons_2010_OECD_pfd.pdf

Berwick, D.M. & Hackbarth, A.D. (2012) 'Eliminating waste in US health care', *Journal of the American Medical Association*, vol. 307, no. 14, pp. 1513–1516.

Bowers, A.P. & Strelitz, J. with Allen, J. & Donkin, A. (2012) *An Equal Start: Improving Outcomes in Children's Centres – An Evidence Review*, Institute of Equity, University College London, London.

Bywaters, P. (2009) 'Tackling inequalities in health: A global challenge for social work', *British Journal of Social Work*, vol. 39, no. 2, pp. 353–367.

Bywaters, P., McLeod, E. & Napier, L. (eds) (2009) *Social Work and Global Health Inequalities*, Policy Press, Bristol, UK.

Commission on the Social Determinants of Health (CSDH) (2008) *Closing the Gap in a Generation: Final Report*, World Health Organisation, Geneva.

Department of Health (2010) *Equity and Excellence: Liberating the NHS. Cm 7881*, The Stationery Office, London.

Elmendorf, A.E. (2010) *Global Health Then and Now. UN Chronicle XLVII, 2.* Available at: http://www.un.org/wcm/content/site/chronicle/home/archive/issues2010/achieving_global_health

Fahy, N. (2012) 'Who is shaping the future of European health systems?' *British Medical Journal*, vol. 344: e1712.

Global Health Strategies Initiatives (2011) *Shifting Paradigm: How the BRICS Are Reshaping Global Health and Development* [online]. Available at: http://www.ghsinitiatives.org/

Gulland, A. (2010) 'Gates Foundation gives $10bn for research and delivery of vaccines', *British Medical Journal*, vol. 340: c650.

Heinonen, T., Yang J., Deane, L. & Cheung, M. (2009) 'Social work in rural China', in P. Bywaters, E. McLeod, & L. Napier, (eds), *Social Work and Global Health Inequalities*, Policy Press, Bristol, UK, pp. 172–177.

Hong, P.Y.P. & Song, I.H. (2010) 'Glocalization of social work practice: Global and local responses to globalization', *International Social Work*, vol. 53, no. 5, pp. 656–670.

Kentikelenis, A. Karanikolos, M., Papanicolas I., Basu, S., McKee, M. & Stuckler, D. (2012) 'Health effects of financial crisis: Omens of a Greek tragedy', *The Lancet*, vol. 378, no. 9801, October 22, pp. 1457–1458.

Labonte, R. & Schrecker, T. (2007a) 'Globalization and social determinants of health: Introduction and Methodological Background (part 1 of 3)', *Globalization and Health*, vol. 3, no. 5. Available at: http://www.globalizationandhealth.com/content/3/1/5

Labonte, R. & Schrecker, T. (2007b) 'Globalization and social determinants of health: The role of the global marketplace (part 2 of 3)', *Globalization and Health*, vol. 3, no. 6. Available at: http://www.globalizationandhealth.com/content/3/1/6

Labonte, R. & Schrecker, T. (2007c) 'Globalization and social determinants of health: Promoting health equity in global governance (part 3 of 3)', *Globalization and Health*, vol. 3, no. 7. Available at: http://www.globalizationandhealth.com/content/3/1/7

Lees, C. & Player, S. (2011) *The Plot Against the NHS*, Merlin Press, Pontypool, UK.

Lethborg, C. & Posenelli, S. (2009) 'Improving psychosocial care for cancer patients', in *Social Work and Global Health Inequalities*, P. Bywaters, E. McLeod & L. Napier (eds), Policy Press, Bristol, UK, pp. 198–208.

Lister, J. (ed) (2011) *Europe's Health for Sale: The Heavy Cost of Privatisation*, Libri Publishing, Faringdon, UK.

Marmot, M. (2010) *Fair Society, Healthy Lives: Strategic Review of Health Inequalities in England post 2010*. Available at: http://www.marmotreview.org

Quinn, N. & Knifton, L. (2009) 'Addressing mental health inequalities in Scotland through community conversation', in *Social Work and Global Health Inequalities*, P. Bywaters, E. McLeod & L. Napier (eds), Policy Press, Bristol, UK, pp. 192–197.

Sherter, A. (2011) 'Highest-paid CEOs: Top earner takes home $145 million'. Available at: http://www.cbsnews.com/8301–505123_162–57343611/highest-paid-ceos-top-earner-takes-home-$145-million/

Sinclair, S., Meawasige, A. & Kinew, K.A. (2011) 'Youth for Youth – a model for youth suicide prevention: Case study of the Assembly of Manitoba Chiefs Youth Council and Secretariat, Canada', in *Social Determinants Approaches to Public Health: From Concept to Practice*, E. Blas, J. Sommerfeld & A.S. Kurup (eds), WHO, Geneva.

Suhrcke, M. & Stuckler, D. (2012) 'Will the recession be bad for our health? It depends', *Social Science and Medicine*, vol. 74, no. 5, pp. 647–653.

Sulman, J., Savage, D. & Way, S. (2001) 'Retooling social work practice for high volume short stay', *Social Work in Healthcare*, vol. 34, nos. 3–4, pp. 315–332.

Thomson, S., Osborn, R., Squires, D. & Reed, S.J. (2011) *International Profiles of Health Care Systems, 2011*. Commonwealth Fund, New York.

Wilkinson, R. & Pickett, K. (2009) *The Spirit Level: Why More Equal Societies Almost Always Do Better*, Allen Lane, London.

World Health Organization (WHO) (2011a) *Closing the Gap: Policy into Practice on Social Determinants of Health*, Author, Geneva.

World Health Organization (2011b) *Rio Political Declaration on Social Determinants of Health* [online], Available at: http://www.who.int/sdhconference/declaration/en/

4

FACING THE CHALLENGES TOGETHER

A future vision for health social work

Linda Haultain

CHAPTER OBJECTIVES

Numerous questions, tensions and professional concerns emerge when we are asked to contemplate future visions for social work in healthcare. When I was approached to author this chapter the editors suggested I consider the question 'what do you expect health social work practice to look like ten years from now?' In order to better respond to this question I turned to the literature, reflected on current health social work practice, considered the policy, economic, political and organisational context in which health social work practice occurs, spoke to colleagues and remembered my own and close families' recent encounters with the health system. I also reflected on the demands and achievements associated with my present professional leadership of health social workers. This process of critical reflection has left me with more questions than answers, and the future vision I have explored and mapped out should be considered tentative at best. This tentativeness is associated with the tensions that emerged during this reflective activity and the stark realisation that the profession will be required to continually navigate and resolve a number of significant challenges in order to ensure a sustainable future. In order to formulate a response to these tests the chapter objectives include:

1. *A brief exploration of the perennial challenges and emerging themes health social workers face;*
2. *An outline of the core functions and roles of health social workers;*
3. *An exploration of some of the professional activities and strategies that will help strengthen and sustain the professions role in a health environment.*

Introduction

Perennial challenges and emergent themes

The health social work literature highlights and reinforces a number of consistent international challenges which reflect my day-to-day experience in the context of a large district health board and teaching hospital in Aotearoa New Zealand. These challenges include the ever-increasing global prominence of market-driven, cost-containment strategies (Berkman, 1996; Judd and Sheffield, 2010; Mizrahi and Berger, 2005); reduced length of hospital stay and pressure for rapid discharge (Sulman *et al.*, 2001); demographic changes such as the aging population (Aldrich, 2010) and an increasingly culturally diverse population (Pecukonis *et al.*, 2003); growing numbers of patients with multiple, chronic health problems (Berkman, 1996); health inequalities (Whiteside, 2004); technological advancements (Pecukonis *et al.*, 2003) and the impact on the profession of a constantly changing health environment (Joubert, 2006; Judd and Sheffield, 2010).

The ever-increasing focus on cost containment, and the requirement to do more with less, intensifies the pressure to consider the impact of our professional activities on patient outcomes. Under these conditions the need to justify and demonstrate the impact of our professional contribution also escalates. This translates into heightened expectations to engage in evidence-based practice (Trinder, 2000), with robust evidence of positive outcomes (Epstein, 2010). When we consider the resource and access issues associated with health inequalities, the need to pay urgent attention to how limited social work resources are effectively utilised becomes paramount.

There is little argument that every person's quality and length of life on the planet is profoundly impacted for better or for worse by socially constructed health inequalities (Bywaters *et al.*, 2009). Proposing that, historically, social policy has maintained a focus on health care because of the 'public good' aspect of health, some argue that public policy in relation to health care has dire consequences based on the amount of public resources we are willing to devote to it. These determinants include who will be cared for and who will miss out, who will be relieved and who will suffer, who will live and who will die (Cheyne *et al.*, 1997).

We see the impact of these social determinants being played out every day in our own countries and communities. Here in New Zealand, although diminishing, the life expectancy gap between Māori (indigenous people of New Zealand) and non-Māori is described by one health commentator as 'still large and "stark"' (Blakely, 2008, p. 10). The international messages are also clear regarding the unequal distribution of toxic experiences, such as bad politics, poor social policy and programmes, and unjust economic arrangements, in short, the social determinants of health (Commission on Social Determinants of Health, 2008).

There is a growing awareness of health inequalities and the contribution health social workers could make to reduce these disparities as articulated by Bywaters and his colleagues (Bywaters *et al.*, 2009). For those of us who work on the front line of the health system there is a struggle to find a balance between the provisions of individually focused interventions, and engaging in activities that are likely to result in larger-scale change. A number of challenges confront us in this context which may hamper our attempts to shift our focus from the micro to the macro.

As long ago as 1996 health social work authors identified what they described as old and new health care paradigms (Berkman, 1996). Berkman maintained that, traditionally, the health system was based on patterns of acute, simple disease which were unpredictable. Conversely the new health care paradigm recognises that increasing volumes of patients are requiring health care for multiple, chronic health conditions. These chronic conditions are understood to be impacted by multiple factors, such as an individual's access to health care, their physical environment, genetic makeup, their social context and psychological functioning (Berkman, 1996; Stone, 2007). In short, many of these elements reflect the social determinants of health, and require health social workers and our medical colleagues to consider alternative approaches to the traditional model as described by Berkman above.

The changing health care paradigm has also impacted on health social work, particularly in the area of hospital-based practice and the increased focus on reduced length of stay. The average length of stay in a New Zealand hospital is less than four days, while some patients experience excessive periods of hospitalisation, particularly the elderly (Sulman *et al.*, 2001). In this context early identification of psychosocial needs, and the rapid assessment and intervention required to support a timely and effective discharge is critical (Sulman *et al.*, 2001). This approach may be in conflict with the need to provide effective responses to the chronically ill patient impacted negatively by the social determinants of health such as poor housing, poverty and limited access to health care.

The link between health inequalities and ethnicity has been firmly established (Gauld, 2003) as is the profession's responsibility to address issues of social justice (Social Work Registration Board, 2008). This responsibility has multiple ways of manifesting in practice, including our ability to provide culturally competent psychosocial assessments that enable social workers to identify and address concerns linked to the social determinants of health. What then does the literature say about the role of health social workers and what has remained milestone knowledge, consistently relied on to support the aims of health social work? What new knowledge has emerged to support our way forward and what challenges do we face as we move forward into the future?

Broad agreements in the health context

Drawing on my doctoral research situated in an acute hospital environment and linking these findings to the literature, current skills and agreed priorities are highlighted. This review provides a firm foundation from which to explore the future roles and responsibilities of health social workers.

It is Rock (2002) who reinforces for us what has remained a largely consistent vision for the first medical social worker developed in 1908 by Cabot and Cannon in the Massachusetts General Hospital. This vision includes the need to understand the patient and their environment, especially; the importance of family and the community including its resources; compliance with medical treatment plans; discharge planning and follow-up and research, particularly related to the needs of the community (Rock, 2002).

Rock contrasts the dominant 20th century biomedical worldview with the more contemporary biopsychosocial approach preferred by health social workers. The former is focused on disease, the reductionism of complex phenomena, a mind/body dualism and a lack of acknowledgement of the social, psychological and behavioural elements of illness. In contrast, 'the biopsychosocial model attempts to integrate a vision of a patient as a person, in-situation, not unlike the social work concept of person–environment fit' (Rock, 2002, p. 11).

While acknowledging the longstanding relevance the biopsychosocial worldview has had in the health context, the economic climate demands that health social workers make decisions about what requests for services are prioritised on a day-to-day basis (Giles *et al.*, 2007). The requirement to allocate social work resources to meet both the needs of the patients and the organisation is acknowledged as a challenge faced by social work practitioners and leaders alike (Giles *et al.*, 2007).

These decisions are being made in a context which is in a constant state of change with diminishing resources *and* an ever-increasing requirement to provide an accountable, effective, evidence-based and outcomes-focused service (Giles *et al.*, 2007). Giles and her colleagues invite us to consider where to begin in an environment that increasingly privileges evidence, outputs and outcomes.

As far back as 1993 Ross challenged the profession to examine the basis of our decision making and to use the evidence generated to help inform the social work administrative functions in health, i.e., the allocation of resources. Further, Ross invited health social workers to take the responsibility for setting these priorities seriously and develop the capacity to justify our decisions based on client need, balanced against the knowledge that we have the ability to meet this need (Ross, 1993).

Giles *et al*'s (2007) study aimed to respond to Ross's invitation by exploring the views of health social workers regarding their clinical priorities and the knowledge drawn on to inform these priority-setting decisions. The outcome of the study was the development of a set of clinical priorities for health social work practice. Making an explicit connection between the clinical priorities and the Australian Association of Social Workers' ethical requirements, each priority has been linked to a corresponding ethical obligation (identified in brackets). The clinical priorities are centred on three primary areas of social work activity: safety and risk (Human dignity and worth); social and psychosocial support (Service to humanity); and access to resources (Social justice) (Giles *et al.*, 2007).

These priorities are closely aligned to, and reinforce, the findings of my doctoral research, undertaken in the acute hospital environment. This study aimed to identify the dimensions of effective health social work, relying on a mixed-method study which sought the opinions of health social workers, nurses, midwives and doctors (Haultain, 2011). By including our medical colleagues as participants I aimed to identify the needs of patients as described by those members of the multidisciplinary team who have the responsibility for identifying and referring patients and their families to health social workers. In a context where meeting the needs of the organisation is imperative, it was reassuring to discover that, for the most part, our views regarding the roles, responsibilities and dimensions of practice associated with effective health social work are congruent across the disciplines. Following the example of Giles and her colleagues I have linked the domains of practice, with the ethical requirements, and practice standards as described by the Aotearoa New Zealand Association of Social Workers.

TABLE 4.1 Service domains and ethical obligations and practice standards

Domain	Definition – the effective health social worker	Relevant elements of the IFSW Statement of Ethical Principles (IFSW, 2012)
Cultural advocacy and support	• is culturally competent, aware and responsive • applies these personal and professional qualities to support patient safety, comfort and engagement with the health service • attends to both patient and family needs • understands the risks and demands associated with cross-cultural service provision • actively assists members of the multidisciplinary team (MDT) to provide a culturally responsive health service	• promote the right to participation • recognise and respect cultural diversity • distribute resources equitably • challenge unjust practices
Medical advocacy and support	• is alert to the patient and their families' understanding of and engagement with the medical context • actively seeks to notice and respond to misunderstanding in close consultation with our medical colleagues	• respect and promote people's right to make their own decisions and choices • promote the right to participation
Emotional advocacy and support	• provides advocacy and support to ensure the emotional distress patients and their *whānau* experience is responded to • engages with warmth, compassion and empathy towards patients and their *whānau* • maintains a non-judgemental approach towards our clients • seeks to use ourselves and our relationships with patients and families to help support change	• uphold and defend each person's emotional integrity and wellbeing • treat each person as a whole • identify and develop strengths • act with compassion, empathy and care

(Continued)

TABLE 4.1 *(Continued)*

Domain	Definition – the effective health social worker	Relevant elements of the IFSW Statement of Ethical Principles (IFSW, 2012)
Practical advocacy and support	• ensures the provision of the basic necessities of life while people are in hospital and upon discharge • has a sound knowledge of resources both internal and external to the hospital • accesses resources to support a safe and timely discharge	• uphold and defend each person's physical integrity and wellbeing • distribute resources equitably
Responding to vulnerability and risk	• is able to identify, assess and respond to the needs of vulnerable patients and their famiy in order to reduce risk, and increase patient safety and wellbeing • vulnerable infants and children • vulnerable adults (due to disability and/or cognitive impairment) • elder abuse and neglect	• uphold and defend each person's psychological and emotional integrity and wellbeing • respect the right to self-determination • recognise the UN Convention on the Rights of the Child (1989) • recognise the UN Convention on the Elimination of all Forms of Discrimination against Women (1979)
Working the ward – dependable service delivery	• provides a dependable, timely service • proactively identifies patients who may require our input • prioritises competing demands in order to meet patient and family needs • assesses and meet needs in a timely manner • solves complex psychosocial problems for the benefit of the patients, their family and the organisation	• maintain professional standards of conduct • develop and maintain the required skills and competence to do our job
Psychosocial assessment with a focus on safe and timely discharge	• undertakes timely assessment of a patient's needs • develops and implements intervention plans • works in consultation to support a safe and timely discharge from the hospital	• uphold and defend each person's physical, psychological, emotional and spiritual integrity and wellbeing

(Continued)

TABLE 4.1 (*Continued*)

Domain	Definition – the effective health social worker	Relevant elements of the IFSW Statement of Ethical Principles (IFSW, 2012)
Team relationships	• develops and maintains relationships with the MDT for the benefit of our patients and their families	• conduct oneself professionally
Team work	• understands the value of team work • works in close consultation with the MDT to support appropriate patient care and outcomes	• maintain professional standards of conduct • challenge unjust practices
Communication	• is an open, clear and concise communicator who understands the importance of timely, accurate and professional communication with members of the MDT, patients and family • provides an information pathway between patients, their families and the MDT	• professional conduct

In light of the longstanding challenges the profession faces in the health context as described earlier in this chapter, the changing health paradigms and population needs, and the belief that the role of health social workers has been clearly defined and endorsed by our medical colleagues, where to from here? Having identified fundamental priorities where does the profession go now, in order to ensure a secure and sustainable future?

Looking to the future – developing our capacity

Our professional forebears have provided us with a solid foundation upon which we are able to build. These achievements include having firmly established the link between the medical and the social circumstances of people's lives, more recently articulated as the biopsychosocial model of health. Further accomplishments include having identified a set of roles, responsibilities and priorities that reflect our ethical obligations, organisational and patient needs. What remains to be done? Now, more than ever before, health social workers must accelerate their capacity to use the resources at the disposal of patients, families and the health system to best effect.

When we consider the changing needs of the population and the constrained resources we have to meet those needs, it is difficult not to think of the elastic band analogy where resources are simply stretched, and stretched to breaking point. This is not what I am advocating. At the risk of sounding like a Pollyanna, I propose we find ways of working smarter, and find ways of applying our social work knowledge, skills and abilities to the patients and their families who need us most.

Almost a decade ago Pecukonis *et al.* (2003), predicted an uncertain future for health social work describing it as being 'at a critical juncture' (2003, p. 1). They argued that a shift from hospital to ambulatory services, an increased focus on primary prevention, and growing numbers of patients with chronic conditions demanded we develop a new set of skills. By way of example they invited us to consider the five-year risk factors associated with cardio-vascular disease: diet, obesity, a sedentary lifestyle, smoking and hypertensions (Pecukonis *et al.*, 2003). They note that all these risk factors reflect lifestyle choices and behaviour which could be positively influenced by social work interventions.

Making a link with other behaviours associated with high levels of risk which have health implications, and therefore are a drain on health resources they draw our attention to family violence, child protection, elder abuse, drug and alcohol dependence, and obesity. Pecukonis *et al.* (2003) claim that all these areas pose national health concerns and argue that all of these fields of practice can, do, and should, benefit from competent health social work practice.

The concept of future-proofing the profession comes to mind as Pecukonis *et al.* make a number of recommendations regarding areas of competence development that health social workers could usefully focus on. They suggest we would benefit from learning about the brain and its influence on behaviour and emotion; understanding human genetics; developing our knowledge of psychopharmacology and developing a greater capacity to respond to physical and mental health concerns (Pecukonis *et al.*, 2003).

Reinforcing calls from other social work authors (Lymbery and Millward, 2001; Rock and Cooper, 2000), Pecukonis and colleagues emphasise the 'assembly line approach' taken by many general practitioners in a primary health setting and argue strongly for the value of health social workers in this health setting. These authors collectively describe health social workers' ability to contribute in the primary health arena as being vast. By way of example they suggest we could coordinate psycho-educational groups for patients with multiple health issues, work with high risk groups such as teenage pregnant women, drug and alcohol abusers, and the victims and perpetrators of domestic violence (Pecukonis *et al.*, 2003).

Other research has demonstrated health social workers' ability to respond effectively to depression, anxiety and to support patient's adjustment to a new diagnosis. This practice was found to result in reduced visits to the physician and improved compliance with diet, nutrition and various other medical regimens (Rock and Cooper, 2000). Co-location of health social workers in the primary health environment was also found to improve working relationships, communication and service coordination (Lymbery and Millward, 2001).

The struggle that countries such as Aotearoa New Zealand have providing accessible, appropriate and engaging health care for Māori is clear (Jansen *et al.*, 2009). The greater impact of the social determinants of health on this population results in a powerful sense of urgency to do something different. Practices which support increased disease prevention and management, health promotion and health literacy are all core elements of the types of practice skills increasingly required to make a difference for this population, whilst also reducing the financial burden associated with the burgeoning of chronic health conditions.

The literature abounds with encouragement to increasingly engage in collaborative, interprofessional and interagency practice as a more effective way of responding to complex patient needs (Zimmerman and Dabelko, 2007). In order to achieve this next level of professional competence and confidence, an increased focus is required in a number of key areas. Highlighting the inherent value of whole-of-government policies, Scott maintains the call for multiple sectors to work together grows increasingly louder (Scott, 2005). Evidence of this increased focus can be found in the recent New Zealand initiatives to develop more effective collaboration between child protection services and health.

An example of a greater focus on interdisciplinary and interagency working is an initiative regarding improved services for vulnerable pregnant women. Largely a primary health initiative driven by health social workers and midwives, pregnant women experiencing coexisting complex social problems are provided with an early intervention, multiagency wrap-around service. This approach enables priorities to be established, collaboration and communication to occur, and plans to be agreed and implemented which have at their centre, the wellbeing of mother and child.

This recent practice experience has highlighted both the enormous benefits and substantial challenges associated with effective interprofessional practice. Stone (2007) asserts that, in the current practice context, a number of factors exist which propel us towards the provision of interprofessional education to engage in more effective interprofessional practice. Reinforcing the shifting, changing and growing health demands he includes the aging population, the move towards ambulatory services, chronic disease and its drain on health resources, the need to maximise efficiency and improve cost-effectiveness as just some of the reasons to improve our capacity in this area (Stone, 2007).

Adding another important layer to the value of collaborative models of practice, Zimmerman and Dabelko contend that some hospitals are moving away from a model of health care delivery which could be described as traditional and towards a more collaborative approach to practice (Zimmerman and Dabelko, 2007). They identify that increased consumer satisfaction, improved service coordination and team performance, and increased levels of treatment compliance have been linked to these collaborative models of practice (Zimmerman and Dabelko, 2007).

When we consider the domains of effective health social work practice identified earlier in this chapter, many of which include our capacity to engage patients and their family, facilitate communication pathways in complex systems and engage in collaborative practices it is little wonder that a number of authors maintain that health social workers are well positioned to take up a leadership role grounded in social work core values and skills. In view of the environment described earlier, how can health social work position itself to ensure a strong and sustainable future?

How do we hold the space necessary to engage in the types of professional activities required to scan the horizon, future-proof the profession, develop skills and practice models, set and maintain standards while also continuing to provide the service, day to day? Clearly these initiatives will demand much from us, both individually and collectively. Unmistakably, it will require those of us in leadership roles to step up to the plate, to engage critically, ethically and humanely to effectively develop organisational and health policy.

Conclusion

While numerous responses to the challenges we face are possible, I suggest that a consolidation of our capacity to cultivate and reinforce the professional contribution we make in the health care context is the way forward. If we are to achieve this, a greater engagement with frontline practitioners is required in order to refocus and extend health social work practice. This is, at times, difficult to imagine when the roles of leadership and management are often at odds with frontline practitioners. Throughout this process of thoughtful reflection I have identified a number of areas of professional activity that, if implemented, are likely to assist us as we go forward into the brave new world of health social work. I suggest the following professional agenda.

- Apply the knowledge we have in relation to health social work roles, responsibilities and priorities to establish systems, set standards, monitor practice and increase practitioner competence;
- Increase our ability as health social work leaders to safeguard high standards of care by embedding clinical governance structures and processes (Degeling et al., 2004);
- Focus on the development of a productive organisational culture and climate (Braithwaite and Travaglia, 2008);
- Develop a learning culture (Gould and Baldwin, 2006) which supports the creation of a practice environment in which excellence can flourish (Braithwaite and Travaglia, 2008);
- Improve our capacity to lead change by learning about change management models and practice i.e. Kotter's model (Kotter, 1996);
- Boost our capacity to access, digest and apply findings from research (Plath, 2006);
- Strengthen our ability to audit, critically review, evaluate and research health social work practice in order to improve practice *and* demonstrate outcomes (Epstein, 2010); and
- Develop partnerships with local universities to grow our capacity to engage in practice-based research (Joubert, 2006).

Having identified and acknowledged the complex and on-going nature of the contextual challenges the profession faces in the health environment we are required to consider the profession's ability to develop, adapt and contribute in these circumstances. This process demands that we anticipate the skills, attitudes, behaviours, strategies and leadership competencies that will be necessary to support this adaptation; and herein lies the challenge. These challenges demand a lot from us as a profession, and time will tell if we have the professional determination, willingness and capacity to undertake the necessary activities to ensure our on-going survival as health social workers.

QUESTIONS FOR REFLECTION

1.   What have been the consistent challenges social workers have faced practising in a context which is dominated by the medical model?
2.   What skills, knowledge, strategies and approaches do health social workers need to develop in order to respond to these challenges?
3.   What role does health social work leadership play in ensuring a professional agenda is articulated and implemented in order to grow health social work practice into the future?

References

Aldrich, R. (2010) 'The aging demographic transition: The impact on elderly and social workers', *Aotearoa New Zealand Social Work Review*, vol. 22, no. 2, pp. 4–12.

Berkman, B. (1996) 'The emerging health care world: Implications for social work practice and education', *Social Work*, vol. 41, no. 5, pp. 541–551.

Blakely, T. (2008) 'Social injustice is killing people on a grand scale', *The New Zealand Medical Journal*, vol. 121, no. 1281, pp. 7–11.

Braithwaite, J. & Travaglia, J. (2008) 'An overview of clinical governance policies, practices and initiatives', *Australian Health Review*, vol. 32, no. 1, pp. 10–22.

Bywaters, P., McLeod, E. & Napier, L. (eds) (2009) *Social Work and Global Health Inequalities*, Policy Press, Bristol, UK.

Cheyne, C., O'Brien, M. & Belgrave, M. (1997) 'Health policy reform: Control or responsiveness?', in *Social Policy in Aotearoa New Zealand: A Critical Introduction*, Oxford University Press, Auckland, New Zealand, pp. 218–240.

Commission on Social Determinants of Health (CSDH) (2008) *Closing the gap in a generation: Health equity through action on the social determinants of health. Final report of the commission on social determinants of health*, World Health Organization, Geneva.

Degeling, P., Maxwell, S., Iedema, R. & Hunter, D. (2004) 'Making clinical governance work', *British Medical Journal*, vol. 329, no. 7467, pp. 679–681.

Epstein, I. (2010) *Clinical Data-mining Integrating Practice and Research*, Oxford University Press, Oxford, UK.

Gauld, R. (ed) (2003) *Continuity Amid Chaos*, University of Otago Press, Dunedin, New Zealand.

Giles, R., Gould, S., Hart, C. & Swancott, J. (2007) 'Clinical priorities: Strengthening social work practice in health', *Australian Social Work*, vol. 60, no. 2, pp. 147–165.

Gould, N., & Baldwin, M. (eds) (2006) *Social Work, Critical Reflection and the Learning Organization*, Ashgate, Aldershot, UK.

Haultain, L. (2011) *From the cleaners to the doctors – exploring the dimensions of effective health social work in the acute hospital.* Unpublished PhD Thesis, Massey University, Albany, New Zealand.

International Federation of Social Workers (IFSW) (2012) *Statement of Ethical Principles* [online]. Available at: http://ifsw.org/policies/statement-of-ethical-principles/

Jansen, P., Bacal, K. & Crengle, S. (2009) *He Ritenga Whakaaro: Maori Experiences of Health Services*, Mauri Ora Associates, Auckland, New Zealand.

Joubert, L. (2006) 'Academic-practice partnerships in practice research: A cultural shift for health social workers', *Social Work in Health Care*, vol. 43, nos. 2/3, pp. 151–161.

Judd, R. & Sheffield, S. (2010) 'Hospital social work: Contemporary roles and professional activities', *Social Work in Health Care*, vol. 49, no. 1, pp. 856–871.

Kotter, J. (1996) *Leading Change*, Harvard Business Review Press, Boston, MA.

Lymbery, M. & Millward, A. (2001) 'Community care in practice: Social work in primary health care', *Social Work Health and Mental Health*, vol. 34, nos. 3–4, pp. 241–259.

Mizrahi, T. & Berger, C. (2005) 'A longitudinal look at social work leadership in hospitals: The impact of a changing health care system', *Health and Social Work*, vol. 30, no. 2, pp. 155–163.

Pecukonis, E., Cornelius, L. & Parrish, M. (2003) 'The future of health social work', *Social Work in Health Care*, vol. 37, no. 3, pp. 1–15.

Plath, D. (2006) 'Evidence-based practice: Current issues and future directions', *Australian Social Work*, vol. 59, no. 1, pp. 56–72.

Rock, B. (2002) 'Social work in health care for the 21st century: The biopsychosocial model', in *Social Workers' Desk Reference*, A. Roberts & G. Greene (eds), Oxford University Press, New York, pp. 10–15.

Rock, B. & Cooper, M. (2000) 'Social work in primary care: A demonstration student unit utilizing practice research', *Social Work in Health Care*, vol. 31, no. 1, pp. 1–17.

Ross, J. (1993) 'Redefining hospital social work: An embattled professional domain', *Health and Social Work*, vol. 18, no. 4, pp. 243–248.

Scott, D. (2005) 'Inter-organisational collaboration in family-centred practice: A framework for analysis and action', *Australian Social Work*, vol. 58, no. 2, pp. 132–141.

Social Work Registration Board (2008) 'Code of conduct guidelines for social workers' [online]. Available at: http://www.swrb.govt.nz/code-of-conduct

Stone, N. (2007) 'Coming in from the interprofessional cold in Australia', *Australian Health Care Review*, vol. 31, no. 3, pp. 332–340.

Sulman, J., Savage, D. & Way, S. (2001) 'Retooling social work practice for high volume, short stay', *Social Work in Health Care*, vol. 34, nos. 3/4, pp. 315–332.

Trinder, L. (2000) 'Evidence-based practice in social work and probation', in *Evidence-based Practice: A Critical Appraisal*, L. Trinder & S. Reynolds (eds), Blackwell Science, Oxford, UK, pp. 138–162.

United Nations General Assembly (1979) *Convention on the Elimination of All Forms of Discrimination against Women* [online]. Available at: http://www.ohchr.org/EN/ProfessionalInterest/Pages/CEDAW.aspx

United Nations General Assembly (1989) *Convention on the Rights of the Child* [online]. Available at: http://www.unicef.org/crc/

Whiteside, M. (2004) 'The challenge of interdisciplinary collaboration in addressing the social determinants', *Australian Social Work*, vol. 57, no. 4, pp. 381–393.

Zimmerman, J. & Dabelko, H. (2007) 'Collaborative models of patient care: New opportunities for hospital social workers', *Social Work in Health Care*, vol. 44, no. 4, pp. 33–47.

5

RISK AND VULNERABILITY DISCOURSES IN HEALTH

Liz Beddoe

CHAPTER OBJECTIVES

1. *Explore how the social construction of risk permeates contemporary social care and health discourses;*
2. *Consider the social construction of vulnerable populations in contemporary health and social policy;*
3. *Critically interrogate the impact of these constructs on the social work profession and its practice with service users;*
4. *Briefly consider the potential for a counter-story.*

Introduction

The present era has been described as the 'risk society' (Beck, 1992). The construct of risk has a strong hold on contemporary society; with many suggesting that risk evokes 'the cultural character of our times' (Petersen and Wilkinson, 2008, p. 1). Essentially the sociological concept of the risk society depicts a world in which people and institutions focus energies on dangers and hazards emanating from the physical and social environments. In this way of understanding contemporary society, risk as a project requires that we all identify, assess and manage risks in everyday life. Thus risks, unaddressed and undiminished, threaten our security, health and wellbeing.

Our current epoch is dominated by 'the meshing of risk, responsibility and prudent choice' (Kemshall, 2002, p. 1). Central to the theoretical debates about the importance of risk are questions about whether the world *is* more hazardous or just feels dangerous, and the extent to which the volume and speed of access to information afforded by information and communication technologies simply raises our awareness of potential hazards. In a 'runaway world' the pace of change is rapid and new technologies bring greater complexity to our lives (Giddens, 1999a). Giddens argued that the manufactured risk of the contemporary era 'is risk created by the very progression of human development, especially by the progression of science and technology' (1999b, p. 4). We are all exposed to a constant flow of information about the dangers inherent in our food, lifestyle and via our interaction with technologies. Our own bodies become a project of regulation and government to ensure we reduce our risk of harm and infirmity. In the field of social policy however, the impact of the risk society cannot be untangled from the doctrines of neo-liberalism.

Neo-liberalism has seen Western nations focus on reducing constraints on the market, freeing up employment practices and blurring the boundaries of private and public services. A major plank of the neo-liberal project is to engineer a shift away from universal or even 'needs' focussed social policies to those which favour targeting of reduced resources on those most at risk. Risk thinking is thus embedded in current notions of welfare and social security and increasingly forms a backdrop to welfare cuts and the partial dismantling of public health care systems. The focus on 'at risk' individuals and categories of people operates as one of the mechanisms policy-makers assert provides a focus on the most vulnerable, while in reality this discourse deflects attention away from the welfare cuts and sanctioning that are rife throughout the developed world. It is not uncommon for those facing diminishing assistance to be told this reduction of support is essential in order to help those who are more at risk.

This chapter will explore some of the current discourses of risk and how this construction permeates contemporary discourses of health and wellbeing. In particular I will explore the social construction of so-called vulnerable populations in contemporary health and social policy and critically interrogate the impact of this construct on the health professionals and their practice with service users.

Theoretical perspectives

For Beck (1992) the notion of the risk society begins where traditional societies and cultures are diminished and replaced by global forces. Traditional risks from the natural environment are superseded by risk related to the consequences of modernisation e.g. technology, mass communications, industrialisation, environmental change, globalisation of markets and financial institutions (Beck, 1992). Beck argues that the central preoccupation of the risk society is no longer with the distribution of wealth ('goods') but with the distribution of risk ('bads'); on who manufactures these risks and upon whom they fall. The rise of the risk society is essentially preoccupied with the 'development of instrumental rational control', promoted in all spheres of life (Elliott, 2002, p. 295).

Beck's thesis is subject to continuing critique, in particular his belief that class theory has outlived its usefulness as a framework for understanding social conditions. Indeed the debates continue to be refreshed as the impact of global events – financial failures, national indebtedness, currency instability, environmental pollution, the impact of climate change – raises again the thorny problem of the uneven spread of the 'bads' associated with such events. Beck (1999, p. 5) reminds us in his recent debate with Curran (Beck, 2013; Curran, 2013) that he had noted earlier that 'pollution follows the poor'. Elliott (2002, p. 312) has invoked cultural and post-modern ideas about identities to argue that Beck inadequately appreciates the 'full significance of interpersonal, emotional and cultural factors as these influence and shape risk-monitoring in contemporary societies'. From a postmodernist perspective, attempts to construct risk as a 'master discourse' are rejected when there is an emphasis on 'the multiple, fragmented, discontinuous and local' (Elliott, 2002, p. 311). A plurality of cultural and political perspectives and indeed epistemological stances serve to reduce any traditional faith in the social institutions of science and medicine and concomitant faith in 'humanly engineered progress' (Elliott, 2002, p. 309). Uncertainty reigns.

Have risks increased? Adams has argued that Beck's distinction between modern risk and traditional dangers is exaggerated (1995, p. 179). Human wellbeing has always been vulnerable to hazards in the natural world. Some argue that what has changed is the complexity and multiplicity of risks and our consciousness of them (Adams, 1995). We live in a world influenced by the conviction that we must keep, and be kept, safe. One of the consequences of a heightened awareness of risk is that we all need to take responsibility for identifying, managing and reducing risk, whether as citizens or agents in corporate organisations. A personal safety plan is recommended for all and fiscal accountability requires organisations to identify the potential for costly risks. Nowhere is this more apparent in our concern for our own health (and for the health of our children).

In modern health care the risk discourse is dominant in the form of surveillance medicine demonstrated by the dramatic increase in focus on risk in the medical journals over the course of the last century (Skolbekken, 2008). The message is that we are all targets as few of us are perfectly healthy and we are all potentially subject to disease. Even in the popular media there is constant exhortation to change our habits to avoid disease and infirmity: we must reduce sugar and fat, we should drink red wine but not too much and so forth. It is our clear responsibility to be regularly tested for many diseases and to assess our bones, blood and organs for signs of deterioration. There is an inherent paradox in all this surveillance. The rationale for such surveillance is protection against our human frailty but one consequence of the Western obsession with health is that we are constantly reminded of our vulnerability (Skolbekken, 2008). We assess our genetic heritage, our lifestyle and the social and physical environments we inhabit and will almost certainly be found wanting. On any given day the number of articles in newspapers and popular magazines that focus on health risks and prevention strategies tells a story of our fearful relationship with our imperfect bodies.

Furedi's (2007) essay on fear suggests that the obsession with risk creates a new category of persons who are at risk and 'to be "at risk"' is no longer just about the probability of some hazard impacting on you; it is also about who you are as a person' (Furedi, 2007, p. 6). Within the realm of social policy whole categories of people, such as children, older people and adolescents are categorised as being at risk. Furedi suggests that a consequence of this obsession with predicting and managing risk has:

> Become something which shapes and makes our identities. To be 'at risk' clearly assigns to the individual a passive and dependent role. Increasingly, someone defined as being at risk is seen to exist in a permanent condition of vulnerability – and this informs the way that we make sense of the threats we face. (Furedi, 2007, p. 7)

It is in this realm that the risk discourse intersects with the interests of social workers in their commitment to ensuring the wellbeing of people and human worth and dignity. Social workers frequently interact with those who have already collected the vulnerable or at risk labels. I argue here for a challenge to the growth in use of vulnerability as a label with which to categorise groups of people and thus impose or deny services through rationing and governing mechanisms.

Vulnerability

In the worlds of health and social care where risk thinking has become dominant, this discourse is underpinned by the belief that in all spheres *rational* control of risk is an achievable goal. The prediction of the likelihood of future harm occurring to services users and/others is central to the risk practices 'mobilized by professionals such as psychologists, psychiatrists, correctional workers and social workers to predict, control and manage the risk of marginalized people who come under their gaze' (Pollack, 2010, p. 5). Such categories of people are then deemed vulnerable, a term which appears frequently in contemporary society and is a tangible manifestation of risk thinking. Categorisation of the vulnerable – whether to likely harm or the potential to harm others – fits this managerial inclination. While we would all share an everyday concern that those who face challenges and disadvantage are supported, recent commentators have suggested that there are contested meanings in the use of the term. Brown (2011, p. 314) argues that rather than being innocent, the concept of vulnerability is 'loaded with political, moral and practical implications' and undermines social justice for those people and groups so characterised. She identifies three main objections to use of the term: firstly, that it is paternalistic and offensive; secondly that it is closely aligned to technologies of social control and lastly that labelling individuals or groups as vulnerable is exclusionary and potentially stigmatising (Brown, 2011).

In the public discourse, policy-makers, the media, community groups and social workers frequently employ this problematic construct of vulnerable groups. Children, youth, people with disabilities and older people are the most likely to be characterised as vulnerable because of their physical (age, bodily features) and social (risk identities, barriers) characteristics. With reference to the relatively recent manifestation of the label 'vulnerable adults', Furedi argues that social policy has constructed a notion of 'biologically mature children who require official and professional support' (2008, p. 655). The relationship between people and risk is redefined in a new paradigm in which people deemed vulnerable are considered unable to manage the uncertainties of life.

Within the current climate of severe curtailment of welfare, the notion of vulnerability appears in the policy language to be connected to attempts by government to target funds, and thus programmes will focus on the most vulnerable who must be protected. The growing identification of at-risk groups however, also poses a problem for politicians with two concomitant and important drivers: firstly the compulsion to reduce risk and avoid costly mistakes that incur public outrage. The second driver is the push towards residual welfare and the focus on a safety-net where resources are narrowly targeted and costs are reduced. Services for children are not immune, while mandated child protection systems continue to grow; more universal parent support programmes may be cut. Services for adults exert less of an emotional claim but fear of public criticism drives the same anxieties about abuse and neglect. It is alongside these political challenges that the notion of adult protection emerges.

Constructing vulnerability: risk and 'adult protection'

'Adult protection' appears to have developed in the UK policy language as a response to inquiries into the abuses of adults. Johnson (2012) indicates that the term drew together previously separate concerns, including sexual exploitation of learning-disabled adults; in-family harm to older adults and harm to adults with health problems inflicted within care facilities. One of the consequences of such categorisations as that there is a risk that vulnerability to harm is associated with some inherent factors – age, learning disability, health or physical disability – thus risking limiting assumptions that people with these characteristics need professional involvement in decisions about their lives. Such assumptions invoke the deficit-focused perspectives, stigma and paternalism (Brown, 2011) that social workers would hope to avoid.

One of the contemporary challenges of working in health and social care is the extent to which these discourses create contradictory forces that are frustrating and limiting for service users. A good example of this is provided by Wills and Chenoweth (2005). Bringing the culture of safety into the foreground, they describe the impact on services for disabled people and their families (p. 53). They note in these examples how attempts to create 'ordinary lives' can be stymied:

> For disabled people and their families reliant on services, risk avoidance policies often limit the capacity of the services to offer ordinary experiences. We have observed for example, that people living in group homes may have fewer outings because of the concern for potential risk to themselves or others. This reflects a retreat from the 'ordinary' to the 'risk-managed' life. (Wills and Chenoweth, 2005, p. 53)

Faulkner (2012) notes that the views of service users on risk management differ from those of practitioners. She conducted qualitative research with services users to explore issues of risk and responsibility. She found that, for many research participants, the risk of losing their independence was of greater concern than any potential risk of harm. Echoing Wills and Chenoweth (2005), Faulkner (2012) found that preserving safety can threaten independence but risk increased institutionalisation, particularly for people in residential care. Clearly, when agencies and practitioners feel constrained there is a risk to quality of life that may be subsumed by fear of mistakes.

The purpose of many forms of categorisations of the vulnerable is to guard against harm and to generate support and access to services. Fawcett (2009) argues that the explicit linking of such categories to services leads individuals to accentuate their vulnerability and focus on deficits rather than abilities in order to obtain support services. One participant in Faulkner's study talked of the balancing act of needing to present as 'enough of a risk to qualify for a service but not too much of a risk that she might be in danger of losing her independence' (Faulkner, 2012, p. 291). These experiences challenge the objectivity of such measures. Fawcett cites Dunn *et al.* (2008) who have drawn attention to the blurring of rights when assessments of risk and vulnerability are argued as objective facts, well beyond the more strictly demarcated tests used to determine mental competency (2009, p. 474).

While there is often a focus on the rights and self-determination of people with disabilities, older people in general are frequently subsumed under the vulnerability construct. Fawcett notes that older women often feature as a vulnerable group, and implicitly as a burden on services and the community, 'serving to promote negative inferences . . . and invalidating strengths and achievements' (2009, p. 475). Older people living alone are particularly prone to become the centre of other adults' anxieties about their wellbeing, with considerable pressure exerted on them to curtail their activities or to accept care services.

Bornat and Bytheway (2010) draw our attention to some of the challenges of later life. The popular ideal of a fulfilling 'third age' is predicated on an expectation of 'individualised lifestyles that assume rational risk management and the maximisation of advantage and choice' (2010, p. 1121). For older adults the threat to autonomy and independence as a significant element of wellbeing can come from financial insecurity, personal health, ill-health or death of a partner, pressures from family members and significant changes in housing and location. Changes in personal circumstances can reduce community engagement and enforced housing changes may sever friendships and social supports of neighbours and services. Older people who become less able to manage independently may be easily labelled 'at risk' and their families or health care providers may exert considerable pressure on them to relocate, despite the potentially harmful social and mental health consequences of relocation.

In health care organisations the management of risk conforms to the trend to attempt to eliminate possible hazards and uncertainties through rational systems. Sociological research, however, illuminates a possible consequence of such systems as clinical governance and as posing a challenge to everyday experiences in health care. Hillman *et al.* (2013) explored the experience of older people on acute hospital wards and found examples where such governance impacted on the interactions between staff and patients with de-humanising effects. They noted that risk anxieties and policies interfered with care, reducing empathy and justifying reducing patient agency and control, with patient dignity a significant casualty (Hillman *et al.*, 2013).

Governmentality and surveillance

One feature of contemporary society theorised in the work of Foucault (1980) is governmentality, or the ethos of governance (Van Loon, 2008). Governmentality in the current context is the manner in which citizens are ruled in exchange for the services provided by government; those utilising services 'must fulfil certain requirements and make themselves available for scrutiny and surveillance' and to fail in this regard is to risk sanctions (Van Loon, 2008, p. 49). The growth of information technology has enabled social and health services to harness enormous quantities of data. In itself this data creates the capacity for intense surveillance of people's lives as data sharing between agencies of the state becomes commonplace. The civil rights and privacy issues are well documented elsewhere and Garrett has warned about 'the "function creep" potential of the databases in a social context where ideas about "problem families" are returning to popular, political and professional debates' (Garrett, 2005, p. 539). Risk and surveillance thus come together in governmentality as risk is employed to identify specific targets for surveillance and intervention, for example teenagers' sexual behaviour (Van Loon, 2008) and people who experience mental illness (Warner, 2008).

Peckover (2013) has recently examined the routine interpersonal violence screening that occurs in health care systems. Such routine screening can be seen to raise professionals' awareness and increase demand for services as more women and children come to attention because of family and interpersonal violence. Such screening mechanisms are popular in social policy because of their facility to target those at risk, for example screening women in pregnancy and sexual health services, but they do raise concerns about the adequacy of responses and they have undoubtedly expanded the 'scope of the professional gaze' (Peckover, 2013, p. 7).

Such intensive surveillance as is offered by data sharing across health, justice and welfare systems engenders many privacy fears too complex to be explored here but of concern to many. And it is into the world of *practice* that many of the consequential activities of surveillance fall. Peckover (2013, p. 80) cites Stanley *et al.* (2010) as reporting that social work services can be overwhelmed by the number of notifications of women and child named at risk by screening systems.

Impact on the social work profession in health and social care

What does this linking of risk thinking and surveillance mean for social workers and other practitioners in health? Risk awareness and risk management are clearly central to the contemporary health and welfare discourse. Both social policy and management practice have addressed risk in social work through myriad tools and technologies for identifying, assessing severity and managing risk in health and social work organisations. Increasingly there is a trend (found disturbing by many commentators) for social policy initiatives to focus resources on technological mechanisms to predict the likelihood of harm, especially when this can be couched as a cost-effective approach to reducing harm. To be able to reliably predict those most at risk, especially children, is of course, an attractive proposition and such capability indeed raises considerable ethical obligations for health professionals and social workers (de Haan, in press). For many observers, concerns fall into several categories: concern about the increasing surveillance of citizens, as explored above; concern about the impact of patronising 'the state knows best' policies on the rights of self-determination of categories of people deemed vulnerable and, lastly, and connected to the latter, the spectre of increasingly defensive practice.

Defensive practice

It is commonly held that anxieties haunt social workers and health services managers as organisations are constantly scrutinised by a mistake-focused media and the phenomenon of public inquires (Butler and Drakeford, 2005). The impact of a culture of blame in health and social policy promotes a greater emphasis on the defensibility of decisions rather than making good decisions (Pollack, 2010, p. 1274). More broadly, social workers have been associated with failures and tragedies and, as a consequence, accepting increasingly micromanaged practice, thus taking responsibility for managing risky behaviour on behalf of an anxious society. Careful identification of risk factors and attempts to apply prediction strategies to management aims to diminish poor outcomes for the organisation as well as service users (Green, 2007).

While defensive practice has perhaps been written about mostly in relation to children and is particularly observable in child protection (see Harris, 1987; Parton, 2006; Stanley, 2007), it can also impact on other groups. As we have seen above, the construction of the notion adult protection has shifted the focus from the *needs* of older adults or people with disabilities or chronic illness to the assessment and management of *risk*. Practice becomes dominated by technicist approaches where risk-assessment systems and check-lists are put in place to minimise the practitioner risk of 'missing something important'. As noted in Hillman *et al.*'s (2013) research, an ethic of care to preserve human dignity is compromised by risk-reduction regimes.

These discourses and the accompanying technologies can be visually represented as creating a 'funnel' effect, as shown in Figure 5.1, where the potent mix of risk and vulnerability discourses, intense media scrutiny and public anxieties about public service failures can trickle down into defensive practice in health and care.

Taylor (2006) studied the influence of risk-management paradigms in health and social services that might impact on professional decision making on the long-term care of older people. His research identified six conceptual paradigms for working

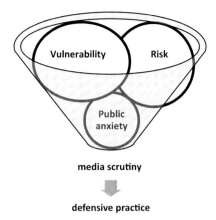

FIGURE 5.1 The anxiety funnel

in this risk-averse environment which will resonate with social workers in many fields of practice. These were described as identifying and meeting needs; minimizing situational hazards'; protecting this individual and others; balancing benefits and harms'; accounting for resources and priorities and lastly wariness of lurking conflicts' (Taylor, 2006, p. 1417). Essentially, these paradigms reflect the balancing act that social workers and other health professionals face when considering the role of self-determination and choice, competing rights and the institutional vulnerabilities that haunt managers. Taylor observed that each paradigm was responsive to different drivers and, where conflicts were identified, workers would shift to an alternative paradigm: The rationale for decision making seemed to be more about what was defensible than what was right.

Conclusions: the counter-story

The examples of research provided in this chapter tell a story of practitioners facing real professional, moral and ethical challenges in this current environment. There is a real danger that uncritical practice may stray far away from the foundational principles of dignity and worth, self-determination and human agency. Stanford has conceptualised the impact of the risk discourse as a 'predominantly morally conservative and repressive social, political and cultural force in contemporary social work' (Stanford, 2008, p. 209). She refers to the 'catastrophe narrative' in which social workers are portrayed as fearful and constrained, 'having been unwittingly co-opted into the conservative politics of risk' (Stanford, 2008, p. 210). It is indeed troubling that social workers may find themselves less able to be 'in the moment' with clients, focussed instead on the ever-present spectre of future harm.

Even so, social workers *do* resist and Stanford's study demonstrated that, while the practice environment is risk saturated, the moral and ethical standpoints of social work offer 'a powerful antidote' against such conservatism and defensiveness (2008, p. 218). Indeed it is vital that we maintain the quality of relationship between the practitioner and client needed to bridge the divide between need- and risk-focussed activities. The counter-story in the profession is, in part, also a revitalisation of relationship-based practice (Ruch *et al.*, 2010). Sawyer *et al.* (2009) studied the practices of health workers through a risk lens and found that the social workers and nurses interviewed were deeply reflective in how they engaged with risk management, drawing on personal and professional values, life experiences and perspectives on mental illness, disability and ageing. Rather than allowing risk thinking to displace a more therapeutic engagement with service users Sawyer *et al.* (2009, p. 377) found that the professionals studied maintained 'a strong sense of agency, a professional ethos and a focus on clients' needs'.

QUESTIONS FOR REFLECTION

1. Thinking about your current workplace, can you observe examples of Taylor's six paradigms in operation?
2. Are there groups labelled 'vulnerable' whose independence might be limited by risk-averse policies and practices?
3. What strategies might social workers employ to resist defensive practice in health and social services?

References

Adams, J. (1995) *Risk*, University College London Press, London.

Beck, U. (1992) *Risk Society: Towards a New Modernity*, Sage, London.

Beck, U. (1999) *World Risk Society*, Polity Press/Blackwell Publishers, Cambridge.

Beck, U. (2013) 'Why "class" is too soft a category to capture the explosiveness of social inequality at the beginning of the twenty-first century', *The British Journal of Sociology*, vol. 64, no. 1, pp. 63–74. doi:10.1111/1468–4446.12005

Bornat, J. & Bytheway, B. (2010) 'Perceptions and presentations of living with everyday risk in later life', *British Journal of Social Work*, vol. 40, no. 4, pp. 1118–1134. doi:10.1093/bjsw/bcq001

Brown, K. (2011) '"Vulnerability"': Handle with care', *Ethics and Social Welfare*, vol. 5, no. 3, pp. 313–321. doi:10.1080/17496535.2011.597165

Butler, I. & Drakeford, M. (2005) *Scandal, Social Policy and Social Welfare*, 2nd edn. BASW Policy Press, Bristol, UK.

Curran, D. (2013) 'Risk society and the distribution of bads: Theorizing class in the risk society', *The British Journal of Sociology*, vol. 64, no. 1, pp. 44–62. doi:10.1111/1468–4446.12004

de Haan, I. (in press) 'Another Pandora's box? Glimpsing hope that predictive risk modelling offers new ways to meet families' needs and keep children safe', paper, University of Auckland, New Zealand.

Elliott, A. (2002) 'Beck's sociology of risk: A critical assessment', *Sociology*, vol. 36 no. 2, pp. 293–315. doi:10.1177/0038038502036002004

Faulkner, A. (2012) 'The right to take risks', *Journal of Adult Protection*, vol. 14, no. 6, pp. 287–296.

Fawcett, B. (2009) 'Vulnerability: Questioning the certainties in social work and health', *International Social Work*, vol. 52, no. 4, pp. 473–484. doi:10.1177/0020872809104251

Foucault, M. (1980) *Power/knowledge: Selected Interviews and Other Writings, 1972–1977*, Harvester, Brighton, UK.

Furedi, F. (2007) *The Only Thing We Have to Fear is the 'Culture of Fear' Itself* [online]. Available at: http://www.spiked-online.com/index.php?/site/article/3053/

Furedi, F. (2008) 'Fear and security: A vulnerability-led policy response', *Social Policy & Administration*, vol. 42, no. 6, pp. 645–661.

Garrett, P.M. (2005) 'Social work's "electronic turn": Notes on the deployment of information and communication technologies in social work with children and families', *Critical Social Policy*, vol. 25, no. 4, pp. 529–553. doi:10.1177/0261018305057044

Giddens, A. (1999a) *Risk: Runaway World Series*, Lecture 2 BBC Reith Lectures [online]. Available at: http://www.bbc.co.uk/radio4/reith1999/

Giddens, A. (1999b) 'Risk and responsibility', *Modern Law Review*, vol. 62, no. 1, pp. 1–10.

Green, D. (2007) 'Risk and social work practice', *Australian Social Work*, vol. 60, no. 4, pp. 395–409.

Green, D. & Sawyer, A.-M. (2010) 'Managing risk in community care of older people: Perspectives from the frontline', *Australian Social Work*, vol. 63, no. 4, pp. 375–390.

Harris, N. (1987) 'Defensive social work', *British Journal of Social Work*, vol. 17, no. 1, pp. 61–69.

Hillman, A., Tadd, W., Calnan, S., Calnan, M., Bayer, A. & Read, S. (2013) 'Risk, governance and the experience of care', *Sociology of Health & Illness*, vol. 35, pp. 939-955. doi:10.1111/1467–9566.12017

Johnson, F. (2012) 'What is an "adult protection" issue? Victims, perpetrators and the professional construction of adult protection issues'. *Critical Social Policy*, vol. 32, no. 2, pp. 203–222. doi:10.1177/0261018311420278

Kemshall, H. (2002) *Risk, Social Policy and Social Welfare*, Open University Press, Buckingham, UK.

Parton, N. (2006) *Safeguarding Children: Early Intervention and Surveillance in a Late Modern Society*, Palgrave Macmillan, Basingstoke, UK.

Parton, N. (2010) '"From dangerousness to risk": The growing importance of screening and surveillance systems for safeguarding and promoting the well-being of children in England', *Health, Risk & Society*, vol. 12, no. 1, pp. 51–64.

Peckover, S. (2013) 'Domestic abuse, safeguarding children and public health: Towards an analysis of discursive forms and surveillant techniques in contemporary UK policy and practice', *British Journal of Social Work*. doi:10.1093/bjsw/bct042

Petersen, A. & Wilkinson, I. (2008) 'Health, risk and vulnerability: An introduction', in *Health, Risk and Vulnerability*, A. Petersen & I. Wilkinson (eds), Routledge, London, pp. 1–15.

Pollack, S. (2010) 'Labelling clients "risky": Social work and the neo-liberal welfare state', *British Journal of Social Work*, vol. 40, no. 4, pp. 1263–1278. doi:10.1093/bjsw/bcn079

Ruch, G., Turney, D. & Ward, A. (eds) (2010) *Relationship-based social work*, Jessica Kingsley, London.

Sawyer, A.-M., Green, D., Moran, A. & Brett, J. (2009) 'Should the nurse change the light globe? Human service professionals managing risk on the frontline', *Journal of Sociology*, vol. 45, no. 4, pp. 361–381. doi:10.1177/1440783309346478

Skolbekken, J.-A. (2008) 'Unlimited medicalization? Risk and the pathologization of normality', in *Health, Risk and Vulnerability*, A. Petersen & I. Wilkinson (eds), Routledge, London, pp. 16–29.

Stanford, S. (2008) 'Taking a stand or playing it safe? Resisting the moral conservatism of risk in social work practice', *European Journal of Social Work*, vol. 11, no. 3, pp. 209–220.

Stanley, T. (2007) 'Risky work: Child protection practice', *Social Policy Journal of New Zealand*, no. 30, pp. 163–177.

Taylor, B.J. (2006) 'Risk management paradigms in health and social services for professional decision making on the long-term care of older people', *British Journal of Social Work*, vol. 36, no. 8, pp. 1411–1429. doi: 10.1093/bjsw/bch406

Van Loon, J. (2008) 'Governmentality and the subpolitics of teenage sexual risk behaviour', in *Health, Risk and Vulnerability*, A. Petersen & I. Wilkinson (eds), Routledge, London, pp. 48–65.

Warner, J. (2008) 'Community care, risk and the shifting locus of danger and vulnerability', in *Health, Risk and Vulnerability*, A. Petersen & I. Wilkinson (eds), Routledge, London, pp. 30–47.

Wills, R., & Chenoweth, L. (2005) 'Support or compliance', in *Allies in Emancipation: Shifting from Providing Service to Being of Support*, P. O'Brien & M. Sullivan (eds.), South Thomson Learning, Melbourne, Australia, pp. 49–64.

6

STRESS, RESILIENCE AND RESPONDING TO CIVIL DEFENCE EMERGENCIES AND NATURAL DISASTERS

An ecological approach

Carole Adamson

CHAPTER OBJECTIVES

This chapter addresses the current theoretical positioning of stress and of resilience, and the contribution of these concepts to health and wellbeing, by developing linkages to the constructs in our social work knowledge base. Using the experience of civil defence emergencies and natural disasters as a focus, an ecological lens is employed to construct a relational understanding of resilience for social work practice. It provides three objectives for the reader:

1. *Firstly, the understanding of ecological and constructivist approaches to social work is refreshed and offered for exploration and critique;*
2. *Secondly, the reader is challenged to develop a perspective on stress and on resilience that incorporates and resonates with social work knowledge and principles;*
3. *Finally, this framework for practice offers the reader the opportunity to apply their own understanding of social work, stress and resilience to a practice setting of civil emergencies and disasters.*

Introduction

The individual and the environment

Central to our current understanding of people's capacity to respond to challenging life events and adversity is the recognition that a focus upon individual coping mechanisms and responses provides a necessary, but not sufficient, knowledge base from which to initiate effective intervention.

This fundamental premise of current social work theory can be captured in the following scenario, concerning a student social worker in a multi-disciplinary mental health team in the months following a major natural disaster. Keen to understand the concept of depression with which a middle-aged service user, Jenny, has been diagnosed, she explores the dimensions of the diagnosis with various colleagues and the literature available in the team: her supervisor asks her to reflect on her findings, which she portrays in Figure 6.1.

She reflects on the drug company-sponsored, waiting-room poster about depression. It depicts the human brain and the effects of various medications on the experience of depression. With the various disciplines, she then explores the physiological, cognitive–behavioural and social elements of Jenny's experience. Jenny's home has been declared uninhabitable following a geological survey of its foundations, but the insurance company is not yet willing to accept that the house itself cannot be lived in. Jenny reports being in limbo: neighbours have mostly moved away, public transport to the suburb has been reduced due to falling demand, and their place of employment has been relocated to a new commercial hub further away from their home. The student begins to tease out the contributing factors (the brain, body, environmental and social influences) that have bearing on Jenny's reality. Additionally, the student's work with the Jenny generates a strong belief that it is the interpretation of experience, woven throughout this systemic appreciation,

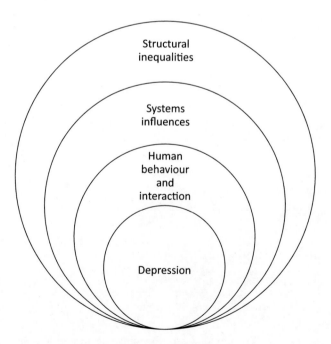

FIGURE 6.1 A multi-systemic approach to depression

which shapes the possibilities for social work intervention. The student explores her understanding of the Jenny's experience in supervision. Is it the shock of the disaster which has triggered the depression? Or is it the loss of friends, neighbours and ready access to resources, or the loss of their home? What role does Jenny's interaction with the insurance company have in creating a sense of hopelessness? How do these factors interact? In which areas of Jenny's life are support and intervention likely to have most benefit and increase their resilience to further experience of depression? The student and her supervisor began to explore the difference between linear and non-linear causality, which reinforces her commitment to understanding ecological perspectives on health and wellbeing (Keenan, 2010). It is an ecological and constructivist perspective that underpins this chapter, articulated through an exploration of disasters and social work practice.

Health, wellbeing and resilience in a disaster context are, it is argued here, a complex mix of systemic impacts within the contexts in which people live. The consolidation of systems approaches within an ecological framework is a foundation of current social work theory and practice: in recognising the complex interaction of the person with their environment, an ecological perspective contributes to an appreciation of resilience as an interactive, dynamic and environmentally aware process. This moves us away from a deficit model focused solely on stress and negative impact and enables strengths-based approaches that honour the cultural, historic and contextual elements that are key to improving health and wellbeing. As discussed by Healy (2005), concepts of non-linearity, self-reinforcing feedback, sensitivity to initial conditions and the creation of generalising patterns borrow from systems, complexity and chaos theories to suggest that our understanding of the causes and response to the impact of stress on health and wellbeing is well grounded in the ecology of human experience.

Ecological perspectives in social work are at times critiqued for their lack of structural awareness, analysis and practice direction (Dominelli, 2012; Hugman, 2009): ignoring the influence of the social determinants of health and inequality is arguably a betrayal of social work's core commitment to social justice and human rights. The challenge for radical or structurally informed social work, however, often mounted by critics who suggest that the person is lost in the political, is to maintain sight of the uniqueness of the individual service user's experience. Fook's (1993) argument for radical casework provided some early bridging of the radical–therapeutic divide. When we are addressing challenges to health and wellbeing in relation to resilience and stressful life events, this attention to the individual is crucial. It is here that a relationship between structural and constructivist approaches can be brokered.

The fundamental philosophical shift that occurred with systems thinking, enabling multi-systemic, multi-layered perspectives in social work assessment and intervention, also laid the groundwork for a constructivist perception of the experience of stress and the social work role in enhancing capacity. Recognising the standpoint of service users and the validity of their experience enables both users and practitioners to value individual and collective narratives of survival and meaning-making (Cooper, 2001) and (alongside radical social work) embeds social work within its values base of social justice and human rights. Structural and radical perspectives, long espoused by social work but at times critiqued as inadequately providing guidance on interpersonal skills, can be re-invigorated by this relational stance of strengths and narrative approaches that link the personal to the political (Denborough, 2008).

What follows is a brief summary of current and emerging stress and resilience research, positioned within social work by our ecologically informed understanding of complexity and mindful of our growing understanding of the social work role following disasters.

The ecology of resilience and stress

The notion of stress within human experience is a metaphor adapted from the hard sciences of engineering (Selye, 1982). It suggests the impact of strain upon systems or structures, with an implication of lowered performance and increased risk. Adopted within, and adapted to, psychosocial contexts, there is now substantial evidence that high levels of stress have an impact on physical and mental health (Krantz and McCeney, 2002; Sapolsky, 1994; Thoits, 2010). Early conceptualisations of the stress response tended to focus upon the individual bearing the impact of the stressors, with the psychological literature focused upon notions of coping (for instance, Lazarus, 1966) and the individual characteristics of those experiencing the stress. This stance resonates with the intellectual characteristics of psychological and social thought during the early developments of human stress research: the dominance of bio-medical constructs characteristically locates the pathology of experience within the individual experiencing the stress. The impact is identifiable and the intervention clearly articulated in terms of cause and effect. Within our student social worker scenario, she questions the weighting that the drug company poster places upon the brain and wonders how the brain interacts with the rest of the Jenny's experience in this current depressive episode.

At the heart of much theoretical tension between the knowledge bases of social work and the positivist perspective of biomedical approaches, this focus upon the individual within stress research has now shifted in favour of an emergent consideration of person and environment interactions more compatible with social work. In addition to research in relation to the physiological and psychological impact of stress upon individual health and wellbeing, there is also a growing evidence base for the impact of the environment upon the individual. From this arises a concomitant demand for environmental responsibility for eliminating the stressors, reducing their impact or creating a salutogenic (health-generating) environment capable of promoting and sustaining health and wellbeing. Research regarding social inclusion, marginalisation and health inequalities is beginning to include recognition of stressors and cognitive–emotional factors in health and wellbeing (Pickett and Wilkinson, 2010). For our student social worker, this signals the need to explore the wider explanations for vulnerability to depression and raises questions about the scope and focus for potential social work interventions.

The development of the concept of resilience can be charted from a similar focus on individual traits and personality through to a more complex understanding of ecological interactions and influences (Bottrell, 2009). The emphasis of current resilience research focuses upon the ecological context as the site for the bi-directional resolution of a stress–resilience interaction that determines unique health and wellbeing outcomes for individuals, families and communities (Keenan, 2010; McEwen and Gianaros, 2010). Cultural specificity (Bottrell, 2009; Ungar, 2008) and challenges to the normative appraisal of resilience (Bonanno, 2004; Ungar, 2004) now form an established constructivist paradigm in resilience research.

An appraisal of the resilience literature will reveal considerable disparity and potential disagreement around the definition of the concept, variously seen as residing within the individual and a process of their adaptation to negative circumstances (for example, Collins, 2007), as a protective factor (Kinman and Grant, 2011) or as an outcome (Masten and Coatsworth, 1998). Most current definitions appear to contain an acknowledgement of positive adaptation to adversity (Luthar and Cicchetti, 2000). Describing resilience as a trajectory following a disaster, Norris *et al.*, (2009) define it as demonstrating a sharp decrease after initially high stress reactions, in contrast to resistance (low and stable levels of symptoms), recovery (a slower decline of symptoms) and chronic stress responses. This plethora of constructions is not surprising: the more that the research evidence is open to examining the complex interaction of environmental systems and the meaning-making processes of the people located within them, the greater the interactive and relational nature of the concept and the greater (or potentially more impossible) the challenge in determining the weighting of influences. The difficulty in defining and measuring resilience in social work practice lies at the heart of our understanding that it is a product of complex person–environment interactions. This conclusion is especially pertinent when we consider the impact of large-scale civil defence emergencies and natural disasters.

That a person's health and wellbeing, or capacity to withstand the adversity thrown up by life events, is a complex interaction of their own personal coping abilities and traits with environmental protective and vulnerability factors is now well established in the literature. Any social work intervention in response to the impact of stress within an individual, family system or community has the imperative to assess the differential exposure to stressors and protective factors within the environment. Just as the vulnerability to depression in our initial scenario will depend upon a matrix of genetic, behavioural, social and structural influences and conditions, so too, our appraisal of stress and resilience factors in those with whom we work now has a full ecological range of research to support our interventions.

Structural inequalities in society are thus on our stress and resilience agenda. Thoits (2010) presents a clear case that differential exposure to stress is the deciding factor in gender, race, class and social inequalities in health. In addition, she argues that minority groups suffer discrimination stress that can exacerbate this inequality even more, and that life course and generational factors will widen these gaps.

These inequalities have clear implications for those groups following an environmental or human disaster that may exacerbate marginalisation and disparity (Bonanno *et al.*, 2007).

The final frontier marking the separation of bio-medical and complex systems research in resilience and stress is in the process of being dismantled with the articulation of bi-directional influences in health and wellbeing that link neurological functioning to socio-economic conditions. Research evidence is mounting that health outcomes and wellbeing at a socio-economic level have links to the experience of chronic stress, articulated at a neurological level through physiological markers such as allostatic load scores and mediated through factors such as social support (McEwen and Gianaros, 2010). Evidence such as this can underscore the social work imperative to reduce entrapment in environmental niches (Rapp, 1998) or 'hotspots' (Gilgun, 2005) and to develop community-level resources whilst maintaining a focus on support for individual health and wellbeing. Such research can generate useful insights into the impact of large-scale social and community experiences such as disaster and civil defence emergencies.

Two core principles emerge to influence our discussion of the importance of a stress and resilience knowledge base for promoting health and wellbeing. Firstly, stress and resilience approaches to practice need to be inclusive of person-in-environment, structural and constructivist elements that address the full range of potential stressors, not just those with a linear cause-and-effect relationship. Our second principle is that an understanding of the bi-directional influences involved in human experience of stress and resilience responses promotes the need for multi-level intervention and removes the imperative that we should focus solely upon the individual as the focus for change. With an understanding of current perspectives of stress and resilience in relation to health and wellbeing, the attention of this chapter now turns to the application of these perspectives to social work practice in working with civil defence emergencies and disasters.

Civil defence emergencies and natural disasters: reframing stress and resilience

There is a significant body of knowledge on current and emerging stress and resilience perspectives to social work practice in civil defence emergencies and disaster settings. Worldwide, there are many examples of the immediate links between natural and man-made disasters and individual and community health and wellbeing. This chapter accesses the core knowledge gained from a national workshop on social work disaster curriculum in New Zealand (Council for Social Work Education Aotearoa New Zealand (CSWEANZ), 2011), initiated by schools of social work primarily as a result of the devastating earthquakes in Christchurch (New Zealand's third-largest city) and the wider Canterbury region in 2010 and 2011. The workshop learned from key informants involved in social work delivery in Christchurch after the earthquakes, as well as people with experience of floods in Fiji, the 2001 Boxing Day tsunami in Thailand, and government officials located in emergency management and civil defence roles. This workshop focused on the narratives of those panellists involved and was not so much designed to be research-informed as narrative-generating.

It is logical that much of our understanding of civil defence emergencies and disaster response is informed by a knowledge base of stress and resilience, as well as allied research from trauma, loss and grief. This workshop considered it to be fundamental that this core knowledge is embedded in social work practice in order to equip social workers in crisis and post-crisis situations. A key principle that emerged from this workshop, however, is that our understanding of stress and resilience needs to be framed within the contextual environment in which these events occur and therefore is to be activated within a community development framework. Figure 6.2 provides one possible model for this, developed out of the CSWEANZ workshop.

Focusing on individual levels, participants stressed the importance of understanding the physiological stress response and of having pre-disaster exposure to stress management strategies and self-knowledge. Several observed that these processes of sustaining and enhancing resilience required not only individual repertoires of mindfulness and reflection but environmental strategies such as flexibility in the changed organisational environments (working hours, adaptation of roles and responsibilities, and permission to return to work to establish or re-establish routine in what has become known as the 'new normal'). Thus, the utilisation of stress and resilience knowledge needs to be framed up on a community development level, linking the personal to the political.

FIGURE 6.2 Incorporating stress and resilience within a civil defence framework

On a social and community level, the workshop generated several narratives of importance. One thread linked the experience of the Christchurch earthquakes to the emerging concepts of resilience concerned with cultural specificity and the risks of a normative appraisal of what constitutes strength and coping (Bottrell, 2009; Ungar, 2004, 2008). Gilgun (2005) reminds us that people are demonstrably resilient in some circumstances and contexts but not in others: this applies to fluctuations in a person's levels of coping and in access to, and appropriateness of, coping resources over time, as we can explore in a knowledge base of stress-vulnerability (or stress-diathesis) models (Falloon and Fadden, 1993; Randal et al., 2009). Panellists stressed the risks inherent in imposing a diagnosis or an assumption of coping or of victimhood on those with earthquake experience. One can be both coping and victim, either simultaneously or over time. Constructions of survivors as in need of counselling, or as heroes, were as unhelpful as government attempts to extract good news stories in order to respond to national curiosity and stress levels. Agency managers quickly ascertained that stress levels of workers were best managed by allowing people back to work in order to gain meaning from action and their recovery efforts; siloed agency functioning based on pre-earthquake norms, patch-protection and structures was broken down in favour of managing what worked and what enabled new priorities and communication channels to function.

This chapter has considered that some of the key messages in emergent constructions of stress and resilience are the structural and bi-directional implications of relating the physiological implications of the stress response to situations of marginalisation and discrimination in society (McEwen and Gianaros, 2010; Pickett and Wilkinson, 2010; Thoits, 2010). One of the key messages given at this workshop was that civil defence emergencies play out along the existing fault lines and fractures in society. In the immediate disaster relief response in Christchurch, it was the central city business district (the CBD) which became the focal point for rescue and recovery operations. This attention was related perhaps to the scale of the immediately visible devastation (collapsed multi-storey buildings), concentrated population and access, but media attention with the CBD also perhaps reflected the national pre-occupation with the destruction of national icons such as the Anglican cathedral. Meanwhile, the badly damaged eastern suburbs, coincidentally the lower socio-economic areas built on flat, swampy ground susceptible to ground oscillation and liquefaction, were less quickly identified as in need and arguably have remained relatively neglected in recovery and re-building initiatives subsequent to the immediate disaster recovery.

Whilst relief efforts on a local, regional and national basis displayed considerable unity and community spirit in the months after the disasters, housing supply, income and strength of pre-existing social networks have provided indicators of recovery progress. Stressors have become individualised as some households and individuals have been able to relocate from red-stickered (that is, condemned) properties whereas others have had no clear message from government and regional relief organisations or insurance companies and remain in a limbo of truncated and restricted futures. Collective pulling together, manifesting in anger, grieving or support, fundamental to resilience, has been eroded and at times replaced by individualised situations that are fundamentally stressful and disempowering, with a resultant impact on health and wellbeing. Emerging anecdotal evidence from mental health services, for example, indicates that levels of psychosis remained static or reduced in the immediate aftermath of this collective disaster, with levels of anxiety disorders, depression and self-harm rising after these collective energies and initiatives had dissipated. Reflecting the focus of our case study at the beginning of this chapter, this corroborates with trauma literature from communities riven by civil war (for instance Adjukovic, 2004) that suggests that there is a limit to the effectiveness of individualised intervention and response in order to mitigate stress and sustain resilient behaviour in the immediate aftermath of major life events. There is a sound research base supporting the use of collectively focused, community development interventions that assume that people are coping and can be resilient with support, and which build social capital through strengthening or re-building social networks of support (Bonanno et al., 2007). Such social and community-level capacity building provides opportunity for individual coping strategies to flourish (with individual support should it be needed). What direction would our student social worker now recommend for Jenny with depression? What balance between individual support and community-level processes are right for this person?

Early intervention after such a disaster, therefore, requires both collective and individual level intervention. Supporting the assistance that individuals' unique situations require are the structural and systemic levels of interventions such as relief efforts at regional, national and international levels in the immediate response period; plans and systems that facilitate interventions for groups and communities, such as hospital-level training and protocols for emergency-level response; the ability of non-governmental local agencies to re-focus their core purpose and become service and communication hubs for the new configurations of community and need. Later support and intervention similarly contains both individual and community level activity, but individual needs may become differentiated and less easily identified as part of collective and community development strategies. The impact of chronic stress upon physical and mental health and wellbeing, for instance, may not be readily recognised as disaster-related (Kario et al., 2003).

The organisation of, and involvement of people in, processes that connect the community and the individual lie at the core of the person-in-environment approach of social work, and as suggested earlier in this chapter, connects us actively with our social work identity as committed to human rights and social justice approaches. Examples from the Christchurch and Canterbury disasters suggests that community initiatives which, whilst not always recognisable as social work activity, will have a direct bearing on recovery and (through our knowledge of stress and resilience) mandate social work to either initiate, participate and/or refer people towards participation. Groups within the community such as university students and local farmers formed 'armies' to deliver practical assistance in the early days of response and recovery; the empty spaces where buildings once stood, so economically, socially and visually debilitating, can be used for temporary shopping malls made out of brightly painted shipping containers and community arts projects, cycle-powered cinemas, dance and poetry (Gapfiller Charitable Trust, 2012). Transitional architecture festivals and events focusing on the strengths and features of local communities serve to develop alternative narratives of resilience and hope and to foster social inclusion.

What is the imperative for social work activity in disasters and civil defence emergencies? Through the learning from this workshop, it has become evident that what is important for those involved in natural disasters is as much the importance of narrative, of the development of contextual and cultural interpretations and meanings about the stress and resilience in civil emergencies, as it is about the application of specific stress knowledge. Strengthened, too, is the argument that structural inequalities can be exacerbated by the stressors of a natural disaster, and that it is by (re-)building the social equity that stressors can most effectively be managed.

If we accept that a multi-level lens (one that recognises both linear and non-linear causation) is best employed throughout all phases of an emergency and recovery period, then the challenge for social work is to work at a community level in a stress- and resilience-informed manner, and to work at individual levels mindful of not only our stress and resilience knowledge base, but of the likely non-linear relationship between individual experience and responses that include community-level activity. Our knowledge of bi-directional influences on stress and resilience, that individual stress and resilience is impacted upon by multi-level psychosocial events and influences, reinforces that we should work at many levels in order to work towards health and wellbeing after such stressful life events. Structural awareness that community-wide disasters impact differentially on the more vulnerable groups in society provides justification for targeted social work initiatives with those made potentially more marginalised and under-resourced, such as older people, those living with pre-existing disabilities or health conditions, and refugees and new settlers.

How do we legitimate social work intervention in these non-clinical and perhaps non-traditional social work roles? From a linear, bio-medical perspective, finding the evidence for community-level intervention challenges cost-benefit accounting practices and evidence-based guidelines derived from clinical research. Such research is indicative of the restrictions potentially imposed by frameworks of evidence-based practice which have as their intellectual basis a requirement to implement positivist methods of inquiry (Adamson, 2001; Webb, 2001). Complex relational and interactive contexts, such as the wellbeing of individuals and communities affected by civil emergencies and disasters, stretch the ability of some scientific methods of inquiry and perhaps suggest that a different form of evaluation (one that incorporates multi-systemic analysis) be employed. Current research regarding health inequalities and social inclusion can be usefully complemented by the perspectives on stress and resilience that we have explored in this chapter.

Stress, resilience and social work practice in civil emergencies and disasters: a summary

Within this chapter, a conceptual argument is proposed with an ecologically informed understanding of stress and resilience theories at its heart. The chapter suggests that there is a natural synergy between the fundamental principles of social work, its key blend of systemic, structural and constructivist theory and the current status of stress and resilience theories when applied to disasters and civil defence emergencies. Key principles emerging from the discussion suggest that the environmental conditions that enable sustainable and resilient functioning and positive outcomes from engaging with adversity are characterised by multi-systemic activity and recognition of bi-directional relationships between people and their environment.

QUESTIONS FOR REFLECTION

1. What is the relationship between systemic, structural and constructivist perspectives in social work?
2. How can an understanding of bi-directional influences (the two-way process of interaction between the person and their environment) help social workers to strengthen a person's resilience?
3. How best can social work position itself in the recovery and rebuilding after disasters?

References

Adamson, C.E. (2001) 'Social work and the call for evidence-based practice in mental health: Where do we stand?', *Social Work Review*, vol. 13, no. 2, pp. 8–12.

Ajdukovic, D. (2004) 'Social contexts of trauma and healing', *Medicine, Conflict and Survival*, vol. 20, no. 2, pp. 120–135. doi: 10.1080/1362369042000234717

Bonanno, G.A. (2004) 'Loss, trauma, and human resilience: Have we underestimated the human capacity to thrive after extremely aversive events?', *American Psychologist*, vol. 59, no. 1, pp. 20–28. doi: 10.1037/0003–066X.59.1.20

Bonanno, G.A., Galea, S., Bucciarelli, A., & Vlahov, D. (2007) 'What predicts psychological resilience after disaster? The role of demographics, resources, and life stress', *Journal of Consulting and Clinical Psychology*, vol. 75, no. 5, pp. 671–682. doi: 10.1037/0022–006x.75.5.671

Bottrell, D. (2009) 'Understanding "marginal" perspectives: Towards a social theory of resilience', *Qualitative Social Work*, vol. 8, no. 3, pp. 321–339. doi:10.1177/1473325009337840

Collins, S. (2007) 'Social workers, resilience, positive emotions and optimism', *Practice*, vol. 19, no. 4, pp. 255–269. doi: 10.1080/09503150701728186

Cooper, B. (2001) 'Constructivism in social work: Towards a participative practice viability', *British Journal of Social Work*, vol. 31, no. 5, pp. 721–738. doi: 10.1093/bjsw/31.5.721

Council for Social Work Education Aotearoa New Zealand (CSWEANZ) (2011) Unpublished record of 'Disaster Curriculum' workshop, Wellington, CSWEANZ. [Author's notes].

Denborough, D. (2008) *Collective Narrative Practice: Responding to Individuals, Groups and Communities who have Experienced Trauma*, Dulwich Centre Publications, Adelaide, Australia.

Dominelli, L. (2012) *Green Social Work: From Environmental Crises to Environmental Justice*, Polity Press, Cambridge.

Falloon, I.R.H. & Fadden, G. (1993) *Integrated Mental Health Care: A Comprehensive, Community-Based Approach*, Cambridge University Press, Cambridge.

Fook, J. (1993) *Radical Casework: A Theory of Practice*, Allen & Unwin, St Leonards, Australia.

Gapfiller Charitable Trust (2012) *Gapfiller* [online]. Available at: http://www.gapfiller.org.nz/

Gilgun, J.F. (2005) 'Evidence-based practice, descriptive research and the resilience–schema–gender–brain functioning (RSGB) assessment', *British Journal of Social Work*, vol. 35, no. 6, pp. 843–862. doi: 10.1093/bjsw/bch216

Healy, K. (2005) *Social Work Theories in Context: Creating Frameworks for Practice*, Palgrave Macmillan, Basingstoke, UK.

Hugman, R. (2009) 'But is it social work? Some reflections on mistaken identities', *British Journal of Social Work*, vol. 39, no. 6, pp. 1138–1153. doi:10.1093/bjsw/bcm158

Kario, K., McEwen, B.S., & Pickering, T.G. (2003) 'Disasters and the heart: A review of the effects of earthquake-induced stress on cardiovascular disease', *Hypertension Research: Official Journal of the Japanese Society of Hypertension*, vol. 26, no. 5, pp. 355–367. doi: 10.1291/hypres.26.355

Keenan, E.K. (2010) 'Seeing the forest and the trees: Using dynamic systems theory to understand "stress and coping" and "trauma and resilience"', *Journal of Human Behavior in the Social Environment*, vol. 20, no. 8, pp. 1038–1060. doi: 10.1080/10911359.2010.494947

Kinman, G., & Grant, L. (2011) 'Exploring stress resilience in trainee social workers: The role of emotional and social competencies', *British Journal of Social Work*, vol. 41, no. 2, pp. 261–275. doi: 10.1093/bjsw/bcq088

Krantz, D.S. & McCeney, M.K. (2002) 'Effects of psychological and social factors on organic disease: A critical assessment of research on coronary heart disease', *Annual Review of Psychology*, vol. 53, pp. 341–369.

Lazarus, R.S. (1966) *Psychological Stress and the Coping Process*, McGraw-Hill, New York.

Luthar, S.S., & Cicchetti, D. (2000) 'The construct of resilience: Implications for interventions and social policies', *Development and Psychopathology*, vol. 12, no. 4, pp. 857–885. doi: 10.1017/S0954579400004156

Masten, A.S. & Coatsworth, J.D. (1998) 'The development of competence in favorable and unfavorable environments: Lessons from research on successful children', *American Psychologist*, vol. 53, no. 2, pp. 205–220. doi: 10.1037/0003–066x.53.2.205

McEwen, B.S. & Gianaros, P.J. (2010) 'Central role of the brain in stress and adaptation: Links to socioeconomic status, health, and disease', *Annals of the New York Academy of Sciences*, vol. 1186, no. 1, pp. 190–222. doi: 10.1111/j.1749–6632.2009.05331.x

Norris, F.H., Tracy, M., & Galea, S. (2009) 'Looking for resilience: Understanding the longitudinal trajectories of responses to stress', *Social Science & Medicine*, vol. 68, no. 12, pp. 2190–2198. doi: 10.1016/j.socscimed.2009.03.043

Pickett, K.E. & Wilkinson, R.G. (2010) 'Inequality: An underacknowledged source of mental illness and distress', *The British Journal of Psychiatry*, vol. 197, no. 6, pp. 426–428. doi: 10.1192/bjp.bp.109.072066

Randal, P., Stewart, M.W., Proverbs, D., Lampshire, D., Symes, J. & Hamer, H. (2009) '"The re-covery model": An integrative developmental stress-vulnerability-strengths approach to mental health', *Psychosis*, vol. 1, no. 2, pp. 122–133. doi: 10.1080/17522430902948167

Rapp, C. (1998) *The Strengths Model: Case Management with People Suffering from Severe and Persistent Mental Illness*, Oxford University Press, New York.

Sapolsky, R.M. (1994). *Why Zebras Don't Get Ulcers: A Guide to Stress, Stress-Related Diseases, and Coping*, W.H. Freeman, New York.

Selye, H. (1982) 'History and present status of the stress concept', in *Handbook of Stress: Theoretical and Clinical Aspects*, L.B. Goldberger & S. Bresnitz (eds) Free Press, New York, pp. 7–17.

Thoits, P.A. (2010) 'Stress and health', *Journal of Health and Social Behavior*, vol. 51, no. 1 suppl, S41–S53. doi: 10.1177/0022146510383499

Ungar, M. (2004) 'A constructionist discourse on resilience: Multiple contexts, multiple realities among at-risk children and youth', *Youth Society*, vol. 35, no. 3, pp. 341–365.

Ungar, M. (2008) 'Resilience across cultures', *British Journal of Social Work*, vol. 38, no. 2, pp. 218–235. doi: 10.1093/bjsw/bcl343

Webb, S.A. (2001) 'Some considerations on the validity of evidence-based practice in social work', *British Journal of Social Work*, vol. 31, no. 1, pp. 57–79. doi: 10.1093/bjsw/31.1.57

7

STIGMA IN HEALTH AND SOCIAL WORK

Towards a new paradigm

Viviene E. Cree

CHAPTER OBJECTIVES

The chapter will examine 'stigma' in health and social care, offering a new way of thinking about how this might be understood and confronted.

1. *It will firstly explore meanings of the concept of stigma in theory and research;*
2. *It will then discuss stigma in specific accounts of social work practice and research;*
3. *It will finally offer a new paradigm for challenging stigma in health and social care.*

Introduction

The concept of stigma is so familiar that it may seem to have lost its potency, if not its meaning altogether. It is rarely defined and is often used alongside or in place of, other popular concepts such as discrimination and exclusion. It is used in so many situations, that it inevitably leads to the question: why bother with such a hackneyed and outdated concept? This chapter argues that it is vital that we revisit the idea of stigma, not as a way of uncovering yet more 'victims' to be pitied or consoled, but instead as part of a transformative agenda for individual and social change in social work and health. The chapter draws on my own experience, first as a social work practitioner for many years, and then as a researcher studying the impact of HIV (parental and own) on children in families in Scotland. This is not, of course, to claim that HIV stigma is the only kind of stigma worthy of examination. Rather, it is to acknowledge that HIV is particularly stigmatised and stigmatising, as will be discussed in more detail. This specific case-study example gives access to rich data on children and young people's views and understandings of stigma and how it operates in their lives. From this, we can make connections with the ways that stigma may operate in other health and social care settings, and hence with how we might confront and challenge stigma.

Theoretical perspectives and research findings

The word stigma is originally a Greek word, first used to refer to a type of mark or tattoo that was cut or burned into the skin of people who were designated as criminals, slaves or traitors; the intention was to identify them visibly as 'blemished or ritually polluted', so that they could be avoided, particularly in public places. Additional layers of meaning were added in Christian times, when stigma was used to refer to 'bodily signs of holy grace' or in medical terms, as 'bodily signs of physical disorder' (Goffman, 1968, p. 11). During the 1950s and 1960s, psychologists studied stigma across a number of physical illnesses, examining, for example, the impact of having a disability or a facial deformity on individuals. The social psychologist Erving Goffman was the first person to consider in detail the *social* effects of having a stigmatised condition, and it is his work, first published in 1963, that remains the principle source for the many subsequent studies of stigma, whether from psychological, social psychological or sociological perspectives.

Goffman's study, *Stigma. Notes on the Management of Spoiled Identity*, begins with the realisation that, when a stranger enters our presence, we quickly make up our minds about them on the basis of verbal and non-verbal cues. If the person has something about them that makes them different to us and 'somehow less desirable', we may reduce them in our minds 'from a whole and usual person to a tainted, discounted one' (1968, p. 12). Stigma is therefore essentially about 'differentness'; we stigmatise those whom we see as different to ourselves. Goffman goes on to make a distinction between 'the discredited' (where the 'differentness' is known about immediately, or has been disclosed) and 'the discreditable' (people whose 'differentness' is not immediately noticeable, or is not disclosed). Most people who have been stigmatised will have experience of both situations, he argues. Goffman identifies three different types of stigma: abominations of the body (physical disabilities, described here as deformities); blemishes of individual character (for example, weak will, domineering character, unnatural passions, dishonesty, etc.); and what he calls the tribal stigma of race, nation, and religion (which is transmitted, he suggests, through lineages, contaminating all members of a family) (1968, p. 14). In the remainder of his book, Goffman explores how those who are stigmatised cope with this experience, individually and socially. He highlights that many people who are afraid of being stigmatised go to great lengths to conceal their differentness and pass as what he calls normals (1968, p. 100). Those who are prepared to admit their differentness may also play down the effects of this, in a process Goffman calls covering (1968, p. 125). Passing and covering behaviour applies equally to those who have a discrediting condition and to their associates who experience 'courtesy stigma' by virtue of their connection with the stigmatised person (1968, p. 44). Most importantly, Goffman points out that it is not only 'normals' who treat stigmatised people with distaste. Instead, those who are stigmatised often incorporate society's views of them and come to discredit themselves. Self-hatred and shame spoils their social identity and their interactions with others, so that they come to see themselves only in terms of their 'spoiled identity'.

Subsequent research, building on Goffman's work, has demonstrated the pervasive effects of stigma on the lives of people with a wide range of health problems and disabilities. Some studies have tackled the issue broadly (e.g. Scambler, 2009; van Brakel, 2006; Weiss et al., 2011). Others have examined the impact of stigma on diseases such as leprosy (e.g. Voorend et al., 2011), HIV/AIDS (e.g. Herek, 1999) and tuberculosis (e.g. Baral et al., 2007), and on conditions such as epilepsy (e.g. Ahmad, 2011; Scambler and Hopkins, 1986). Others have explored stigma associated with mental health and illness (e.g. Corrigan et al., 2011; Gormley and Quinn, 2009; Horsfall et al., 2010), and within this research, significant attention has been given to the stigma around dementia and Alzheimer's disease (e.g. Benbow and Reynolds, 2000). There are now new topics for investigation, reflecting current social issues and anxieties about health, including studies of Hepatitis C stigma (Paylor and Mack, 2010). Studies have also investigated the stigma experienced by caregivers of those with a variety of health problems, physical and mental (e.g. Gray et al., 2010; MacKenzie, 2006; Phelan et al., 2011). It has, moreover, been identified that courtesy stigma may be experienced by practitioners as well as family members.

Interestingly, there are occasions when the power of stigma has been deliberately employed as a tactic in public health education campaigns, as a strategy to reduce certain (alleged undesirable) behaviours and encourage other (more desirable) behaviours. So the infamous 'AIDS. Don't Die of Ignorance' 1986 television advertisements in the UK featuring a blackened tombstone were an intentional attempt by government to shock people into changing their sexual behaviour. The campaign was held to be so successful that it was replicated across Europe. Smoking serves as another example. In order to discourage smoking (for good reasons), smoking bans have been introduced in public places across the UK. Increasingly, those who continue to smoke are treated as undesirable. They may feel guilty about their smoking habits, and in consequence, (it is hoped) decide to stop smoking, for the good of themselves and others (see Bell et al., 2010). But what are the potentially negative consequences of these campaigns? There is little doubt that the 'Don't Die of Ignorance' advertisements encouraged the idea that HIV was a 'gay plague'. As Green and Sobo (2000) have asserted, AIDS became the threat to encourage people away from what were perceived to be 'dangerous identities' (Green and Sobo, 2000). More recently, it has been suggested that campaigns which promote healthy eating may actually increase the anxiety and depression of those who struggle with their weight (see Puhl and Heier, 2010; Schafer and Ferraro, 2011).

I will now turn to my own experience of social work practice and research in order to unpack some of these issues further.

Stigma in practice

I began my professional career in the UK as a youth and community worker in the 1970s, later retraining as a social worker in the early 1980s. Youth and community workers (also known as community education workers) tended to work at that time with a broad population of service users: young people attending youth clubs, parents and children using playgroups, adults coming for evening classes, older people playing indoor bowls during the daytime. There was no targeting of individuals or groups and no stigmatising either; the community centre was a resource for all in the neighbourhood who chose to use it.

Statutory social work operated very differently, then and now. By its very nature, social work stigmatises: its central purpose is 'to work on behalf of society to help individuals and groups who are vulnerable and marginalised' (Cree, 2010, p. 6). As a social worker in the 1980s, working on an intermediate treatment (IT) project for adolescents identified as at risk of prison or removal from home, I was conscious that it seemed unfair to our neighbours in the community that 'the bad kids got all the goodies'; whilst little or no services existed for 'ordinary' kids in the neighbourhood, the problem kids accessed our centre with its pool tables and craft room, its minibus and its trips to various outdoor pursuits. In return for this special treatment, they were labelled (and came to label themselves) as trouble with a capital T. Later, working as a social worker with young mothers and their children, the impact of stigma was felt just as strongly. Here the young women's social isolation and lack of self-confidence were the product of years of being stigmatised through class, gender, education and poverty – poverty of aspiration as well as poverty of income and possessions. There is an interesting connection here with Bourdieu's (1986) ideas about cultural and social capital; the young mothers had little of either cultural or social capital, and as a result, had few resources on which to draw. Those who had social workers felt, and were, different from others in the community. In some ways, this was positive because their knowledge of 'the system' meant that they were able to mediate, and, to a degree, resist the stigmatising effects of being service users. But in other ways, their identification as clients of social workers meant that that had failed – failed society and failed themselves. One of our achievements from this time was that, with the support and hard work of the women themselves, we set up a project that was open to *all* women and children in the community, not just those identified as 'in need'. We secured a tenancy for a council house free of charge from our local authority and persuaded a voluntary organisation to fund a group worker and crèche worker (see Cree and MacDonald, 1985). It is difficult to imagine that such an initiative might be financed today in the current economic climate. But we did succeed then, and the project turned out to be hugely important to the local community when HIV/AIDS struck soon afterwards, and young people with whom we were working became ill and were dying. (There had been a lot of intravenous drug use through the 1970s and into the 1980s in the neighbourhood, as later depicted in the 1996 book and film *Trainspotting*; see also Robertson *et al.*, 1986.) The fear and panic in the community was immense, felt by local people and practitioners alike; there could have been no clearer example of the special stigma associated with HIV. Some years later, I began a research study focused on the experiences of the children who had been born around this time. This became a concern that I have continued to be interested in over the last 10 years.

Children infected and affected by HIV[1]: a case-study of stigma in action

It is widely accepted that stigma is particularly strong in relation to HIV/AIDS. Research conducted from the 1990s onwards has noted that HIV/AIDS demonstrates all three types of stigma described by Goffman: 'abominations of the body', 'blemishes of character' and 'tribal stigma of race, nation and religion' (see Herek, 1999).

I have led two research studies on the impact of HIV on the lives of children and young people in Scotland. The first, conducted between 1999 and 2002, developed as a response to what was perceived as a gap in knowledge about children affected by HIV in Scotland (Kay et al., 2002; Cree et al., 2006). It was known that significant numbers of children and young people were living with parents with HIV, and that some were accompanying their parents on visits to health and social work agencies. It was not, however, known what issues this raised for them, and what supports they felt they needed. The study comprised three elements: surveys of health and social work services for children affected by parental HIV throughout Scotland; a survey of HIV education and support in secondary schools in Dundee, Edinburgh and Glasgow; and interviews with 28 children and young people affected by parental HIV in Dundee, Edinburgh and Glasgow (three key sites of HIV prevalence in Scotland). The second study was designed as a 10 year follow-up to the first, updating what was known and this time exploring both infected and affected children's views and experiences (Cree and Sidhva, 2009). This study also had three components: a scoping study focusing on findings from research in the last 10 years; an epidemiological survey of infected and affected children; and interviews with 48 informants (practitioners, parents and carers, and infected and affected children).

Importantly, neither study set out to be an examination of HIV stigma. Instead, the research agenda was open: we set out to explore the impact of HIV on children and young people; to find out what social supports these children and young people drew on; and to examine their perceptions of HIV services (both adult-centred and child-centred services) to find out what (if anything) had made a positive difference in their lives. Children and young people took part. Nevertheless, in both studies, stigma had a major influence not just on the lives of the children and young people, but also on the research itself, impacting on everything we did (and were able to do), from accessing informants to conducting the research and disseminating findings. This has been discussed in an earlier research paper (Cree et al., 2004) and some of the discussion from that article is explored again here.

Accessing informants

We had considerable difficulty in accessing children and young people to take part in both studies. In the first study, we only targeted children whom we were assured knew that their parent/s had HIV. This, of course, raised a number of thorny issues. What *did* the children know? What did they *understand* of what they had been told? We felt it was unethical to speak to children who did not know about their parent's diagnosis; another study conducted at the same time in London by Lewis (2001) for the National Children's Bureau took a different view of this, interviewing children who knew their parents were ill, but not that the illness was HIV. What better illustration can there be of the stigma that surrounds HIV?

In the second study, we met children who were HIV positive, as well as those affected by parental HIV. We also interviewed African parents and children (all the children and young people in the first study had been white and Scottish). This brought a new layer of stigma, because those who took part in the research were quite literally terrified that their friends, neighbours and churches in the African community would get to hear about their HIV status. They were afraid that they might be ostracised, and for a group of people who were already struggling with the difficulties of being asylum seekers and refugees, this was a massive risk. (This issue is also discussed in Cree, 2008, and Sinyemu and Baillie, 2005.)

Findings from the research

Although none of the children and young people who took part in the studies used the word stigma to describe their experience, all demonstrated its impact one way or another. Most commonly, they told us that they did not want to be treated differently to other young people. They knew their lives were different in many aspects, but they wanted to be seen as the 'same as the others', as we titled the final report of the second study. One young woman in the first study put this eloquently. She said:

> I wanted to be treated the same. . . . I didnae want like anybody, all the rest of my teachers or anything, to know, in case they treated me different, in case they thought they had to treat me different, and they didnae. I was just the same as everybody else.

The desire not to be treated differently is, of course, strongly connected with the wish to be, and to be seen to be, normal. Some children and young people played down the impact of parental HIV on their lives; as one young girl stated firmly, 'My dad is just a plain normal dad'. Her mother had already died of AIDS, and her father had episodes of acute illness. Was she attempting to pass as a normal, or covering (using Goffman's terminology)? Or did her father do such a good job of passing and covering that she saw little of his pain and discomfort? Or was her response simply age-appropriate? It is known that younger children may have limited understanding of the concept of illness (see Siegal and Peterson, 1999). As researchers, we puzzled over these questions at an intellectual level, but we were also acutely aware that, had we been social workers, we would have had to make a full assessment and, if necessary, do something about this. This highlights a key distinction between social work researchers and practitioners.

In spite of the warnings from parents and risk of rejection, most children and young people in our studies had told a best friend, in a process that has been called selective disclosure. Scambler and Hopkins (1986) note that secret-giving is recipro- cal and is at the heart of the process of making someone a close friend. Some young people described being open about parental HIV only in specific settings, most notably in HIV support agencies. Here they were able to share their joys and anxi- eties without fear of recrimination or 'slagging'. This, however, was not possible for African children in the second study. At the time of the research, no agencies were offering specialist support for children infected, or affected, by HIV in Glasgow.

The main finding to come out of both these studies was that if we are to reduce and even remove the stigma around HIV, we must find ways of being able to talk about it. It is secrecy and fear that bring shame and exclusion. Changes in HIV diagnosis and treatment also offer opportunities here. Thanks to the introduction of antiretroviral treatment, HIV is now a chronic, long-term illness, at least in the developed (minority) world where medicines are accessible. The young people in our studies who were living with HIV (their own or a parent's) refused to see them- selves as victims; instead, they were getting on with the job of living their lives and taking charge of their situation as best they could.

Disseminating the findings

The message we took from the children, young people, parents and practitioners in our research was that HIV needs to be normalised; this was therefore what we set out to convey in our dissemination events that marked the end of both studies. We wanted to shout from the roof-tops that HIV is an illness like any other, that every- one has something that makes them different and special, and that there is no place for stigma in health and social work. Children and young people attended both dis- semination events, and prepared their own feedback to be shared with others; our final report in 2009 was launched by the singer Annie Lennox, as a further way of opening out the topic to as many people as possible. One of the lessons we learned was that the impact of the research went on long after the studies were completed. For example, one 15-year-old whom we had interviewed for the study went on a year later to conduct a newspaper interview entitled, 'The day mum told me she had HIV'. This was a courageous act by both her and her mother; they had agreed that they needed to stand up and be counted and that nothing would change until they took the initiative themselves.

Towards a new paradigm

This research, and my experience in practice, tell me that conventional casework approaches to health and social care may make things worse for people, because stigma feeds on the secrecy that is central to the individualising or personalising of problems. Looking forward, I believe that we must instead embrace a *social* model of health and illness; one that sees health and illness as *social* phenomena that cannot be separated from wider social and structural issues such as class, gender, age, ethnicity and poverty. From this perspective, it will be no surprise to discover that poor people are sicker than rich people; that structural inequalities are central to health and illness (see Graham, 2000). The search for a new paradigm therefore suggests that we need to find ways of opening up conversations between and within individuals, groups and communities, bringing people together to confront and challenge stigma and discrimination, admitting our own weaknesses and humanity in the process.

This new approach builds on three important antecedents. As far back as 1959, the sociologist C. Wright Mills argued that unemployment, war, marriage and problems of the city needed to be understood as 'public issues' as well as 'personal troubles', and because of this, individual solutions would never be enough to bring about lasting improvement, for individuals or for society. Then in the late 1960s and 1970s, 'second-wave' feminists argued that what had been viewed up till then as private and personal problems such as domestic violence, rape and child sexual abuse needed to be understood politically; the rallying cry was that 'the personal is political' (see http://www.carolhanisch.org/ for a discussion of this).

More recently, the disabled people's movement has introduced the idea of 'the social model of disability'. This suggests that it is not individuals who are disabled, but society that disables individuals, by making it impossible for them to lead full lives as citizens, through systemic barriers and discrimination, both direct and indirect (see Oliver, 1983). Taken together, the general point remains: health and illness require a *social* understanding and a *social* response.

Stigma, I have argued, is an inevitable part of human nature and health and social care practice. The challenge for us is not to collude with this – and therefore to make things worse – but instead to confront and challenge assumptions, question the status quo and walk alongside people to help them build on their strengths. As human beings, we all require support from others at some point in our lives, and at the same time, we all have power – power to resist and power to transform our lives and society (Foucault, 1977). Our goal in working with others should, in consequence, be empowerment, not pity; transformation, not further victimisation (Cree, 2013).

Conclusion

This chapter has argued that the effects of stigma on individuals and groups in health and social work are real and damaging. At the same time, it has been argued that the best way to challenge stigma is to refute it; to confront secrecy and denial head-on and demand fair and equal treatment for all, whatever their illness or condition. This approach suggests a new paradigm for working in health and social care, one which recognises that we may all, at some point in our lives, require specialist help and support, and that there should be no barriers to seeking help, and no shame attached to receiving it. Instead, we are all part of society, and have a responsibility to care for each other within society.

QUESTIONS FOR REFLECTION

1. How far do you think health and social work agencies reinforce stigma?
2. What might they do to challenge stigma?
3. What do you think *you* might do to mitigate the effects of stigma with the people you work with?

Note

1. The term 'affected by HIV' is commonly used to refer to those with a parent or carer with HIV. These children may be uninfected, or, as is more likely, untested for HIV.

References

Ahmad, M. (2011) 'Epilepsy: Stigma and management', *Current Research in Neuroscience*, vol. 1, no. 1, pp. 1–14.

Baral, S.C., Karki, D.K. & Newell, J.N. (2007) 'Causes of stigma and discrimination associated with tuberculosis in Nepal: A qualitative study', *BMC Public Health*, vol. 7, pp. 211–221.

Bell, K., Salmon, A., Bowers, M., Bell, J. & McCullough, L. (2010) 'Smoking, stigma and tobacco "denormalization": Further reflections on the use of stigma as a public health tool.' A commentary on *Social Science & Medicine*'s Stigma, Prejudice, Discrimination and Health Special Issue (vol. 67, no. 3), *Social Science & Medicine*, vol. 70, 795–799.

Benbow, S. M. & Reynolds, D. (2000) 'Challenging the stigma of Alzheimer's disease', *Hospital Medicine*, vol. 61, no. 3, pp. 174–177.

Bourdieu, P. (1986) 'The forms of capital', in *Handbook of Theory and Research for the Sociology of Education*, J.G. Richardson (ed), Greenwood Press, New York, pp. 241–258.

Corrigan, P., Roe, D. & Tsang, H. (2011) *Challenging the Stigma of Mental Illness*, Wiley, Chichester, UK.

Cree, V.E. (2008) '*It's Good to Go for a Test*', Report of the Evaluation of Waverley Care's HIV Testing Campaign in Glasgow, Waverley Care, Edinburgh, Scotland.

Cree, V.E. (2010) *Sociology for Social Workers and Probation Officers*, 2nd edn. Routledge, London.

Cree, V.E. (2013) 'New practices in empowerment', in *New Politics of Critical Social Work*, M. Gray, M. & S. Webb (eds), Palgrave Macmillan, Basingstoke, UK.

Cree, V.E., Kay, H., Tisdall, K. & Wallace, J. (2004) 'Stigma and parental HIV', *Qualitative Social Work*, vol. 3, no. 1, pp. 7–25.

Cree, V.E., Kay, H., Tisdall, K. & Wallace, J. (2006) 'Listening to children and young people affected by parental HIV: Findings from a Scottish study', *AIDS Care* vol. 18, no. 1, 73–76.

Cree, V. & MacDonald, M. (1985) 'A place to be themselves', *Community Care*, vol. 577, pp. 14–15.

Cree, V.E. & Sidhva, D. (2009) '*I Want to be Like the Others': A Cross-Sector Needs Assessment of Children Infected and Affected by HIV in Scotland*, Waverley Care, Edinburgh, Scotland.

Foucault, M. (1977) *Discipline and Punish: The Birth of the Prison*, Pantheon Books, New York.

Goffman, E. (1968) *Stigma: Notes on the Management of a Spoiled Identity*, Penguin, Harmondsworth, UK.

Gormley, D. & Quinn, N. (2009) 'Mental health stigma and discrimination: The experience within social work', *Practice: Social Work in Action*, vol. 21, no. 4, 259–272.

Graham, H. (2000) *Understanding Health Inequalities*, Open University Press, Buckingham.

Gray, B., Robinson, C., Seddon, D. & Roberts, A. (2010) Patterns of exclusion of carers for people with mental health problems: The perspectives of professionals', *Journal of Social Work Practice*, vol. 24, no. 4, pp. 475–492.

Green, G. & Sobo, E.J. (2000) *The Endangered Self: Managing the Social Risks of HIV*, Routledge, London.

Herek, G.M. (1999) 'AIDS and stigma', *American Behavioral Scientist*, vol. 42, no. 7, pp. 1106–1116.

Horsfall, J., Clearly, M. & Hunt, G.E. (2010) 'Stigma in mental health: Clients and professionals', *Issues in Mental Health Nursing*, vol. 31, pp. 450–455.

Kay, H., Cree, V., Tisdall, K. & Wallace, J. (2002) *Listening to Children and Young People Whose Parent or Carer Is HIV Positive*, University of Edinburgh & Children in Scotland, Edinburgh.

Lewis, E. (2001) *Afraid to Say: The Needs and Views of Young People Living with HIV/AIDS*, National Children's Bureau, London.

MacKenzie, J. (2006) 'Stigma and dementia: East European and South Asian family carers negotiating stigma in the UK', *Dementia*, vol. 5, no. 2, pp. 233–247.

Mills, C.W. (1959) *The Sociological Imagination*, Oxford University Press, Oxford.

Oliver, M. (1983) *Social Work with Disabled People*, Macmillan, Basingstoke, UK.

Paylor, I. & Mack, H. (2010) 'Gazing into the scarlet crystal ball: Social work and hepatitis C', *British Journal of Social Work*, vol. 40, no. 7, pp. 2291–2307.

Phelan, S.M., Griffin, J.M., Hellerstedt, W.L., Sayer, N.A., Jensen, A.C., Burgess, D.J. & van Ryn, M. (2011) 'Perceived stigma, strain, and mental health among caregivers of veterans with traumatic brain injury', *Disability and Health Journal*, vol. 4, no. 3, pp. 177–184.

Puhl, R.M. & Heuer, C.A. (2010) 'Obesity stigma: Important considerations for public health', *American Journal of Public Health*, vol. 100, no. 6, pp. 1019–1028.

Robertson, J.R., Bucknall, A.B.V., Welsby, P.D., Roberts, J.J.K., Inglis, J.M., Peutherer, J.F. & Brettle, R.P. (1986) 'Epidemic of AIDS related virus (HTLV-III/LAV) infection among intravenous drug abusers', *British Medical Journal*, vol. 292, no. 6519, pp. 527–529.

Scambler, G. (2009) 'Health-related stigma', *Sociology of Health & Illness*, vol. 31, no.3, pp. 441–455.

Scambler, G. & Hopkins, A. (1986) 'Being epileptic: Coming to terms with stigma', *Sociology of Health & Illness*, vol. 8, no 1, pp. 26–43.

Schafer, M.H. & Ferraro, K.F. (2011) 'The stigma of obesity: Does perceived weight discrimination affect identity and physical health?' *Social Psychology Quarterly*, vol. 74, no. 1, pp. 76–97.

Siegal, M. & Peterson, G.C. (1999) *Children's Understanding of Biology and Health*, Cambridge University Press, Cambridge.

Sinyemu, E. & Baillie, M. (2005) *HIV Becomes Your Name*, Waverley Care, Edinburgh, Scotland.

van Brakel, W.H. (2006) 'Measuring health-related stigma: A literature review', *Psychology, Health & Medicine*, vol. 11, no. 3, 307–334.

Voorend, C.G.N., van Brakel, W.H., Cross, H., Augustine, V. & Ebenso, B. (2011) '*Report of the Stigma Research Workshop for the development of scientific consensus papers and field guidelines on health-related stigma*,' held in Amsterdam, the Netherlands, from 11–14 October, *Leprosy Review*, vol. 82, pp. 188–201.

Weiss, M.G., Ramakrishna, J. & Somma, D. (2011) 'Health-related stigma: Rethinking concepts and interventions', *Psychology, Health & Medicine*, vol. 11, no. 3, pp. 277–287.

8

THE NATURAL ENVIRONMENT AND WELLBEING

Uschi Bay

CHAPTER OBJECTIVES

1. *Explore the role of the natural environment for health and wellbeing in social work practice;*
2. *Indicate how the natural environment can be a source of distress and disease and social work's response;*
3. *Promote a rethinking of wellbeing practices that recognises the interdependence of people and nature in social work practice.*

   Never in history have humans spent so little time in physical contact with animals and plants, and the consequences are unknown. (Katcher and Beck, 1987, pp. 175–183, cited in Pryor et al., 2005, p. 4)

Introduction

My contention is that, ontologically, people and nature are not separate and for this reason the wellbeing of both the natural environment and people is fostered through an interrelationship that is marked by an on-going respectful interdependence. This conceptualisation influences how the natural environment is incorporated into social work practice at personal, individual, group, community, policy and planning levels. Many examples of social work practice at these various levels posit wellbeing as internal to people, as a state of being rather than as a relation with the natural environment, and in so doing relegate nature to the status of a resource. When the natural environment is appropriated as some raw material to be preserved, protected, used or made economically or agriculturally productive, it means that nature is primarily treated as a context for people's 'wellbeing practices'

(Haraway, 1995). The challenge in social work theory and practice is to overcome the dichotomy of social versus natural, of culture versus nature, and to develop a 'people as place' conception that also considers wellbeing as a relational concept (see Bell, 2012; White, 2010; Zapf, 2009).

As a relational concept, wellbeing is not something that someone has or aims for as an attained state, rather 'people become who and what they are in and through their relatedness to others' and in relation with nature (White, 2010, p. 164). Wellbeing practices, in what Haraway (1995, p. 188) calls 'White Capitalist Patriarchy' – 'that turns everything into a resource for appropriation' can be affirming of capitalism, militarism, colonialism and consumerism. In this way wellbeing practices may be 'profoundly de-politicising and can strengthen ideologies of individual choice' (Haraway, 1995, p. 188). Further discourses of wellbeing can strengthen the construct of 'citizen-subjects', opening individuals up to be governed more effectively through their 'self-responsible self-monitoring' (Sointu, 2005, cited in White, 2010, p. 167). In this way medical discourses might 'responsibilise' individuals for their wellbeing practices and indirectly lead to people being blamed for their lifestyles and bad habits. It is important that social workers have regard for a broader understanding of wellbeing practices as relational, and critically consider the way that wellbeing discourses frame the individual as responsible for their health, especially in the current neo-liberal policy contexts evident in many nations. For social work theory and practice the challenge is to promote a 'people as place' notion that foregrounds the interrelation between the natural environment and human wellbeing (Zapf, 2009). My hope is that newly developed ways of thinking in social work can prioritise the conditions for the mutual flourishing between people and the natural environment.

In the first section of this chapter I will outline the relation between human contact with the natural environment and psychological, social, economic and ecological wellbeing gained as indicated in previous research. There are many examples of how the interrelationship between direct social work practice and nature are related to mental wellbeing and to positive overall health outcomes (Heinsch, 2012). Even so, human contact with nature is not always benign and natural disasters can have a serious impact on human wellbeing. The recovery process after natural disasters can, at times, lead the people impacted upon to innovate and create new ways of living that are far more ecologically sustainable (Besthorn, 2012b).

Humans have destroyed and altered parts of the natural environment in unprecedented ways over the last half century. These changes have led to increases in prosperity for many, but also to problems of pollution, toxic waste and environmental degradation resulting in species extinction of both flora and fauna (Millennium Ecosystem Assessment, 2005, p. v). Climate change is also attributed to human activity on the planet (Solomon *et al.*, 2007). Human wellbeing is likely to be dramatically negatively impacted by global warming and the changes this will bring to the natural environment. Social workers are encouraged by leaders in environmental social work or green social work to engage with the issues and changes that arise from the current and predicted climate events on a range of levels; individual,

group, community, policy analysis and advocacy as well as through social and political action or support of social movements (Coates and Gray, 2012; Peeters, 2012).

Nature as a resource for individual health and wellbeing

In this section the beneficial relationship between the natural environment and
psychological, emotional, cognitive, spiritual, physical and social wellbeing will be
discussed. There is a growing consensus among various helping professionals that
'positive non-threatening interactions with nature can enhance various dimensions
of well-being' (Burns, 2009, p. 240). According to Heinsch (2012, p. 311), numerous research studies from disciplines other than social work attest to the 'health-
enhancing qualities of nature'. Her recent literature review highlighted many ways
the natural environment as a resource can be incorporated into social work practice
in various contexts. Social workers are also aware that modern lifestyles do not
always promote people contact with nature, plants and animals. Hence nature as a
resource for direct practice becomes even more important. Thinking about nature
as not just manifest in wild spaces, but in indoor plants, private, public and community gardens, green spaces, parks and streetscapes in urban settings is central to devising strategies to improve or enhance individual family and community wellbeing.

A brief overview of some of the relevant research for direct social work practice
including nature as a resource shows 'that nature had a particularly calming influence on people experiencing high-level crisis, as in response to death, divorce or
any other severe loss' (Heinsch, 2012, p. 311). There is a therapeutic value attributed
to people's contact with nature in nature therapy. The use of nature as an element
in the treatment of Attention Deficit Hyperactivity Disorder (ADHD) in children
is considered effective in reducing their symptoms (Kuo and Faber Taylor, 2004).
The use of bush adventures for young people with substance abuse or self-reported
mental health issues has also proved effective (Pryor et al., 2005). Research related
to depression and strategies for managing mild and moderate levels of depression
indicate that time in nature is a factor in positively dealing with this aspect of life
(Peacock et al., 2007). Some eco-psychologists aim to devise strategies that promote clients to engage in more nature-based interactions, 'for the enhancement of
individual well-being, environmental well-being, the well-being of the relationship between the two' (Burns, 2009, p. 243). In work with couples, Burns (2009)
might recommend a couple visit natural environments that were part of their early
relationship to recapture aspects of their connection to each other. These diverse
findings encourage social work practitioners to consider the value of incorporating
nature as a resource in devising strategies with individuals suffering from mental
health issues, loss, grief, stress, tension, substance abuse and for hyperactivity in
children.

Direct involvement with nature is linked to human physical and emotional wellbeing. People engaging in activities like walking, gardening, horse riding, hiking and
farming are strong components in 'contemporary ecotherapy' (Bursi, 2007, cited
in Heinsch, 2012, p. 312). Research supports the restorative benefits of walking

mindfully in nature every day (Young, 2010). Berman *et al.*'s study (2008) found a rise in cognitive functioning following a 50–55 minute walk in nature (Heinsch, 2012, p. 312). The link between walking in nature and decreases in anxiety and depression again suggest that social workers, in devising strategies to assist people with these issues, can call on these findings to support the use of nature as a resource to promote physical, cognitive, emotional and spiritual wellbeing.

Contact with nature is considered vitally important for children's wellbeing. Children with ADHD had significantly reduced symptoms after participating in 'green outdoor activities' regardless of urban or rural setting, age, sex, income or diagnosis (Kuo and Faber Taylor, 2004). In a national study, Faber Taylor and Kuo (2009) found that walking in nature improved children's concentration significantly. This suggests to social workers and parents that a regular walk in the park or in another natural space as a common after-school or weekend activity may be a really important strategy for children and adolescents suffering from ADHD. There is also a strong link between increases in cognitive functioning and contact with nature for children with learning difficulties.

In the United States there is an explosion of new grassroots groups developing campaigns to increase children's contact with nature. Katcher and Beck (1987, cited in Pryor *et al.*, 2005) contend that this is the first time in human history that people have spent so little time in physical contact with nature, with animals and plants. The grassroots reaction to increase children's contact with nature may be thus both a welcome and warranted response to some major lifestyle changes effected through an increasingly capitalist and consumerist focus in the world. This is also the first time in human history that over half the world now lives in cities (United Nations Population Fund, 2007). These changes no doubt contribute to how regularly children access and engage with nature and the types of natural environments available to them.

For social work, the issue of access to, and availability of, green areas for structurally disadvantaged groups is an issue not only in direct practice but also in community work, policy and planning work. Mass *et al.* (2006) found that 'lower socioeconomic groups, such as older people, young people . . . gain greater benefits from the presence of green areas in their living environment than other groups' (cited in Heinsch, 2012, p. 311). It is also common that structurally disadvantaged people reside in the most depleted or abused natural environments. Natural settings high in species richness, in the variety of plants and range of bird species are associated with increased psychological benefits (Fuller *et al.* 2007, cited in Heinsch, 2012, p. 312). Residing in areas close to large green spaces with high species richness relates to people reporting increased perception of general wellbeing. Often poorer people and disadvantaged groups reside in areas that are less likely to offer access to nature in ways that would offer maximum benefits to their overall psychological, cognitive, emotional, physical and spiritual wellbeing.

Social workers may initiate the use of nature as a resource in institutional settings by bringing nature directly into various institutional settings like nursing homes, hospitals, prisons and schools, through gardening and pet therapy. The benefit of nature for human wellbeing is related not only to being close to or being in nature, but can also be indirectly attained just by viewing nature. Research indicates that even viewing videos of 'natural landscapes had a calming effect on participants in as little as 20 seconds' (Van den Berg *et al.*, 2003, cited in Heinsch, 2012, p. 311). This has implications for the use of displays of nature in institutional settings and in pain management. Images of nature (moving or static) can be used in many settings to enhance people's emotional, and possibly spiritual, wellbeing through indirect contact with nature.

Companion animals have been shown to bring increased social interaction in institutional settings (Churchill *et al.*, 1999; Bruck, 1999, both cited in Heinsch, 2012, p. 315) and to significant improvements in prison inmates' social skills (Fournier *et al.* 2007, cited in Heinsch, 2012, p. 315). Community gardens are considered to provide not only a place to congregate with other residents but also as a place to learn about growing food – often leading to exchanges of knowledge as well as swapping of healthy produce. Community development workers indicate that community gardens can be a focal point for celebration of food, culture and even provide support to people who are struggling financially to cover food costs (Wakefield *et al.*, cited in Norton, 2012, p. 306).

Natural environment and human distress

In this chapter, so far, I have illustrated the recognised health and wellbeing benefits of nature as a resource, especially in relation to emotional, cognitive and physical wellbeing on a personal level. These wellbeing aspects of contact with nature have all been presented as positive and as health enhancing; however, contact with nature can also be negative. Some people fear nature or associate it with danger on psychological, emotional or physical levels; or fear and avoid certain elements or activities in nature like swimming, horse riding or climbing. My point here is that human contact and interaction with the natural environment is not unproblematic nor is it always benign or beneficial.

Nature can wreak havoc on human lives and livelihoods and cause distress and dis-ease. Social work practitioners are involved in addressing people's distress and disease through crisis intervention with survivors of natural disasters and through disaster relief service provision. Social work scholarship contributes to understanding the efficacy, gendered aspects and increases in violence in families and communities as important facets of post disaster relief services and the role of community functioning in recovery processes locally and globally (Alston, 2009; Winkworth *et al.*, 2009)

Natural disasters like frequent floods, long and severe droughts, earthquakes, tsunamis, mud slides, tornadoes, cyclones, typhoons, severe wind, hail and electrical storms all impact people around the world in specific locations at various times. Social work professionals are engaged in both assisting individuals and communities to prepare for, and recover from, natural disasters through direct practice interventions, group work, community work, policy analysis and through research to enable human wellbeing post-disaster (see Coates and Gray, 2012).

Recovery from natural disasters often correlates for people with their sense of attachment to a place. Many people rebuild after floods, fires or earthquakes and some use the opportunity post-disaster to improve the sustainability of their ways of living. For example, Fred Besthorn outlined the example of a small town, Greensburg, Kansas in the United States flattened by a tornado on May 5, 2007, at the 2012 Joint World Conference on Social Work and Social Development in Sweden. Besthorn (2012b) highlighted the unexpected way that local residents used this tragedy as an opportunity, through a process of debate, taking over six months and including all residents, to decide to rebuild Greensburg in a totally 'green' way. Greensburg is the first and only all-green city in the United States and reflects an extraordinary recovery that prioritises sustaining the environment that sustains the residents. In a sense, the community of Greensburg could be considered to be resilient because of the local residents' ability to create a new way of life.

In the natural disaster recovery literature, the definition of resilience is related to the 'ability to survive future natural disasters with minimum loss of life and property, as well as the ability to create [a] sense of place among residents; a stronger, more diverse economy; and a more economically integrated and diverse population' (Vale and Camponella, 2005, cited in Winkworth *et al.*, 2009, p. 6). There is growing recognition of the importance of community-led, self-organising groups enacting participatory democracy at a local level not only in relation to recovery from natural and man-made disasters, but also in promoting sustainable development and sustainable living (Besthorn, 2012b; Hopkins, 2010).

Community-led recoveries through processes of participatory democracy and with a focus on sustaining the environment are also being encouraged through transnational grassroots movements like transition town movements that originated in Kinsale, Ireland, in 2005 to address twin concerns about Peak Oil and Climate Change (Hopkins, 2010; Seyfang, 2009). Several kinds of climate change community groups aim to reduce dependence on finite extractive resources such as coal, gas and oil, and aim for judicious management of water while seeking renewable energy to reduce carbon emissions. Other related alternative movements include the 'slow food movement' (Fonte, 2002), including food sovereignty initiatives, civic food networks in Brazil and Spain and the international peasant farmer movement, La Via Campesina. These movements are all in various ways engaged in promoting the health of humans and nature through sustainable land use practices, production and sale of organic and local foods, and through protecting farm land from overuse, the debilitating effects of mono-cultural agricultural production and agrotoxins. These movements posit that the health of people is interrelated with the health of the land. Struggles over land use and the use of commons and land rights more broadly are part of the political aspects of the relationship between human and natural environmental wellbeing.

Research into the effects of environmental disasters and the impacts on various population groups has highlighted the multiple interacting variables that compound the effects of natural disasters on groups whose livelihood is dependent directly on natural resources. Social work scholars have identified the interaction between various contextual factors and specific population groups who are considered at risk of reduced wellbeing in relation to natural disasters. For instance, Margaret Alston (2012) makes a case for understanding the factors influencing the marked increased risk of suicide amongst rural male farmers during times of extended drought in Australia. Vandana Shiva (2006) indicates that male farmer suicides increased in India in relation to corporate influences – where infertile seeds needing chemical fertilisers were promoted at the cost of farmer's sovereign rights over seeds. Tampering with nature through developing hybridised and non-renewable seeds, the various world trade agreements and patents on possibly commonly owned natural resources also reduced farmer self-sufficiency and ability to farm without mounting debts. These two examples further indicate that the relations between nature, human wellbeing and livelihoods are complex, multiple and mediated socially, culturally, economically and politically, as well as being gendered (Alston, 2012).

Destruction of the natural environment and human wellbeing

It has become increasingly apparent that human actions impact on the natural world in ways that are problematic. Over the last 50 years 'humans have changed ecosystems more rapidly and extensively than in any comparable period of time in human history. . . . This has resulted in a substantial and largely irreversible loss in the diversity of life on Earth' (Millennium Ecosystem Assessment, 2005, p. v). These consequences of humans' destructive interactions with nature are also a source of distress and 'dis-ease' for human wellbeing. The aim of the Millennium Ecosystem Assessment, carried out between 2001 and 2005, 'was to assess the consequences of ecosystems change for human well-being and to establish the scientific basis for actions needed to enhance the conservation and sustainable use of ecosystems and their contributions to human well-being' (Millennium Ecosystem Assessment, 2005, p. v). There is growing evidence that human actions have led to the 'irrevocable loss of thousands of animal and plant species' (Besthorn, 2012a, p. 253).

One key aspect of the health and wellbeing of the planet and thus human health and wellbeing relates to the massive increase in deforestation across the globe. 'An estimated 13 million hectares of the world's forested areas – almost exclusively in the tropical regions – are deforested annually' (CSIRO, 2008). It is known that 'Pristine forests are home to over half of all terrestrial species in the world and their loss would impoverish the planet' (ScienceDaily, 2007). Over the last few years economic considerations and issues around climate change have stimulated ideas around using forests for carbon sequestration thus paying Indigenous peoples or other landholders to keep their forests intact as carbon sinks. Yet there are other risks with this idea, such as when large tracts of forest catch fire and release more carbon into the air. Canada's forests have been affected by bushfires and insect outbreaks that have 'transformed them from CO_2 sink to a CO_2 source' (Canadell 2008, cited in ScienceDaily, 2007). The interdependencies between economic uses of forests and human wellbeing is complex and human actions may have unexpected outcomes that undermine the earlier benefits of using natural resources in unsustainable ways. For example, the Millennium Ecosystem Assessment noted that 'an international demand for timber may lead to a regional loss of forest cover, which increases flood magnitude along a local stretch of a river' (2005, p. vii). Exponents of the therapeutic use of nature also posit a relationship between humans and nature that assumes 'that a healthy and sustainable environment is dependent on healthy human relationships with nature' (Pryor *et al.*, 2005, p. 3).

Apart from the destruction of natural environments further changes to the ecosystems include the introduction of various toxic waste products and pollution. In the 1980s some social workers joined with the environmental movement to highlight the 'negative impacts on people of industrial pollution, the dumping of industrial waste and agricultural practices – spraying and run off – resulting in exposure to toxins in water, soil and air' (Coates and Gray, 2012, p. 230). From a structural perspective coining the term 'environmental racism' indicates the close relationship between degraded, poisoned and dangerous environments and the usually low socio-economic and minority racial groups directly negatively affected by the destruction of their immediate natural environment.

The introduction of toxic waste has often impacted specifically on Indigenous groups in various parts of the world (Coates and Gray, 2012). The impact on children of pollution, degradation and toxic waste is also important for social workers to consider at local, nation and transnational levels (Buka *et al.*, 2006). Children are usually more susceptible to toxic waste and poisons in the air, water, land and food which is now often grown with application of chemical fertilisers and covered in chemical sprays for preservation during transport.

One of the major concerns in relation to nature and human wellbeing in the 21st century is the issue of climate change. The scientific consensus is that humans have contributed to carbon emissions leading to global warming (Oreskes, 2004, p. 1686). The Intergovernmental Panel on Climate Change (IPCC) established by the United Nations and the World Meteorological Organisation to evaluate scientific evidence of climate change is clear that human activities are modifying the Earth's climate (McCarthy, 2001). Social workers are responding to the climate change challenges through research, integrating knowledge about the importance of developing holistic understandings to address the transformations required to maintain a planet that can support life. This major challenge is linked to social work's ontology and epistemology and calls for a holistic paradigm shift and political engagement. Peeters (2012) argues that it is necessary to 'search for an alternative to the dominant idea that well-being follows primarily from material prosperity and economic growth' (p. 290).

Implications for practice

There is growing consensus that positive interactions with nature promote human wellbeing especially at personal and interpersonal levels and within institutional and community settings. The therapeutic use of nature has, as its central focus, human contact with nature. I have also made some references to the fact that companion animals, pet ownership, bush adventures and community gardens as forms of engaging with nature or the natural world are found to increase positive social skills and social interactions in institutions, group therapy and local neighbourhoods.

Social work practitioners engaging with children may also consider how applicable increased access to nature is when devising strategies to address learning difficulties. Research and policy advocacy are key roles here for social workers in promoting specifically children's wellbeing; possibly this kind of work is most effectively undertaken through collaboration with other professionals also working from a holistic health and wellbeing perspective. Policy analysis and policy advocacy to promote sustainable living is another key area social workers in all areas of practice can contribute – whether this is in, for example, housing, mental health, child welfare or family services. As Peeters (2012, p. 295) suggests, sustainable development requires major transformations that will be necessary across society and social workers can play a significant role in these change processes.

It is also crucial practitioners undertake research into the ways natural disasters and related events interact with social, economic and political systems and impact on people's wellbeing. Transition to an ecological sustainable way of living requires inter-professional collaboration in research to inform social change as well as social work practice at interpersonal, group, community and policy levels. Green and McDermott (2010, p. 2415) contend 'social work must build on its existing knowledge by engaging with the way natural scientists and knowledge theorists now explain the world'. The transition to a more sustainable way of living will thus also require transdisciplinary collaboration to address the complexity of current social and ecological problems.

Currently, social work theorists are proposing a paradigm shift with the aim of comprehensively transforming 'social work epistemology into a cohesive, holistic framework that can adequately account for interrelationships, co-operation, experiential knowledge, collective concerns and participation in the context of social work efforts to work for social justice outcomes using an emancipatory, human rights approach' (Bell, 2012, p. 416), and call for 'a new vision of human and planetary well-being' (Peeters, 2012, p. 290).

Conclusion

Social work as a profession is engaged in 'enhancing and maintaining human life and wellbeing' (Green and McDermott, 2010, p. 2430). Social workers are increasingly recognising the interdependence between people and nature as mutually constitutive (Besthorn, 2012a; Peeters, 2012; Norton, 2012). This shift towards holism is required to enable social workers to engage with the current and urgent 'social-ecological crisis' (Peeters, 2012, p. 295). This is the challenge facing social work: to holistically understand the 'person-in-environment' or 'people as place' and continually work at the 'borders of social, economic, biological and political systems' (Green and McDermott, 2010, p. 2430) in order to work towards a new meaning of wellbeing that is inclusive of all life.

QUESTIONS FOR REFLECTION

1. Is it necessary to shift towards holism conceptually before it is possible to address the current 'social-ecological crisis'?
2. What would a new meaning of wellbeing that is inclusive of all life look like? Can you articulate the key aspects needed to achieve this kind of vision?
3. In direct social work practice, how might the interdependence between people and nature be taken into account? What strategies might you use?

References

Alston, M. (2009) 'Drought policy in Australia: Gender mainstreaming or gender blindness?', *Gender Place And Culture*, vol. 16, no. 2, pp. 139–154.

Alston, M. (2012) 'Rural male suicide in Australia', *Social Science and Medicine*, vol. 74, no. 4, pp. 515–522.

Bell, K. (2012) 'Towards a post-conventional philosophical base for social work', *British Journal of Social Work*, vol. 42, no. 3, pp. 408–423.

Besthorn, F. (2012a) 'Deep ecology's contribution to social work: A ten-year retrospective', *International Journal of Social Welfare*, vol. 21, no. 3, pp. 248–259.

Besthorn, F. (2012b) *Social Work and the Environment* [online]. Available at: http://swsd2012. creo.tv/tuesday/fred_h_besthorn/d3p4-fred_h_besthorn

Buka, I., Koranteng S. & Osornio-Vargas, A. (2006) 'The effects of air pollution on the health of children', *Paediatric Child Health*, vol. 11, no. 8, pp. 513–516.

Burns, G.W. (2009), *Happiness, Healing Enhancement: Your Casebook Collection for Applying Positive Psychology in Therapy*, John Wiley, Hoboken, NJ.

Coates, J. & Gray, M. (2012) 'The environment and social work: An overview and introduction', *International Journal of Social Welfare*, vol. 21, no. 3, pp. 230–238.

CSIRO Australia (2008, June 19) *Tropical Forest Sustainability: A Climate Change Boon* [online]. Available at: http://www.csiro.au/Organisation-Structure/Divisions/Marine – Atmospheric-Research/TropicalForestsAndClimateChange.aspx

Faber Taylor, A. & Kuo, F.E. (2009) 'Children with attention deficits concentrate better after walk in the park', *Journal of Attention Disorders*, vol. 12, no. 5, pp. 402–409.

Fonte, M. (2002) 'Food systems, consumption models and risk perception in late modernity', *International Journal of Agriculture and Food*, vol. 10, no. 1, pp. 13–21.

Green, D. & McDermott, F. (2010) 'Social work from inside and between complex systems: Perspectives on person-in-environment for today's social work', *British Journal of Social Work*, vol. 40, no. 8, pp. 2414–2430.

Haraway, D. (1995) 'Situated knowledges: The science question in feminism and the privilege of the partial perspective', in *Technology and the Politics of Knowledge*, A. Feenberg & A. Hannay (eds), Indiana University Press, Indianapolis.

Heinsch, M. (2012) 'Getting down to earth: Finding a place for nature in social work practice', *International Journal of Social Welfare*, vol. 21, no. 3, pp. 309–318.

Hopkins, R. (2010) *Transition – How Far Can We Go? From Oil Dependency to Local Resilience* [online]. Available at: http://www.slideshare.net/transitionderby/rob-hopkins-in-derby

Kuo, F.E. & Faber Taylor, A. (2004) 'A potential natural treatment for Attention-Deficit/ Hyperactivity Disorder: Evidence from a national study', *American Journal of Public Health*, vol. 94, no. 9, pp. 1580–1586.

McCarthy, J.J. (ed) (2001) *Climate Change 2001: Impacts, Adaptation, and Vulnerability*, Cambridge University Press, Cambridge.

Millennium Ecosystem Assessment (2005) *Ecosystems and Human Well-being: Synthesis*, Island Press, Washington, DC. Available at: http://www.millenniumassessment.org/documents/document.356.aspx.pdf

Norton, C.L. (2012) 'Social work and the environment: An ecosocial approach', *International Journal of Social Welfare*, vol. 21, no. 3 pp. 299–308.

Oreskes, N. (2004) 'Beyond the ivory tower: The scientific consensus on climate change', *Science 3*, vol. 306, no. 5702, p. 1686. doi: 10.1126/science.1103618

Peacock, J., Hine, R. & Pretty, J. (2007) 'Got the blues, then find some greenspace: The mental health benefits of green exercise activities and green care', *MIND Week Report*, February.

Peeters, J. (2012) 'The place of social work in sustainable development: Towards ecosocial practice', *International Journal of Social Welfare*, vol. 21, no. 3, pp. 287–298.

Pryor, A., Carpenter, C. & Townsend, M. (2005) 'Outdoor education and bush adventure therapy: A socio-ecological approach to health and well-being', *Australian Journal of Outdoor Education*, vol. 9, no. 1, pp. 3–13.

ScienceDaily (Nov. 15, 2007) *Single-largest Biodiversity Survey Says Primary Rainforest is Irreplaceable*. Available at: http://www.sciencedaily.com/releases/2007/11/071114111144.htm

Seyfang, G. (2009), *Green Shoots of Sustainability: The 2009 UK Transition Movement Survey*, University of East Anglia, UK.

Shiva, V. (2006) *Farmer Suicides, the US–India Nuclear Deal, Wal-Mart in India and More*. Available at: http://www.democracynow.org/2006/12/13/vandana_shiva_on_farmer_suicides_the

Solomon, S., Qin, D., Manning, M., Chen, Z., Marquis, M., Averyt, K.B. Tignor, M. & Miller H.L. (eds) (2007) *Contribution of Working Group I to the Fourth Assessment Report of the Intergovernmental Panel on Climate Change*, Cambridge University Press, Cambridge.

White, S.C. (2010) 'Analysing wellbeing: A framework for development practice', *Development in Practice*, vol. 20, no. 2, pp. 158–172.

Winkworth, G., Healy, C., Woodward, M. & Camilleri, P. (2009) 'Community capacity building: Lessons from 2003 Canberra brushfires', *The Australian Journal of Emergency Management*, vol. 24, no. 2, pp. 5–12.

United Nations Population Fund (2007) *State of the World Population 2007, Unleashing the Potential of Urban Growth*. Available at: http://www.unfpa.org/swp/2007/english/introduction.html

Young, R.D. (2010) 'Restoring mental vitality in an endangered world: Reflections on the benefits of walking', *Ecopsychology*, vol. 2, no. 1, pp. 13–22.

Zapf, M.K. (2009) *Social Work and the Environment: Understanding People and Place*, Canadian Scholars Press, Toronto.

PART II

Diverse communities

Culture, identity, spirituality and health

9

INDIGENOUS[1] AUSTRALIAN SOCIAL-HEALTH THEORY

Decolonisation, healing – reclaiming wellbeing

Lorraine Muller

> *Our knowledge 'is not alpha and omega but Circular and Reformative.' If you cut the tail off a snake (keelback) its tail grows back but the scales have a slightly different pattern. Contemporary Indigenous culture/knowledge is like the newly grown tail. Colonisation and invasion 'cut the tail off' our culture, and although wounded, the snake (culture and knowledge) survived, lying low while it regenerated its new tail that is the same as the old one, with a slightly different pattern. Our culture/knowledge is as vigorous as before, yet wiser and knowledgeable of its assailant and its ways.*
>
> (As explained to me by a Clever man.)

This chapter is a short story of a journey of the recuperation of our knowledge, using decolonisation as a framework for research, and how it assists in the healing and reclaiming of wellbeing.

CHAPTER OBJECTIVES

This chapter shares the research path taken in documenting Indigenous Australian social-health theory:

1. *The process of colonisation is discussed;*
2. *Ways of healing from colonisation's negative effects is then examined;*
3. *Decolonisation is demonstrated as a framework for research that is relevant to both the colonised and coloniser community, for both are afflicted by the ideology of colonisation.*

Introduction

Recovery of knowledge, a pathway of rediscovery

We, Indigenous Australians, Aboriginal and Torres Strait Islanders, have a very rigorous and academically sound theoretical base. Until recently, this knowledge was held and transferred orally, meaning that, when engaging with tertiary studies, our students could not draw on our theory as an academic source. Collectively, a group of social health workers, those for whom the social, emotional (including Spiritual) and physical wellbeing of our people is central to their practice, and community members, determined that we needed our theory in an academic format. Making our theory available to our students, workers and interested non-Indigenous colleagues became the topic of my qualitative doctoral research.

Initially, I assumed our theory would be a practice theory, rather than the meta-theory, entwined with examples of practice, that emerged as the study progressed. Documenting our theory took me on a circuitous path where I realised the truth that meta-theory and methodology are interconnected and entangled and both are products of the researcher's world view which, in turn, informs the process of research and establishes what is acceptable as theory (Overton, nd; Overton and Ennis, 2006). Sometimes described as relational theory/methodology, Indigenous theory and methodologies have significant difference, as they have a decolonising aim and clear connection to Country (lands) (Kovach, 2010, pp. 30–36).

Process is as important as the outcome when conducting Indigenous research and Aboriginal Grounded Research (AGR) (Fejo, 1994, p. 16; King, 2005) providing a collaborative, respectful approach with emphasis on proper process and methods of inquiry. A central aspect of AGR was a large group of significant knowledge holders who collectively made up a guiding expert panel, who ensured that the documented knowledge was appropriate to be shared and endorsed its validity and the cultural integrity of the findings.

Knowledge was shared with me in semi-structured individual interviews via email, chance encounters, by telephone and in two large focus groups. Forty-two people shared their knowledge in formal interviews/focus groups, in addition to numerous informal interviews and the 38 expert panel members. My responsibility, as primary researcher, was to discern what knowledge was to be shared, or not shared, drawing on the expert panel as required, and present it in an academically sound, yet readable, format.

Research principles and protocols were not immediately clear, for I was documenting insider knowledge, and had not realised the full extent of the 'ways of being' (ontology), 'ways of knowing' (epistemology) and 'ways of doing' (methodology) differed from non-Indigenous epistemology and ontology (Martin, 2008, p. 72). Langton (2003, p. 121) explains, that '[f]rom the inside, a culture is "felt" as normative, not deviant. It is European culture which is different for an Aboriginal person'. Engaging in reciprocal learning, a circular teaching/learning process, with my non-Indigenous primary supervisor also helped me articulate our values and protocols more fully (Gair and Muller, 2009).

Genuine two-way sharing of knowledge is a sign of mutual respect and understanding – Indigenous research requires a climate of mutuality (Eckermann *et al.*, 2006; Kovach, 2010). In addition to reciprocity and mutuality, respect based on the 'truth' that everyone is intrinsically equal, formed the fundamental precept for my research. Other key protocols and values identified are: the survival and protection of our knowledge is a political process; one only speaks for oneself unless one has explicit permission otherwise; consensus; use of plain language and deep listening (Dadirri) (Ungunmerr-Baumann, 2002); a time-rich approach; consultation and full disclosure; respect for gender and age; and, with knowledge comes responsibility (Muller, 2010).

Circular learning reflects the responsibility to knowledge. Knowledge and responsibility are inseparable; custodians of knowledge have an obligation to ensure that knowledge is respected, nurtured, and shared where appropriate (Gair and Muller, 2009, pp. 141–143). Sharing knowledge on the basics of our theory is part of my responsibility for having that knowledge shared with me. As interviews progressed, I shared the collective knowledge from previous discussions, fulfilling my obligation as both teacher and learner.

Writing and organising the shared knowledge, taking our oral theory to a written format, presented difficulties. I tried many Western ways of coding and analysing the data with limited success. I was 'growled' at by a few people for using language that was seen to be 'too white', because 'we see things not as black and white but more colourful' (in Muller, 2010, p. 153). I was trying to shove our knowledge into a non-Indigenous box where it was simply not going to fit. Finally, I returned to the transcripts of the research conversations where the answer was waiting for me: 'It has to be linked to culture, in a cultural way, by giving an example first, then ask how the learner understands it, building on from there' in multiple, intertwined and knotted together layers (2010, p. 153).

Capturing the essence of our complex theory was daunting and Kovach's (2010, p. 10) assurance that, when using 'Indigenous methodologies – start where you are, it will take you where you need to go' resonated with my experience. Decolonisation provided the framework for research.

Decolonisation: a framework for research

In this section I draw on Poka Laenui's (also known as Hayden Burgess) five stages of colonisation that he suggests are evident in all colonised countries: 1) *Denial and Withdrawal*; 2) *Destruction/Eradication*; 3) *Denigration/Belittlement/Insult*; 4) *Surface Accommodation/Tokenism*; 5) *Transformation/Exploitation*, as well as his proposed 'five stages of decolonisation' (Laenui, 2000, 2007). These stages are not necessarily sequential or separate.

Laenui's proposed five stages of decolonisation are 1) *Rediscovery and Recovery*; 2) *Mourning*; 3) *Dreaming*; 4) *Commitment*; and 5) *Action* (Laenui, 2000, 2007), but I found that something was missing. Translated to an Australian context, 'Dreaming' incorporated our deep Spiritual concept of 'the dreaming'. Compiling the knowledge shared in my study, it became evident there was an additional stage of decolonisation, a stage of *Healing/Forgiveness – Reclaiming Wellbeing and Harmony*, a phase for self-care, that nestles between the Mourning phase and the Dreaming phase. Reclamation of Spiritual wellbeing, where resilience is nurtured and healing occurs, happens in this stage. The identification of a sixth stage of decolonisation was a significant outcome of my research (Muller, 2013).

The six stages of Decolonisation (Laenui's five and the new stage) that formed the framework for my research are:

1. ***Rediscovery and recovery***
   This is a foundation phase of rediscovering history, traditional practices and languages, reconnecting with Country and kin: it is a time of renewed sense of identity, of recovering knowledges (Laenui, 2000, 2007). People may arrive at this stage by curiosity, accident, desperation, escape, coincidence, fate, or as I found in my research, Spirituality.

2. ***Mourning***
   In this phase, feelings of anger and injustice need time for expression in order for healing to begin; sadly, some people become lost in this phase, unable to move towards healing (Laenui, 2000, p. 4).

3. ***Healing/forgiveness – reclaiming wellbeing and harmony***
   Healing/Forgiveness – reclaiming wellbeing, is a pivotal stage of decolonisation – it is a time for self-care, healing. This is a stage of reflection and the reclaiming of Spiritual wellbeing that builds resilience. Healing is a significant focus for social-health workers and is central to the theory that informs our work.

4. ***Dreaming and 'the Dreaming'***
   This is a stage of strengthening and revaluing our philosophy and knowledge. Laenui sees this phase as the most crucial for recovery, describing it as *Building the Master Recovery Plan* (2000), however, in an Australian context this is more about drawing on the ancient and contemporary wisdom of our peoples.
   The *Dreaming* and *Dreamtime* are words that, in Australia, relate to Aboriginal philosophy, Spirituality, creation and Country.

5. ***Commitment***
   From the Dreaming phase comes the stage of establishing a commitment to a direction for social change (Laenui, 2000).

6. ***Action***
   This is a phase for pro-active, not reactive, action (Laenui, 2000).

All six stages of decolonisation provided the framework for translating our theory and I will discuss these phases later in this chapter because there is no linear path in explaining our theory where all things are interconnected. Digressing slightly I return to the primary task of documenting our theory.

Knowledge shared: an overview of our theory

Theory can be a topic that fills social workers with dread; often seen as an abstract academic concept, difficult to relate to everyday practice, with mumbles and diversions used to stifle any further conversation (Healy, 2005, p. 95). I did not find this among Aboriginal and Torres Strait Islander workers; we yarn about theory – the values and principles that inform our ways of working.

Talk of theory invariably included aspects of our philosophy and Spirituality, carefully interwoven with practice examples, deep learning and humour. Adaptation and incorporation of selective non-Indigenous practice under the governance of our philosophy and theoretical framework, was also evident.

Below is a brief, select, overview of Indigenous Australian social-health theory under headings that cannot do justice to the interconnectedness of such themes. However, social-health theory must be situated in the current reality, that racism continues to influence life and work and it is part of our everyday lives.

Racism

Experiences of racism were so commonplace in my research conversations that it was almost overlooked. Stories of racism held a twist of humour, usually against the perpetrator. As one person put it, 'Blackfellas gotta laugh at these things, if we don't we'd always be crying' (in Muller, 2010, p. 156). However, serious health implications arise from racism (Paradies, 2007; Paradies *et al.*, 2008) and 'continuing racism in Australian society presents a serious social problem with psychological, ethical and physiological ramifications' (Pedersen and Barlow, 2008, p. 148).

Racism in the workplace and academy was particularly relevant because a complainant against racism commonly suffers retaliation and repercussions such as demotion, and/or retrenchment. In academia, 'systemic biases' act to limit the 'the valuing of Indigenous knowledge systems' and that 'racism and paternalism work against both equal participation in research and the valuing of Indigenous knowledge systems' (Dwyer and Silburn, 2009, pp. 5–13). As the late Puggy Hunter was quoted as saying, 'every-time we share knowledge, non-Indigenous people become the experts – we are just informants' (in Muller, 2010). Immigrants, or new settlers, including non-white settlers, also enact racism against Indigenous Australians. As new settlers seek to gain integration and acceptance into mainstream Australian society they sometimes adopt the prejudices of mainstream society. Racism underpins the ideology of colonisation: decolonisation challenges racism and can act to neutralise it.

Spirituality

'Spirituality is something that was always there, it is not something that is talked about freely like Christianity; it is part of who you are'

'Spirituality does not need a religion attached to it'

'Spirituality is what makes a person'
(research conversations in Muller, 2010, p. 167)

Spirituality, the experience of the sacred, and Connectedness is an integral aspect of Aboriginal philosophy and featured strongly in my research conversations. The sacred is the domain of spirit that 'resides in the relationship between the human spirit and the natural life force' (Graham, 2008, p. 186). Spirituality is incorporated into everyday ways of working; it is relied on for connecting with others' Spirituality.

I discuss Spirituality, as shared with me, in relation to the theory that informs practice in what I refer to as 'everyday Spirituality'.

Our Spirituality's focus is on the present, connecting with the spiritual essence surrounding oneself and accepting guidance/trust in its influence in the future, not seeking to escape the present (Graham, 2008, p. 191) while also incorporating the past, present and future.

A 'deep yearning' is referred to in the absence of sufficient Spirituality: there is a 'yearning they hold in the depths of their stomachs . . . a sense of being lost' that causes some to 'turn to drugs, alcohol and suicide' (Purcell, 2002, p. 215). Robb explains the 'restlessness that is expressed by physical and mental torture' as 'this yearning for your people, your land and your Dreaming' for we 'are born from Spirituality' and the 'Dreaming has much more meaning when that part of your soul becomes restful, knowing and content' (Robb, 1996, p. 144). 'Coming into one's [S]pirituality' is a wondrous experience but it can pose a risk of a mental health diagnosis if not understood.

Consciousness of Spirituality can be nurtured from, or before, conception, or develop over time. Some people speak of coming into their Spirituality over a few weeks/months, and/or almost instantaneously. Coming into one's Spirituality results in a new sense of being able to tap into another source, to connect more deeply with country and ancestral entities: it is talked of as a life-changing event.

Spirituality is 'about connecting with all living beings/organisms in the world in harmonic ways. . . . it is about tapping into the still places I go to when I am on Country . . . about finding the calmness in the busy spaces of my life' according to Senimelia Kingsburra (in McEwan and Tsey, 2009, p. vi).

Respect

Respect is the thread that ran throughout this research; respect is based on the basic premise that regardless of status or occupation each soul is intrinsically equal. Everyone is 'acknowledged to have something unique to offer, because of his or her spiritual identity and personal experience of life' (Graham, 2008, p. 192).

Respect, as we use the word, refers to a multiplicity of rules that dictate behaviour, towards self, others, and country; it also dictates the complex recognition of knowledge, moral behaviour and eldership/seniority. Respect also informs, but is not limited to, childrearing practices and social interactions within and between groups and peoples. Respect is a thread that is entwined with ancient law, philosophy, and Spirituality, that informs an appropriate code of conduct. Respect underlines our need to seek consensus.

As I listened, learned and reflected on the knowledge shared with me, it became evident that something more was happening. People were thanking me, saying that in sharing their knowledge and receiving others' knowledge, they were able, and had more confidence to, express their practice: some said they received healing from the process. This was when I recognised the healing stage of decolonisation.

Healing – reclaiming wellbeing, a stage of decolonisation

'*Reviving ancient knowledge from the ashes of colonialism is critical to . . . the healing agenda*'

(Sinclair, 2004, p. 53)

Threads of the healing phase are evident in the first rediscovery/recovery stage, as a critical review of the history and ideology of colonisation is often the beginning of engaging with the process of decolonisation. History demonstrates how the ideology of colonisation saw the creation of settler myths presented as history and how these myths assisted with the implementation of colonisation.

Contrary to popular coloniser myths that we were uncivilised, nomadic, hunter-gatherers, with no permanent housing, farms, or social order, a decolonised examination of history debunks these as fabrications. Early European settler/explorers journals record stone houses, villages, extensive farming and trading routes that traversed the country of Australia (Gammage, 2011; Kerwin, 2006) and a sophisticated social structure in which men and women had equal but different roles and children were protected (Atkinson, 2002; Robertson, 2000; Tatz, 1999). Knowledge of the history of colonisation is an important aspect of social-health theory and features strongly in workers' practice. History helps promote understanding and connection with our past, present and future.

Anger and pain can arise from stories uncovered in the rediscovery stage, as one moves to the mourning stage. Engaging with the other phases of decolonisation can assist people who risk becoming stuck in this phase. Stories of resistance to the barbarity of colonisation, including those by our non-Indigenous allies, can help one enter the healing/forgiveness phase where wellbeing can be reclaimed.

Healing is a contentious term as Feeney notes, the concept of healing implies that it is possible to fix lives that have been irrevocably shattered, when it obviously is not (Feeney, 2009). As a phase of decolonisation, healing and/or forgiveness does not mean forgetting past wrongs, or forgoing justice, nor does it mean absolving, but it refers to the 'spiritual or emotional healing' which can lead to physical healing (Dillon, 2008, p. 6).

> Healing is part of life and continues through death and into life again. . . . It can be experienced in many forms such as mending a wound or recovery from illness . . . it is about renewal. . . . Healing gives us back to ourselves. Not to hide or fight anymore. But to sit still, calm our minds, listen to the universe and allow our spirits to dance on the wind. . . . Healing is not just about recovering what has been lost or repairing what has been broken. . . . Healing keeps us strong and gentle at the same time. It gives us balance and harmony, a place of triumph and sanctuary for evermore. (Milroy, 2000, cited in Mackean, 2009, p. 522)

Reclaiming Wellbeing reflects the belief that wellbeing is our normative state, and refers to decolonising our minds of the coloniser's negative construction of our identity and 'recovering our sense of wellbeing and equanimity' (in Muller, 2010, p. 252). It is a stage where harmony can be found.

Joining the dots

It is not possible, in a single chapter, to do justice to the depth of knowledge that was shared in this study; such as men's and women's way of working, learning circles, connection to community, the use of humour and catering, to give a brief idea.

Our theory is about connectedness, between our theory and decolonisation. To give a brief idea of how our theory acts I draw on the issue of catering, expanding on it to join the dots.

Catering and food was quite prescriptive, in a best practice model. Meetings and gatherings are planned according to the attendees' needs, and water is always available. Consideration for Elders' need for softer foods and place of origin can dictate that a curry/stew is available, and fish may be required for people from saltwater country. Ever present is the impact diabetes has wrought on our peoples so the menu is centred around a healthy diabetic diet. At times, it is easier to tell caterers that everyone is diabetic.

Drawing on the relationship between how white rice was used in the process of colonisation (history) to the epidemic of diabetes, decolonisation offers a way of conceptualising the need for changing diet as a process of healing.

White rice was one of the cheap foods, empty of nutrition, used by colonisers to usurp Australia's original people from their lands and remains a staple food alongside other 'foods of colonisation'. However, researcher Qi Sun et al. (2010) found large consumption of white rice directly contributed to diabetes thereby enabling a connection with colonisation, white rice and health to be made. Making the connection between the foods of colonisation and poor health can assist people review their consumption of nutrient poor foods such as white rice. Sharing an understanding of how these foods have impacted on our health and wellbeing can help shift attitudes towards changing to a healthier diet, into a positive act of resistance to colonisation. Decolonisation offers an opportunity for pro-active change.

Decolonisation and our non-Indigenous allies

> '[T]he impact of colonialism has been huge. . . . It's made them into the people they are today, [but] . . . Many are trying to run away from their own history'. . . .
> (Watson in Aboriginal and Torres Strait Islander Healing Foundation Development Team, 2009)

Laenui explains that 'colonisation and decolonisation are social processes even more than they are political processes' (2000, p. 1) and these complex processes require personal and social action and participation. In the process of rediscovery, I realised colonisation would not have been possible without the acceptance by the settlers of the myths inherent in the ideology of colonisation, such as the acceptance of the righteousness of racial superiority and dispossession.

Colonisation has changed the lives of Indigenous peoples and many of us are linked socially, genetically or emotionally to peoples in the settler community; our past, present and future are linked. Non-Indigenous practitioners also need knowledge of Indigenous history and the role social workers have played in colonisation (Harms *et al.*, 2011, p. 161) making the healing phase important for non-Indigenous peoples. Koolmatrie and Williams (2000, p. 164) stress that non-Indigenous workers need to 'Deal with the issue of what your people have done to our people, what your ancestors have done to our ancestors . . . [for] Unless you are healed, don't bother to come in and work with *us* because you'll only make *us* worse'.

Framing research on decolonisation

Decolonisation, while an integral aspect of Indigenous methodologies, can provide a research framework, particularly for our allies. Kovach notes that Indigenous academics should rightly take on the role of 'educating their non-Indigenous contemporaries' or risk Indigenous students, particularly those wishing to use Indigenous methodologies, continuing to be misunderstood (Kovach, 2010, p. 31). Kevin Gilbert also talked of the need for teaching, 'because you have to heal the Whitefella' . . . 'we have to grow the Whitefella up' (1996, p. 61). Sharing our knowledge, that which is appropriate to share, offers the opportunity for educating/healing non-Indigenous peoples.

Decolonisation offers an opportunity for research that is relevant to both the coloniser and colonised community. While Kovach (2010) rightly identifies that Indigenous theory/methodologies have a decolonising aim, it is our meta-theory that dictates and establishes what are acceptable protocols and values in our specific Indigenous research methodologies and theory.

Adapting the framework of the six stages of decolonisation, and an understanding of the five stages of colonisation used in my research can present opportunities for other applications. This approach provides a framework for research that can be used for applications by our non-Indigenous allies as they walk beside us in our quest to untangle the mess caused by colonisation.

Conclusion

Like the rejuvenated snake that introduced this chapter, this is a story of a research project where we, Indigenous Australians, are recovering our knowledge; translating select aspects of our oral theory into an academically usable format. Decolonisation provided a framework for this resurgence of our knowledge and resulted in the identification of a new stage in decolonisation, which is healing and the reclaiming of wellbeing.

Sharing an insight into how our theory links to practice, I demonstrated the healing opportunities available when taking a path of decolonisation. Decolonisation offers an opportunity for healing in both the colonised and coloniser community, for both are afflicted by the ideology of colonisation. Colonisation was/ is enacted by the settler society, therefore decolonisation is particularly relevant for the colonising community.

As Indigenous knowledge is rejuvenated the challenge now is for non-Indigenous people to decolonise their minds and overcome the 'systemic biases' in academia where 'racism and paternalism work against both equal participation in research and the valuing of Indigenous knowledge systems' (Dwyer and Silburn, 2009, pp. 5–13). Decolonisation is everybody's business.

> You see, that mouth of the snake . . . our people have retreated into the belly of the snake. It's our consolidation of our Aboriginality, a renewing of our identity. Only recently have we begun emerging from the mouth of the snake with renewal and consolidation of who we are. (Watson in Aboriginal and Torres Strait Islander Healing Foundation Development Team, 2009, 1.2.1)

QUESTIONS FOR REFLECTION

1. Reflect on the role that colonisation has had on the social, emotional and physical health and wellbeing of you and the people you work with.
2. Rediscovery and recovery of decolonised history is a foundation of decolonisation. What opportunities can you envisage by connecting decolonisation and history to address current health issues?
3. What opportunities can you see for using decolonisation as a framework for health and wellbeing research?

Note

1. 'Indigenous' means Indigenous Australian – people who identify themselves as Aboriginal and/or Torres Strait Islander people. In this chapter, non-Indigenous people are the 'other', highlighting the many times adjectives are used to 'other' Indigenous peoples—as strangers in their own lands.

References

Aboriginal and Torres Strait Islander Healing Foundation Development Team (2009) *Voices from the Campfires: Establishing the Aboriginal and Torres Strait Islander Healing Foundation* [online]. Available at: http://www.fahcsia.gov.au/our-responsibilities/indigenous-australians/programs-services/recognition-respect/voices-from-the-campfires-establi shing-the-aboriginal-and-torres-strait-islander-healing-foundation

Atkinson, J. (2002) *Trauma Trails: Recreating Song Lines – The Trans-generational Effects of Trauma in Indigenous Australia*, Spinifex Press, North Melbourne, Australia.

Dillon, A. (2008) 'Does the apology bring about healing?', *Aboriginal and Islander Health Worker Journal*, vol. 32, no. 4, p. 6.

Dwyer, J. & Silburn, K. (2009) *Review of the NHMRC Road Map: A Strategic Framework for Improving Aboriginal and Torres Strait Islander Health Through Research. Final Consultation Report* [online]. Available at: http://www.nhmrc.gov.au/_files_nhmrc/file/your_health/indigenous/r45_road_map_final_consultation_report.pdf

Eckermann, A., Dowd, T., Chong, E., Nixon, L., Gray, R. & Johnson, S. (2006) *Binan Goonj: Bridging Cultures in Aboriginal Health*, 2nd edn. Elsevier, Marrickville, Australia.

Feeney, M. (2009) *Reclaiming the Spirit of Well Being: Promising Healing Practices for Aboriginal and Torres Strait Islander People: Discussion Paper*, The Stolen Generation Alliance [online]. Available at: http://www.earlytraumagrief.anu.edu.au/uploads/Feeney_HealingDiscussion Paper_2009–1.pdf

Fejo, L. (1994) 'The strong women, strong babies, strong culture program', *Aboriginal and Islander Health Worker Journal*, vol. 18, no. 6, p. 16.

Gair, S. & Muller, L. (2009) 'Circular movement in teaching and learning for Indigenous social work education', in *Social Work Education in the Asian Pacific Region: Issues and Debates*, C. Noble, M. Henrickson & Han Y. (eds), Vulgar Press, Bayswater, Australia, pp. 125–148.

Gammage, B. (2011) *The Biggest Estate on Earth: How Aborigines Made Australia*, Allen & Unwin, Sydney, Australia.

Gilbert, K. (1996) 'God at the campfire and that Christ fella', in *Aboriginal Spirituality: Past Present Future*, A. Pattel-Gray (ed), HarperCollinsReligious, Blackburn, Australia, pp. 54–65.

Graham, M. (2008) 'Some thoughts about the philosophical underpinnings of Aboriginal worldviews', *Australian Humanities Review – Ecological Humanities: Classic Essay*, vol. 3, no. 2, pp. 181–194.

Harms, L., Middleton, J., Whyte, J., Anderson, I., Clarke, A., Sloan, J. Hagel, M. & Smith, M. (2011) 'Social work with Aboriginal clients: Perspectives on educational preparation and practice', *Australian Social Work*, vol. 64, no. 2, pp. 156–168.

Healy, K. (2005) *Social Work Theories in Context: Creating Frameworks for Practice*, Palgrave Macmillan, Basingstoke, UK.

Kerwin, D.W. (2006) *Aboriginal dreaming tracks or trading paths: The common ways.* Unpublished Doctoral Thesis, Griffith University, Queensland, Australia.

King, C. (2005, 31 August) 'Decolonising Research from an Australian Indigenous Research Perspective', paper presented at the *7th Indigenous Research Forum*, Cairns, Australia.

Koolmatrie, J. & Williams, R. (2000) 'Unresolved grief and the removal of indigenous Australian children', *Australian Psychologist*, vol. 35, no. 2, pp. 158–166.

Kovach, M.E. (2010) *Indigenous Methodologies: Characteristics, Conversation, and Contexts*, University of Toronto Press, Toronto, Canada.

Laenui, P. (also known as Hayden Burgess) (2000) 'Processes of decolonization', in *Reclaiming Indigenous Voice and Vision*, M. Battiste (ed), UBC Press, Vancouver, Canada, pp. 150–160. Available at: http://www.opihi.com/sovereignty/colonization.htm

Laenui, P. (also known as Hayden Burgess) (2007) 'Welcome Remarks' paper presented at *Indigenous Voices in Social Work: Not Lost in Translation*, Makaha, Oahu, HI.

Langton, M. (2003) 'Aboriginal art and film: The politics of representation', in *Blacklines: Contemporary Critical Writing by Indigenous Australians*, M. Grossman (ed), Melbourne University Press, Melbourne, Australia, pp. 109–124.

Mackean, T. (2009) 'A healed and healthy country: Understanding healing for Indigenous Australians', *The Medical Journal of Australia*, vol. 190, no. 10, pp. 522–523.

Martin, K. (2008) *Please Knock Before you Enter: Aboriginal Regulation of Outsiders and the Implications for Researchers*, Post Pressed, Teneriffe, Australia.

McEwan, A. & Tsey, K. (2009) *The Role of Spirituality in Social and Emotional Wellbeing Initiatives: The Family Wellbeing Program at Yarrabah*, CRCATH, Cooperative Research Centre for Aboriginal Health, Casuarina, Australia.

Muller, L. (2010). *Indigenous Australian* social-health theory. Unpublished Doctoral Thesis. James Cook University, Townsville, Australia.

Muller, L. (2013) Forthcoming, Allen and Unwin, Sydney, Australia.

Overton, W.F. (nd) *Metatheory & Methodology in Developmental Psychology* [online]. Available at: http://csudh.edu/dearhabermas/metatheorybk01.htm

Overton, W.F. & Ennis, M.D. (2006) 'Cognitive–developmental and behavior–analytic theories: Evolving into complementarity', *Human Development*, vol. 49, no. 3, pp. 143–172.

Paradies, Y. (2007) 'Racism', in *Social Determinants of Indigenous Health*, B. Carson, T. Dunbar, R.D. Chenhall & R. Baillie (eds), Allen & Unwin, Crows Nest, Australia, pp. 65–80.

Paradies, Y., Harris, R. & Anderson, I. (2008) 'The Impact of Racism on Indigenous Health in Australia and Aotearoa: Towards a Research Agenda', *Discussion Paper Series: No 4* (p. 38), Cooperative Research Centre for Aboriginal Health, Casuarina, Australia.

Pedersen, A. & Barlow, F.K. (2008) 'Theory to social action: A university-based strategy targeting prejudice against Aboriginal Australians', *Australian Psychologist*, vol. 43, no. 3, pp. 148–159.

Purcell, L. (2002) *Black Chicks Talking*, Hodder, Sydney, Australia.

Robb, L. (1996) 'A homeless spirit', in *Aboriginal Spirituality: Past Present Future*, A. Pattel-Gray (ed), HarperCollinsReligious, Blackburn, Australia, pp. 113–121.

Robertson, B. (2000) *Aboriginal and Torres Strait Islander Women's Task Force on Violence Report*, Queensland Department of Aboriginal and Torres Strait Islander Policy and Development, Brisbane, Australia.

Sinclair, R. (2004) 'Aboriginal social work education in Canada: Decolonizing pedagogy for the seventh generation', *First Peoples Child and Family Review: A Journal on Innovation and Best Practices in Aboriginal Child Welfare Administration, Research, Policy and Practice*, vol. 1, no. 1, pp. 49–61.

Sun, Q., Spiegelman, D., van Dam, R.M., Holmes, M.D., Malik, V.S., Willett, W.C. & Hu, F.B. (2010) 'White rice, brown rice, and risk of type 2 diabetes in US men and women', *Archives of Internal Medicine*, vol. 170, no. 11, pp. 961–969.

Tatz, C. (1999) 'Genocide in Australia', *AIATSIS Research Discussion Papers No 8*. Australian Institute of Aboriginal and Torres Strait Islander Studies, Canberra, Australia.

Ungunmerr-Baumann, M.-R. (2002) *Dadirri: Inner Deep Listening and Quiet Still Awareness* [online]. Available at: http://www.liturgyplanning.com.au/documents/main.php?g2_view=core.DownloadItem&g2_itemId=4832

10

WHAI ORA – MĀORI HEALTH

Jim Anglem

CHAPTER OBJECTIVES

1. *To make explicit links between European colonisation and the decline in Māori health;*
2. *To document colonial legislative history and its subsequent impact on Māori wellbeing;*
3. *To guide social work practitioners on areas to consider in work with Māori clients and community.*

   The aim of this chapter is to provide readers with a view that is strongly held by many Māori that, unless one has knowledge of New Zealand's shared history, it is likely there will be a diminished capability for those entrusted with the health care of Māori and other minority ethnic groups. The link between the history of Māori since colonisation and subsequent unfavourable health outcomes is undeniable. Continued stereotyping and prejudice arguably occur through ignorance, not necessarily ill-will. Thus, developing opportunities to examine and discuss some of the events of New Zealand's past will, it is hoped, provide opportunities for those engaged in health and the social services to view all clients without bias.

Introduction

In 1986 a seminal government report, Puao te Ata Tu (The Report of the Ministerial Advisory Committee on a Māori Perspective for the Department of Social Welfare) was released (Department of Social Welfare [DSW], 1986). This report was to influence major change in New Zealand social work practice and was the culmination of widespread criticism of several government departments, DSW in particular, noting a monocultural approach to policy and service delivery that was described as institutional racism. The commission, charged with the investigation into the alleged racism, travelled the length of the country and met with Māori families and communities. The themes that emerged were consistent and were described as *ngeri* (a litany of sound). This 'sound' was a euphemism for families across the country expressing their anger and disappointment at the way they believed staff at the DSW had treated them. Several important recommendations emerged, which remain as relevant today for health and social service providers as they were nearly 30 years ago when the report was developed.

A key point in the findings of Puao te Ata Tu was that those people who were entrusted with the care of children, and Māori children in particular, had little familiarity with New Zealand history. The authors of the report were strongly of the view that staff in the (then) Department of Social Welfare should have a greater knowledge of our shared history rather than knowledge of *te reo Māori* (the Māori language). The reasons for the emphasis on history are based on the belief that the New Zealand school curriculum identified Māori as a 'deficit' people, deficient in health, housing, education and employment. There was an implicit belief that this had always been the case until the white immigrants arrived from Europe. With their arrival, and after the Māori Wars, now called the Land Wars, the new migrants were able to assist Māori improve their otherwise 'uncivilised' lives. Many Māori believed the history taught in New Zealand's schools was either absent or inaccurate, and, that if all people understood 'our' history it would be of greater benefit than a somewhat pitying view that many held. Additionally, an increased interest by many non-Māori in learning the Māori language was more likely to further alienate Māori who, mostly, were not conversant with their language.

Puao te Ata Tu thus remains a fundamental beginning point for any discussion that analyses Māori welfare and health. The question that should be asked is: 'Have Māori always suffered from poor health?'

Evidence suggests that this is not the case, so it seems a sensible approach to explore this evidence with a view to understanding the factors that contribute to the obviously poor health of Māori people, when compared to other counterparts within Aotearoa in the 21st century. Within this chapter there is the intention to unravel some of the realities of Māori health and secondly, to debate some of the arguments raised about Māori privilege.

History and Māori health

This chapter will attempt to explore Māori health and examine why it is currently in a relatively poor state within Aotearoa when compared with other New Zealand residents (Harwood, 2010). This state is particularly concerning when early English visitors such as Captain James Cook observed and wrote in his journal in 1769, '[i]n all our visits to their [Māori] towns where young and old, men and women, crowded about us, we never saw a single person who appeared to have any bodily complaint, nor did we perceive the slightest eruption upon the skin or any marks that any eruption had left behind' (Cook, 1900, p. 46).

Savage, in *Some Account of New Zealand* wrote, 'The men are usually five feet eight inches to six feet [1.75 to 1.82] . . . and probably, in many instances, live to a

great age' (Savage, 1807, pp. 16–17). This old age that Savage refers to can be reinforced by Herries Beattie, a prolific writer on the South Island and Māori, who in
one of his many books, *Maori Place Names of Canterbury* 'identifies the ages of 24 of
52 Māori elders whom he interviewed as being between 62 and 96 with an average
of 75, all of whom were born in the 1880's or earlier' (1945, pp. 119–120). It is only
now, within the last decade, that Māori life expectancy has reached or exceeded the
life-span of many of the elders whom Beattie had interviewed.

It has been a commonly held belief that, because of a poor diet, Māori did not
live as long as non-Māori at the beginning of the 19th century. There is a strong
body of evidence that refutes that view, although the arrival of increasing numbers
of migrants after 1840 brought disease, land dispossession and war – which certainly
detrimentally affected the health and wellbeing of the indigenous population. It
is clear too, however, that despite the often-stated idea that Māori were naïve in
matters of trade and commerce, that in many parts of the country, Māori enjoyed
wealth and success, which in turn supported education, health and strong communities. Several observers wrote of the burgeoning trade, the impressive agricultural
outputs as well as coastal trade especially in the Wanganui and Waikato areas as
described in Paul Temm's *The Waitangi Tribunal* (Temm, 1990, pp. 20–23). During
the period leading up to 1860, Richard Taylor wrote in New Zealand and of its
inhabitants: 'This was the golden age [1858] of Māori agriculture and growth. Peace
and prosperity seemed assured' (Taylor, cited in Temm, 1990, p. 23).

The decline of Māori health and the rise of racism

A few years after the observations recorded above, a palpable increase in overt
racism became apparent and, in 1863, Governor Grey ordered the invasion of the
Waikato, 'for a rebellion that never took place' (Temm, 1990, p. 23). Although Māori
fought to defend their lands the British-trained troops prevailed against farmers and
traders and the consequence of the inevitable loss of the wars was huge confisca-
tions of land as punishment. This resulted in Māoridom being 'deprived of their
capital – the land – on which they had already built such prosperity. They were
reduced to poverty, living in shacks and eking out a living as best they could. Sickness and disease were rampant' (Temm, 1990, p. 23).

In 1877, as though there were a need to reinforce the superiority of the white
colonists, Judge James Prendergast in the now infamous case of Wi Parata v. the
Bishop of Wellington, ruled that the Treaty of Waitangi 'was worthless – a . . .
nullity . . . between a civilised nation and a group of savages' (King, 2003, p. 235).

Between this period and deep into the 20th century, Māori were subjected to
an avalanche of legislation that stripped away Māori land and Māori dignity. These
legislative Acts were developed as a growing number of Parliamentarians became
impatient with Māori who resisted attempts to give up their land and cultural assets.
Such Acts included:

- *The Māori Prisoners Act in 1880* which authorised the continued imprison-
  ment of many Taranaki Māori who had been in prisons in the South Island

for 13 months without having been tried, even although the minister, Bryce, declared that if they had been tried they would probably only have received 24 hours in custody. This act ensured that they could be kept in prison indefinitely (Scott, 1975).

- *The Native Land Purchase and Acquisition Act of 1893* enabled the governor to take any native land for settlement whether it was agreed to by the owners or not. It is difficult to find anything that was other than discriminatory and ugly about this piece of legislation (Durie, 1998).
- *The Land Titles Protection Act of 1902* reversed the findings of the Privy Council's findings of 1901 regarding the ruling in Wi Parata v. The Bishop of Wellington. When the Privy Council in London overturned the ruling of 1877 which had declared the Treaty to be a mere nullity as a consequence of Wi Parata's challenge, the view of New Zealand's government was unequivocal. It immediately instigated the Land Titles Protection Act, thus ensuring that Māori could no longer use the Privy Council to embarrass the government over its decisions (Temm, 1990).
- In *1907 The Tohunga Suppression Act* was passed, ironically on the advice of the Māori medical officer. (A *tohunga* is an elder, trained in the arts of Māori medicine, architecture and design, agriculture and fishing and was a storehouse for family and tribal histories.) This act was passed with eagerness by the government which was more interested in political advantage rather than the misplaced medical concerns of the 25-year-old Māori medical officer. This act was viewed by many Māori as an attack on *tikanga* (Māori knowledge and traditions) (Durie, 1998).
- *The Public Works Act of 1908* authorised the taking of Māori land, without compensation, for roads and railways. The same act allowed for Pakeha land owners to negotiate about whether to agree to have their land taken or not, but if it were taken, they would be compensated. In their book *Healing Our History*, Consedine and Consedine have argued that this act and others, too, can be referred to as 'White Privilege' (Consedine and Consedine, 2005, p. 209).
- *The Native Land Act of 1909* reinforced the taking of Māori land for public works and was specific that no compensation was to be paid. Some scholars argue that this particular land act was the turning point in land alienation although all of the previous land acts had ensured that there would be some satisfaction for the insatiable greed by Pakeha for land (Durie, 1998).

Tohunga Suppression Act 1907

This particular act deserves some closer examination as it outlawed the very people who, for centuries, had been the advisors on all matters spiritual and physical, on mental health and relationships, on planting and on fishing, on weather and on navigation. They were the tribes' mentors and guides. All societies have such people and they may occur in various capacities, for example, as psychologists and meteorologists and as counsellors. There was a clear intolerance of the government to allow Māori culture except when they deemed it appropriate such as at ceremonies (Durie, 1998). The effect on most Māori was devastating as almost all communities had access to, and intimate relationships with, tohunga.

The question of who owns knowledge and ideas was, in effect, determined by government when it outlawed tohunga. The explanation appearing in the act that 'every person who gathers Māoris [sic] around him by practising on their superstition or credulity, or who misleads or attempts to mislead any Māori by professing or pretending to possess supernatural powers in the treatment or cure of any disease, or in the foretelling of future events' is committing an offence was a staggering blow to those Māori who were steeped in tikanga (cultural beliefs). Arguably ministers of religion, counsellors and psychiatrists could be identified as practising many of the behaviours that were considered to be illegal by Māori. It became obvious that many indigenous practices were considered inferior and offensive while practices that were developed in European (Western) environments were considered normal and acceptable.

The practice of Whangai outlawed

The Whangai system of adoption was outlawed in 1909 as it identified another fundamental difference between the values imported from Britain and those of Māori. This difference was the status of children, who, like women, were mere chattels of men in the eyes of the law according to Westminster. Thus children were the property of a family and recognised as such by law. In Māori society however, such inequity did not occur. All children were made aware of their whakapapa, but they also belonged to a whanau (wider family), not a specific nuclear family.

In the period that led up to the passing of the legislation that rejected whangai as a practice, it became apparent that many Māori families had taken care of, and raised, non-Māori children. In the commentary supporting the discussion regarding the Act on Whangai forbidding Māori adopting Pakeha children, ironically, there was commentary about 'indifferent European parents' and 'heartless European mothers' who abandoned their children and imposed upon the 'generosity and goodness' of 'good hearted Māori women who possessed a great deal of human tenderness' (Mikaere, 1994). Nevertheless, it was deemed appropriate for Pakeha (European) mothers to adopt Māori children while denying Māori the right to continue to provide care for either their own or children of other ethnicities.

Māori population reaches its nadir

As a consequence of the legislative acts that cascaded onto Māori during the latter part of the 19th and the early 20th century it should not be surprising that this period saw the total population of Māori at its lowest totals since the arrival of James Cook in 1769.

At the signing of the Treaty of Waitangi estimates vary over the population of Māori. Most of the guesses are between 100,000 and 150,000 and the non-Māori population at this time was about 2,000. Māori at this time owned nearly 30 million hectares.

Sixty years later the population had decreased to less than 45,000 and the land that Māori owned was a mere 4 million hectares. There was a belief that Māori were a dying race and as a consequence Prime Minister Seddon cynically agreed that Māori could have some social welfare benefits because, 'as a dying race' the cost to the government would be short term (McClure, 1998, pp. 25–26). When statistics a short time later showed that the trend was reversing and that Māori numbers were steadily climbing he was less than pleased.

The selected legislative acts described above have had the effect of placing many Māori in servitude, denying Māori human rights and perhaps creating an attitude by non-Māori New Zealanders that Māori did not deserve the status of equality that existed at the time of the signing of the Treaty of Waitangi.

It is this attitude (Puao te Ata Tu refers to this as 'Institutional Racism') that has been at the centre of the debate over why Māori health in New Zealand is so relatively poor.

Disparities in health care

The disparities in health statistics have been the subject of much research over the past 20 years and Professor Mason Durie has been a leading figure in the illumination of such differences. While there have been improvements made in the general health of Māori there remains a significant gap between the health and the treatment of health between the Māori population and the non-Māori population. Durie notes that serious disparities and particular concerns exist about the relatively high rates of respiratory disease and diabetes as well as the high Māori rates of cancer of the lung, stomach and cervix and the increasing admission rates to psychiatric hospitals (Durie, 1998).

More recent health statistics indicate that the incidents of preventable deaths (deaths that may have been avoided had access to medical assistance been available) were more than two-and-a-half times higher for Māori than for non-Māori (Ministry of Health, 2012).

White women have much lower rates of lung, breast or cervical cancer but are more likely to survive these diseases (Ministry of Health, 2010). New Zealand's hospitals, too, are places where differing treatments between ethnicities are apparent. According to research, rates of ischaemic heart disease (a leading cause of death for both Māori and non-Māori in New Zealand) show that Māori have twice the mortality rate of non-Māori (Ministry of Health, 2009). It appears that, on the basis of mortality rates, access to surgical interventions depends on ethnicity, as white New Zealanders seem more frequently to be given the option of life-saving surgery (Curtis *et al.*, 2003, cited in Dew and Davis, 2005, p. 64; Ministry of Health, 2013)

It has been suggested that, within the largely white and Western model of medicine practised in New Zealand that stereotypical attitudes exist determining the type of treatment Māori receive compared with non-Māori. Such attitudes are reported to exist among administrative staff responsible for recording patient appointments. It is known that some health professionals are less than subtle in their behaviour towards some ethnic groups resulting in some patients not wishing to return (Maidment *et al.*, 2011), thus reinforcing an often repeated criticism that Māori patients will not attend follow-up consultations or treatments.

There seems little doubt that the histories of medical care in New Zealand for Māori have not created the trust of the system enjoyed by the non-Māori community and, at the heart of that lack of trust, are residual attitudes amongst professional and non-professional people in the system, tainted by a disturbing degree of prejudice.

The social work response

The International Federation of Social Workers (IFSW) in Montreal, Canada in July 2000 identified that social work practice was based on respect for equality, worth and dignity for all people (IFSW, 2000). The General Meeting that promoted this ideal further suggested that social workers, in their work, address injustices, inequities and barriers as well as personal and societal problems. Jordan (1997, p. 98) likened social workers to 'blue helmeted United Nations troops serving as peace keepers in a civil war . . . attacked by both sides'.

In New Zealand such values as espoused above have been adopted but with a clear Indigenous relationship highlighted by the Aotearoa New Zealand Association of Social Workers' statement that social work operates under a bicultural model which has due regard for the Treaty of Waitangi.

This relationship places social workers in an unambiguous position in New Zealand. There is an obligation, not only to support the disproportionate numbers of Māori who are the recipients of a lower level of health, but to support the strategies adopted by Māori for the improvement of health care. In other words to be 'blue helmeted' soldiers who are prepared to be fired on by all sides.

Mason Durie has written on many occasions that he believes that the solutions for improving Māori health lie with Māori. Thus the role of the social worker is to support kaupapa (strategies) that are designed to do just that. It should be no surprise that all recent strategies that deal with problems of Māori health have been addressed in *Puao te Ata Tu*.

Believing the evidence

As a former university teacher, I was regularly challenged by many non-Māori students who genuinely were unable to believe the experiences of Māori and Pacific Island students and who wanted to provide some other explanation for what seemed clear examples of blatant racism. Some students have been mystified by claims of discrimination and prejudice, and while acknowledging the evils of racism, see it only in abstract terms. Thus, when faced with recounted examples, these students are likely to want to find some argument that explains away the charge of racism.

This is not to suggest any real failings in such students, merely that, for many, the starkness and ugliness of racism are difficult to accept. Cultural differences are real, however, and it is the responsibility of the social worker to respond to these differences. Some basic concepts regarding Māori health should be acknowledged and, where there is uncertainty, a key point to keep at the forefront of one's mind is that there are always *kaumatua* (men and women who are elders and cultural experts) to consult.

Some cultural commentators, such as Inoue (2007), writing about cultural fluency, have suggested that working cross-culturally requires a mixture of respect, empathy, interest and a non-judgemental, tolerant attitude, plus a sense of a humour. Such identified qualities should enhance communication and increase professionalism.

Māori wellbeing (health)

For many Māori, individual wellbeing can only be achieved if there is strength and vitality within the whanau (family), the physical environment and the spiritual world that they are in. The ideals of health and wellbeing should be seen also within the context of Mason Durie's *Te Whare Tapa Wha* (the four sides of a house) which he developed in 1982, and the extension of that idea proposed by Rose Pere in 1984 which she called *Te Wheke* (the octopus) (Durie, 2001). Each model identified the various ways that elements such as *wairua* (spiritual wellbeing), *whanau* (family), *hinengaro* (thoughts and feelings) and *tinana* (physical health) are inter connected and each without the support of the other elements will create weaknesses. Such an approach, widely accepted now as part of generic health care plans, was contrary to the bio-medical model that has dominated medical practice in New Zealand.

At the heart of Māori health is *mana*. Mana is about self-worth and personal dignity. Some have argued that *mana* is often misinterpreted to mean status and, although it does mean that, it derives more from a sense of *whakaiti* (humility) than it does from merely attaining a position of importance. At a broader level it is about authority, at a personal level, however, it is the essence of being a confident and healthy, achieving person. It is difficult to maintain this level of existence if your family has been humiliated through land loss or unemployment or if your family has become dysfunctional and no longer communicative (Ministry of Justice, 2001).

As an ethically driven social worker, best practice might arguably include the many ideas that Inoue (2007) included in her thoughts on cultural fluency and, if so, they would ensure that the enhancement of *mana* was key in the approach towards a client. Conversely, if intervention should mean that *mana* was compromised, logic would suggest that the intervention was flawed.

Wairua involves the somewhat difficult notion of spirituality, in the sense of someone being described as having spiritual wellbeing. It is well documented in literature that interconnectedness with family, culture and work may create a sense of wellbeing and a relationship with higher powers. *Wairua* is sometimes associated with *mauri* (life force) which is a consideration of fields of energy that people and objects have. Accordingly, *wairua* pervades all Māori values and is best seen as a link between life and death (Ministry of Justice, 2001). *Wairua* can also be linked with ideas of fear, love and amazement; such feelings can be regarded as spiritual but for many people these are important in terms of their feelings of wellbeing. It behoves health professionals then, to have regard to wairua as it surrounds us and is not simply related to religion.

Tapu and *noa* should always be considered together as one. *Tapu* is about special or sacred states such as ceremonies involving illness, death, grief or carving or when special occasions require rituals to be carried out. The other, *noa,* is the opposite. If food is *tapu* (not to be touched or eaten) until it is blessed, then *noa* is the state of the food after a *karakia* (incantation like a prayer to acknowledge the importance of food and the special environment in which the food is to be consumed). *Noa* means freedom and safety, but only in relation to the concept of *tapu.* If *tapu* can be seen as a 'stop sign' then *noa* is the 'go sign'.

Whakamaa is often considered to be acute embarrassment, but to think of it in such fundamental terms is to miss the serious connotations that lie with it. Sometimes it can be seen as deep anxiety or depression. It is often the result of a mental deterioration following an acute loss of *mana*. Such a situation may be best left for *kaumatua* or *tohunga* to consider. It is certainly not a matter of requiring the sufferer to 'just snap out of it!'

The above examples of important Māori values are indicative of some of the complexities of cross-cultural encounters that social workers may face. It is not necessary for social workers to be familiar with all of these but it is important for social workers to understand when they have reached an impasse and when cultural expertise is needed.

Conclusion

Racism is, in the view of much New Zealand and international literature, the most insidious and debilitating phenomenon affecting the health of the Māori population. It sits at the centre of the unsatisfactory medical interventions and the consequent poor (relative to New Zealand's white population) health that Māori in New Zealand endure. A key role of social workers is to challenge the climate of discrimination that is endemic in the health arena in New Zealand to ensure that being Māori does not mean that your chances of being sick increases. It also asserts that an understanding of Māori concepts and experiences facilitates cultural identity being regarded as strength. The emphasis on racism and in particular, institutional racism, in Puao te Ata Tu, remains fundamentally important within the health sector. Perhaps equally important in improving health outcomes is the need to assist clients to realise their potential by identifying *mana*-enhancing strategies.

QUESTIONS FOR REFLECTION

1. Is racism an overstated problem within Aotearoa New Zealand?
2. Should we be focusing more on multicultural issues than bicultural ones?
3. Identify the most significant skills a social worker might need to work successfully cross-culturally.
4. How does a social worker reconcile the often-stated view that Māori are a privileged ethnic group in Aotearoa New Zealand?
5. To ensure appropriate consultation occurs, it is important that the correct questions are asked of the correct people. For example most hospitals will have *Kaumatua/Kuia* (although *Kaumatua* is a term that is inclusive of women, the term *Kuia* (or *Taua* within Kai Tahu) is used by some organisations to denote a similarly skilled woman) but other organisations may not. It is therefore, important that social workers know where to find *mana whenua* (tribal group with central authority for Māori issues) administrative offices. Do you know where to find such a group?

References

Beattie, H. (1945) *Maori Place-names of Canterbury*, Otago Daily Times, Dunedin, New Zealand.

Consedine, R. & Consedine, J. (2005) *Healing Our History*, Penguin Books, Auckland, New Zealand.

Cook, J. (1900) *The Journals of Captain James Cook on his Voyages of Discovery*, Hakluyt, London.

Department of Social Welfare (DSW) (1986) *Puao te Ata Tu, Ministerial Advisory Committee Report on a Maori Perspective for the Department of Social Welfare* [online]. Available at: http://www.msd.govt.nz/documents/about-msd-and-our-work/publications-resources/archive/1988-puaoteatatu.pdf

Dew, K. & Davis, P. (eds) (2005) *Health and Society in Aotearoa New Zealand*, Oxford University Press, Auckland, New Zealand.

Durie, M. (1998) *Te Mana Te Kawanatanga: The Politics of Maori Self Determination*, Oxford University Press, Auckland, New Zealand.

Durie, M. (2001) *Mauri Ora: The Dynamics of Maori Health*, Oxford University Press, Auckland, New Zealand.

Harwood, M. (2010) 'Rehabilitation and indigenous peoples: The Maori experience', *Disability and Rehabilitation*, vol. 32, no. 12, pp. 972–977.

Inoue, Y. (2007) 'Exploring the effect of cultural fluency on health literacy among foreigners', *Journal of Intercultural Communication* [online]. Available at: http://www.immi.se/intercultural/

International Federation of Social Workers (IFSW) (2000) *Definition of Social Work* [online]. Available at: http://ifsw.org/policies/definition-of-social-work/

Jordan, B. (1997) 'Social work and society in the politics of social work', in *Blackwell Companion to Social Work*, M. Davis (ed), Blackwell Publishers, Oxford, pp. 8–23.

King, M. (2003) *The Penguin History of New Zealand*, Penguin Books, Auckland, New Zealand.

Maidment, J., Egan, R. & Wexler, J. (2011) 'Social work with older people from culturally and linguistically diverse backgrounds: Using research to inform practice', *Aotearoa New Zealand Social Work*, vol. 23, no. 3, pp. 3–15.

McClure, M. (1998) *A Civilised Community*, Auckland University Press, Auckland, New Zealand.

Mikaere, A. (1994) 'Maori women: Caught in the contradictions of a colonised reality', *Waikato Law Review*, vol. 2, no. 125, pp. 125–150.

Ministry of Health (2009) *Mortality and Demographic Data 2005* [online]. Available at: http://www.health.govt.nz/publication/mortality-and-demographic-data-2005

Ministry of Health (2010) *Unequal Impact II: Māori and Non-Māori Cancer Statistics by Deprivation and Rural-Urban Status 2002–2006* [online]. Available at: http://www.health.govt.nz/publication/unequal-impact-ii-maori-and-non-maori-cancer-statistics-deprivation-and-rural-urban-status-2002–2006

Ministry of Health (2012) *Avoidable Mortality and Hospitalisation* [online]. Available at: http://www.health.govt.nz/nz-health-statistics/health-statistics-and-data-sets/maori-health-data-and-stats/tatau-kahukura-maori-health-chart-book/nga-punaha-hauora-tutohu-health-system-indicators/avoidable-mortality-and-hospitalisation-0–74

Ministry of Health (2013) *The Health of Maori Adults and Children* [online]. Available at: http://www.health.govt.nz/publication/health-maori-adults-and-children

Ministry of Justice (2001) *He Hinatore ki te Ao Maori: A Glimpse into the Maori World* [online]. Available at: http://www.justice.govt.nz/publications/publications-archived/2001/he-hinatore-ki-te-ao-maori-a-glimpse-into-the-maori-world

Pere, R. (1984) *Te Oranga o te Whanau: The Health of the Family*. Maori Health Planning Workshop, Hoani Waititi Marae, Auckland, New Zealand.

Savage, J. (1807) *Some Account of New Zealand*, London Union Printing Office, London.

Scott, D. (1975) *Ask That Mountain*, Reed Publishing, Auckland, New Zealand.

Temm, P. (1990) *The Waitangi Tribunal: The Conscience of the Nation*, Random Century, Auckland, New Zealand.

11

PACIFIC HEALTH

Yvonne Crichton-Hill, Tanya McCall and Genevieve Togiaso

CHAPTER OBJECTIVES

1. *To profile the Pacific population and define Pacific health;*
2. *To identify the factors that influence Pacific health and wellbeing;*
3. *To provide suggestions for health practice with Pacific people.*

Introduction

In New Zealand there is a history of concern over the health status of Pacific peoples, who have poor health compared with the rest of the New Zealand population. A range of conceptual models have been developed to contribute to our understanding of how health interventions with Pacific communities might best be delivered. There is little doubt that initiatives focused on improving the health status of the Pacific population need to continue.

While Pacific health social work is developing, people working with Pacific peoples in mainstream or in Pacific non-government organisations face a number of challenges. For those working in mainstream organisations, models of health practice may be driven by values and beliefs that are not responsive to Pacific communities. Pacific agencies also face a challenge in that the number of qualified Pacific social workers in employment is limited. However, despite lacking qualifications, ethnic minority workers may still provide services that are culturally competent. Agencies across sectors can struggle to find qualified and experienced health practitioners (Vu *et al.*, 2011).

In this chapter we explore the range of factors that influence Pacific health. To begin we discuss the profile of the Pacific population in New Zealand before moving on to explore the meaning of the term 'wellbeing'. The remainder of the chapter discusses ideas for health social work practice with Pacific populations.

The Pacific population in New Zealand

In order to support or improve the quality of care of the Pacific population we must understand the cultural and ethnic diversity of Pacific people. The settlement of Pacific peoples in New Zealand is relatively recent. The heaviest periods of migration occurred in the 1960s and 1970s. The Pacific population is approximately 7% of the total New Zealand population (Minister of Health and Minister of Pacific Island Affairs, 2010), and the population is youthful; the median age is 21.1 years (Statistics New Zealand, 2008). This is lower than the median age of the general New Zealand population which is 38 years for females and 36 years for males (Statistics New Zealand, 2012).

Approximately three out of five Pacific people in New Zealand are New Zealand born (Statistics New Zealand, 2010). For this reason Pacific people are no longer considered to be migrant (Helu *et al.*, 2009). The largest Pacific ethnic group living in New Zealand is Samoan, followed by Cook Islands Māori, Tongan, Niuean, Fijian, Tokelauan and Tuvaluan (Statistics New Zealand, 2010). The majority of Pacific peoples living in New Zealand live in Auckland (67%), followed by Wellington (13%). Approximately 7% of Pacific people living in New Zealand reside in the South Island (Statistics New Zealand, 2010).

Profiling and defining Pacific health

Much of what is written about Pacific health makes grim reading. This is not entirely surprising as, nationally, Pacific peoples have poorer health status across a wide variety of measures when compared with the total New Zealand population (Ministry of Health, 2012). Despite being able to access the same healthcare services as other New Zealanders, Pacific peoples endure persistent disparities in health outcomes and health care. Diabetes is three times more prevalent among Pacific peoples than among other New Zealanders. Cardiac heart disease mortality is similarly high, with Pacific peoples having the highest mortality and hospital discharge rate for stroke. Infant mortality rates are 40% higher for the Pacific population than the national average (Tukuitonga, 2013).

Health is described as 'a state of complete physical, mental and social well-being and not merely the absence of disease or infirmity' (World Health Organisation, 1946, p. 100). This definition necessitates an exploration of the meaning of the term 'wellbeing' which is a broad concept that can be applied to many areas including economic, social, material and psychological (King, 2007). The concept of wellbeing is difficult to define and measure and can mean different things to different people. Diener (1984) suggested that there are three components to wellbeing. The first is that wellbeing comes from individual experience; it is therefore subjective. Secondly, wellbeing refers not only to a lack of negative factors, but also the presence of positive aspects. Finally, the determination of wellbeing requires a holistic assessment of the individual and their context and incorporates a number of domains including income, education, work, housing and health (Cotterell *et al.*, 2009).

Exploring wellbeing in a Pacific community

In November 2011, Pacific Trust Canterbury (PTC) embarked on a journey to engage the Canterbury Pacific community in defining the concept of wellbeing. The engagement process was part of developing a Pacific-appropriate 'Whanau Ora'; that is, a framework for health practice with Pacific families. Whanau Ora is a New Zealand government initiative that was introduced in 2010 with the aim of building resilient and capable families 'empowered to transform their own futures by taking control of their lives' (Ministry of Health, 2011, p. 4) thereby being less reliant on state agencies.

PTC began operating in March of 1999, started delivering community services in 2000 and opened a general practice clinic in 2003. The organisation is the sole Pacific South Island Whanau Ora provider that provides health, social and educational services ranging from general practice to delivering community health service contracts including: Well Child, Mothers and Pepe (babies), Adult and Youth Mental Health; Outreach Immunisation; Alcohol and Drug Services; Social Work; Smoking Cessation; Nutrition and Physical Activity; Engaging and Transitioning into Early Childhood Education; and Earthquake Support Coordination (following the 2010 and 2011 Canterbury earthquakes in New Zealand).

To explore Pacific community definitions of wellbeing, PTC held nine fono (meetings) with different Pacific communities, attended by over 500 people. The fono were carefully structured to ensure that facilitators were not dictating to, or putting words in the mouths of, the community about their perspectives of wellbeing. The objectives of the meetings were to find out what community groups already knew about PTC particularly with regard to service delivery; to identify any areas for service improvement; and to connect the communities with the concept that Pacific people can be happy, healthy and prosperous through thriving, not just surviving. The questions asked of the communities were:

What is important for you in your life to achieve wellbeing?
What gets in the way of achieving these things?

Participants were asked to categorise and rank their responses, and encouraged to explore the barriers to achieving what they perceived as wellbeing and to discuss how PTC could support them to reduce those barriers. Throughout the discussion process each ethnic-specific group was divided into smaller groups specific to men, women, and young people and discussion occurred in each group's ethnic-specific language.

The top five barriers to wellbeing were identified as: money; social and family; education; intergenerational factors; and work. The top five factors influencing wellbeing were identified as family, health (both mental and physical), education, finance and spirituality (church). These responses resonate with Pacific literature that describes wellbeing as holistic, including spiritual aspects alongside physical, psychological, mental and emotional dimensions (Ministry of Social Development, 2012). The fono also identified resilience as a central component of wellbeing.

These factors were common across all the ethnic-specific Pacific groups; however, a number of differences were also highlighted, demonstrating that a 'one size fits all' approach cannot be applied. The differences between the groups support the need for an individual assessment and care approach, where all approaches are tailored to the individual and their fānau/family rather than them needing to fit with whatever approach health practitioners are using. In their examination of Samoan, Cook Island, Tongan and Niuean wellbeing using census data, Cotterell *et al.*, (2009) suggested that in 'relation to income, employment and housing . . . differences in levels of wellbeing exist among the four Pacific ethnicities examined' (p. 110). Pacific peoples cannot be seen as a homogenous group when considering public policy measures.

However, considering individualised, ethnic-specific approaches are only one part of what is required to enhance Pacific health and wellbeing. An understanding of the interaction between social factors and Pacific health is also necessary.

The social determinants of health

Population health is significantly influenced by broad social factors. These social determinants of health include income, education and employment (Adler and Stewart, 2010; National Advisory Committee on Health and Disability, 1998). According to Solar and Irwin (2010), there are three key elements of a conceptual framework for the social determinants of health: socio-economic and political; structural; and intermediary.

Firstly, the *socio-economic and political* context includes consideration of the influence on health of aspects such as a government course of action; economic policy; social policy in relation to housing, employment, and land; and public policy in relation to health and education.

Secondly, *structural* determinants refer to a society's institutions and the implementation of policies. Structural aspects include factors such as class, power, prestige and community status, and experiences of discrimination. These aspects, when combined with a person's socio-economic position (education level, occupation and level of income) influence health status. Low household income is often associated with poor nutrition; less consideration for preventive health measures; increased uptake of smoking; reduced right of entry to quality education; unemployment; fewer options for coping with disabilities; and increased likelihood of being convicted of a criminal offence (Durie *et al.*, 2010).

Pacific peoples are, according to the Minister of Health and the Minister of Pacific Island Affairs (2010), more likely to live in areas of higher economic deprivation than other ethnic groups. According to Statistics New Zealand and the Ministry of Pacific Island Affairs (2010) a significant number of Pacific children and young people live in overcrowded homes. Pacific people are also less likely to leave high school with a qualification; however, this has improved over recent years with increasing numbers of Pacific people entering university (Minister of Health and Minister of Pacific Island Affairs, 2010). In the employment sphere, Pacific people, along with Māori, have higher rates of unemployment than other ethnic groups.

These first two elements of the framework combine to generate health inequalities where health, wellbeing and disease are distributed unequally across different social groups (Solar and Irwin, 2010). The literature indicates that Pacific peoples occupy low socio-economic positions and are therefore more likely to experience poor health outcomes.

The final element in the conceptual framework of social determinants is *intermediary determinants*. Structural determinants operate through a range of intermediary factors stemming from unequal, stratified societies, and include levels of difference in exposure to health-compromising conditions; vulnerability to certain health conditions; disparity in access to resources; and differences in health outcomes. The intermediary factors include material circumstances, biological and behavioural aspects, psychosocial influences and the impact of the health system.

As the Commission on the Social Determinants of Health states: 'In essence, health inequalities are health differences which are: socially produced; systematic in their distribution across the population; and unfair' (2007, p. 7). An example of socially produced, systematic differences that create health inequity can be found in the distribution of resources in poorer areas. These areas areas have fewer supermarkets and more fast food outlets per kilometre than wealthier areas. Pearce *et al.*, (2007) conclude that 'there is a strong association between neighborhood deprivation and geographic access to fast food outlets in New Zealand' (p. 375). Similar findings were reported by the Obesity Action Coalition (2009) who examined food security for Pacific people in New Zealand. Overseas studies indicate that areas with larger populations on welfare have fewer grocery stores than middle-income areas (Algert *et al.*, 2006; Cotterill and Franklin, 1995).

In other areas in New Zealand there are similar examples of inequity in resource distribution. A related correlation between wealthy and poorer areas was found in relation to the density of liquor outlets in an urban area in Auckland (Alcohol Advisory Council of New Zealand, 2012) where significant populations of Māori and Pacific peoples live. The effect of income inequality on health reflects both a lack of resources held by individuals and systematic under-investments across a wide range of community infrastructures.

In order to redress health inequities, power must be given to socially disadvantaged groups; therefore, in order to reduce inequities in Pacific health, Pacific people must be provided with the resources to seek their own solutions.

Perspectives and practice

Strong cultural links can influence beliefs about health and illness, and access and use of health services in New Zealand (Minister of Health and Minister of Pacific Island Affairs, 2010). Culture and the interrelationship between the individual, family and the community as an influence on health status cannot be ignored.

Individual

Many Pacific peoples draw their individual sense of health and wellbeing from the quality of their relationships within their collective contexts: immediate and extended family, and community.

> It is difficult, because there is no such thing as a Samoan person who is independent [of others], [tu'otasi] . . . we can try and explain the Palagi concept of self but this is futile. We will eventually return to the connections between people [va fealoaloa'i]. You cannot take a Samoan out of the collective context. I cannot say that I am a person, just me; [because] then I will be nothing without my other connections. (Tamasese *et al.*, 2005, p. 303)

Decisions on matters affecting an individual's health are generally made through consultation. Health is generally considered to be a family concern as opposed to an individual matter (Tukuitonga, 1990 cited in Ministry of Health, 2008). Health is not merely a state of individual wellbeing; the health of an individual and the health of the family are inextricably linked. The Pacific concept of self and wellbeing is therefore located in the centre of the collective, rather than the individual.

Family

Family plays a significant role in the health and wellbeing of Pacific peoples. Family refers to not only the nuclear family, but also to the extended family. In this context, family may therefore include family members related through adoption (legal or customary) and marriage (Kingi, 2008). For many Pacific peoples, an individual's role is defined by the family, so personal contribution to the family in turn defines the individual (Mauri Ora Associates, 2010). Family is the centre of the community and way of life (Minister of Health and Minister of Pacific Island Affairs, 2010). It is from family that a Pacific person derives a sense of identity and the understanding of obligations to look after one another. This emphasises how family is an integral part of 'culture' and 'caring', given that wellness and illness is perceived as a collective experience within the family (Robinson *et al.*, 2006) and aligns with the Māori concept of whanau ora, thereby recognising that health and wellbeing are influenced by the collective as well as the individual (Ministry of Health, 2002).

Community

Traditional Pacific cultural values evolved in village/island environments where co-operation and communalism were necessary for survival. For Pacific peoples, the importance of community, that is, the connectedness between the individual, family and community, and the importance of community connection and its impact on Pacific health, cannot be overstated. Factors that embody family and community strength include social connectedness, positive values and behaviours, positive role modelling and security of cultural identity (Tait, 2009).

For example, many Pacific families are strong participants in church and community activities, which create and reinforce strong social connections and therefore resilience (Tait, 2009). There have been a number of health initiatives which have successfully built on the strengths of Pacific communities, such as the MeNZB™[1] campaign for Pacific children, and Pacific church initiatives to increase physical activity and healthy eating (Minister of Health and Minister of Pacific Island Affairs, 2010).

Practice

The social work profession promotes social change, problem solving in human relationships and the empowerment and liberation of people to enhance wellbeing. Utilising theories of human behaviour and social systems, social work intervenes at the point where people interact with their environments. Principles of human rights and social justice are fundamental to social work (International Federation of Social Workers, p. 1).

In order to action the principles indicated in the above definition, social workers must understand the complex connections that occur between people and their environments, and the connections between private troubles and public issues (Blok, 2012). This process necessitates an understanding of the social, economic, political and historical context that shape lives.

Ethnic-specific approaches to health are gaining popularity within New Zealand. The development of these approaches acknowledges that social work health interventions based predominantly on Western practice may not be useful with Pacific peoples. Furthermore, as Southwick (2001) argues in relation to the nursing profession in New Zealand, predominant values and beliefs can be ingrained in a profession's ideas about how to do the work. These taken-for-granted ideas are oppressive as they are 'deemed to be the necessary and sufficient standard for what counts as knowledge for all cultures in the New Zealand context' (Southwick, 2001, p. 121).

It is through developing an understanding of unique individual, family and community cultures, that social workers can avoid homogenous, one-size-fits-all approaches in practice. Ethnic-specific Pacific approaches to the connectedness of people and their environments explicitly recognise the relationship between 'people and their lived and ancestral homes, their divinities and god(s), their natural and cosmological environments, and their ancestors' (Ministry of Social Development, 2012, p. 9).

Nga Vaka o Kaiga Tapu (Ministry of Social Development, 2012) is a Pacific framework aimed at addressing family violence in Pacific families and communities. This overarching framework is supported by seven approaches representing the seven Pacific nations of the Cook Islands, Fiji, Niue, Samoa, Tokelau, Tonga and Tuvalu. The content of each focuses on Pacific values and beliefs which can be applied to social work practice with Pacific populations more broadly in health settings.

The heart of the overarching conceptual framework is the idea that all Pacific people seek to achieve 'wellbeing, peace and harmony' (Ministry of Social Development, 2012, p. 2). To this end the conceptual framework is strengths-based in its approach, and relational; that is, the framework recognises that 'all people and things are interconnected and interdependent' (p. 2).

In Nga Vaka o Kainga Tapu (Ministry of Social Development, 2012), a number of beliefs are shared by all the ethnic-specific approaches including family as the site of cultural preservation or the site where culture can be misrepresented; language as the entry point to understanding worldviews which can be distorted through translation into English. Thus, social work practitioners should be able to converse in the particular Pacific language of the individual, family or community they are working with.

Pacific models of health – Fonofale

Although there are a number of diverse Pacific models of health, the common thread is the inclusion of key concepts that are integral to Pacific cultures including the relation/connectedness between the individual, family and community (Agnew *et al.*, 2004; Ministry of Social Development, 2012).

> If I become mentally unwell, everything else is not well. If I become physically unwell, everything else is not well. I cannot say, 'I will leave my spirituality while I go and get on with my physical function', or 'I will put aside my mental function while I undertake my spiritual duty'. The whole person is all parts. The person cannot be divided by anyone. (Tamasese *et al.*, p. 303)

One example of a connected approach to health is the 'Fonofale' model developed by Fuimaono Karl Pulotu-Endemann to explain the key features Pacific peoples consider important for maintaining good health, and which are distinct from approaches to health within mainstream New Zealand culture (Mental Health Commission, 2001). The Fonofale model incorporates the most important Pacific values including family, culture and spirituality as well as physical and mental health, and other factors that impact on health. The model also views Pacific health as being impacted upon by the environment, time (current and historical) and political and socio-economic contexts. The model uses the metaphor of a traditional Samoan house or fale (house). The key parts to the fale include family as the foundation, culture as the roof, the four pou (poles) being physical, spiritual, mental and other which may include, but is not limited to, gender, sexuality/sexual orientation, age and socio-economic status. The fale is encompassed and impacted on by environment, time and context.

The Fonofale model is dynamic in that all facets have an interactive relationship with each other in the same way the individual, family and community are synergistic.

Pacific peoples share a set of values which are based on family, community and culture. The beliefs held by Pacific peoples about individual health, family and community influence health choices and behaviours. If health policies and strategies are to be responsive to the health needs of Pacific peoples, they must take into account the significant role that family, community and culture play in contributing to the health outcomes of Pacific peoples.

Conclusion

The enhancement of the health of our Pacific population must begin with recognition of the factors that contribute to the current state of Pacific health. These factors, which include the influence of socio-political contexts, structural and intermediary determinants, must be considered alongside Pacific perspectives of health and wellbeing, and Pacific values and beliefs. Furthermore, a range of strategies for Pacific health social work is needed to ensure that the rich diversity of Pacific populations is not homogenised by one-size-fits-all approaches.

Social workers have the opportunity to challenge the current health inequities that exist for our Pacific population not only through their work with individuals and families, but through advocating and networking for integrated culturally responsive health services across the health sector. Social workers can also contribute to social change by arguing, strategically on behalf of their Pacific communities, for the sensitive and equitable distribution of resources.

QUESTIONS FOR REFLECTION

1. Why is it important for health social workers to understand the health challenges facing Pacific populations?
2. How might a non-Pacific social worker engage with Pacific individuals, families and communities?
3. What knowledge and skill areas for development do you have in relation to working with the Pacific population?

Note

1. MeNZB is a vaccine against a specific strain of Group Meningococcus used to control an epidemic of meningococcal disease in New Zealand.

References

Adler, N. & Stewart, J. (2010) 'Health disparities across the lifespan: Meaning, methods and mechanisms', *Annals of the New York Academy of Sciences*, vol. 1186, pp. 5–23.

Agnew, F., Pulotu-Endemann, F.K., Robinson, G., Suaalii-Sauni, T., Warren, H., Wheeler, A., . . . & Schmidt-Sopoaga, H. (2004) *Pacific Models of Mental Health Service Delivery in New*

Zealand ('PMMHSD') Project [online]. Clinical Research and Resource Centre, Waitemata District Health Board Auckland. Health Research Council of New Zealand, Auckland, New Zealand. Available at: http://www.sfauckland.org.nz/site/supportingfamilies/files/Information/Pacific_Models_Report_Final_Sept_2004.pdf

Alcohol Advisory Council of New Zealand (2012) *The Impacts of Liquor Outlets in Manukau City. Report No. 3. The Spatial and Other Characteristics of Liquor Outlets in Manukau City*, Alcohol Advisory Council of New Zealand, Wellington, New Zealand.

Algert, S.J., Agrawal, A. & Lewis, D.S. (2006) 'Disparities in access to fresh produce in low income neighborhoods in Los Angeles', *American Journal of Preventative Medicine*, vol. 30, no. 5, pp. 365–370.

Blok, W. (2012) *Core Social Work: International Theory, Values and Practice*, Jessica Kingsley Publishers, London.

Commission on Social Determinants of Health (2007) *A Conceptual Framework for Action on the Social Determinants of Health*, World Health Organisation, Geneva.

Cotterell, G., von Randow, M. & McTaggart, S. (2009) 'Using census data to examine changes in wellbeing for Samoan, Cook Island, Tongan and Niuean households', *Social Policy Journal of New Zealand*, vol. 35, pp. 93–111.

Cotterill, R.W. & Franklin, A.W. (1995) *The Urban Grocery Store Gap*, University of Connecticut Food Marketing Policy Centre, Storrs CT.

Diener, E. (1984) 'Subjective well-being', *Psychological Bulletin*, vol. 95, no. 3, pp. 542–575.

Durie, M., Cooper, R., Grennel, D., Snively, S., & Tuaine, N. (2010) *Whanau Ora: Report of the Taskforce on Whanau-Centred Initiatives*, Ministry for the Community and Voluntary Sector, Wellington, New Zealand.

Helu, S.L., Robinson, E., Grant, S., Herd, R., & Denny, S. (2009) *Youth '07. The Health and Wellbeing of Secondary School Students in New Zealand: Results for Pacific Young People*, University of Auckland, Auckland, New Zealand.

International Federation of Social Workers (n.d.) *Definition of Social Work* [online]. Available at: http://ifsw.org/policies/definition-of-social-work/

King, P. (2007) *The Concept of Wellbeing and its Application in a Study of Ageing in Aotearoa New Zealand*, Family Centre Social Policy Research Unit Wellington, University of Waikato, Hamilton, New Zealand.

Kingi, P. (2008) 'Viewpoint: Cultural determinants of health', in *The Health of Pacific Children and Young People in New Zealand*, E. Craig., S. Taufa, C. Jackson & D. Yeo Han (eds), Ministry of Health, New Zealand Child and Youth Epidemiology Service, Auckland, New Zealand, pp. 29–33.

Mauri Ora Associates & SAEJ Consultancy (2010) *Best Health Outcomes for Pacific Peoples: Practice Implications*, Medical Council of New Zealand, Wellington, New Zealand.

Mental Health Commission (2001) *Pacific Mental Health Services and Workforce: Moving on the Blueprint*, Mental Health Commission, Wellington, New Zealand.

Ministry of Health (2002) *He Korowai Oranga: Maori Health Strategy*, Ministry of Health, Wellington, New Zealand.

Ministry of Health (2008) *Improving Quality of Care for Pacific Peoples*, Ministry of Health, Wellington, New Zealand.

Ministry of Health (2011) *Whanau Ora: Transforming our Futures*, Ministry of Health, Wellington, New Zealand.

Ministry of Health (2012) *Tupu Ola Moui Pacific Health Chart Book 2012*, Ministry of Health, Wellington, New Zealand.

Minister of Health & Minister of Pacific Island Affairs (2010) '*Ala Mo'ui: Pathways to Pacific Health and Wellbeing 2010–2014*, Ministry of Health, Wellington, New Zealand.

Ministry of Social Development (2012) *Nga vaka o kaiga tapu: A Pacific Conceptual Framework to Address Family Violence in New Zealand*, Ministry of Social Development, Wellington, New Zealand.

National Advisory Committee on Health and Disability (1998) *The Social, Cultural and Economic Determinants of Health*, National Health Committee, Wellington, New Zealand.

Obesity Action Coalition (2009) *Food Security for Pacific Peoples in New Zealand*, Obesity Action Coalition, Wellington, New Zealand.

Pearce, J., Blakely, T., Witten, K. & Bartie, P. (2007) 'Neighborhood deprivation and access to fast food retailing. A national study', *American Journal of Preventative Medicine*, vol. 32, no. 5, pp. 375–382.

Robinson, G., Warren, H., Samu, K., Wheeler, A., Matangi-Karsten, H. & Agnew, F. (2006) 'Pacific healthcare workers and their treatment interventions for Pacific clients with alcohol and drug issues in New Zealand', *New Zealand Medical Journal*, vol. 119, no. 1228, pp. 52–62. Available at: http://www.nzma.org.nz/journal/119–1228/

Solar, O., & Irwin, A. A. (2010). *A Conceptual Framework for Action on the Social Determinants of Health*. Social Determinants of Health Discussion Paper 2 (Policy and Practice). Geneva: World Health Organisation.

Southwick, M.R. (2001) *Pacific women's stories of becoming a nurse in New Zealand: A radical hermeneutic reconstruction of marginality*. Unpublished Doctoral Thesis, Victoria University of Wellington, New Zealand.

Statistics New Zealand (2008). *Quick Stats about Pacific Peoples: Population Structure* [online]. Available at: http://www.stats.govt.nz/Census/2006CensusHomePage/QuickStats/quickstats-about-a-subject/pacific-peoples/population-structure.aspx

Statistics New Zealand (2010) *Subnational Ethnic Population Projections* [online]. Available at: http://www.stats.govt.nz/browse_for_stats/population/estimates_and_projections/subnational-ethnic-population-projections/pacific.aspx

Statistics New Zealand (2012) *National Population Estimates: March 2012 Quarter*, Statistics New Zealand, Wellington, New Zealand.

Statistics New Zealand & Ministry of Pacific Island Affairs (2010) *Demographics of New Zealand's Pacific Population*, Statistics New Zealand, Wellington, New Zealand.

Tait, R. (2009) *An Outcomes Framework for Pacific Peoples in New Zealand: Report for the Ministry of Pacific Island Affairs*. Available at: http://www.mpia.govt.nz/assets/documents/news-archive/2009/Framework-report-final.pdf

Tamasese, K., Peteru, C., Waldegrave, C. & Bush, A. (2005) 'Ole Taeao Afua, the new morning: A qualitative investigation into Samoan perspectives on mental health and culturally appropriate services', *Australian and New Zealand Journal of Psychiatry*, vol. 39, no. 4, 300–309.

Tukuitonga, C. (2013) 'Pacific people in New Zealand', in *Cole's Medical Practice in New Zealand* (12th edn), I. St George (ed), Medical Council of New Zealand, Wellington, New Zealand, pp. 66–82.

Vu, C.M., Schwartz, S.L. & Austin, M.J. (2011) 'Asian community mental health services at 35: A pioneering multi-ethnic service organization (1973–2008)', *Journal of Evidence-Based Social Work*, vol. 8, nos. 1–2, pp. 124–142.

World Health Organization (1946) *Preamble to the Constitution as adopted by the International Health Conference*, New York, 19–22 June, 1946; signed on 22 July 1946 by the representatives of 61 States (Official Records of the World Health Organization, no. 2, p. 100) and entered into force on 7 April 1948. Available at: http://www.who.int/about/definition/en/print.html

12

GAY, LESBIAN, BISEXUAL, TRANSGENDER, TRANSSEXUAL PEOPLE AND DISCOURSES OF HEALTH AND WELLBEING

Joy Phillips

> *All persons are equal before the law and are entitled without any discrimination to the equal protection of the law. In this respect, the law shall prohibit any discrimination and guarantee to all persons equal and effective protection against discrimination on any ground.*
>
> Article 26, International Covenant on Civil and Political Rights
> (Office of the High Commissioner for Human Rights, 1976)

The introductory quote is significant in our quest for a more just and inclusive society that recognises, embraces and celebrates difference and diversity including sexuality and gender. Just as our sexuality and gender identity shapes our everyday life, these elements influence our lived experiences in sickness, health and wellbeing. The focus of this chapter is on gay, lesbian, bisexual and transgender and transsexual people represented in the acronym GLBT health and wellbeing discourses. The problematic nature of such an acronym will be interrogated. The significant health and wellbeing disparities and issues impacting on GLBT people including access and equity in health care will be explored and linked to social work theory and praxis. This analysis will occur through an examination of Australian and international health and gerontology research literature including government reports.

CHAPTER OBJECTIVES

1. Deconstruct the acronym 'GLBT/Q¹ in terms of representation, meanings, and ideology in both social work practice and GLBT health and wellbeing;
2. Critically interrogate the research literature on GLBT/Q health and wellbeing;
3. Identify disparities and inequities between GLBT and wider population;
4. Provoke critical thinking and dialogue on and with GLBT people.

Introduction

Breaking the silence, telling our tales, is not enough.

We can value the process and the courage it may require without believing that it is an end in itself. (Rich, 1986, p. 144)

Indeed, breaking the silences is a process, as suggested by Rich. It is not an end in itself but rather a continuum – a continuum in breaking the silence and in/ visibility, to provoke critical thinking and debate on and with lesbians, gay women and men, bisexual women and men and transgender/transsexual people in our practice as social workers in the various settings to bring about change and transformation. I acknowledge my subjectivity and positioning in writing this chapter as a white Anglo-Saxon, ageing lesbian feminist. I am currently undertaking my PhD research investigating residential aged care service provision for ageing same-sexattracted women and lesbians in the state of Victoria, Australia. My research project is exploring both the perspectives of ageing same-sex-attracted women and lesbians accessing and residing in such facilities, and the insights and experiences of managers working with government aged care policies in the residential aged care context.

I have not always been out and proud. Instead, I have oscillated between being inside and outside of the closet at different stages of my life. My way of knowing and becoming as a lesbian locates itself within poststructuralism. I have never considered myself, or identified as a heterosexual woman although I married and have five children from that marriage. Are you asking yourself: 'what is the meaning of becoming a lesbian?' Within this context, what makes me a lesbian is a selfidentification process and as such, is a political choice. It is a political choice in the sense of disrupting and subverting the hegemony of the heteropatriarchy and heteronormativity discourses in our society. My subjectivity as a lesbian is fluid, multiple, contested, contradictory and always becoming. I do not identify as 'queer' because it is amorphous and in my view, lacks political power due to the failure to name myself a lesbian. What assumptions underpin the notion that the concept 'queer' lacks political power to me as a lesbian?

The GLBT acronym

Sexuality [and gender] may be thought about, experienced, and acted on differently according to age, class, ethnicity, physical ability, sexual orientation and preference, religion, and region. (Vance, 1992, p. 17)

How we know and interpret the world, and our place in it, is through language, where symbolic meanings are shared and defined, and communication is established and maintained. It is important to recognise that meaning in language is neither fixed, neutral or value-free and as poststructuralists argue, meaning is situated, multiple, fluid and open to interpretation (Crotty, 1998). Further, Foucault (1980) states that language and discourse are always intimately linked with power, knowledge, authority and legitimisation. What does this mean in terms of the GLBT acronym that is currently in vogue? Is the acronym's meaning fixed, neutral and value-free? Are concepts such as 'lesbian', 'gay man', 'bisexuality', 'sexual identity' and 'identity formation' ethnocentric?

The GLBT acronym is dominant in Australian research literature while the acronym LGBT dominates the United Kingdom and North American research literature. The question as to why the word 'lesbian' predominates instead of 'gay' in these countries is interesting to speculate upon; nonetheless, it demonstrates how different political contexts construct power relations. What does the acronym represent? Could the acronym be a form of assimilation? Does it represent the lived experiences of all the individuals who live within each categorisation; those crossing boundaries of categorisation or those outside of the categorisation? Could there also be a difference between their public/private/personal depending on the degree of outness? What implications does this have for social work practice?

One of the challenges for social workers is to understand what the acronym represents and within what context. Does it represent sexual and/or gender identities? Culture? Community? Is each category fixed and homogenous? Where do new categories such as 'genderqueer', 'heteroflexible', 'asexual/homoromantic', 'gender bending', or 'gender blending' locate themselves in terms of the acronym. These new identity formations name the richness and great diversity that exists within the GLBT acronym. Indeed, what are the implications for social work practitioners working with GLBT people?

Social work practitioners need to engage in deconstructing categories in the GLBT acronym and the potentially dichotomous ways of thinking about identity. Practitioners need to work actively to deconstruct language as a strategy for thinking and reimaging categories and classifications to contest and recreate power, space, boundaries, across time and geography. Social work practitioners need to challenge and expose dominant discourses for any discriminatory or oppressive assumptions, ideas and beliefs that underpin them and develop counter-discourses based on notions of fairness, equality and social justice (Mullaly, 2002).

'Coming out' of the closet

> In the case of silence, each one of us draws the face of her own fear – fear of contempt, of censure, or of some judgment, or of recognition, of challenge, of annihilation. But most of all, I think, we fear that very visibility without which we also cannot truly live. (Lorde, 1984, p. 42)

In/visibility is a key factor for most marginalised, identity-based groups such as GLBT people which hampers socio-political and economic/legal[2] change and transformation. The closet is a metaphor for a space or place, and, as such, is a fundamental feature of GLBT social life because coming out is a lifelong process when heterosexuality is the norm; GLBT people must decide when, where and how to disclose their sexuality and gender identity (Phillips and Marks, 2006). The closet is a place where you can be out of sight, in silence, and invisible; it can be a site of oppression, but it can also be a site of contestation and resistance. Sedgwick (1990) argues that the closet, in addition to being the 'defining structure for gay oppression in this century' has marked many binary impasses (natural/unnatural; public/private; health/illness; same/different) that are central in epistemologies of twentieth-century Western culture, where visibility plays an important role (p. 71). Therefore, there are risks, regardless of one's positioning in terms of the closet, which have implications on the health and wellbeing of GLBT individuals.

Coming out is possibly the first major step in a GLBT individual's life to disclose aspects of their identity, and, depending on the level of outness, to oneself, family, friends, school, workplace and society that will impact on their health and wellbeing. There are many factors influencing individuals' disclosure of their sexuality and gender identity. For example, safety concerns, past experiences, fear of disapproval, stigma, lack of validation or discrimination (Dyson, 2007); it is influenced by risk and benefit – the higher the risk and/or low in benefit leads to low disclosure and vice-versa (Symonds and Gleitzman, 2006). Coming out is hampered by one's current single status or a lack of compatibility with a partner's level of disclosure comfort, and the greater the religious influence, the significantly lower the likelihood to disclose (Dane *et al.*, 2010).

Coming out at any age is not without its risks, as noted above. During our lifetime, we pass through transitional periods where we are most vulnerable. One of those critical life stages is passing from childhood to adulthood. A study in the US associated with LGB individuals coming out to their parents reports higher levels of risk behaviours and poor health conditions than those who had not come out (Rothman *et al.*, 2012). In Australia, young people aged 16–24 were more likely to hide their sexuality or gender identity at home and in public, including educational institutions, than any other group (Leonard *et al.*, 2012). Young people are at an increased risk of homelessness because of rejection by their family and friends; multiple risk-taking behaviours; depression; low self esteem; emotional pain; unhappiness; and incidence of suicidal and self-harming behaviours (Hillier *et al.*, 2005).

The other critical life stage is from adult independence to old age and fragility. In Australia, there is evidence to suggest that ageing GLBT people who may have been out for most of their lives are 'de-gaying' their homes and going back into the closet upon entering aged care service provision (Barrett, 2008). The major factors for lesbians and gay men going back into the closet include:

> fear of physical and emotional abuse if sexual orientation or gender identity is disclosed, a reduced standard of care as a consequence of prejudicial attitudes on the part of some carers; being forced back into the closet as a consequence of the perceived threat of homophobia . . . abuse, lack of physical intimacy because of taboos against displays of same-sex affection and the attitude of religious service providers as they become increasingly involved in the delivery of aged care services. (McNair and Harrison, 2002, p. 43)

In the United Kingdom, it is suggested that older lesbians and gay men are not silent by choice, they are often silenced by policy and practice which actively excludes and marginalises their needs and perspectives (Ward *et al.*, 2008). The concerns and issues of LGBT ageing people in the US are similar to those in the UK and Australia. Additionally, some states in the US have built aged care facilities catering to lesbian and gay men (Grant, 2010).

Why GLBT health and wellbeing matters

> The World Health Organisation defines health as 'a state of complete physical, mental and social well-being and not merely the absence of disease or infirmity.' (WHO, 2007, p. 2)

The WHO model of health has bought about a paradigm shift from a biomedical to a social model of health at both national and international levels. Mental health, according to WHO (2007, n.p.), is 'a state of wellbeing in which the individual realises his or her own abilities, can cope with the normal stresses of life, can work productively and fruitfully, and is able to make a contribution to his or her community'. There are many determinants of health and wellbeing that are complex and interrelated such as sexuality, gender, culture, ethnicity, socio-economic status, environment, social connectedness, location, biology and genetics (Mulé *et al.*, 2009).

All human beings have to deal with illness, disease, sickness and death. Indeed, health and wellbeing matters. GLBT people have increased vulnerability and risk of a range of health conditions, due in part to their experiences of heterosexism, homophobia, discrimination, oppression and abuse (Mulé *et al.*, 2009) (See Table 12.1). The literature comparing the general health and wellbeing of sexual and gender identity minorities with that of heterosexuals indicates there are some disparities such as higher rates of obesity in lesbians and increased anal cancer in gay and bisexual men (Rainbow Health Ontario, 2008). In Australia, the level of self-reported general health by sexuality indicates that non-heterosexual females had lower levels of general health than the general population, while bisexual females, and those with another identity reported lower levels of general health than lesbians (Leonard *et al.*, 2012). The results for non-heterosexual males were similar to non-heterosexual female levels of self-reported general health. Young people, both non-heterosexual females and males, rate their health as noticeably poorer than their counterparts in the general population (Leonard *et al.*, 2012).

A major concern for GLBT individuals accessing health care services is disclosure of their sexuality and gender identity due to heterosexism, homophobia, oppression, discrimination and abuse (McNair and Harrison, 2002). The development of a homosexual identity and coming out in the various social contexts impacts on health, especially mental health and wellbeing. The reconstruction of a self-identity can be a very painful experience and may invoke self-loathing, fear, confusion and isolation. Trans people may also find it challenging to deal with the decision or not to transition (Diversity Works, 2010). The way GLBT people cope varies according

TABLE 12.1 Factors increasing vulnerabilities and risks (Adapted from Mulé *et al.*, 2009)

Vulnerabilities and risks	
Barriers to accessing mainstream health care services	Mental health (depression, eating disorders, addictive behaviours, suicide ideation and attempts)
Lack of GLBT-appropriate health and social services	
Invisibility – in health-prevention/promotion initiatives	
Compromised treatment	Lack of connectedness/isolation
Fear of consequence upon disclosure	Lack of community
Heteronormativity	Homophobia
Lack of factual information can actually contribute to ill health	Stigma

to life experiences, psychological frameworks, how connected they are, as well as past encounters with health care services (Cox *et al.*, 2009). Some GLBT people display adaptive, positive and varied coping skills, know how to care for their health needs, are connected and live happily despite adversity. However, others experience increased reliance on destructive coping and survival skills due to their experiences of hetero-sexist discrimination and abuse; substance addiction; suicidal ideation; self-harming; depression; anxiety; disordered eating patterns; low self-esteem or fragmented inter-personal relationships (Cox *et al.* 2009). See Table 12.2 for a snapshot of some of the experiences of coming out and becoming GLBT.

TABLE 12.2 Oppression/discrimination: internalisation, individual and externalisation, societal (Adapted from Mulé *et al.*, 2009)

GLBT-marginalisation/ stigmatisation (internalisation)	*Individual Acts*	*Systemic discrimination-societal (externalisation)*
Guilt/shame – internalised homophobia	Violence	Heteronormativity assumes the heterosexual experience is the only legitimate one
Fear – pervasive personal insecurity	Hate crimes/ victimisation	Ignorance of GLBT sexuality and gender
Low self-esteem	Prejudice	In/visibility of GLBT people
Stress – closetry/being 'outed'/ self-denial	Bullying	Devaluing/negating GLBT culture and shunning relationships
Invisibility – lack of role models	Peer/parents/sibling rejection	Lack of understanding/ knowledge of health issues
Inner turmoil and psychic pain	Abuse	Barriers to access to mainstream health care
Hypervigilance/over-achieving	Humiliation	Social/legal exclusion
Social isolation/alienation/ disconnectedness	Ridicule	Erasure from research
Depression/mental health issues – anxiety, self-harming	Hostile environments	Lack of health services for GLBT people and lack of community resources

GLBT people reported in Australia that their mental health continues to be significantly poorer than the general population (Leonard *et al.*, 2012). Lesbian and gay youth are two to six times more likely to attempt suicide than heterosexual youth (ACTION, 1998). Young lesbians are more at risk of committing suicide than gay men because they often feel more isolated (ACTION, 1998). Transgender females and males both experience higher rates of almost all types of non-physical and physical abuse than all of non-heterosexuals (Leonard *et al.*, 2012). Gay men experience victimisation and aggression in public places, whereas lesbians experience aggression in their homes (ACTION, 1998). The recent *Private Lives 2* report indicates just over half of the people in their Australian research ($N = 3835$) were in a relationship, and non-heterosexual women are more likely than non-heterosexual men to be partnered (Leonard *et al.*, 2012). GLBT individuals rely on their friends and partners as their primary sources of emotional support and health information but, in times of illness, the biological family was most likely sought (Leonard *et al.*, 2012).

Practice implications for social work

It is imperative for practitioners to challenge discourses that pathologise GLBT identities and health issues. Social workers need to promote the social structures that link the personal factors which impact on GLBT identities, psychosocial development and life experience with facilitating health and wellbeing. Social workers also need to take action in addressing GLBT access and equity in the health care context by challenging systems that reinforce unequal power relations impacting on GLBT people in recognition that policy, legal and institutional change and transformation is necessary for a more just and fair society. This agenda includes advocating for people in same-sex relations to be able to exercise the same rights as heterosexual couples to authorise medical treatment, access information and visit their partner in institutional care such as a hospital or an aged care facility. It is important for practitioners to incorporate culturally safe and inclusive principles into practice when working with GLBT individuals, couples and families (see Table 12.3).

Conclusion

> [S]exuality [and gender identity] as a source of pleasure and as an expression of love is not readily recognized for a population that have been traditionally marginalized in society. (Tepper, 2000, p. 285)

Health and wellbeing matters, and GLBT people have increased vulnerability and risks associated with their health and wellbeing when the hegemony of heteropatriarchy and heteronormativity does not embrace and celebrate difference and diversity in sexuality and gender. GLBT people will continue to experience barriers, and equity and access issues in the health care context due to discrimination, oppression and marginalisation which directly affects their health, wellbeing outcomes and social inclusion. Social work practitioners have an influential role in exposing and

TABLE 12.3 Features of culturally safe and inclusive practice (Barrett, 2011; Val's Café, Gay and Lesbian Health Victoria, 2010)

• Provide a welcoming environment for GLBT individuals (display posters, symbols and material in the foyer of institutions such as hospitals, aged care facilities, doctors' waiting rooms or counsellors' room)
• Communicate using open, inclusive and gender neutral language (Do you have a partner? Are you in a relationship? What is your partner's name? Is there anyone you would like to bring with you to your next appointment?)
• Do not assume but provide prompts to elicit information (In our service we see a lot of straight and gay people . . .)
• Frame assessments within a non-heterosexual model of family formations and relationships, and expressions of sexuality and gender
• Non-judgemental approach when GLBT are open about their sexuality, gender and sexual orientation
• Understand and have knowledge on GLBT health and wellbeing issues
• Exercise legal obligations towards GLBT individuals under the law such as *Equal Opportunity Act, Victorian Charter of Human rights and Responsibilities Act*
• Model recognition and positive acceptance of the diversity of intimate and caring relationships, and family formations outside of the heterosexual two-parent model
• Refer to the professional social work Code of Ethics to ensure that practice is non-discriminatory and anti-oppressive

challenging unequal power relations, social structures and discourses that promote discriminatory or oppressive assumptions, ideas and beliefs regarding GLBT people in the health setting.

QUESTIONS FOR REFLECTION

1. What attitudes, assumptions and ideologies influence your perceptions of GLBT people?
2. What language can you use to avoid assumptions that negate the significance of identity, recognition, acceptance and affirmation in your practice?
3. Can you identify homophobic practices within social work itself?
4. How can you ensure your practice is culturally safe and inclusive to GLBT people?

Acknowledgement

Many thanks go to Sandie Price for her editing and comments in the writing, and those LGBTIQ individuals in breaking their silences and invisibility of heteropatriarchy and heteronormativity by participating in research.

Notes

1. The term 'same-sex-attracted' is problematic for those individuals whose biological sex and/or gender identity do not align with assumptions that all people are born either

strictly male or female, and our sex defined at birth is consistent with a person's gender identity (Lamond, 2010).

2. This is most evident in Australia in the current debates on same-sex couples having the same legal right to marry as opposite-sex couples. There have been some positive shifts made in the recognition of same-sex couples in the *Family Law Amendment (De Facto and Other Measures) Act and the Same-Sex Relationships (Equal Treatment in Commonwealth Laws – General Law Reform) Act 2008*. Recognition and validation by families, communities and society to same-sex couples are important because same-sex couples face stressors that opposite-sex couples do not. These include internalised homophobia, issues of disclosure, intimate same-sex violence, oppressions, stigma, prejudice and discrimination, all of which have the potential to impact on GLBT people's health and wellbeing (Leonard, 2002). Further, this is complicated and influenced by ethnicity, race, class and/or religion.

References

ACTION (1998) *ACTION for Lesbian Gay and Bisexual Youth in Calderdale*, Calderdale [online]. Available at: http://www.lesbianinformationservice.org/support.htm

Barrett, C. (2008) *My People, A Project Exploring the Experiences of Gay, Lesbian, Bisexual, Transgender and Intersex Seniors in Aged-care Services*, Matrix Guild Victoria Inc., Fairfield, Australia. Available at: http://www.matrixguildvic.org.au

Barrett, C. (2011) *We Live Here Too: A Guide to Lesbian Inclusive Practice in Aged Care*, Matrix Guild Victoria Inc., Fairfield, Australia.

Cox, N., Dawaele, A., Vanden Berghe, W. & Vinchke, J. (2009) 'Acculturation strategies and mental health in gay, lesbian and bisexual youth', *Journal of Youth and Adolescence*, vol. 39, no. 10, pp. 1199–1210.

Crotty, M. (1998) *The Foundations of Social Research, Meaning and Perspective in the Research Process*, Allen & Unwin, Crows Nest, Sydney, Australia.

Dane, S.K., Masser, B.M., MacDonald, G. & Duck, J.M. (2010) *Not So Private Lives: National Findings on the Relationships and Well-being of Same-sex Attracted Australians* [online]. Available at: http://www.notsoprivatelives.com/not-so-private-lives-prints.pdf

Diversity Works (2010) *Research Project on Lesbian, Gay, Bisexual and Trans People who Live, Work, Socialize, and/or Use Services in West London* [online]. (Original research project undertaken by Roy A.) Available at: http://www.ealingcvs.org.uk/documents/reports/diversity%20works%20final%20full%20report.pdf

Dyson, S. (2007) *Practised ways of being: Theorising lesbians, agency and health* (Unpublished Doctoral Thesis). Available at: http://www.lib.latrobe.edfu.au/thesis/public/adt-LTU20080630.162510

Foucault, M. (1980) *Power/knowledge: Selected Interviews and Other Writings, 1972–1977*, Harvester, Brighton, UK.

Grant J.M. (2010) *Outing Age, Public Policy Issues Affecting Lesbian, Gay, Bisexual and Transgender Elders* [online]. Available at: http://www.thetaskforce.org/reports_and_research/outing_age_2010

Hiller, L., Jones T. & Mitchell, A. (2005) *Writing Themselves in Again: Six Years On: The 2nd national report on the sexuality and wellbeing of same sex attracted young people in Australia*, Australian Research Centre in Sex, Health and Society (ARCSHS), La Trobe University, Melbourne Available at: http://www.glhv.org.au/files/writing_themselves_in_again.pdf

Lamond, A. (2010) 'Register details not yet finalized', *Sydney Star Observer*, 19 May.

Leonard, W. (2002) *Introductory Paper: Developing a Framework for Understanding Patterns of Health and Illness Specific to Gay, Lesbian, Bisexual, Transgender and Intersex (GLBTI) People in What's the Difference? Health Issues of Major Concern to Gay, Lesbian, Bisexual, Transgender* and Intersex (GLBTI) Victorians, Rural and Regional and Aged Care Services Division, Victoria Government Department of Human Services, Melbourne, pp. 1–11. Available at: http://www.dialog.unimelb.edu.au/lesbian/pdf/Whats%20the%20difference.pdf

Leonard, W., Pitts, M., Mitchell, A., Lyons, A., Smith, A., Patel, S., Couch, M. & Barrett, A. (2012) *Private Lives 2: The Second National Survey of the Health and Wellbeing of GLBT Australians* [online]. Available at: www.glhv.org.aureport/private-lives-2-report

Lorde, A. (1984) *The Transformation of Silence into Language and Action in Sister Outsider, Essays and Speeches*, Crossing Press, New York.

Mail, P.D. & Safford, L. (2003) 'LGBT disease prevention and health promotion: Wellness for gay, lesbian, bisexual and transgender individuals and communities', *Clinical Research and Regulatory Affairs*, vol. 20, no. 2, pp. 183–204.

McNair, R. & Harrison, J. (2002) 'Life stage issues within GLBTI communities', in Ministerial Advisory Committee on Gay and Lesbian Health (MACGLH) (2002) *What's the Difference? Health Issues of Major Concern to Gay, Lesbian, Bisexual, Transgender and Intersex (GLBTI) Victoria*, Research Paper, Rural and Regional Health and Aged Care Services, Melbourne, Australia.

Mulé, N.J., Ross, L.E., Deeprose, B., Jackson, B.E., Daley, A., Travers, A. & Moore, D. (2009) 'Promoting LGBT health and wellbeing through inclusive policy development', *International Journal for Equity in Health*, vol. 8, no. 18. Available at: http://www.equityhealthj.com/content/8/1/18

Mullaly, B. (2002) *Challenging Oppression, A Critical Social Work Approach*, Oxford University Press, Oxford.

Office of the High Commissioner for Human Rights (1976) *International Covenant on Civil and Political Rights* [online]. Available at: http://www2.ohchr.org/english/law/cc pr.htm#art26

Phillips, J. & Marks, G. (2006) 'Coming out, coming in: How do dominant discourses around aged care facilities take into account the identity and needs of ageing lesbians?' *Gay and Lesbian Issues and Psychology Review*, vol. 2, no. 2, pp. 67–77.

Rainbow Health, Ontario (2008) *LGBT Health Issues* [online]. Available at: www.rainbowhealthontario.ca/lgbtHealth/lgbtHealthIssiues.cfm

Rich, A. (1986) 'Resisting amnesia: history and personal life', in *Blood, Bread, and Poetry: Selected Prose, 1979–1985*, W.W. Norton, New York.

Rothman, E. F., Sullivan, M., Keyes, S. & Bolhmer, U. (2012) 'Parents' supportive reactions to sexual orientation disclosure associated with better health: Results from a population-based survey of LGB adults in Massachusetts', *Journal of Homosexuality*, vol. 59, no. 2, pp. 186–200.

Sedgwick, K.E. (1990) *Epistemology of the Closet*, University of California Press, Berkeley, CA.

Symonds, S. & Gleitzman, M. (2006) Risk and benefit: What meanings do these terms have for non-heterosexual individuals? Personal email communication 13 February, 2008.

Tepper, M.S. (2000) 'Sexuality and disability: The missing discourse of pleasure', *Sexuality and Disability*, vol. 18, no. 4, pp. 283–290.

Val's Café, Gay and Lesbian Health Victoria (GLHV) & ALSO Foundation (2010) *Val's Café Audit, A Tool to Measure GLBTI (Gay, Lesbian, Bisexual, Transgender & Intersex) Inclusive Practice in Aged Care Services* [online]. Available at: http://www.glhv.org.au/files/Val'sCafeNationalAgedCareAudit-blue.pdf

Vance, C.S. (1992) 'Pleasure and danger: Toward a politics of sexuality', in *Pleasure and Danger, Exploring Female Sexuality*, C.S. Vance (ed), Pandora/Harper Collins, London, pp. 1–27.

Ward, R., River, L. & Fenge, L.A. (2008) 'Neither silent nor invisible: A comparison of two participative projects involving older lesbians and gay men in the United Kingdom', *Journal of Gay & Lesbian Social Services*, vol. 20, nos. 1–2, pp. 147–165.

World Health Organization (WHO) (1946) *WHO definition of Health, Preamble to the Constitution of the World Health Organization as adopted by the International Health Conference*, New York, 19–22 June, 1946; signed on 22 July 1946 by the representatives of 61 States (Official Records of the World Health Organization, no. 2, p.100) and entered into force on 7 April 1948. Available at: http://www.who.int/about/definition/en/print.html

World Health Organization (WHO) (2007) *Mental Health: Strengthening Mental Health Promotion* [online]. Available at: www.who.int/mediacentre/factsheets/fs220/en/index.html

13

DISABILITY-INCLUSIVE SOCIAL WORK PRACTICE

Helen Meekosha and Karen Soldatic

CHAPTER OBJECTIVES

1. *To provide an overview of recent developments in the area of disability and social work practice;*
2. *To describe ongoing issues within social work education in relation to disabled people;*
3. *To provide an overview of new and emerging literature in the area of social work and disability health and wellbeing;*
4. *To provide students with an opportunity to understand the impact of this new research through the use of real world case studies.*

Human services traditionally conceive, discuss and treat disability within a diagnostic perspective that emphasises individual deficiency. (Meekosha and Dowse, 2007, p. 102)

Introduction

As the opening quote of this chapter suggests, the relationship between disabled people and social workers has had a long and difficult history. While new paradigms of social work have emerged over recent years, the realm of disability-inclusive practice within the profession remains the 'road less travelled' (Morgan and Roulstone, 2012). This is a curious feature of social work practice, particularly given that other areas of diversity and inclusion have been at the forefront of social work innovation (see Briskman *et al.*, 2009).

However, new research is emerging, much of it from disabled social workers themselves, which provides innovative and novel strategies for social workers to effectively work *with* disabled people. Social work practitioners can work as allies of disabled people, supporting disabled people's participation and inclusion (Johnson, 2009). While social workers face considerable constraints due to government policy, expectations and funding, there remains some room to move (MacDonald and Marston, 2006). Social workers engaged in inclusive disability practice do have some discretionary powers to respond to, and work with, disabled people in enabling ways (Soldatic and Meekosha, 2012b).

There is now also a greater imperative for social workers to adopt inclusive disability practices within their social worker 'tool box'. The 2006 United Nations Convention on the Rights of Persons with Disabilities (UNCRPD) explicitly identifies issues of respect, dignity, rights and the provision of real choices as central for disabled people's citizenship (Kayess and French, 2008; Oliver *et al.*, 2012). The UNCRPD was the result of over 20 years of activism by the global disability social movement for disabled people's rights to be framed under the broader rubric of human rights (Barton, 2013). The rights of disabled people are now becoming core concerns of government policy (OECD, 2009) and, within a profession that is largely funded by governments, social workers are required to engage with this ethos. We see this in Australia where new disability funding and service models are being developed, such as the National Disability Insurance Scheme (Productivity Commission, 2011). While these new policy and service initiatives have their critics (Leipoldt, 2009), they are very much supported by disabled people and their support base (Count Us In, 2013). These nascent funding and service models will, no doubt, have implications for social work practice with disabled people, and suggest that social work educators will be required to explore new ways to incorporate these initiatives into their curriculum.

In this chapter, we first provide an overview of the historical relationship between social work and disability. Then we briefly discuss social work education as it currently stands and some of the issues it faces in being inclusive of disability. This contextual discussion will help the reader to understand the case studies presented later. The context in which social workers meet with, and intervene in the lives of, disabled people can be seriously fraught and troubled. The case studies in this chapter clearly detail the constraints, limitations and possibilities of an enabling and inclusive practice with disabled people living in rural and remote locations across Australia.

Social work and disability: a historical relationship

Disabled people's experience of social work has been a mixed one at best. In the early history of social work, disabled people were characterised by their deficiencies and practical intervention amounted to control with some limited assistance, although often assistance has been traditionally given to the family and/or carers of the disabled person. Social workers were responsible for admitting disabled people to institutions, but at the same time they were in a subservient role to the medical profession. Institutionalisation aimed to suppress the manifestations of disability that could not be 'cured' by medication and seclusion.

A philosophy of de-institutionalisation, normalisation and social role valourisa-tion (Nirje, 1969) gradually started to trickle into the profession of social work. Change was not simply driven by an enlightened attitude on the part of the pro-fession, however, nor only by social protests of disabled people but by economic, social and political realities. With de-institutionalisation, social workers acted 'as a conduit between institution and community, helping to move people out' (Bigby and Atkinson, 2010, p. 11). Yet care in the community, as it became widely known, was not to become the 'normal life' envisaged by the reformers. Private troubles still remained private troubles and did not become public issues, as the necessary fun-damental structural change was not on the agenda of social workers. Group homes became smaller institutions situated in the community, but disabled people did not necessarily become part of the community and remained subject to the power and authority characteristic of contemporary society (Levinson, 2005).

Alongside the activism of the global disability movement that led to the UNCRPD, a primary area of change that has affected social work practice in disability in the last 20 years has been the establishment of disabled people's organisations (DPOs), or what is commonly known within the field as disability service-user led organisations (Barnes and Mercer, 2006). In Australia, these organ-isations have flourished, particularly during the late 1980s (Soldatic and Meeko-sha, 2012c). The organisational policies and practices of these services and support networks are directed by disabled people, although able-bodied professionals may be employed (Barnes and Mercer, 2006). Key issues for disabled people are slowly being addressed through the ongoing pressure that DPOs place on national govern-ments. As an example, the Australian Government recently announced the senate inquiry into the involuntary and coerced sterilisation of disabled people (Australian Parliament, 2013), which effectively responds to the years of activism and advocacy by Women With Disabilities Australia (WWDA) for disabled women's full con-trol over their reproductive rights (WWDA, 2013). Unfortunately, too often, social workers and other professionals have promoted involuntary sterilisation to control disabled women's menstruation and as a means to contain their reproduction, in turn denying disabled women the right of motherhood (Frohmader *et al.*, forth-coming). Further, many of the submissions to the Queensland Government Inquiry of 2012–13 into child protection practices identified social workers as one of the main groups determining that disabled mothers were 'unfit' to be mothers.

For social workers who have been supporting disabled people's inclusion and participation, significant changes in international and national policy, and models of service delivery and support, are applauded and welcomed (Roulstone, 2012). However, many social workers have not adapted their practices in line with these progressive changes. Changing long-held views and practices in the profession is no easy task, particularly in a world of increasing government funding cutbacks, rapid global and social change, uncertainty and instability. Current government policy is highly contradictory – on the one hand adopting progressive human rights frameworks to further disabled people's citizenship, while simultaneously making access to disability support systems and payments much more stringent

(Soldatic and Meekosha, 2012a). The predominance of neo-liberal economic ideas in shaping social policy will have a direct impact upon social work practice in the field.

The values and goals of social work are not incompatible with the struggles of disabled people for social justice and self-determination (Stainton *et al.*, 2010, p. 1). As Hallahan, a social work academic with lived experience of disability, argues, social workers in striving for legitimacy, 'must reflexively embrace our status as "constructive troublemakers"' (2010, p. 118). There should be a high level of congruence between social workers as 'troublemakers' striving for a more responsive system to disabled people's long historical struggles for rights, respect and equality. Given these shared values and aims, a central question is: why does disability inclusive practice remain a difficult issue for social workers? Roulstone (2011) contends that this may have to do with social work education, rather than the immediate values and ideals of the profession itself.

Social work education, training and disability

The work of Oliver suggests that social work, as a profession and system of knowledge, has had a poor record in effectively supporting the social inclusion of disabled people (Oliver *et al.*, 2012). While the profession more broadly has embraced issues of race, sex, gender and cultural diversity, it faces a 'conundrum of whether or not to embrace and fully integrate disabled people into the diverse tapestry of its membership and even its leadership' (Mackelprang, 2010, p. 89).

Social work education has tended not to embrace the teaching of disability within the curriculum (Morgan, 2012). When included, disability is too often situated as an individual problem or a medical deficit (Beresford and Boxall, 2012). Here, the disabled client is depicted as in need of individual intervention and rehabilitation. That is, the focus of what social workers can do for disabled people has largely been about trying to change the disabled person rather than seeking to understand how social support systems exclude disabled people (Soldatic and Meekosha, 2012b). Thus, broader structural issues of exclusion, discrimination and oppression, core concerns in improving disabled people's health and wellbeing, appear tangential to social work practice (Meekosha and Dowse, 2007).

While including disabled people's perspectives in the curriculum, as Roulstone (2011) has suggested, remains an important challenge around the globe, there are educators undertaking this task. Morgan (2012) has demonstrated that embedding disability sociological perspectives into the social work curriculum has extended benefits, expanding students' learning into other issues of diversity. Disability, therefore, has great power in shifting old thinking and values within the profession. Social work education needs to reflexively engage with disabled people as experts of social work practice to critically understand the impact of the profession's interaction in disabled people's lives (Beresford and Boxall, 2012).

Social work and disabled people's health and wellbeing

Over the last decade a growing body of research has emerged that indicates the role of social work in maintaining the health and wellbeing of the general community. Trevillion (2007) strongly suggests that social workers play a critical role in facilitating the highest levels of health and wellbeing for disabled people. One aspect of this role is negotiating equitable access to a range of resources for disabled people, such as funding for disability aids and equipment within the home, for workplace supports, and/or to a range of community supports (Cambridge *et al.*, 2005).

Access to available resources and supports enables disabled people to live in their homes and participate in their communities with a level of independence and freedom, ensuring that they are neither socially isolated nor completely dependent on informal carers, family members and friends (Soldatic, 2010). Galvin (2004) has found that maintaining independence from informal care and support is vitally important for disabled people's health and wellbeing. Her research in New Zealand and Australia demonstrates that disabled people are able to maintain higher levels of mental wellbeing when they have formal control over their disability supports. Primarily, this is due to lower levels of stress associated with having the financial means to meet their needs, without having to rely on family members or loved ones and consequently to feel gratitude to them.

In many countries, social workers are the frontline practitioners who assess disabled people's eligibility for different government programmes, services, funding and supports (Cambridge *et al.*, 2005). This can be both within the health and hospital systems and within the broader community, where greater numbers of disabled people are deciding to live. For example, within the hospital system, medical practitioners frequently call on social workers to ensure that the appropriate supports are in place for disabled people returning to their homes after periods of hospitalisation. This can involve working with a range of other professionals, such as occupational therapists or physiotherapists, to arrange home-care assessments for support and the necessary home aids and equipment (e.g., hoists and shower chairs) so disabled people can return to their homes without having to rely on unpaid, informal support structures (Galvin, 2004).

Most disabled people rely on social workers providing fair, equitable and reasonable assessments of their personal living situations and identifying opportunities for community participation. While locating appropriate local GP care and support is important, identifying recreational community facilities and ensuring accessible transport so that disabled people can attend these local activities are critical for maintaining disabled people's health and wellbeing (Dzidic *et al.*, 2013). Page *et al.* (2004) argue that the role of frontline disability workers should be targeted at this level of health engagement – that is, the everyday physical activity, community participation and socialisation that enhances mental wellbeing.

As disabled people increasingly remain in the community, researchers in the UK have found that social work practice has significantly changed given the diverse range of tasks now required of social workers in the disability health arena.

Cambridge *et al.* (2005) suggests that this requires new case-management skills from social workers, as they must manage a diverse set of professional relationships to ensure disabled people can access community resources that contribute to their long-term physical and mental wellbeing.

Social work and disabled people in rural communities

In this section, we draw upon two case studies to give readers an opportunity to understand the experiences of disabled people living in rural and remote Australia and the implications this has for their health and wellbeing. Importantly, working with disabled people in rural communities can be both challenging and empowering for social workers. On one hand, there may be a range of informal community supports available to support rural disabled people's inclusion (Bowles, 2012). On the other hand, there are a range of limitations in rural life which researchers such as Lindsay Gething (1997) describe as creating a 'double disadvantage' for disabled people. For social workers supporting disabled people, this can mean such things as a lack of immediately available resources, minimal and/or restricted service availability, and working with little professional support. Inter-professional work is vital to ensure that the broad-ranging needs and supports of disabled people are realised in rural areas (Evers *et al.*, 1994, p. 147).

As with many other countries, disability in Australia is more prevalent in rural areas (Australian Bureau of Statistics (ABS), 2003). In rural and remote Australia, 36% of the population is over 65 (Davis and Barlett, 2008). Two-thirds of Aboriginal people live in rural and remote Australia (ABS, 2006). According to the most up-to-date information, almost half of Aboriginal people have a chronic illness or disability (ABS, 2010), with little access to adequate or appropriate services and supports (Productivity Commission, 2011). Up to 40% of children in many Aboriginal communities are affected by chronic otitis media, which causes hearing loss and delays speech and language development (Coates *et al.*, 2002), yet these children have poor access to specialist care and support teachers in school. It cannot be assumed that contemporary values and models of intervention in social work can be applied without understanding cultural and contextual factors. Decisions concerning responsibility for care of disabled adults and children in Aboriginal communities, for example, may differ substantially from the mainstream norms of social work.

Moreover, there are invisible populations of disabled people within rural locations, such as children of temporary migrant workers on 457 visas[1] and disabled asylum seekers, who have no entitlements to services and supports at all (Soldatic *et al.*, 2012). We see this in our first case study of Ernesto.

Ernesto is a 7-year-old boy living with his parents in rural Australia on the fringes of Australia's largest mining area. His parents are temporary migrant workers (457 visas) from the Philippines working in the tourism industry. Ernesto was born with cerebral palsy and requires a wide range of supports to ensure that he meets his expected developmental milestones. Even though the family receives health insurance from their employer, unfortunately, many of the disability support items that Ernesto needs are outside the boundaries of this health insurance coverage. The family must therefore pay for each hospitalisation associated with Ernesto's cerebral palsy though they can ill afford the climbing outstanding hospital bills. To help pay for these bills, Ernesto's mother has started part-time casual work. She feels that many of Ernesto's health issues would be addressed if he was entitled to access appropriate disability supports in the same way as other disabled children in the local community.

Ernesto's case, which may appear unusual, is, in fact, not that unlikely. There are many temporary migrant workers in rural Australia who are employed for their specialist skills and knowledge for the benefit of the Australian economy. Even though Ernesto was in the public hospital system, it was the local disability advocate, rather than the local social worker, who extended the parameters of her work mandate to support the family. This case raises serious questions for rural social work practitioners, such as:

1. What can you do for 'invisible' cases that come across your path as a social worker in a rural community?
2. How can you build the case for access to the necessary supports that they need?
3. What may be the limits to this social work support?

Social work practitioners are faced with a host of additional barriers and challenges in rural and remote locations. The limited availability of adequate services and funding is compounded by place-specific risks of drought, flooding and bush fires. These natural disasters place intense strain on a community's resources and, in turn, create growing inequality within rural communities across a spectrum of social and economic indicators (Alston, 2007).

While the natural landscape of rural and remote communities raises particular issues, the socio-cultural environment raises another set of issues for disabled people. Pini and Soldatic (2012) argue that disability directly challenges dominant understandings of 'the rural' as encompassing strength, toughness and impenetrability. These discourses about rurality which are so important in informing the experience of disability in rural spaces, are largely ignored in the social work literature, as have been the experiences and views of disabled people themselves, even while the discipline has witnessed a shift to questions of difference and inclusion in such locations.

For disabled rural women, these ideas can be particularly isolating and exclusionary and they begin to remove themselves from community events and supports as they cannot contend with these local expectations (Pini and Soldatic, 2012). The balancing of self-care to maintain health and wellbeing is weighed against the expectation of community service and contribution – which many disabled people are not in a position to participate in due to environmental barriers, harsh travel conditions and limited resources. Our next case study illustrates how rural disabled women experiencing violence and abuse are particularly marginalised by discourses of rural resilience.

> Maria is a 55-year-old woman living in a rural part of Australia. She had a stroke, which affected her mobility, speech and cognitive functioning when she was 50. She has two grown children, one who lives interstate and one who lives three hours' drive away and has mental health issues. She is able to drive locally using a modified vehicle, but is concerned that she will not be able to afford another vehicle when this one fails. She is officially separated from her husband who lives in another part of her house and lives on a disability support pension. However, she is dependent on her former husband for many household tasks such as shopping and cooking. She feels she is controlled by him and abused in an emotional way. She has to constantly be grateful for her care or he becomes angry. She depends on him to drive her to see her daughter with mental health issues. She had been allocated care and assistance in the home, but her husband cancelled the services. She feels 'trapped' and 'suffers in silence'. The house has not been modified and she has difficulty managing the stairs to get to her bedroom.

Maria's situation is not unusual. One of the key concerns raised by women in our study suggests that because of ideas of rural closeness, community support and strength and resilience, rural disabled women were thought to be well supported by both their informal carers and their immediate, yet small, community. Some key issues to critically think through may include:

1. What would be the role of the social worker in this case?
2. What further information would you need to ascertain?

The challenges to the rights and needs of disabled people within a rural context are not insurmountable; however, they require persistence and creative thinking.

Summary and conclusions

In this chapter we have provided a brief historical overview of disabled people's struggles for rights and citizenship to contextualise their experiences of social work practice and how changing ideas about disabled people are, in turn, changing social work practice. We feel that this history, together with the new and emerging trends in the area, is particularly important to better inform social work practice so that it is more inclusive of disabled people.

We then explored the tenuous relationship between social work education and disabled people and supported Beresford and Boxall's (2012) contention that social work education requires greater integration of disabled people, both as service-users to enrich curriculum and as students who will go on to practise in the profession.

Finally, to illustrate the complex issues facing social work practitioners when working with disabled people, we drew upon two case studies from recent research carried out in rural and remote Australia. Rural and remote communities represent some of the greatest challenges for social workers where complex issues are compounded by over-stretched community resources and inconsistent provision of support. As an outcome of the case studies, readers will have been able to identify the types of intervention and skills required in these isolated environments. In all, the case studies suggest that social workers need to develop a diverse range of reflective practices in these landscapes. This includes examining social workers' potential role as disability rights' collaborators and allies. In particular, developing skills in community development including the mobilisation of services, resources and support networks is especially important in rural areas (Pugh, 2003).

QUESTIONS FOR REFLECTION

1. How would social workers work with disabled people to plan for natural disasters such as bush fires and flooding? Consider both planning for an emergency and the recovery period of rebuilding a community.
2. What practice skills would a social worker need for intervening in domestic violence in a rural community where there are a lack of resources and refuges for disabled women in crisis?
3. Disabled people of diverse groups in rural areas may have access to different types of government funding and resources which rural social workers need to be aware of in order to ensure these groups are not disadvantaged. How can social workers work interprofessionally to ensure they can effectively serve diverse client groups?

Acknowledgement

The research case studies within this chapter are drawn from an Australian Research Discovery Grant: *Disability in Rural Australia*.

Note

1. 457 visas are a visa category that allows for temporary employer sponsorship of skilled workers within specialised areas of industry. The 457 visa holder does not have full access to Australian health and social care systems as they are provided with employer-based insurance systems. However, as Soldatic *et al.* (2012) have argued elsewhere, the disabled children of such workers are particularly disadvantaged when based in rural locations.

References

Alston, M. (2007) 'Globalisation, rural restructuring and health service delivery in Australia: Policy failure and the role of social work?', *Health and Social Care in the Community*, vol. 15, no. 3, pp. 195–202.

Australian Bureau of Statistics (2003) *Ageing and Carers*, Cat. no. 4430.0, Australian Bureau of Statistics, Canberra, Australia.

Australian Bureau of Statistics (2006) *Population Characteristics, Aboriginal and Torres Strait Islander Australians*, Cat. no. 4713.0, Australian Bureau of Statistics, Canberra, Australia.

Australian Bureau of Statistics (2010) *The Health and Welfare of Australia's Aboriginal and Torres Strait Islander Peoples*, Cat. no. 4704.0, Australian Bureau of Statistics, Canberra, Australia.

Australian Parliament (2013) *The Involuntary or Coerced Sterilisation of People with Disabilities in Australia, Senate Committee, Australian Parliament, Canberra* [online]. Available at: http://aph.gov.au/Parliamentary_Business/Committees/Senate_Committees?url=clac_ctte/involuntary_sterilisation/index.htm

Barnes, C. & Mercer, G. (2006) *Independent Futures: Creating User-led Disability Services in a Disabling Society*, Policy Press, Bristol, UK.

Barton, S. (2013) *Weird and Wonderful: The Rise and Fight of the Disability Rights Movement*, Fertile Films, Melbourne, Australia.

Beresford, P. & Boxall, K. (2012) 'Service users, social work education and knowledge for social work practice', *Social Work Education: The International Journal*, vol. 31, no. 2, pp. 155–167.

Bigby, C. & Atkinson, D. (2010) 'Written out of history: Invisible women in intellectual disability social work', *Australian Social Work*, vol. 63, no. 1, pp. 4–17.

Bowles, W. (2012) 'Caregiving in small rural and regional towns', in *Social Work in Rural Australia*, J. Maidment & U. Bay (eds), Allen & Unwin, Sydney, Australia, pp. 106–118.

Briskman, L., Pease, B. & Allan, J. (2009) 'Introducing critical theories for social work in a neo-liberal context', in *Critical Social Work*, J. Allan, L. Briskman & B. Pease (eds), Allen & Unwin, Sydney, Australia, pp. 3–14.

Cambridge, P., Forrester-Jones, R., Carpenter, J., Tate, A., Knapp, M., Beecham, J. & Hallam, A. (2005) 'The state of care management in learning disability and mental health services 12 years into community care', *British Journal of Social Work*, vol. 35, no. 7, pp. 1039–1062.

Coates, H., Morris, P., Leach, A. & Couzos, S. (2002) 'Otitis media in Aboriginal children: Tackling a major health problem', *The Medical Journal of Australia*, vol. 177, no. 4, pp. 177–178.

Count Us In (2013) 150 shades of grey – a very different take on the NDIS Legislation, Count Us IN Campaign, media release, 1 February [online]. Available at: http://everyaustraliancounts.com.au/150_shades_of_grey_a_very_different_take_on_the_ndis_legislation/

Davis, S. & Barlett, J. (2008) 'Healthy ageing in rural Australia: Issues and challenges', *Australasian Journal of Ageing*, vol. 27, no. 92, pp. 56–60.

Dzidic, P., Soldatic, K., Bishop, B., Galardi, G., Tye, M., Fleay, P., Westbrook, P., Curr, P. & Jordan, C. (2013) *Sport and Recreation Inclusion for People with Disabilities*, Curtin University, Perth, Australia.

Evers, H., Cameron, E. & Badger, F. (1994) 'Inter-professional work with old and disabled people', in *Going Inter-professional: Working Together for Health and Welfare*, A. Leathard (ed), Routledge, London, pp. 143–157.

Frohmader, C., Meekosha, H. & Soldatic, K. (forthcoming) 'Unruly mothers or unruly practices? Disabled mothers surviving oppressive state practices in Australia', in *Mothering with Disabilities*, G. Filax & D. Taylor (eds), Demeter Press, Toronto, Canada.

Galvin, R. (2004) 'Challenging the need for gratitude: Comparisons between paid and unpaid care for disabled people', *Journal of Sociology*, vol. 40, no. 2, pp. 137–155.

Gething, L. (1997) 'Sources of double disadvantage for people with disabilities living in remote and rural areas of New South Wales, Australia', *Disability & Society*, vol. 12, no. 4, pp. 513–531.

Gilroy, J. (2009) 'The theory of the cultural interface and Indigenous people with a disability in NSW', *Balayi: Culture, Law, and Colonialism*, vol. 10, pp. 44–59.

Hallahan, L. (2010) 'Legitimising social work disability policy practice: Pain or praxis?', *Australian Social Work*, vol. 63, no. 1, pp. 117–132.

Johnson, K. (2009) 'Disabling discourses and enabling practices in disability politics', in *Critical Social Work*, J. Allan, L. Briskman & B. Pease (eds), Allen & Unwin, Sydney, Australia, pp. 188–200.

Kayess, R. & French, P. (2008) 'Out of darkness into light? Introducing the Convention on the Rights of Persons with Disabilities', *Human Rights Law Review*, vol. 8, no. 1, pp. 1–34.

Leipoldt, E. (2009) A National Disability Insurance Scheme – A barrier to service? *Online Opinion*, 12 October [online]. Available at: http://www.onlineopinion.com.au/view.asp?article=9539

Levinson, J. (2005) 'The group home workplace and the work of know-how', *Human Studies*, vol. 28, no. 1, pp. 57–85.

MacDonald, C. & Marston, G. (2006) 'Room to move? Professional discretion at the front-line of welfare-to-work', *Australian Journal of Social Issues*, vol. 41, no. 2, pp. 171–182.

Mackelprang, R.W. (2010) 'Disability controversies: Past, present, and future', *Journal of Social Work in Disability & Rehabilitation*, vol. 9, no. 2–3, pp. 87–98.

Meekosha, H. & Dowse, L. (2007) 'Integrating critical disability studies into social work education and practice: An Australian perspective', *Practice*, vol. 19, no. 3, pp. 169–183.

Morgan, H. (2012) 'The social model of disability as a threshold concept: Troublesome knowledge and liminal spaces', *Social Work Education: The International Journal*, vol. 31, no. 2, pp. 215–226.

Morgan, H. & Roulstone, A. (2012) 'Editorial', *Social Work Education: The International Journal*, vol. 31, no. 2, pp. 137–141.

Nirje, B. (1969) 'The normalization principle and its human management implications', in *Changing Patterns in Residential Services for the Mentally Retarded*, R. Kugel & W. Wolfensberger (eds), President's Committee on Mental Retardation, Washington, DC, pp. 179–196.

Oliver, M., Sapey, B. & Thomas, P. (2012) *Social Work with Disabled People*, 4th edn, Palgrave Macmillan, London.

Organisation for Economic Co-operation and Development (OECD) (2009) *Sickness, Disability and Work: Keeping on Track in the Economic Downturn*, OECD Directorate for Employment, Labour and Social Affairs, London.

Page, A., Soldatic, K., O'Connor, W. & Johnson, M. (2004) *Increasing Healthy Lifestyles Among People with Intellectual Disabilities*, Healthway, Perth, Australia.

Pini, B. & Soldatic, K. (2012) 'Women, chronic illness and rural Australia: Exploring the intersections between space, identity and the body', in *Rural Women's Health*, B. Leipert, B. Leach & W. Thurston (eds), University of Toronto Press, Toronto, Canada, pp. 385–402.

Productivity Commission (2011) *Disability Care and Support*, Inquiry report No. 54, Australian Government, Canberra, Australia.

Pugh, R. (2003) 'Considering the countryside: Is there a case for rural social work?', *British Journal of Social Work*, vol. 33, no. 1, pp. 67–85.

Roulstone, A. (2011) '*Can the UK social work curriculum begin to embrace more enabling understandings and practices with disabled people?*' Paper presented at Disability Symposium, Lancaster University, Lancaster, UK.

Roulstone, A. (2012) '"Stuck in the middle with you": Towards enabling social work with disabled people', *Social Work Education: The International Journal*, vol. 31, no. 2, pp. 142–154.

Soldatic, K. (2010) *Disability and the Australian neoliberal workfare state*. Unpublished Doctoral Thesis, University of Western Australia, Perth.

Soldatic, K. & Meekosha, H. (2012a) 'Disability and neoliberal state formations', in *Routledge Handbook of Disability Studies*, N. Watson, A. Roulstone & C. Thomas (eds), Routledge, London, pp. 195–210.

Soldatic, K. & Meekosha, H. (2012b) 'Moving the boundaries of feminist social work education with disabled people in the neoliberal era', *Social Work Education: The International Journal*, vol. 31, no. 2, pp. 246–252.

Soldatic, K. & Meekosha, H. (2012c) 'The place of disgust: Disability, gender and class in spaces of workfare', *Societies*, vol. 3, no. 2, pp. 139–156.

Soldatic, K., Meekosha, H. & Somers, K. (2012) 'Finding Ernesto: Temporary migrant labour and disabled children's health', *International Journal of Population Research*, vol. 2, no. 1, pp. 1–9. doi:10.1155/2012/696753 Available at: www.hindawi.com/journals/ijpr/2012/696753/

Stainton, T., Chenoweth, L. & Bigby, C. (2010) 'Social work and disability: An uneasy relationship', *Australian Social Work*, vol. 63, no. 1, pp. 1–3.

Trevillion, S. (2007) 'Health, disability and social work: New directions in social work research', *British Journal of Social Work*, vol. 37, no. 5, pp. 937–946.

Women With Disabilities Australia (WWDA) (2013) *Dehumanised: The Forced Sterilisation of Women and Girls with Disabilities in Australia, Submission to the Australian Senate Inquiry into the Involuntary or Coerced Sterilisation of People with Disabilities in Australia* [online]. Available at: http://www.aph.gov.au/Parliamentary_Business/Committees/Senate_Committees?url= clac_ctte/involuntary_sterilisation/info.htm

PART III
Messages from research

14

COLLABORATIVE PRACTICE AND FAMILY MEETINGS IN CHILDREN'S HEALTH

Andrew Thompson and Carole Adamson

CHAPTER OBJECTIVES

1. *To describe the context of family meetings and family decision-making in the children's health setting;*
2. *To identify issues for social work led research in this area;*
3. *To consider the ethical underpinning of collaborative practice in the area of family decision-making in children's health.*

Introduction

Family-centred care is at the heart of collaborative practice in a children's health environment and family meetings are the central component of good decision-making at the interface between the medical system and the child's family (Fineberg *et al.*, 2007; Hansen *et al.*, 1998).

Every day, within a hospital setting, families are called on to make difficult decisions for their children: decisions about treatments that might benefit their child's quality of life, decisions that might impose a burden of care, and heart-breaking decisions about life and death. This chapter draws upon practitioner-generated research in the area of family decision-making and collaborative practice within children's health and aims to enhance our understanding of the sensitivities, skills and knowledge that are crucial for effective practice in the area. The chapter serves to illustrate the rationale for practitioner-driven research that can bridge the gap between strong theory bases and best practice: it specifically addresses how social work and its collaborative practice can contribute to the resilience of families whose child is faced with serious and end-of-life health conditions.

The motivation for practitioner-led research in the area of family decision-making in child health is often impelled by a strong sense of what can be done better. The lead author and the researcher for this chapter, Andrew, had been working as a social worker in a New Zealand children's hospital since 1995 and has facilitated and attended numerous family meetings. He recalls:

> I can remember my first experience as a health social worker in a family meeting. The family of a six year old girl had just received a devastating cancer diagnosis from her doctor. The parents collapsed into a state of shock and grief. I can still recall being overwhelmed with sadness and feeling powerless to help. I could not find the words to provide any comfort and was silenced in the awful wake of the diagnosis. I was not prepared for that experience and wanted to provide more effective support for the family.

Breaking bad news to families who have a critically ill child is one of the hardest of tasks for medical staff and one of the most traumatic experiences for parents. The communication of bad news to a family can be perceived as a psychological assault upon their resilience: a father wrote after a family meeting saying, 'Hope is dashed! Hope is such an incredible commodity, keeps you going, and to lose it is an almost physical blow, one feels weak and shaky' (Thompson, 2009). The social work role emerges as a crucial component in such decision-making when engaging with, and supporting, families during this time.

It is this imperative to find answers that has motivated the research described within this chapter. The research was driven by a desire to improve family and medical team communication and collaboration during family meetings, underpinned by practice experience that family-centred decision-making enhances families' abilities to resiliently face critical decisions.

'Whanau/Family meetings in the Paediatric Intensive Care Unit (PICU): Content, process, and family satisfaction' (Thompson, 2009), was a three-year project collecting data and information about the process and content of family meetings. (*Whanau* is the Māori word for extended family and is in common usage within New Zealand as a term that both complements and extends a Western understanding of the composition of family.) Initially critical care and family meeting literature was collected and local and international consultation occurred with inter-disciplinary health professionals involved in paediatric intensive care. Following ethics approval, a study of 15 family meetings in the PICU of a New Zealand children's hospital was implemented. The overarching questions driving this study were: 'What is the content and process of a family meeting in the PICU'; 'what factors influence family satisfaction?'

During this chapter we will use the term family meetings (sometimes in the literature termed family conferences): these are different in form and purpose from the concept of family group conferences which have evolved in child protection and youth justice social work practice. When we use the term multidisciplinary team (MDT), we refer to the medical team (physicians), nursing team, other health professions (such as social work, physiotherapists and other registered health professionals) and support workers (for instance, chaplains and cultural support workers).

The family in the context of health

Prior to describing the research and the knowledge derived from the research, the importance of the family meeting in the context of health is considered. As social workers we recognise that children are nested within their families and that family is the 'nexus of almost all people's social, economic, political and cultural lives' (Crothers and McCormack, 2006, p. 6).

Nexus refers to the bonds, the interwoven connectedness of the family as they respond and adapt to the changing environment. The family is a system of interconnected relationships: Minuchin and Minuchin (1974) drew our attention to the internal and external factors that constantly impact on the family as they strive to maintain equilibrium.

One of these factors impacting on the family is health. When a child becomes unwell and requires hospitalisation, the whole family is affected. Using an ecological lens, these changes will occur at the micro level in the family, but it is at the exosystem level that the family meeting occurs and it is at this level that there is great potential for positive change that can impact upon all ecological levels. The opportunity to conduct a family meeting broadens the perspective of the medical team as they gain further insight into the psychological, spiritual, social and physical context of the patient and their family, a process at the heart of social work practice. When we address the whole family in the health environment then we see the patient more fully and are able to collaborate, respond and intervene on multiple levels. Social work theory suggests that a multi-level intervention 'encourages a more holistic examination of the multiple factors within a family system that interact to produce problems' (Crichton-Hill, 2009, p. 183), and in addressing these levels, social work can strengthen the resilience of a family system. The definition of a family meeting in children's health is now explored, prior to a discussion of the complexities of collaborative practice.

Defining the family meeting

For the purpose of this chapter, the family meeting is defined as the forum where the child's family and the multi-disciplinary team meet and discuss together the child's medical condition, make plans for future care, and consider the wellbeing of the family. This definition recognises that children are nested within their family group, that the family also requires support in facing the future, and that the child's wellbeing can best be affirmed within a resilient family. The ability to 'discuss together' during a family meeting promotes shared or collaborative decision-making and exemplifies family-centred care.

Such a family meeting is organised when important medical information is to be communicated to the family and decision-making is required. These meetings may include a new diagnosis; discharge; complications with treatment; a relapse; or the withdrawal of medical treatment with curative or palliative intent. The communication between the family and the MDT during these critical phases involves particularly complex and highly sensitive discussions that require a high level of clinical skill. These conversations often occur in the setting of one or more family meetings attended by several family members and staff, including doctors, nurses, social workers and cultural support workers. Family meetings may occur at the child's bedside, in meeting rooms or less formally in hallways and in conditions where family members are often traumatised (Azoulay et al., 2005; Dyregrov et al., 2003).

Family meetings are a demonstration of family-centred care in the child health environment and, significantly, place the family, rather than the hospital staff, at the centre of the health care delivery system (Hostler, 1991). This is a significant change from historical practice that restricted parental visits to once or twice a day. Today, children's hospitals often have accommodation for parents and the architecture of the building often reflects a commitment to family-centred care. The family are no longer considered as visitors in the hospital by the medical team but are viewed as active participants in the care of the patient, as partners with the medical team with trust and collaboration encouraged (Lautrette et al., 2006).

The 'Initiative for Paediatric Palliative Care' (Browning and Solomon, 2005) identified six domains of high quality family-centred care in the paediatric health environment including: support of the family unit; communication with the child and family about treatment goals and plans; discussions about ethics and shared decision-making; the relief of pain and other symptoms; continuity of care; and grief and bereavement support. Collaborative practice may reduce fear and anxiety in the family and patient and at its best, create an environment of mutual respect and understanding between the family and the MDT.

The contribution of this practitioner-led research project to the understanding of family-centred decision-making and collaborative decision-making is now addressed, with a brief description of the method, design and participant populations prefacing a discussion of the key findings.

Family meetings in the paediatric intensive care unit

The research project under consideration in this chapter took place in 2008 in a paediatric intensive care unit (PICU) in a university-affiliated children's hospital in New Zealand. The hospital has 176 beds of which 16 were in the PICU. The lead author was in an ideal position to undertake the study having established effective working relationships in the PICU whilst employed as a social worker at the hospital with the Consult Liaison Psychiatry Team, coordinating and providing clinical support to the Bereavement Service and the Paediatric Palliative Care Team.

The PICU Family Meeting mixed method research (Thompson, 2009) utilised purposive sampling: the distinctive characteristics of the 121 participants were that the family members involved had a child in the PICU with a life-threatening medical condition and the medical team participants were all caring for a child with a life-threatening condition. The research required organisational approval from the

District Health Board managing the hospital and sign-off was granted by the Chief Medical Officer. An application for ethical approval to proceed with the study was lodged with the New Zealand Ministry of Health and this was also granted. The 15 family meetings required the consent of 68 family members and 53 medical staff.

Each meeting was digitally recorded to enable qualitative analysis, and families were asked about their satisfaction with the meeting using a Likert scale questionnaire for quantitative purposes. Data was collected, transcribed and then analysed using a coding framework developed by Curtis et al. (2002). Questionnaire scores were compared with demographic information and meeting attributes (length of meeting, time spent talking by participants and number of participants) to identify any associations that might predict increased satisfaction from family participants. The findings were combined and compared with the recent literature and recommendations for guidelines for family meetings were proposed.

Not all families admitted to the PICU were eligible for inclusion in the study. Those families where there was risk of litigation or alleged child protection issues were excluded from the study. This exclusion was to avoid the possible use of meeting recordings for future legal proceedings. Those family members who were known to the researcher in his capacity as a social worker were also excluded from the study. This was to ensure that the researcher was not a participant in the study and could not influence the data or the process of a meeting.

The foundation for this research was the study by Curtis et al. (2002) which had a sample of 51 family meetings from four adult hospitals. The research reported here had a sample size of 15 family groups from a children's hospital, which may have limited the potential of the study to demonstrate widely applicable findings. However, the participation of 15 family groups and medical staff can be regarded as a good-sized sample for such a sensitive topic (Sandelowski, 1995).

In conducting the study, the research acknowledged the possibility of a 'Hawthorne effect' that could influence the findings, as the medical team and family may have altered their behaviour or modified their responses because they realised they were being recorded and scrutinised (Campbell et al., 1995). The Hawthorne effect postulates that the performance of individuals improves whilst they are aware of being observed for research purposes. If this was the case here, then the health professionals involved would respond with their best practice and this could only benefit the family and do no harm.

There were a number of methodological challenges related to this research, including risks of re-traumatisation and gaining consent of the medical professionals for recording such crucial meetings. Resolution of these challenges was achieved by attention to ethical and collaborative processes. There was sensitivity concerning how to ask families about their satisfaction with a family meeting without intruding on their grief or re-traumatising them by asking them to revisit a difficult memory. In order to find out how satisfied family members were with the family meeting, it was decided to question them immediately after the meeting closed. Consideration was given to contacting families after discharge from the PICU but there was a strong possibility the family might be grieving for their child and any contact might be intrusive if it was not directed towards supporting them.

In addition, families might use the questionnaire to rate their satisfaction with their stay in the PICU rather than their satisfaction with one family meeting. It was decided that, at the close of each meeting, two key members of the family would be given a brief questionnaire to rate their satisfaction. This was kept as short as possible to minimise intrusion and the family was reassured that their questionnaires would be confidential and not shown to medical staff.

Recording the meetings was an ethical challenge from both the families' and the medical professionals' perspectives. Participant families and MDT members were offered the opportunity to review the recording of their meeting. During the rigorous ethics process it was decided that participants should be able to listen to their meeting recordings and should also be offered counselling support should they be re-traumatised by the experience. One family requested their meeting recording and an experienced social worker accompanied them as they listened.

In consultation with international experts, the researcher has learnt, on an anecdotal basis, that past attempts to record and code family meetings in the PICU had been unsuccessful due to an inability to get consent from medical staff. The researcher was aware of these potential difficulties and planned a series of meetings to discuss the research proposal with a number of key staff before embarking on the study. There were no objections from the medical team members who were familiar with his social work practice and consented at an early stage to engage in the research. The only concern from the medical team was that recording meetings would increase medico–legal risk. This was addressed after consultation with the hospital lawyer who allayed their concerns. Collaboration was the key to recruiting health professionals at this stage and considerable time was spent explaining the research and exploring participants' concerns.

The next part of this chapter explores the findings from the research and the implications of the findings on the practitioner's social work practice.

Findings from the research

The mixed methods coding framework developed by Curtis *et al.* (2002) was applied to the 15 transcripts generated by the study and answered one of the major research questions by describing the content and process of whanau/family meetings in the PICU. The framework was used to identify the frequency and content of 28 codes that are specific to the PICU (Thompson, 2009). This provided evidence-based data that later informed the development of guidelines for whanau/family meetings in the PICU and training materials for medical, nursing and other health professionals. Curtis *et al.* (2002) identified six domains of a family meeting in the adult ICU and these were replicated in the PICU (Figure 14.1). These illustrate the process of a family meeting and served as a framework for the presentation of the 28 codes in this research.

Both quantitative and qualitative data were extracted from the family meetings data. A significant finding from the quantitative data concerned the length of family meetings and amount of time spent talking by a family within these meetings.

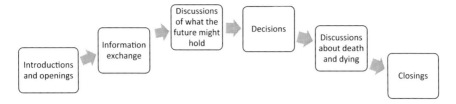

FIGURE 14.1   The process of family meetings in the PICU (Thompson, 2009)

When satisfaction scores were correlated with meeting length, the data indicated that family meetings of between 10 to 40 minutes scored highest for satisfaction (Thompson, 2009). Longer meetings (over 40 minutes) were associated with lower family satisfaction, a finding that had been noted in two previous studies where longer meetings, it was tentatively suggested, may be associated with increased patient/doctor conflict and misunderstandings (Curtis, 2004; McDonagh *et al.*, 2004). A number of studies in the adult intensive care unit indicate that the more time a family spends talking during a family meeting, the more satisfied they are (McDonagh *et al.*, 2004). There was no association in this study between increased proportion of time spent talking by family members and increased satisfaction, leading to the conclusion that satisfaction hinged more upon length of meeting than the time the family spent talking.

From the qualitative analysis of the family meetings, the researcher developed an understanding of practice approaches by health professionals that appeared to enhance communication. These are summarised in Table 14.1.

The combination of qualitative frameworks and quantitative measures used in this practitioner-led research provided an evidence base for the researcher to introduce guidelines and training resources that were then accepted for practice by the PICU multi-disciplinary team. The close synergy between the 'Ten helpful approaches to communication' as outlined in Table 14.1 and the ecological basis to a social work knowledge base suggests that social work has a major contribution to make within the practice of family meetings in children's health.

From the training sessions and presentations emerged a major point for professional discussion regarding decision-making within family meetings. Medical staff frequently raised the question of who has the responsibility for making decisions within meetings: the final section of this chapter introduces a model to illustrate decision-making and collaborative practice within family meetings that is reflective of the research findings and of a social work perspective in health.

Collaborative practice and family meetings

Collaborative practice within the context of family meetings is a contested issue, one reflected by the responses of health professionals to the findings of the research. What does it mean to work together, to collaborate in decision-making? As social workers, can we encourage families to work alongside the multi-disciplinary team

TABLE 14.1 Ten helpful approaches to communication in the Paediatric Intensive Care Unit

Approach	Commentary
Acknowledge spirituality	If the family requests, open with a prayer or karakia (Māori for prayer). The research found that this approach at the opening of a meeting was a great leveller and was honouring of the family present. For some it afforded the acknowledgement and presence of a greater power in preparation for the difficult decisions ahead.
Use open-ended questions	This enabled the family to find their voice, share their understanding and acknowledged the experience and expertise of the family. Open-ended questions may encourage collaboration and understanding.
Acknowledge emotion when it is expressed or spoken	The expression of care and empathy by health professionals appeared to be valued greatly by parents and this is supported in the literature (Meyer et al., 2006).
Express uncertainty	Expressing uncertainty may be perceived by some as a weakness in a health professional, but family members appeared to respond to measured uncertainty in health professionals as an expression of hope and humanity especially when the possible death of a child was being discussed.
State trustworthiness	Stating trustworthiness ensured that the family knew that the medical team were honest and transparent.
Use scenarios to present options to families	The use of scenarios gave the family permission to consider both life and death. It opens up the opportunity for the family to talk about possibilities.
Pause	A pause allows the family time to process, time to grieve, time to consider, time to respond and time to question.
Address guilt and regret	Addressing guilt and regret is helpful when the family blames themselves for their child's condition.
Shifting position from expert to learner (about the family)	The ability to balance knowledge and experience without overpowering the family requires the health professional to take on a naïve position as they learn about the family and their wishes.
Family meetings require a team response	The traditional role of the doctor as someone who facilitates the meeting, delivers the medical information and supports the family may be over. The communication of bad news is a complex task, with a number of roles requiring skilled responses at multiple levels: the social worker may facilitate the meeting, the doctor may deliver and explain the medical information, the nurse may support the family and check on their understanding.

or expect either health professionals or family members to accede to each other's views? The following discussion begins to tease out some of the issues concerning the medical ethic of autonomy in decision-making, issues of professional power and the family context as a driver for collaborative practice.

Decision-making in health is underpinned by the ethical principle of autonomy, which refers to the right of the individual to make his or her own decisions. This right is based on the individual's competence or capacity to act as they seek to understand the medical information that they are given by the healthcare provider

(McConnell *et al.*, 2004), but is not without contention within the context of family meetings. The ethic of autonomy is contentious when an individual's rights are held by a surrogate decision-maker, such as a caregiver, a family group, friends or even a community. It is also contentious when the cultural norms of a family are not shared or understood by the medical team.

International studies indicate a range of positions on the spectrum of decision-making (Yaguchi *et al.*, 2005). Orfali (2004) noted that in France, a paternalistic model of doctor-led decision-making was adopted as parents were considered too emotional to make decisions, whereas the American model of decision-making appeared to favour parents as the appropriate decision-makers. The role of the doctor in this context was to provide information and treatment options. A similar European and North American pattern was noted by Carnevale *et al.* (2007) in France and Quebec (Canada), with paternalistic decision-making operating in France and a more varied decisional authority in Quebec, with parents the most common decision-makers. Decision-making is a contested, culturally sensitive issue and was reviewed by five European and North American critical care societies who issued a joint consensus statement advocating shared decision-making about life support in Intensive Care Units (Carlet *et al.*, 2004). The consensus stated that decision making was a shared responsibility between the medical team (the treating physician) and the patient's family. Within multi-cultural contexts in which children's health services often operate, tensions between different decision-making processes, with variables in professional/clinical and family/cultural positions in regard to autonomy, may become stumbling blocks to effective communication and positive outcomes.

Where the principle of autonomy interacts with culture, it may also affect a family or community's perception of their right to make decisions on behalf of one of their members. A collectivist culture (such as Māori, the indigenous peoples of New Zealand, and Pasifika, communities from the Pacific Islands) encourages individuals to see themselves as part of a larger community and put the needs of the community before the individual. An individualist culture encourages individuals to exercise their uniqueness, make personal choices and strive for personal autonomy (Littlewood, 1999). This cultural complexity of decision-making is illustrated in Figure 14.2. The vertical axis in Figure 14.2 expresses the spectrum of cultural decision-making from individualist to collectivist and the horizontal axis represents the spectrum of decision-making in the health environment from medical-professional-led decision-making to patient or family-led decision-making. The mid-point on this spectrum is shared decision-making, where the family and medical team work together to achieve a consensus (Curtis and White, 2008). This spectrum illustrates the range of positions that decision-making can occur. The position on the spectrum will depend on the views and preferences of the medical team and the culture of the family.

The ecological practice that enables social workers to take roles as active agents in the space between different systems and to focus on the relational aspects of effective practice indicates a key role for the social worker in establishing who the

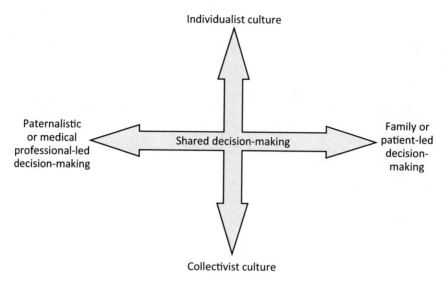

FIGURE 14.2 The spectrum of decision-making

decision-makers are before engaging in a family meeting. This can be a difficult task in the hospital setting when the patient may be supported by a number of medical specialists who have different or competing ideas about what is in the patient's best interests. Family members might also have different perspectives on the patient's condition and the social worker will need to establish who can speak on behalf of the family, negotiating familial decision-making processes as well as those established within the clinical practice of the health setting.

This chapter has provided an opportunity to describe the process and outcomes of a piece of practitioner-led research within the field of collaborative practice and family meetings in children's health. It has served to firmly embed the legitimacy of practice inquiry and the research activity that follows this. Practitioner-led research is an integral part of the social work role and fits into the established paradigms that describe social work practice. Payne (2005) has illustrated the scope of the social work role using a triangle with each of the three corners representing a view of social work practice: reflexive-therapeutic, individualist-reformist and socialist-collectivist. We see the position of this research as sitting between the discourse of individualist-reformist and socialist-collectivist. In this health context, practitioner-led research has an emancipatory and transformational function. Conducting the research provided an evidence-based platform for the lead author to influence the practice of his colleagues and enter into a dialogue about best practice with families facing end-of-life decisions. This also led to invitations to speak at national and international health care events including conferences and seminars that have directly influenced health care delivery to families.

This chapter has outlined some key areas for consideration in the manner in which crucial family meetings in children's health are conducted. We have also described a process of research that required collaborative intent between the researcher and the researched: without collaboration the research would not have been completed.

QUESTIONS FOR REFLECTION

1. How is collaborative decision-making articulated within different cultures, especially in terms of decision-making roles and power-sharing?
2. How might social workers articulate their crucial role in family meetings?
3. How can the function of practitioner-led research be strengthened in your work environment?

References

Azoulay, E., Pochard, F., Kentish-Barnes, N., Chevret, S., Aboab, J., Adrie, C., . . . & Schlemmer, B. (2005) 'Risk of post-traumatic stress symptoms in family members of intensive care unit patients', *American Journal of Respiratory and Critical Care Medicine*, vol. 171, no. 9, pp. 987–994.

Browning, D.M. & Solomon, M.Z. (2005) 'The initiative for pediatric palliative care: An interdisciplinary educational approach for healthcare professionals', *Journal of Pediatric Nursing*, vol. 20, no. 5, pp. 326–334.

Campbell, J.P., Maxey, V.A. & Watson, W.A. (1995) 'Hawthorne effect: Implications for pre-hospital research', *Annals of Emergency Medicine*, vol. 26, no. 5, pp. 590–594.

Carlet, J., Thijs, L.G., Antonelli, M., Cassell, J., Cox, P., Hill, N., . . . & Thompson, B.T. (2004) 'Challenges in end-of-life care in the ICU – statement of the 5th international consensus conference in critical care'. Brussels, Belgium, April 2003, *Intensive Care Medicine*, vol. 30, no. 5, pp. 770–784.

Carnevale, F.A., Canoui, P., Cremer, R., Farrell, C.A., Doussea, A., Seguin, M., . . . & Lacroix, J. (2007) 'Parental involvement in treatment decisions regarding their critically ill child: A comparative study of France and Quebec', *Pediatric Critical Care Medicine*, vol. 8, no. 4, pp. 337–342.

Crichton-Hill, Y. (2009) 'Working with families', in *Practice Skills in Social Work and Welfare: More than Just Common Sense*, J. Maidment & R. Egan (eds), Allen & Unwin, Crows Nest, Australia, pp. 181–201.

Crothers, C. & McCormack, F. (2006) 'Towards a statistical typology of New Zealand households and families: The efficacy of the family life cycle model and alternatives', Families Commission Blue Skies Report 15/06. Families Commission, Wellington, New Zealand.

Curtis, J.R. (2004) 'Communicating about end-of-life care with patients and families in the intensive care unit', *Critical Care Clinics*, vol. 20, no. 3, pp. 363–380.

Curtis, J.R., Engelberg, R.A., Wenrich, M.D., Nielsen, E.L., Shannon, S.E., Treece, P.D., . . . & Rubenfeld, G.D. (2002) 'Studying communication about end-of-life care during the ICU family conference: Development of a framework', *Journal of Critical Care*, vol. 17, no. 3, pp. 147–160.

Curtis, J.R. & White, D.B. (2008) 'Practical guidance for evidence-based ICU family conferences', *Chest Journal*, vol. 134, no. 4, pp. 835–843. doi:10.1378/chest.08–0235

Dyregrov, K., Nordanger, D. & Dyregrov, A. (2003) 'Predictors of psychosocial distress after suicide, SIDS and accident', *Death Studies*, vol. 27, no. 2, pp. 143–165.

Hansen, P., Cornish, P. & Kayser, K. (1998) 'Family conferences as forums for decision making in hospital settings', *Social Work in Health Care*, vol. 27, no. 3, pp. 57–74.

Hostler, S. (1991) 'Family-centered care', *Pediatric Clinics of North America*, vol. 38, no. 6, pp. 111–113.

Lautrette, A., Ciroldi, M., Ksibi, H. & Azoulay, E. (2006) 'End-of-life family conferences: Rooted in the evidence', *Critical Care Medicine*, vol. 34, no. 11, pp. S364–S372.

Littlewood, W. (1999) 'Defining and developing autonomy in East Asian contexts', *Applied Linguistics*, vol. 20, no. 1, pp. 71–94.

McConnell, Y., Frager, G. & Levetown, M. (2004) 'Decision making in pediatric palliative care', *Palliative Care for Infants, Children and Adolescents: A Practical Handbook*, Johns Hopkins University Press, Baltimore, MD, pp. 69–111.

McDonagh, J.R., Elliott, T.B., Engelberg, R.A., Treece, P.D., Shannon, S.E., Rubenfeld, G.D., . . . & Curtis, J.R. (2004) 'Family satisfaction with family conferences about end-of-life care in the intensive care unit: Increased proportion of family speech is associated with increased satisfaction', *Critical Care Medicine*, vol. 32, no. 7, pp. 1484–1488.

Minuchin, S. & Minuchin, S. (1974) *Families and Family Therapy*, Harvard University Press, Cambridge, MA.

Orfali, K. (2004) 'Parental role in medical decision-making: Fact or fiction? A comparative study of ethical dilemmas in French and American neonatal intensive care units', *Social Science and Medicine*, vol. 58, no. 10, pp. 2009–2022.

Payne, M. (2005) *Modern Social Work Theory*, 3rd edn. Palgrave Macmillan, Basingstoke, UK.

Sandelowski, M. (1995) 'Sample size in qualitative research', *Research in Nursing & Health*, vol. 18, no. 2, pp. 179–183.

Thompson, A.P. (2009) *Whanau/family meetings in the paediatric intensive care unit: Content, process, and family satisfaction.* Unpublished Master's Thesis, Massey University, Auckland, New Zealand.

Yaguchi, A., Truog, R.D., Curtis, J.R., Luce, J.M., Levy, M.M., Melot, C. & Vincent, J. (2005) 'International differences in end-of-life attitudes in the intensive care unit: Results of a survey', *Archives of Internal Medicine*, vol. 165, no. 17, pp. 1970–1975.

15

IMPROVING PUBLIC SPACES FOR YOUNG PEOPLE

The contribution of participatory research

Phil Crane

CHAPTER OBJECTIVES

1. *To examine the contribution of public spaces to the wellbeing of young people;*
2. *To explore how participatory action research can be used as a process tool for contextually responsive, collaborative, iterative and multi-method community level practice;*
3. *To consider how the addition of a spatial frame to practice can open up unexpected alliances and opportunities for enhancing the wellbeing of people.*

Introduction

'Space' and 'place' in social and community work

In recent years there has been a revisiting of the meaning of 'person-in-environment' within social and community work. An argument has been made for greater recognition of the spatial environment, and within this 'place', as a focus for practice (Kemp, 2011; McKinnon, 2008). Zapf's notion of living 'well in place' (2009, p. 194) provides a useful starting point for considering how the places and spaces within which people live support and promote wellbeing. Many relationships and community connections are rooted 'in place' (Zapf, 2009, p. 75 citing Chaskin, 1997, p. 522; Jack, 2010), and processes of exclusion and marginalisation are often produced and reproduced spatially (Sibley, 1995; Smith and Low, 2006). Social theory has tended to privilege considerations of time, and change over time, with space generally assumed to be simply a venue for living (Fairbanks II, 2003).

The relationship between people and public space has been the subject of concerted attention over the past decades particularly in the disciplines of human geography and urban sociology. Public space research and literature seek to understand how social, political, economic and cultural processes condition these spaces and the relations that manifest in them (Smith and Low, 2006). This is complex terrain. People's access to a wide range of spaces is increasingly affected by processes of privatisation and corporatisation which have blurred the simple public–private distinction. Privately owned and managed spaces such as shopping centres now routinely host essential public services such as transport inter-changes, police shopfronts and public libraries. Conversely publically owned urban spaces such as town squares, pedestrian thoroughfares and footpaths have become increasingly commodified and effectively privatised through zoning laws and leasing arrangements which permit certain uses and not others, and the use of management strategies which privilege consumption and discourage use for other purposes. In addition, public spaces often play an important role in promoting visual, corporate and municipal images, images which may not be consistent with the incorporation of 'fringe groups' (Laughlin and Johnson, 2011, p. 440) or value social interaction (Schmidt and Nemeth, 2010). Drawing on Smith and Low (2006), there are complex politics in how urban public spaces are understood, configured, managed and experienced, amid long-held concerns that the availability of such spaces not under heavy surveillance and control is being eroded (Davis, 1992; Flusty, 1994). Meanwhile new urbanism has promoted the view that the built environment can be designed and planned so as to promote community when this may not be the case (Crane and Dee, 2001). The implications of these politics around public space for people living on the margins and for how social work understands community level practice are profound.

Wellbeing, young people and public space

Spatial autonomy and opportunities for social interaction are widely shared reasons why young people utilise public spaces, and without their friends the same spaces are often seen as 'boring' (Travlou, 2007, p. 74). A study of young people's views of public space in Toronto found three specific criteria comprising social character, namely that public spaces are ones that are easily accessible, engender a sense of belonging and are venues to find and be with friends (Laughlin and Johnson, 2011, pp. 442–445). Whilst young people are heavy and visible users of public space they have no legal capacity to own or modify it, meaning they must occupy and appropriate the spaces they use, their claims communicated to others including other groups of young people through frequency, regularity and traditions of occupancy (Childress, 2004). The development of social and cultural identities is for many young people intertwined with being in public spaces where they can be seen, engage with peers, be free from parental supervision and watch others (Malone, 2002; White and Wyn, 2008). The relationship between young people and authorities vested with managing space contains embedded tensions, which manifest most clearly when young people's use does not align with formally or implicitly endorsed purposes.

There is also enormous variability in the way young people of different ages, social and geographic locations engage with, and move through, the urban landscape. While some broad generalisations can be made, the key to understanding how particular young people use and relate to public spaces requires space-specific investigation, consistent with the finding that young people create their own microgeographies within communities (Matthews and Limb, 1999).

A wide range of studies have identified neighbourhood-level factors affecting wellbeing (Holland *et al.*, 2011). Wyn (2009), in an overview of young people's health, cites studies which indicate that safe neighbourhoods are associated with better psychological wellbeing and educational achievement of young people (citing Meyers and Miller, 2004), and that there exists a direct association between a young person's level of social support and health risk factors (citing Australian Institute of Health and Welfare, 2007).

Young people's wellbeing is, in part, dependent on their access to the resources they require, to the establishment and maintenance of relationships of trust (Eckersley *et al.*, 2005) and to feeling valued and appreciated (Wilkinson and Marmot, 2003). Yet various studies and surveys indicate that the experience many young people have of public spaces is often of negative attitudes to their presence by adult others and perceived unfair treatment by authorities. Behaviour not deemed consistent with the primary purposes of a space is often criminalised, and in some jurisdictions a person's mere presence in public spaces for non-endorsed purposes, such as being without a place to live and non-consumption, is criminalised through the use of police move-on powers and 'street cleansing' strategies, labelled as 'anti-social' (Nemeth, 2006), and/or designed out (Owens, 1999). Whether this represents a 'punitive turn in urban social policy' (DeVerteuil *et al.*, 2009, p. 646), or reflects historical continuity is an interesting question. What is not in doubt is that young people, and some young people in particular, are constructed in the media as threats, problems and sources of anxiety to the community (Bessant and Hil, 1997). Yet exclusion is not simply a result of how others see and respond to young people. Young people may be met with hostility by other young people, and some will avoid areas because of the way sub-groups occupy space with youth–youth relations reflecting significant micro-cultural tensions and effecting behaviour and perceptions of inclusion/exclusion.

Perhaps the most substantial effort to identify indicators that make communities good or alienating to grow up in has been through two projects of the United Nations, namely the eight-nation Growing Up In Cities (GUIC) study (Driskell, 2002), and the Child Friendly Cities Initiative (CFCI) (UNICEF, 2009). These initiatives are founded on a commitment to children's rights, including their authentic participation and sustainability (Malone, 2006), and have generated various indicators of subjective wellbeing, that is, 'how people think and feel about their lives' (Rablen, 2012, p. 297). The multi-nation GUIC study elicited young people's relationship to their community, public life and public space across a diversity of geographic and cultural locations. A number of characteristics emerged as having a positive or negative impact on 10–15-year-olds' sense of wellbeing. Positive indicators of environmental quality for children and young people were found to include feeling welcome and valued in their community; safety and freedom of movement; a variety of interesting activity options; cohesive community identity (clear geographic boundaries and community level activities); safe green areas (formal or wild); provision of basic needs such as food, water, electricity, medical care, sanitation, security of tenure where family members have legal rights over properties they own or rent; peer gathering places that are safe and accessible where they can meet others/play; and a tradition of community organising and mutual help (Chawla, 2002, pp. 228–229).

The UNICEF Child Friendly Cities Initiative (CFCI) responded to concerns about the living conditions for children, global trends of rapid urbanisation, decentralisation, growing responsibilities being given to municipalities and communities and the increasing importance of cities and towns within political and economic systems (Malone, 2006). It has since morphed into the global 'child friendly cities' movement.

Participatory action research as a framework for public space practice

White's 1990 book *No Space of Their Own* explored the increasing regulation and policing of young people and the spaces they occupied, expressed in policy as an emphasis on 'skill formation' and 'law and order' (p. 211). White explicitly identified public spaces as important to young people as spaces to congregate but also as venues where the autonomous activities of working-class young people were curbed. Since then various public space projects carried out with local government agencies and their youth and/or community development teams have illuminated key features of community-level applied research such as the interweaving of substantive inquiry and strategic elements, using a mix of methods that inform each other (Holland *et al.*, 2011), and the need for a suite of complementary initiatives from different disciplines and vantage points (Crane, 2000). Social and community development workers within local government, periodically supported by consultants and academics, have played key roles in these processes.

Many public space projects have used what has been variously termed as collaborative inquiry, participatory research, or participatory action research (PAR) approaches. PAR attempts to generate relational and reflective knowledge that would not be accessible without the active engagement of the people who are participants in the context being researched (Kenny, 2006), and uses such knowledge to inform change within the immediate research context and/or at higher levels of policy and systems (Burns, 2007; Jupp, 2007; Park, 1999). In this sense PAR is a constructivist approach to knowledge production where meanings about issues and aspects of life differ across people and contexts, and can inform actions which are both context relevant and personally engaging. The emphasis in PAR is on engagement typified by reciprocity (Maiter *et al.*, 2008), and the iterative and ongoing development of strategies based on the understandings generated, the experience of which inform revised strategies and new lines of inquiry.

The values of social work fit well with PAR. Values of collaboration and viewing young people as part of the community rather than simply as objects for management and control also reflect critical realist notions of there being an objective social world albeit one where people's perspectives and contexts are active constituents in social relations (Bhaskar, 1975). The effect of this epistemological position is consistent with the stated values of social work to both take a people and community-centred (social ecological) approach whilst respecting human rights and working towards an 'objectively real' social justice. PAR also draws on processes and strategies which fit a particular community context where many of those participating do not consider themselves as researchers. In contracted projects using PAR there will generally be one or more facilitators of the inquiry process, sometimes consultants, who bring additional research expertise to the process. Participatory action research has been used for a variety of large-scale processes as well as a variety of health and wellbeing oriented community-level projects (Minkler, 2000). The defining feature of PAR processes is how inquiry and action inform each other in an iterative process where new relationships, understandings and practices are not only goals but are emergent, their development providing the basis for the next wave of relationship, understanding and strategy development. Ife (2002) argues PAR is underpinned by the same principles as community development and is fully consistent with the notion of praxis.

The PAR process involves interlinked cycles of observation, reflection, planning and action (Carr and Kemmis, 1986). A developed version of this cyclic character of PAR is depicted in Figure 15.1.

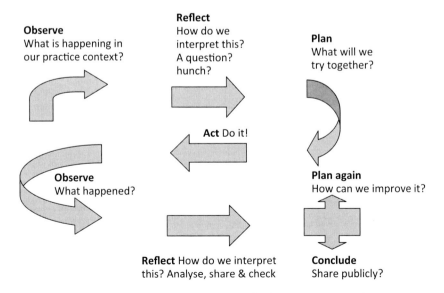

Observe
What is happening in our practice context?

Reflect
How do we interpret this? A question? hunch?

Plan
What will we try together?

Act Do it!

Observe
What happened?

Plan again
How can we improve it?

Reflect How do we interpret this? Analyse, share & check

Conclude
Share publicly?

FIGURE 15.1 An extended PAR cycle (Crane and O'Regan, 2010, p. 11)

A mixed response approach to public space practice: the case of Redland City

From 2009 to 2011 Redland City Council in south-east Queensland sponsored a range of inter-related policy, planning, applied research and strategic initiatives around young people's use of public and community accessed spaces, some drawing on Australian Government 'Safer Cities' funding. Providing a policy foundation was the Cities 'Strong Communities' policy where strong community was defined as a 'connected community with access to the full range of options required for a rich community life and an active attachment to place' (Redland City Council, 2009, p. 1). This policy provided a degree of legitimacy for various youth and public-space strategies and projects.

In 2009 the Capalaba Stakeholders Group was established by Council as a response to tensions and complaints about young people's 'anti-social' behaviour in and around the two main shopping centres in that suburb's central business district (CBD). The Stakeholders Group was the consultative mechanism for the development of a negotiated approach to understand and respond to these tensions. Membership included various sections of Council, managers and security from the local shopping centres, other businesses, police, residents and youth services. The elected Councillor chaired the Group, and the Council's community development team provided support. A small team at the Queensland University of Technology led by the author was engaged to facilitate the development of protocols to respond to the tensions, reporting to the group. While the outcome was initially envisaged as the development of one or more shopping centre protocols, it became apparent that the needs identified and responses required went beyond the confines of the shopping centres and a broader set of principles and guidelines were developed for use in the CBD and with application to other public spaces across the city. In respect of the Capalaba CBD area the result of the project, according to those involved, was an improved social climate in public spaces, evidenced by fewer tensions and enhanced communication.

The research approach employed by the consultants combined a participatory action research process with a strategic framework for public space practice. Previous work by the author and colleagues with Brisbane City Council had given rise to a practice approach referred to at the time as 'local government integrated planning' (White, 1998) where integration involves considering the role that the interlinked domains of design, planning, management and policy each play in the development of youth friendly urban public spaces (Crane, 2000). The underlying logic is that single-domain, time-limited attempts to deal with tensions are unlikely to be sufficient or result in sustainable change. This 'mixed response' approach to public space practice was further refined during the work with Redlands City (Crane *et al.*, 2011) with revised key domains of response depicted in Figure 15.2.

Prior to commencement of the project the Council community development team had undertaken a survey of 2148 young people aged 12–17 from local high schools to ascertain their perceptions of safety and community attitudes. The survey

Policy/legislation   Management

Inquiry/research   Human services

Community
engagement   **Public Space Practice**   Spatial design

Activation   Planning
Facility
provision

FIGURE 15.2 A mixed response approach to public space practice

(reported in Crane, 2010) found that, whilst most young people said they felt safe, more than a quarter did not believe the community was concerned about their safety. More young people thought the community had a negative rather than positive view of what they were doing in public spaces. Males and older young people were more likely to believe they were seen negatively. Those young people who had a positive view of community attitudes also tended to feel safer in their own suburb and more generally in the city. Optimum feelings of safety were indicated by: a moderate frequency of presence by authorities; a view of young people as recipients of protective and control services; an appreciation of young women's concerns; and a view by young people that authorities were fair in their dealings with them. The survey demonstrated that local young people were aware of, and were impacted by negative community views and the style of policing they experienced. The survey provided initial influential voice for young people, and legitimacy across a diversity of stakeholders for taking a considered approach.

The various strategies developed and activities undertaken during the project are described in Table 15.1 using the categories from the above mixed response model.

Discussion

The paucity of quality evaluation studies means it is difficult to estimate the level of impact of such projects and component strategies on the experience and well-being of young people. In the Redlands case observable mechanisms and relationships were developed that were not previously present. These include benchmark surveying of young people's and residents' sense of safety, the development of agreed youth and public space principles and processes to inform how tensions and issues are responded to by the Council's community development team, additional facilities for use by young people, and additional information for young people. Perhaps most importantly there is enhanced local evidence and awareness that relations between young people and others in the community should be appreciated as important. There is evidence of increased willingness and capacity for a

TABLE 15.1 A mixed response approach to public space practice in Redland City

Interlinked domains	Strategies
Community engagement	Convened a Stakeholders Group comprised of diverse local agencies and individuals
	Held a series of public community forums to provide updates and opportunities for discussion
	Developed a youth engagement strategy to inform the spatial design, management and programs to be offered at a new youth space (involved touring other youth spaces and workshop)
	Developed an information card to provide information on local services, young people's rights in respect of police, where to get legal assistance, youth spaces in the city and how to link into the youth forum
Inquiry/research using a wide variety of methods	Youth and Public Space Survey ($N = 2148$)
	Community Safety Survey of residents over 18 ($N = 229$)
	Semi-structured interviews of stakeholders from the CBD ($N = 20$)
	On-going small group discussions with young people who use the CBD public spaces
	Observations of key spaces
	Collection of local information and statistics (e.g. crime)
Activation of spaces	Gained funding for a local youth service to provide an empathetic presence/passive activity on Thursday evenings in the public space where tensions existed
Management	Police, shopping centre management and youth service collect information on what is happening in public spaces and share this at the Stakeholder Group. The type and level of intervention needed is more consciously considered and youth friendly
Spatial design	The spatial design of the CBD and 'The Steps' area identified as contributing to tensions and Council advised to address through re-design in CBD Master Plan
Facility provision	Council provides a venue and funding for a local youth space. The local library considers how it could better orient to teenagers. Discussion commenced on what facilities could be put on the adjacent green space to the 'The Steps'.
Human services	Discussion at and input by the city youth services network
	Enhanced linkages between some providers
	New youth space provides a potential 'soft entry point' young people to access specialist youth services
Policy	Young people endorsed new policy of keeping one side of 'The Steps' clear of gathered groups.
	The document produced from project becomes new operational level policyused by the Community Development team at Council to inform public space practice in other parts of the city and to inform Councils Community Safety Strategy (personal communication from Community Development Team Redland City Council, June 2012).

diversity of agencies and people to be involved in collaborative dialogue, and of reduced tensions between young people and authorities. Further empirical investigation is needed to ascertain any sustained shifts in young people's views and experience.

The Redlands initiatives provide insight into how practice at the local level can make progress on improving the relationship between young people seen as problematic in their use of public space, and others who plan, manage and use these spaces. Achieving and sustaining movement to a more relationally supportive local environment for young people requires a suite of interlinked strategies and targets, rather than reliance on short-term projects which use single-domain responses. Consistent with asset-based approaches to community development, there needs to be a fundamental regard for the existing and potential strengths within communities (Healy, 2006).

Social and community workers should be interested in the role of place and of particular spaces in their clients' wellbeing. Asking action inquiry questions important to people is an implicit part of community practice and can usefully employ PAR as a guiding process framework. Action inquiry questions are phrased in such a way that they invite learning through doing. For example '*What would it take to . . .* improve how public spaces in this area contribute to the wellbeing of young people?' Or '*What would it take to . . .* improve the relationship between young people and others in the community?' or '*How can we . . .* reduce tensions in the local park between young people and residents?'

There are of course substantial limitations to participatory inquiry approaches. The neo-liberal contract regime, within which much social and community work is institutionally situated, provides challenges and barriers to creating the space for collaborative engagement and action. The engagement and prominence of powerful stakeholders (local government, business, police) means much public space practice is not located within disadvantaged communities themselves. The power of various participants in such applied research is unequal and there can often be conversations occurring *about* others rather than *with* others. There is evidence to suggest that young people who are the most marginalised are less likely than other young people to gain from public space initiatives (Crane *et al.*, 2000).

A second limitation is that such projects are often not sustained over time but are grounded in a short term reactive need to 'fix' a problem, that being the assumed problematic behaviour of young people. Where a more inclusive agenda is evident this is often via time limited projects. How to institutionalise improved arrangements and relations in respect of those young people most marginalised is a substantial challenge.

A third limitation arises from what could be termed 'populist romanticism' about participatory processes (Greenwood *et al.*, 2006, p. 93). Just because a participatory process is used does not mean the inquiry necessarily has substantive or strategic value. Participatory approaches must be modest about their claims to unearthing particular types of knowledge, empowering participants and achieving change (Jupp, 2007, p. 2838). Participatory research often seeks to maximise the participation of those members of communities most affected by issues but this is often uneven and difficult to sustain. The location of the facilitator/researcher within an institutional context (such as a local government, university or local government) with more relative power can limit the reciprocity that is experienced and achieved (Maiter *et al.*, 2008), and contains the challenge of who owns the knowledge and intellectual property produced (Greenwood *et al.*, 2006).

Conclusion

This chapter has argued that a spatial perspective is an important element of appreciating locality related aspects of young people's wellbeing. Further practitioners need ways of working with people in communities that acknowledge and activate the knowledge and capacities of those on the margins, whilst also engaging more powerful stakeholders and decision makers.

This chapter has also outlined a framework for public space practice. Reflecting the broader trend to develop more 'joined up' responses, practitioners need to draw on a mix of strategic levers that influence how spaces and places can foster rather than erode people's wellbeing. PAR provides a process for how this work can be undertaken, an approach that is essentially trans-disciplinary, iterative and developmental.

Whilst the disparities arising from uneven power cannot be wished away, the use of PAR can increase local understandings and transparency, and to some extent temporarily destabilise exclusionary dynamics. Practitioners can foster the development of communicative spaces so that new options can emerge. Engaging with and enhancing commitment at the local level involves the nuanced skills of bridging between diverse logics and discourses, domains of practice, and institutional structures without losing sight of the core values that underpin community development. Such practice, if it incorporates a spatial frame, can open up unexpected alliances and possibilities for enhancing the wellbeing of people.

QUESTIONS FOR REFLECTION

1. How can we as practitioners foster an approach to place and the key public spaces within this which enhances sociability and wellbeing?
2. How can we encourage and facilitate a complimentary suite of community resources and responses to be brought to bear on the complexity of 'living well in place'?

References

Bessant, J. & Hil, R. (eds) (1997) *Youth, Crime and the Media: Media Representations of and Reactions to Young People in Relation to Law & Order*, Australian Clearinghouse for Youth Studies, Hobart, Australia.

Bhaskar, R. (1975) *A Realist Theory of Science*, 2nd edn. Verso, London.

Burns, D. (2007) *Systemic Action Research: A Strategy for Whole System Change*, Policy Press, Bristol, UK.

Carr, W. & Kemmis, S. (1986) *Becoming Critical: Education, Knowledge and Action Research*, Falmer Press, London.

Chawla, L. (2002) *Growing Up in an Urbanising World*, UNESCO Publishing/Earthscan, Paris.

Childress, H. (2004) 'Teenagers, territory and the appropriation of space', *Childhood*, vol. 11, no. 2, pp. 195–205.

Crane, P. (2000) 'Young people and public space: Developing inclusive policy and practice', *Scottish Youth Issues Journal*, vol. 1, pp. 105–124.

Crane, P. (2010) *Their Space, My Space, Our Space? Report of the 2009 Redland City Council Youth and Public Space Survey*. Redland City Council: Redlands [online]. Available at: http://eprints.qut.edu.au/view/person/Crane,_Philip.html

Crane, P., Adkins, B. & Marston G. (2000) *Brokering Inclusion: The Myer Centre Youth Protocol*, unpublished report, Brisbane City Council: Brisbane, Australia [online]. Available at: http://eprints.qut.edu.au/view/person/Crane,_Philip.html

Crane, P. & Dee, M. (2001) 'Young people, public space and new urbanism', *Youth Studies Australia*, vol. 20, no. 1, pp. 11–18.

Crane, P., Dee, M. & Spencer, A. (2011) *Redland City Youth and Public Space Report: Provisions for Good Practice*, unpublished report, Queensland University of Technology, Brisbane, Australia [online]. Available at: http://eprints.qut.edu.au/view/person/Crane,_Philip.html

Crane, P. & O'Regan, M. (2010) *On PAR: Using Participatory Action Research to Improve Early Intervention*, Australian Government, Canberra, Australia.

Davis, M. (1992) 'Fortress Los Angeles: The militarisation of urban space', in *Variations on a Theme Park: The new American city and the end of Public Space*, M. Sorkin (ed), Noonday Press, New York.

DeVerteuil, G., May, J. & Von Mahs, J. (2009) 'Complexity not collapse: Recasting the geographies of homelessness in a "punitive" age', *Progress in Human Geography*, vol. 33, no. 5, pp. 646–666.

Driskell, D. (2002) *Creating Better Cities with Children and Youth*, UNESCO Publishing, Paris.

Eckersley, R., Wierenga, A. & Wyn, J. (2005) *Flashpoints & Signposts: Pathways to Success and Wellbeing for Australia's Young People*, Mental Health and Wellbeing Unit, Victorian Health Promotion Foundation, Australia.

Fairbanks II, R. (2003) 'A theoretical primer on space', *Critical Social Work*, vol. 4, no. 1. Available at: http://www.uwindsor.ca/criticalsocialwork/a-theoretical-primer-on-space

Flusty, S. (1994) *Building Paranoia: The Proliferation of Interdictory Space and the Erosion of Spatial Justice*, LA Forum for Architecture and Urban Design, Los Angeles.

Greenwood, D., Brydon-Miller, M. & Shafer, C. (2006) 'Intellectual property and action research', *Action Research*, vol. 4, no. 1, pp. 81–95.

Healy, K. (2006) 'Asset-based community development: Recognising and building on community strengths', in *Skills for Human Service Practice: Working with Individuals, Groups and Communities*, A. O'Hara & Z. Weber (eds), Oxford University Press, South Melbourne, Australia, pp. 247–258.

Holland, S., Burgess, S. Grogan-Kaylor, A. & Delva, J. (2011) 'Understanding neighbourhoods, communities and environments: New approaches for social work research', *British Journal of Social Work*, vol. 41, no. 4, pp. 689–707.

Ife, J. (2002) *Community Development: Community-based Alternatives in an Age of Globalisation*, 2nd edn, Pearson Education Australia, Frenchs Forest, Australia.

Jack, G. (2010) 'Place matters: The significance of place attachments for children's wellbeing', *British Journal of Social Work*, vol. 38, no. 2, pp. 755–771.

Jupp, E. (2007) 'Participation, local knowledge and empowerment: Researching public space with young people', *Environment and Planning*, vol. 39, no. 12, pp. 2832–2844.

Kemp, S. (2011) 'Recentring environment in social work practice: Necessity, opportunity, challenge', *British Journal of Social Work*, vol. 41, no. 6, pp. 1198–1210.

Kenny, S. (2006) *Developing Communities for the Future*, 3rd edn, Thompson, South Melbourne, Australia.

Laughlin, D. & Johnson, L. (2011) 'Defining and exploring public space: Perspectives of young people from Regent Park, Toronto', *Children's Geographies*, vol. 9, nos. 3–4, pp. 439–456.

Maiter, S., Simich, L., Jacobson, N., & Wise, J. (2008) 'Reciprocity: An ethic for community based participatory action research', *Action Research*, vol. 6, no. 3, pp. 305–325.

Malone, K. (2002) 'Street life: Youth, culture and competing uses of public space', *Environment and Urbanization*, vol. 14, no. 2, pp. 157–168.

Malone, K. (2006) 'United Nations: A key player in a global movement for child friendly cities', in *Creating Child Friendly Cities: Reinstating Kids in the City*, B. Gleeson & N. Sipes, (eds), Routledge, London, pp. 13–32.

Matthews, H. & Limb, M. (1999) 'Defining an agenda for the geography of children: Review and prospect', *Progress in Human Geography*, vol. 23, no. 1, pp. 61–90.

McKinnon, J. (2008) 'Exploring the nexus between social work and the environment', *Australian Social Work*, vol. 61, no. 3, pp. 256–268.

Minkler, M. (2000) 'Using participatory action research to build healthy communities', *Public Health Reports*, vol. 115, no. 2–3, pp. 191–197.

Nemeth, J. (2006) 'Conflict, exclusion, relocation: Skateboarding and public space', *Journal of Urban Design*, vol. 11, no. 3, pp. 297–318.

Owens, P. (1999) 'No teens allowed: The exclusion of adolescents from public spaces', *Bulletin of People–Environment Studies*, vol. 12, no. 1, pp. 21–24.

Park, P. (1999) 'People, knowledge and change in participatory research', *Management Learning*, vol. 30, no. 2, pp. 141–157.

Rablen, M. (2012) 'The promotion of local wellbeing: A primer for policymakers', *Local Economy*, vol. 27, no. 3, pp. 297–314.

Redland City Council (2009) *Policy document: Strong Communities*. Corporate POL-3087. [online]. Available at: http://www.redland.qld.gov.au/SiteCollectionDocuments/Policies/POL-3087.pdf

Schmidt, S. & Nemeth, J. (2010) 'Space, place and the city: Emerging research on public space design and planning', *Journal of Urban Design*, vol. 15, no. 4, pp. 453–457.

Sibley, D. (1995) *Geographies of Exclusion: Society and Difference in the West*, Routledge, London,.

Smith, N. & Low, S. (2006) 'Introduction: The imperative of public space', in *The Politics of Public Space*, S. Low & N. Smith (eds), Routledge, New York.

Travlou, P. (2007) 'Mapping youth spaces in the public realm: Identity, space and social exclusion', in *Public Space – Open Space*, C. Ward Thompson & P. Travlou (eds), Taylor and Francis, London.

UNICEF (2009) *Child Friendly Cities Promoted by UNICEF National Committees and Country Offices* – Fact Sheet, September 2009 [online]. Available at: http://www.childfriendlycities.org/documents/view/id/65/lang/en

White, R. (1990) *No Space of Their Own: Young People and Social Control in Australia*, Cambridge University Press, Cambridge.

White, R. (1998) *Public Spaces for Young People: A Guide to Creative Projects and Positive Strategies*, Commonwealth Attorney-General's Department, Canberra, Australia.

White, R. & Wyn, J. (2008) *Youth and Society: Exploring the Social Dynamics of Youth Experience*, 2nd edn, Oxford University Press, South Melbourne, Australia.

Wilkinson. R. & Marmot, M. (2003) *The Solid Facts*, World Health Organization, Copenhagen, Denmark.

Wyn, J. (2009) *Youth Health and Welfare: The Cultural Politics of Education and Wellbeing*, Oxford University Press, South Melbourne, Australia.

Zapf, M. (2009) *Social Work and the Environment: Understanding People and Place*, Canadian Scholars' Press, Toronto, Canada.

16

AGEING IN RESILIENCY

Learning from the experiences and perceptions of migrant older adults

Hong-Jae Park

CHAPTER OBJECTIVES

1. *To deepen an understanding of the experiences and perceptions of migrant older adults in the global age;*
2. *To apply a life-span development approach to elder abuse and neglect in the family;*
3. *To highlight the importance of recognising the resilience that underlies the health and wellbeing of older people.*

Introduction

Social work with older people is an area of practice that has been relatively under-developed, although the profession ought to be at the forefront of the efforts to deal with the issues associated with ageing and ageing populations. Working with older people requires not only understanding individuals' experiences and perceptions, but also making sense of the context within which they are embedded (Tanner, 2010). A life-span development approach can provide an effective framework that allows practitioners to develop a better understanding of older people's developmental issues relating to their circumstances. This integrated approach to ageing and old age highlights the claim that both individual characteristics and environmental factors are equally important in achieving successful ageing and resilience.

Along with the population ageing, globalisation across nations is an important aspect of social work practice with older people. Issues associated with old age and older people become more complex than before as many people move to another country to live or stay. Some older people may have their children or grandchildren overseas, while others may relocate themselves to another country in the desire to be close to their family or to have a new life. Such migration of individuals or of family units creates transnational families in which caring for aged parents via long distances poses a range of challenges (Phillips, 2007). Intergenerational family relationships are influenced by the dispersion of family members and networks within the transnational context (Lunt *et al.*, 2006).

Older migrant adults are those older people who have retired in their own country and then moved to another nation in their later life. These people may face 'double' challenges in adapting and adjusting to the combined process of ageing and resettlement in a new country (International Longevity Center, 2006). Ageing 'in place', remaining where people have lived for a long time, may not be a feasible option for older migrants, as they need to re-start in the place where both the culture and language are different (Treas and Mazumdar, 2004). In some cases, stress in later-life migration increases intergenerational conflict thus causing elder mistreatment (Thomas, 2003). Studies have shown that elder mistreatment, such as a failure of undertaking caregiving obligations or perhaps the exploitation of finances, has occurred among Asian migrant families in the United States (Le, 1997; Tatara, 1999).

This chapter explores the experiences and perceptions of older Korean people in New Zealand in relation to the issues of elder mistreatment and filial piety. The author acknowledges that older migrants face a range of challenges as they have moved to another culture in later adulthood. At the same time, the author asserts the claim that classifying older migrants just as a fragile or at-risk group does little to help us understand how people transcend adversity. This chapter, therefore, attempts to identify the factors that allow older people to achieve and maintain resilience under adverse circumstances.

The study on the issues of filial piety and elder mistreatment

The study that is the subject of this chapter involved gaining an understanding of the issues of filial piety and elder mistreatment among Korean families in New Zealand (Park, 2011). The objectives of the study were to explore older people's experiences and perceptions of elder mistreatment, and to examine their help-seeking patterns towards the problem. The cultural heritage of filial piety (care and respect for older people) was also studied in order to learn about the relationship between the cultural values and elder mistreatment within the migrant context in which Korean families in the study were situated.

Contextual background of the study

Koreans form the third-largest Asian ethnic group in New Zealand, following Chinese and Indian groups. They have been established as the fastest-growing minority community in the country from the early 1990s. The latest census data show that the number of Korean residents has increased by more than 30 times from 930 in 1991 to 30,792 in 2006 (Statistics New Zealand, 2007). Although Korean people comprise less than one per cent in the New Zealand population, they play an important role in promoting the movement of people, products and cultures between the two nations (Collins, 2006).

Older people aged 65 and over account for only two per cent of the Korean residents in New Zealand. The number in this age group is increasing as the majority of the first immigrant generation reaches old age. Korean older people are either those people who retired in their homeland first and then moved to New Zealand to live with their family, or migrant older adults who came to the country at a younger age and then reached the age of retirement (Park, 2011). They were born overseas and, therefore, are likely to live in a transnational family context where family members are dispersed between different countries.

Research design and process

The study was designed to explore the issues of elder mistreatment and filial piety through collecting data from Korean migrants residing in New Zealand. A mixed methods approach was deployed combining qualitative and quantitative studies at different stages of the investigation. The study was approved by the appropriate ethics bodies.

There were three sources of data collection: qualitative interviews with 20 key informants; a structured survey with 50 older people; and in-depth interviews with 10 older people. First, a contextual study with key informants in the Korean community was undertaken to map the social and cultural context where older Koreans were placed. The participants in the key informant study consisted of community leaders, religious leaders, health professionals, social workers and other key actors in the community. A survey study of Korean elders was then conducted to examine their perceptions of elder mistreatment and filial piety and their help-seeking patterns. The survey contained multiple open-ended questions with reference to six scenarios of elder mistreatment. Finally, the lived experiences of elder abuse and neglect were investigated with older people who were, or had been, mistreated in their transnational family setting. The focus of these phenomenological interviews was less an investigation of each participant's experience and more of an explanation of the phenomenon distilled from the individuals' stories.

The fieldwork for this study was extremely difficult and complex, as elder abuse and neglect is a taboo issue particularly in a 'small' minority community. There was a significant conflict between research interests and the loyalty to the community being studied. For example, the biggest concern for a few participants was to reveal abuse cases, because doing so might damage their community's 'face' (reputation) as a model migrant community. Investigating the hidden problem of elder mistreatment also required a culturally sensitive approach that focused on open and honest relationships with participants through applying the principles of respect and filial piety at the community level. Ethical practice, including protecting privacy, confidentiality and boundaries, was central to maintaining such trustful relationships in the process of collecting data within real-life situations.

The data collected were managed in a cross-cultural context which required an alternative approach to the data analysis process, rather than relying on existing code-based analysis techniques. Data were analysed through a two-fold analytical approach. In the first-stage of analysis, quantitative data were analysed using SPSS analysis while a concept-mapping technique was employed for qualitative data. In the second phase of data analysis, the concept-mapping technique was applied again to enhance the integrated interpretation of both qualitative and quantitative data in the bilingual research setting. This theme-centred method used conceptual diagrams to create concepts and explore their relationships, with a focus on the broader cultural and social context (Rubin and Babbie, 2008). Core concepts were identified by creating, adjusting, and recreating main ideas from the raw data in which the two languages, Korean and English, were complementarily used. Key themes emerged from the conceptual profile that contained several clusters of concepts and networks of ideas.

Learning from the experiences and perceptions of older adult migrants

Immigration in later life causes migrant older adults to face multiple challenges due to the mixed effects of resettlement and ageing processes in a new place. Some may experience disadvantage and discrimination in the host society as they tend to be alienated from the mainstream language and culture (Thomas, 2003). Moving to another culture may contribute to weakening family obligations and duties towards older people among immigrant families (Lee, 2007). Under these circumstances, the migrant context of older adults often represents a fertile land where seeds of elder abuse are planted much more easily than in the homeland.

Elder mistreatment as a hidden health and social problem

Elder abuse and neglect in the migrant setting is a traumatic event that has an adverse impact on the health and wellbeing of older migrants. It undermines older people's adaptive processes to a positive ageing experience in a new environment. The causes and consequences of elder mistreatment among migrant families are particularly complex and unknown (Nerenberg, 2008; Peri *et al.*, 2008).

The findings from the study show that elder mistreatment occurs among Korean immigrant families in New Zealand. Psychological abuse was commonly identified by the older people who participated in interviews. Elder neglect was another type of mistreatment among them, despite the fact that the person who sponsored his or her parents had a social and legal obligation to support them. Financial abuse or exploitation also occurred during the resettlement process of older migrants and their families. This observation of abuse cases in the Korean population in New Zealand reinforces the claim that elder abuse and neglect in the Korean culture occurs indiscriminately whether older people live in their home country or abroad (Kim, 2005). The findings from this study add further evidence to the commonly cited notion that elder abuse and neglect happens in every culture, within every ethnicity (WHO, 2008).

The occurrence of elder mistreatment among Koreans in New Zealand was closely related to the decrease of family solidarity and kinship ties in family arrangements in both the homeland and within the host nation. It was observed that immigration affected not only the size and composition of family networks, but also the practice of care and support for ageing parents. The traditional cultural norms associated with filial piety were likely to become eroded in the migrant context, in which individualist ideas were more dominant than family-centred practices. Such changes in family structures and value systems often contributed to the development of elder mistreatment in the transnational family setting.

Any type of elder mistreatment incurs emotional harm. Although the consequences of elder abuse and neglect vary significantly from person to person, the problem can seriously impact upon an older people's emotional and psychological wellbeing. As in all family violence, elder abuse is likely to be a threat to the emotional life of elderly parents, no matter what types of harm are occurring in their family relationship. The results from this study show that all the participants in the in-depth interviews had experienced emotional distress and mental health difficulties, regardless of the type of mistreatment they faced. For example, financial abuse gave rise to psychological and emotional consequences, although it initially involved improper exploitation of an older person's finances.

Beyond emotional harm, elder mistreatment, as a major traumatic event, can cause somatised physical health problems. Some participants in the study identified *Hwa-byung* [see Box 16.1], an anger syndrome, as a major problem that affected both their physical and psychological health and wellbeing. Those participants stated that they had experienced somatised physical symptoms such as heat

---

BOX 16.1

HWA-BYUNG, A UNIVERSAL OR ENCULTURATED ANGER SYNDROME?

Hwa-byung (literally 'fire-illness') is a culture-bounded anger syndrome in the Korean culture. Min (2009) argued that ' "suppression and control have been strong social codes of behaviour in the traditionally familial, collective, and Confucian culture of Korea'" (p. 13). The disease has been listed in Appendix 1, the Glossary of Culture-bound Syndromes in the DSM-IV in 1994. The symptoms of Hwa-byung are associated with suppressed emotions of anger, sighing, a feeling of unfairness and other somatised symptoms. Its symptom profile is different from that of depression, although the two disorders share some common features (Min, Suh and Song, 2009). People with Hwa-byung tend to internalise emotional distress and suffering, keeping them within, and, as a result, these emotions come out in other somatised ways (Park, Kim, Schwarts-Barcott and Kim, 2002). It is considered, in this study, that elder abuse and neglect in the family can be a serious risk factor for Hwa-byung, regardless of whether the syndrome is universal or culture specific.

sensation, pushing up in the chest, pain in the heart, sleep problems, chronic indigestion and heart palpitation, along with having felt fear, anger, shame, a sense of unfairness and of helplessness. The older persons who diagnosed themselves with *Hwa-byung* were likely to suppress and inhibit their anger caused by elder abuse in order to maintain harmonious family relationships and 'family face' (honour) in the community.

Coping with elder mistreatment in a foreign country

Responses to elder mistreatment at an individual level are closely related to older people's perceptions about the situation they face. What people perceive can be a fundamental aspect of how they understand, feel and act upon the problem (Moon and Williams, 1993). In the study, the perceptions of the Korean older people reflected their thoughts and understandings about elder mistreatment, as well as their feelings about filial piety within their family. Those participants who perceived an action as abusive were more likely to seek help from others than when they did not perceive abuse or harm in that situation. In other words, help-seeking behaviour was unlikely to happen if an older person did not perceive a situation as being abusive or was not aware of a situation being abusive.

Elder abuse and neglect is a taboo issue that is likely to be hidden as a family matter or secret. An 'iceberg' theory of elder mistreatment highlights the notion that the majority of elder abuse cases remain underreported (National Center on Elder Abuse, 1998). Some abused elders may be reluctant to reveal abuse outside the family, while others may be afraid of losing their relationship with the abusive child (Bonnie and Wallace, 2003; Brandl *et al.*, 2007). In this study, all the participants who were mistreated did not want to report the abuse to the police or elder abuse services. Most respondents in the survey also stated that they would not reveal their family problems to a social service organisation.

Although older people tend to avoid disclosing elder mistreatment, they would want the abuse to stop (Nerenberg, 2008). Some may try to reduce harm without having their children blamed or face the risk of criminal prosecution by reporting. The findings of the study show that most abused people preferred not to reveal the abuse they faced, but did try to actively manage the situation by their own efforts, for example, self-care strategies and seeking to resolve the problem without help or assistance from other people. Types of self-help or self-care among the participants included confronting the abuse, fleeing from the abusive situation, being tolerant to whatever happened, keeping themselves busy with other things, praying to God or sacrificing themselves for the sake of family harmony.

Apart from self-helping strategies, help-seeking is another process which can be used by abused persons. There are different types of help or support available for them; some types of help can be directly relevant to elder mistreatment, while others can be indirectly useful for coping with the problem. Help can be either formal or informal, depending on who provides it. It was a common finding that older Korean people accepted 'indirect help' from other family members, relatives or friends in the face of an abusive relationship, while they tended not to seek 'direct help' from formal abuse services or authorities.

In this study, virtually every abused person had coped with elder mistreatment despite his or her difficult family circumstances. The participants experiencing abuse were remarkably resilient and willing to restore their damaged family relationships. According to those elders, they had experienced a set of emotional processes that consisted of resentment, repression, forgiveness and resilience. Being resilient in experiencing elder mistreatment was closely related to older adults' sense of personal and social responsibility for themselves and their family members. The ways of responding to and coping with elder mistreatment were affected by their efforts to preserve family face. Many abused elders considered a non-legal approach to solving the problem of elder abuse, while maintaining a sense of resilience by using feasible resources, such as religious or social networks.

Being resilient through being connected

Since people are interconnected by nature, most aspects of elder mistreatment are likely to be matters of interpersonal and social connectedness. Although self-care and help-seeking strategies can be good sources of coping for the people who are suffering from elder mistreatment, the availability of those patterns is likely to be influenced by the extent of their social networks. The findings of the study show that the capacity to overcome the problem tended to be determined by support and help from such networks, in addition to the individual's skills, knowledge and perception. The participants' strategies to cope with elder mistreatment were sought from different layers of networks, including family members, friends and neighbours in the community.

As people age, their social networks can be gradually limited to immediate or close networks (Santrock, 2011). Older people are likely to focus their attention on family or other immediate networks (Carstensen *et al.*, 2006). In particular, Korean older people hold the values which favour close interaction and mutual assistance within their families and tend to identify themselves with the family, rather than with religion, work or any other factors (Oxford Institute of Ageing, 2007). In this study, older migrants were likely to use their family to connect with the outside world due, in part, to experienced cultural and language barriers. Consequently, the family was considered as an essential institution that formed an important network, providing a potential pool of psychological and social resources for those older migrants.

Not only does the family become a site of elder mistreatment, but it can also be a source of healing. In the study, for instance, when abuse occurred in a relationship between a parent and a child, other family members appeared as the mediating force for resolving issues. Family members, other than the abuser, often provided the abused elder with informal help and support. The cultural traditions associated with filial piety and family support had an impact on the emphasis of family networks and relations. The majority of the respondents in the survey interpreted the norm of filial piety as a desirable tool to foster and sustain positive relationships within their family network. They tended to perceive filial piety as, much more than physical or financial support to aged parents, having multi-dimensional aspects of care and concern, such as behavioural and emotional support, parent-honouring attitudes and respect in words and actions (Sung, 2005).

When family networks are not as supportive as they once were, the role of community-based groups becomes imperative in fulfilling the needs and interests of older people. The findings of the study highlight the importance of *Noin-daehaks*, supporting groups for older people, in the Korean community in New Zealand. These senior groups, mainly run by Korean ethnic-based churches, provided older people with opportunities for education, spiritual and socialising activities, entertainment, exercise and a hot meal for lunch. Some older people who had difficulties within the family often utilised these community-based groups as their major support system in the new environment. Attending *Noin-daehaks* often allowed older migrants to develop and maintain a thread of social networks outside the family. Those support groups often made it possible for older people to compensate for their loss of social and family support caused by elder mistreatment in their transnational life.

Implications for social work practice

Social work practice with older migrants should be based on an understanding of human development and the context in which they are embedded. Later-life immigration requires older people's adaptation to the ageing process in a new society where they are not familiar with the local language and culture. Difficulties in adjustment, including the lack of dominant language competency, can threaten the health and wellbeing of older migrants (Min *et al.*, 2005). Living away from the homeland-based family members can pose a range of challenges, such as a lack of potential caregivers, in the transnational family relationships. Under such challenging circumstances, elder abuse and neglect can be a devastating life event that adversely affects older migrants' physical, psychological and socio-emotional development.

A life-span development approach, emphasising development and growth across the life course, would provide practitioners with a framework that helps them identify not only the individual's developmental and relationship issues but also the social and cultural context where elder abuse and neglect occurs. This multidimensional approach is based on the premise that human development continues from conception to old age within the environmental conditions that affect individual and family growth and change (Crawford and Walker, 2007). A critical feature of the approach is an integrated or holistic consideration of various aspects of elder abuse and neglect, including the biological, psychological, socio-emotional, spiritual, moral and the cultural, within its context. From this perspective, elder mistreatment in the family can be seen as a product, or a process, of the relationships between generations throughout their life stages. Social and cultural factors also influence, not only the family relationships, but also the development of elder abuse and neglect.

Theories and knowledge associated with life-span development can serve as a base for practitioners in assessing elder mistreatment among older migrants and planning adequate intervention and prevention strategies for the problem. For example, ideas related to ecological systems are useful to understand the combined effects of environmental and behavioural determinants of older migrants and their families (Balgopal, 2000). Considering the reciprocal impact of people and environmental systems is essential to identifying the risk and protective factors for elder mistreatment among older people living in a foreign country. At the same time, the emphasis on resilience and competence across the life course pertains to the strengths-based framework of social work practice in working with older people, families and communities (Sisneros *et al.*, 2008). It is necessary for practitioners to pay attention to the strengths and resilience of older migrants, rather than focusing on their deficits and weaknesses.

In working with older migrants, the goal of intervention should include promoting resilience and support systems at multiple levels. The roles of social work practitioners are to help those people build social connections and to promote participation in their community and society. For older migrants, their ethnic community is not just an ecological context, but an essential source of strength for growth and opportunities for belonging. The community, consisting of various ethnic-based groups and organisations, can be utilised as a rich repository of culture, language, religious values and social activities for older people (Berg-Weger, 2010). Practitioners need to work closely with those ethnic-based community groups to prevent and tackle the problem of elder mistreatment among migrant families.

Conclusion

The discussion in this chapter is based on the experiences and perceptions of older people from an ethnic minority background in New Zealand. Although migration in later life can be an opportunity for older people to live in an overseas country, it can also cause them to experience a range of challenges and difficulties within the transnational family context. Elder mistreatment among older migrants is a complex issue involving ageing, globalisation and social connectedness. As the traditional norms of filial obligations toward older people are eroding among migrant families, the role of community-based groups and organisations is crucial for the survival and connectedness of older migrants. Such community-based support becomes an essential resource for the resilience that older people can maintain during their ageing process in their host society.

For older migrants, resilience is related to adaptation and adjustment to both ageing and resettling processes in a foreign country. It is evident from this study that the resilience of older adult migrants comes from not only individual and family strengths but also social resources from the wider context at community, societal and cultural levels. The life-span perspective foregrounds the protective factors that may mediate the negative outcomes experienced by older migrants. It serves as a theoretical and practical framework that emphasises the multidimensional attribute of resilience and successful ageing among migrant older adults.

QUESTIONS FOR REFLECTION

1. What are your attitudes to older people and your own ageing?
2. What resources may be available for fostering the resilience of older people from an ethnic minority group in your community?
3. What practice challenges do you anticipate when working with those experiencing elder mistreatment?

References

Balgopal, P.R. (2000) *Social Work Practice with Immigrants and Refugees*, Columbia University Press, New York.

Berg-Weger, M. (2010) *Social Work and Social Welfare: An Invitation*, 2nd edn. Routledge, New York.

Bonnie, R.J. & Wallace, R.B. (2003) *Elder Mistreatment: Abuse, Neglect, and Exploitation in an Aging America*, National Academy Press, Washington, DC.

Brandl, B., Dyer, C., Heisler, C., Otto, J., Stiegel, L. & Thomas, R. (2007) *Elder Abuse Detection and Intervention: A Collaborative Approach*, Springer, New York.

Carstensen, L.L., Mikels, J.A. & Mather, M. (2006) Aging and the intersection of cognition, motivation and emotion', in *Handbook of the Psychology of Aging*, J. Birren & K.W. Schaie (eds), Academic Press, San Diego, pp. 343–362.

Collins, F.L. (2006) *Learning to cross borders: Everyday urban encounters between South Korea and New Zealand.* Unpublished Doctoral Thesis, University of Auckland, Auckland, New Zealand.

Crawford, K. & Walker, J. (2007) *Social Work and Human Development*, 2nd edn. Learning Matters, Exeter, UK.

International Longevity Center (2006) *Ageism in America*, Anti-Ageism Taskforce, New York.

Kim, M.H. (2005) *Coming the Aged Society in Korea: Challenges and Responses*, Ewha Woman's University, Seoul, South Korea.

Le, Q.K. (1997) 'Mistreatment of Vietnamese elderly by their families in the United States', *Journal of Elder Abuse & Neglect*, vol. 9, no. 2, pp. 51–82.

Lee, Y. (2007) 'The immigration experience among elderly Korean immigrants', *Journal of Psychiatric and Mental Health Nursing*, vol. 14, no. 4, pp. 403–410.

Lunt, N., McPherson, M. & Browning, H. (2006) *Les Familles et Whanau sans Frontiers: New Zealand and Transnational Family Obligation*, Families Commission, Wellington, New Zealand.

Min, S.K. (2009) 'Hwabyung in Korea: culture and dynamic analysis', *World Cultural Psychiatry Research Review*, vol. 4, no. 1, pp. 12–21.

Min, J.W. & Moon, A. & Lubben, J.E. (2005) 'Determinants of psychological distress over time among older Korean immigrants and non-wave panel study', *Aging & Mental Health*, vol. 9, no. 3, pp. 210–222.

Min, S.K., Suh, S.Y. & Song, K.J. (2009) 'Symptoms to use for diagnostic criteria of Hwa-Byung, an anger syndrome', *Psychiatry Investigation*, vol. 6, no. 1, pp. 7–12.

Moon, A. & Williams, O. (1993) 'Perceptions of elder abuse and help-seeking patterns among African-American, Caucasian American, and Korean-American elderly women', *The Gerontologist*, vol. 33, no. 3, pp. 386–395. doi:10.1093/geront/33.3.386

National Center on Elder Abuse (1998) *The National Elder Abuse Incidence Study: Final Report,* Author, Washington, DC.

Nerenberg, L. (2008) *Elder Abuse Prevention: Emerging Trends and Promising Strategies*, Springer, New York.

Oxford Institute of Ageing (2007) *The third annual HSBC Future of Retirement study*, HSBC (Hong Kong and Shanghai Banking Corporation), London.

Park, H. (2011) *Western thoughts, Eastern feelings: A study of filial piety and elder mistreatment among Korean immigrants in New Zealand.* Unpublished Doctoral Thesis, University of Canterbury, Christchurch, New Zealand.

Park, Y., Kim, H., Schwartz-Barcott, D. & Kim, J. (2002) 'The conceptual structure of Hwa-byung in middle-aged Korean women', *Health Care Women International*, vol. 23, no. 4, pp. 389–397.

Peri, K., Fanslow, J., Hand, J. & Parsons, J. (2008) *Elder Abuse and Neglect – Exploration of Risk and Protective Factors*, Families Commission, Wellington, NZ.

Phillips, J. (2007) *Care*, Polity, Cambridge.

Rubin, A. & Babbie, E.R. (2008) *Research Methods for Social Work*, 6th edn. Thomson/Brooks/Cole, Belmont, CA.

Santrock, J.W. (2011) *Life-span Development*, 13th edn, McGraw-Hill, New York.

Sisneros, J., Stakeman, C., Joyner, M.C. & Schmitz, C.L. (2008) *Critical Multicultural Social Work*, Lyceum Books, Chicago.

Statistics New Zealand (2007) *2006 Census Population and Dwellings Tables: Culture and Identity* (Table Builder). Available at: http://www.stats.govt.nz

Sung, K. (2005) *Care and Respect for the Elderly in Korea: Filial Piety in Modern Times in East Asia*, Jimoondang, Gyeonggi-do, Korea.

Tanner, D. (2010) *Managing the Ageing Experience: Learning from Older People*, Policy Press, Bristol, UK.

Tatara, T. (1999) *Understanding Elder Abuse in Minority Populations*, Brunner/Mazel, Philadelphia.

Thomas, T. (2003) 'Older migrants and their families', *Family Matters*, vol. 66 (Spring and Summer), pp. 40–44.

Treas, J. & Mazumdar, S. (2004) 'Kin-keeping and caregiving: Contributions of older people in immigrant families', *Journal of Comparative Family Studies*, vol. 35, no. 1, pp. 105–122.

World Health Organization (WHO) (2008) *A Global Response to Elder Abuse and Neglect: Building Primary Health care Capacity to Deal with the Problem Worldwide: Main Report*, Author, Geneva, Switzerland.

17

REFUGEE RESETTLEMENT

Considerations of health and wellbeing

Jay Marlowe

CHAPTER OBJECTIVES

1. *To maintain critical perspectives on risk, vulnerability and wellbeing related to people's experiences from refugee backgrounds;*
2. *To examine professional assumptions about trauma and highlight the need to understand the diverse pathways that people respond to adverse circumstances;*
3. *To discuss how a salutogenic focus can help identify potential ways of promoting health and wellbeing;*
4. *To acknowledge the need for collaborative practices when working with refugee communities.*

Introduction

The process of migrating to a new country as a refugee involves adapting to different social and cultural realities, building new hopes and dreams, and may also involve responding to experiences of loss and trauma. Having refugee status affords access to critical support and resources from the 148 states signatory to the United Nations 1951 Convention Relating to the Status of Refugees and its 1967 Protocol (UNHCR, 2012). Australia and New Zealand are signatory to this convention and offer annual permanent resettlement opportunities for approximately 13,000 and 750 refugees respectively. The settlement process often means that people from different backgrounds are essentially thrust from one cultural reality into another without much preparation for this transition. This experience may involve adapting to different norms, legal expectations and social constructions on particular phenomena such as parenting practices, gender roles, perspectives on health, meanings of community, conceptualisations of time and many others.

Whilst refugees can make invaluable contributions to their new host society, this chapter will illustrate how the refugee label can have contemporary pathologising inclinations and become a person's master status above and beyond any other marker of identity. This master status is often informed through experiences of trauma and can contribute to othering discourses in settlement contexts if not approached critically and cautiously. Through discussing a research project with resettled Sudanese men living in Australia, this chapter provides further insight into understandings of trauma, what it means to consider these experiences and to look beyond this focus to maintain a salutogenic focus towards health and wellbeing.

Literature review – health, wellbeing and critical engagement with trauma

There is not one path that refugees traverse when moving from one place to another. In particular, caution must be used when considering the applicability of the 'refugee experience' to individuals and communities, as Turton (2003) and Ager (1999) acknowledge that refugees experience a diverse multitude of backgrounds and pathways as forced migrants. Despite this awareness, it is worth noting some of the important general considerations that many refugees face or have experienced. Refugees often have had to leave their homes and communities involuntarily, which may include: leaving behind loved friends and family; taking dangerous escape paths with unknown destinations; taking very few (if any) material possessions; living in refugee camps for indefinite periods; lacking documentation that proves their identity or qualifications; not being able to say good-bye; and, importantly, not knowing if they can ever return home.

Currently, the United Nations High Commissioner for Refugees (UNHCR) estimates that there are more than 10.5 million refugees and 34 million people of concern worldwide (UNHCR, 2012). Across this diverse grouping of people, there may be more differences than similarities between what made a person a refugee, as they can come from any ethnic background, age, socioeconomic status, religion or corner of the globe. The term 'refugee' was formally defined by the 1951 United Nations Convention Relating to the Status of Refugees as:

> A person who is outside his or her country of nationality or habitual residence; has a well-founded fear of persecution because of his or her race, religion, nationality, membership of a particular social group or political opinion; and is unable to avail himself or herself of the protection of that country, or to return there, for fear of persecution. (UNHCR, 2012)

A person looking to obtain refugee status must satisfy this definition. The UNHCR notes that less than 1 per cent of the world's refugees will be offered an opportunity for resettlement in places such as Australia, New Zealand, the United

States, Canada, Scandinavia and the United Kingdom. The remaining 99 per cent either integrate into a country of first asylum, return home once it is relatively safe or live predominantly as displaced people in urban centres and refugee camps. Whilst few people from refugee backgrounds will have the chance for resettlement, this protection is absolutely vital for people who are in situations where their safety and wellbeing cannot be ensured.

The resettlement transition may mean that people's identity can come into question as they try to interpret their past sense of self in the contexts of life in a new host country. Men and women, for example, may have to reconsider gender roles and what masculinity/femininity actually means (Marlowe, 2012) and how parenting practices are negotiated (Deng and Pienaar, 2011; Milos, 2011). Children often find themselves caught between home and host cultures and must find ways to navigate competing demands and expectations on their behaviour, values and identity (Valtonen, 2008). Whilst these transitions may incorporate loss, it must also be remembered that resettlement can present many gains that may include meaningful work, education and the opportunity to live one's life without the fear of persecution.

It is important to emphasise the notion of a 'well-founded fear' in the UNHCR definition as refugees may have experienced considerable trauma. Refugees have often been exposed to a number of highly distressing and life-threatening situations including: flight from country, experiencing/witnessing violence, chronic and acute health concerns, detainment and torture and forced marches. Many autobiographical accounts document these challenging circumstances and the diversity of people's experiences (Deng *et al.*, 2005; Reid and Schofield, 2011). These stories document numerous traumatic events and, if not approached cautiously and carefully, these experiences can become a master status for refugees in resettlement contexts (i.e. refugees are traumatised people). It is these conclusions that can be very problematic because, if refugees are understood by host societies as traumatised (often through media presentations) then it is likely that they will not be given as many chances to participate in public life through employment, education and opportunities to meet the wider community living around them (Marlowe, 2010a). Part of the trauma critique, particularly from a bio-medical paradigm, is that it takes a predominantly pathological focus and does not consider other elements of a person's life that also warrant further consideration. For example, there are other important relevant areas of inquiry, such as documenting people's responses to these experiences, their sources of hope and local knowledges to healing and recovery. These understandings can help progress understandings of refugees as *victims surviving in society* towards a more inclusive focus of *peers being capable to participate within it*.

The critique of an overly dominant focus on trauma in relation to forced migration studies is not new. Whilst the experiences of trauma and loss are absolutely essential to consider and honour, there is a danger that people from refugee backgrounds can be pathologised in settlement contexts – usually in the form of negative mental health outcomes (Pupavac, 2008). This critique on trauma and refugees occurs in fields such as psychiatry (Bracken *et al.*, 1997), anthropology

(Malkki, 1995), sociology (Zetter, 2007), psychology (Miller *et al.*, 2006) and social work (Briskman and Fiske, 2009; Kohli, 2006; Westoby and Ingamells, 2010). These authors are not denying the importance of understanding the impacts of trauma in people's lives. Rather, the argument is that much of current research and practice takes an unnecessarily narrow focus on trauma when it could be cast wider to include notions of wellbeing alongside the impacts of adverse experiences. Whilst having traumatic experiences is a risk factor for negative mental health outcomes, the forced migration literature generally demonstrates that the overwhelming vast majority of refugees do not develop long-term psychiatric problems (Murray *et al.*, 2008; Summerfield, 2005). The focus, therefore, can extend beyond trauma to consider how it is that so many people are able to maintain their health and wellbeing despite what they have been through and how they have reduced the impacts of trauma in their lives (White, 2006). This salutogenic focus makes it possible to move beyond (but not discount) the experiences of trauma to also consider people's pathways to healing.

This chapter presents a research project with South Sudanese men who had resettled in Adelaide, South Australia. There have been two major civil wars between North and South Sudan that account for more than forty years of protracted conflict since 1956. In 2011, South Sudan became an independent country and emerged from decades of fighting that has created one of the world's largest diasporic communities (see Johnson, 2003, for an account of South Sudan's history and associated civil wars). From these experiences, millions of South Sudanese people have been exposed to considerable trauma in different forms. There are now estimates that more than 30,000 Sudanese people have resettled in Australia and represent one of the country's fastest growing groups according to the last census (Robinson, 2011). This study looked to collaboratively understand how South Sudanese men conceptualise trauma, and importantly, how they are able to respond to these experiences to highlight their agency, local knowledges and capacities to make meaning in the wake of challenging circumstances.

Research design

This study involved interviewing 24 Sudanese men who had resettled in Adelaide as former refugees and necessitated an ongoing interaction with their community over several years (Marlowe, 2009; Marlowe, 2010b). The in-depth interviews documented the men's perspectives on trauma and their experiences of forced migration and resettlement. The interviews were conducted in English, and the participants often held positions of community leadership. Analysis was carried out through a process of initial and focused coding, writing memos, theoretical sampling and using the constant comparative method as per constructivist grounded theory (Charmaz, 2006). In total, 70 interviews with the 24 participants were conducted. This information was triangulated through ethnographic field data from attending numerous community events by invitation (celebrations, church services and mourning services).

Returning to the previous discussion on how people may carry different social constructions from those of the researcher and/or broader society, this study was built upon on a constructionist epistemological stance, which maintains that meaning is neither objectively known nor subjectively interpreted. Rather, meaning is *constructed* as individuals (both the participants and researcher) encounter their world through the interpreted and discursive perspectives of culture, family, friends, society and history (Schwandt, 2003). This perspective becomes salient with the South Sudanese people living in Australia as they emphasise different understandings between their home country and Australia. The constructionist stance further highlights the need to elevate Sudanese voices, where possible, to capture their perspectives instead of relying upon imposed professional and popular discourses about them.

Participant voices on trauma and responding to it

There is no question that participants in this study were exposed to significant experiences of trauma. Many had lived for years in refugee camps and had been displaced far from friends and family whom, to this day, do not know if they perished in the civil war. One man speaks about being one of the 'Lost Boys' who had to walk thousands of kilometres across deserts to find a relatively safe haven in a refugee camp across Sudan's border:

> When the attack came to my community, and I feel my life threatened, I ran and my kin ran in a different direction, and that was the way to separation. From there we hid. There was no food and we went to Ethiopia.

This journey across to Ethiopia (and others went to Kenya, Egypt and other neighbouring countries) was extremely dangerous with uncertain outcomes. This experience almost inevitably incorporated elements of loss as it required leaving behind important friends, family, familiar landscapes and traditions. Once these people found relatively safe havens in the refugee camps, there were limited basic resources, inadequate housing, poor education facilities and few, or no, employment pathways.

Whilst these experiences were common in refugee camps, many participants were keen to highlight that the limited opportunities for self-determination were often replicated in settlement contexts:

> You know, because the most important thing is that our people are from a very different background. The experiences that they have been through are the hardest ones. And the experience that they are getting here [in Australia], for some it is worse than what they were experiencing [in the refugee camps].

A significant challenge for resettlement in Australia has been the experience of discrimination. Many participants noted difficulties in finding work, making friends outside their community and also feeling that they did not belong within the wider Australian society. In many respects, what participants noted as being the hardest experiences to endure in their forced migration journey were similar in resettlement contexts: separation from loved ones, discrimination, unemployment and challenges securing an education.

Many of participant statements thus illustrate that understandings of trauma are not always what is often generally assumed as the most difficult when considering the 'refugee experience' (i.e. forced marches, experiences of violence, of being child soldiers, torture etc.). Whilst these experiences would be identified as traumatic (and important to acknowledge), participants were keen to express that the limited opportunities to pursue and improve their future for themselves and their families were often the most difficult. Correspondingly, the men noted social and agential responses that helped them to work through traumatic experiences.

Responding to trauma – community resilience, education and employment

When Sudanese people arrived in Australia, they invested in finding opportunities for greater self-determination and the ability to contribute to their families, community and the wider society (see Harris and Marlowe, 2011). They placed their hopes on resettlement, and their comments on community support, education and employment provide insight as to how people are able to respond to traumatic experiences in meaningful ways.

The community presents a clear social pathway of responding to trauma; as its members often came together to mutually support one another. This social connection was highly evident at community events in which the group helped to shoulder the burden of individual difficulties.

> So problems become a shared kind of community problem so it is not an individual problem. When you take problem from an individual problem to a community problem, you have lessened that effect of it. (Participant 24)

This collective value is evidenced by a Sudanese proverb repeated in interviews and at community events: *a problem shared is a problem halved*. Respondents consistently maintained the value of community with respect to resolving problems and spending time together as a resonant approach to mediating trauma (past and present). I directly observed these responses at community celebrations, church services and gatherings to discuss local issues. When a person died in their community, there would often be more than 100 people present to support the bereaved. The role of the church served to bring people together where they could not only talk about the past but their strategies and hopes for a happier future. In these forums, elders would share their cultural knowledge and offer stories to give sustenance and advice to help their community respond to current settlement challenges.

Alongside community responses, most participants highlight the importance of paid work as a man's role in Sudanese society is to provide financially for the family. Limited opportunities for employment can challenge a person's self-concept and ability to support their family and community. Correspondingly, participants identified education as a means to self-sufficiency, supporting family through skilled employment and the hope for a better future. This opportunity gave participants hope. One participant acknowledges the importance of education and how it can help to 'build you up':

> Without education you will not have a good job. Without education you have got no word to say in your society or the community. Because education helps you to see and think different things, it **builds you up**.

This 'building up' provides the opportunity, or at least the hope, of being able to make a difference and improve one's life in future contexts. 'Building up' is a present- and future-focused expression. Rather than speaking of themselves as damaged in some way from war trauma, participants emphasise the injustice of not receiving an education and how it impacts their lives today. These findings are not suggesting that negative mental health outcomes arising from trauma are not possibly present. However, it does highlight that, alongside considering people's past traumatic experiences is the need to consider the practicalities of living in the present, which may include helping them to negotiate issues such as affordable housing, sourcing meaningful employment, becoming confident in the English language and securing educational training. Once these considerations are more fully met, people can often find their own ways to respond to past adversities.

Discussion – implications for social work practice

The participant statements arising from this work, and many others, carry important messages for social work practice. The multiple dislocations of the refugee experience often only represent a starting point to consider what is often uncritically labelled as 'traumatic'. As the participants emphasised, the most challenging experiences were not the initial events from forced migration that is usually the focus within the media (experiences of violence, destitution, child soldiers, etc.). Rather, the most difficult aspects were the playing out of their experiences over time usually in terms of limited opportunities to exercise their own self-determination and to support their respective community. The interplay of context and response, rather than just focussing on traumatic events themselves, provides the awareness that engaging with trauma can be embedded in a process which necessitates an examination of the past *and* present (Marlowe and Adamson, 2011). Maintaining a holistic and collaborative incorporation of a refugee's experiences and perspectives therefore provides a solid foundation for addressing the complexities of trauma within a salutogenic and wellbeing focus.

The Sudanese community has numerous pathways for responding to past and present difficulties. It reinforces their local knowledges about healing and recovery and demonstrates that the social work profession can also play integral roles in working towards people's hopes and aspirations. Participants repeatedly noted how, in resettlement contexts, the hope for a better future has helped them to work through and move beyond traumatic experiences. Social work practice with refugee communities incorporates the question of where each professional is situated on a non-linear continuum from working towards practical outcomes (such as securing employment and negotiating new systems in resettlement contexts), clinically based therapeutic interventions, addressing discrimination, community capacity-building initiatives to policy-level implementation. The fact that our work can occur on so many levels and numerous fields of practice highlights the need for practitioners to avoid the dichotomy between private/public domains and interpersonal/structural dynamics. Our work is not about exclusively embracing one or the other. Rather, it calls for more coordinated and collaborative ways of working together (professionally and within communities) so that the 'big step' of social justice is informed on the ground and supported from broader structural analyses and actions.

These conclusions point to the need to consider what is meant when we talk of a salutogenic perspective. The term 'salutogenesis' was coined by medical sociologist Aaron Antovoksy in 1979 who suggested that the primary emphasis of health care should be on the development of *promoting health* rather than placing the major attention on pathology or disease. Such a shift meant that, instead of starting from a disease or problem-focussed perspective, the beginning point was actually upon looking at people's and communities' health potential and to support pro-active measures that would promote and create conditions of optimal social, physical and mental wellbeing (see Becker *et al.*, 2010, p. 32). Salutogenic principles do not deny the presence or importance of pathology, although its health focus means that it looks for the precursors to wellbeing rather than having a primary emphasis on reducing risk and treating disease. There is certainly value in a wellbeing focus as this chapter has highlighted how refugees can often be predominantly ensconced within a 'traumatic' purview. A salutogenic perspective with refugee groups, however, requires a balancing act as taking a strict focus on wellbeing may potentially marginalise people's very real experiences of trauma. The challenge is determining when, and if, it is appropriate to discuss a person's traumatic experience(s) and how this process can be done in safe, collaborative and respectful ways.

A salutogenic focus also requires thinking beyond health – or at least going beyond how it is most typically viewed. This shift means taking into account issues such as housing, education, employment, relations with the wider society, the lived experience of social policy and how the environment around us can have a direct relationship with our notions of wellbeing. Ager and Strang (2008) wrote a paper on refugee integration and presented an associated framework that is arguably the most-referenced paper in the study of forced migration. They note that successful integration needs to include the foundations of health, education, employment, linguistic competencies and housing. People also need meaningful relationships with people from their own communities and also with the wider society. And finally, they suggest that all of this needs to be underpinned by a rights framework and citizenship whereby people are able to participate as peers in civil society. A salutogenic focus with refugees needs to consider these additional domains in order to critically evaluate the strengths that exist within refugee communities, to consider areas that need further capacity building and identify the potential sites of oppression that may be present within this framework. In this sense, salutogenic and pathogenic perspectives can be complementary when social work adopts a praxis that critically evaluates professional and organisational practices.

As evidenced in the participants' transcripts and in the broader literature, refugee communities do not choose to be welfare dependent, unemployed or isolated from the broader society. They speak about the importance of jobs, education, securing a better life for their children and a sincere desire to contribute to public life. They iterate the importance of having stronger relationships outside their cultural community and how they would further embrace opportunities to participate as peers in civil society. These comments reinforce the assertion that refugee communities (and their individual members), the government and wider society all play important roles in creating opportunities for meaningful settlement.

Realising the empowerment of community also goes beyond building the Sudanese people's capacities. We too, as social work practitioners and researchers, need further capacity – it is not a one-way interaction and highlights that work with refugees is not just about understanding their experiences; it also necessitates self-reflection. The discourse about supporting people coming from refugee backgrounds needs a more profound conceptualisation so that it is about a mutual exercise of working together and acknowledging the need to reflect critically upon our own personal and professional assumptions and practices. Whilst there is much rhetoric that espouses words of empowerment, fostering resilience and community capacity building – actual practice and policy-related decisions can fall short of such endeavours if our practice is not reflexively and critically embraced (Mowbray, 2005).

Whilst acknowledging that some people experience adverse mental health outcomes from traumatic events, the wellbeing literature that focuses on health provides an important reminder that most refugees do not suffer from long-term psychological problems nor are they irrevocably damaged people. The participants' comments from this study underscore their multiple pathways of responding to trauma and illustrate that the different refugee and resettlement experiences that people carry with them are best understood from within their own narratives. This awareness reinforces the necessity to collaboratively acknowledge and honour the trauma story whilst at the same time to look for stories of agency, hope and survival.

Conclusion

The social work profession is well placed to recognise and address both the concerns and wellbeing of people who are potentially vulnerable and marginalised within society. It is within this landscape that people's private pains can be seen as public issues (Mills, 1959; Schwartz, 1969). By thinking outside the domain of personal expressions of pain and trauma, it becomes possible to consider the larger social, cultural, political and economic structures that impact upon people's daily lives. Recognising the politics of power and who has a voice, such an analysis is critical when working as practitioners and researchers with refugee populations.

Overall, this study echoes other scholars' voices who also call for us to ask critical questions about our assumptions of trauma and how our training informs associated responses (Briskman and Fiske, 2009; Dominelli, 2002). There is no one 'refugee experience' – rather it is a question of the diversity of every person's experience and history. It is also necessary to acknowledge that, whilst the refugee experience almost inevitably incurs experiences of loss and trauma, we must recognise that a traumatic experience and a traumatised person are very different things. People have amazing indigenous knowledges and capacities to respond to the transgressions of the past. Our professional knowledge base provides a secure foundation to critically self-reflect, whether we are migrants/refugees ourselves or not, and offers an important reminder to first engage and listen to people who may carry different histories, traditions and experiences from our own.

QUESTIONS FOR REFLECTION

1. How do the people you work with conceptualise trauma in their own lives? Do these constructions fit with your practice wisdom, assumptions and professional training? What informs your own perspectives on trauma, health, wellbeing and identity?
2. In what unique ways do people from refugee and migrant backgrounds challenge and respond to the effects of trauma? How might a salutogenic focus assist in identifying these responses and help optimise the pre-cursors to social, physical, mental and spiritual wellbeing? How might this awareness relate to individual, family, community, cultural and structural based analyses?
3. How can social workers and other allied professionals better work with people and communities from refugee backgrounds with regard to responding to trauma and promoting health and wellbeing in holistic, collaborative and empowering ways?

References

Ager, A. (1999) 'Perspectives on the refugee experience', in *Refugees: Perspectives on the Experience of Forced Migration*, A. Ager (ed), Continuum, New York, pp. 1–23.

Ager, A. & Strang, A. (2008) 'Understanding integration: A conceptual framework', *Journal of Refugee Studies*, vol. 21, no. 1, pp. 166–191.

Becker, C., Glascoff, M. & Felts, W. (2010) 'Salutogenesis 30 years later: Where do we go from here?', *International Electronic Journal of Health Education*, vol. 13, no. 1, pp. 25–32.

Bracken, P., Giller, J. & Summerfield, D. (1997) 'Rethinking mental health work with survivors of wartime violence and refugees', *Journal of Refugee Studies*, vol. 10, no. 4, pp. 431–442.

Briskman, L. & Fiske, L. (2009) 'Working with refugees', in *Social Work: Contexts and Practice*, 2nd edn. M. Connolly & L. Harms (eds), Oxford University Press, Oxford.

Charmaz, K. (2006) *Constructing Grounded Theory*, Sage, London.

Deng, A., Deng, B., Ajak, B. & Bernstein, J. (2005) *They Poured Fire on Us from the Sky: The True Story of Three Lost Boys from Sudan*, Public Affairs, New York.

Deng, S.A. & Pienaar, F. (2011) 'Positive parenting: Integrating Sudanese traditions and New Zealand styles of parenting. An evaluation of Strategies with Kids – Information for Parents (SKIP)', *Australasian Review of African Studies*, vol. 32, no. 2, pp. 160–179.

Dominelli, L. (2002) *Anti-oppressive Social Work Theory and Practice*, Palgrave Macmillan, New York.

Harris, V. & Marlowe, J. (2011) 'Hard yards, high hopes: The educational challenges of African refugee students in Australia', *International Journal of Teaching Learning and Higher Education*, vol. 23, no. 2, pp. 186–196.

Johnson, D. (2003) *The Root Causes of Sudan's Civil Wars*, James Currey Publishers, Oxford.

Kohli, R. (2006) 'The sound of silence: Listening to what unaccompanied asylum-seeking children say and do not say', *British Journal of Social Work*, vol. 36, no. 5, pp. 707–721.

Malkki, L. (1995) 'Refugees and exile: From "refugee studies" to the national order of things', *Annual Review of Anthropology*, vol. 24, pp. 495–523.

Marlowe, J. (2009) 'Accessing "authentic" knowledge: Being and doing with the Sudanese community', *Australian Community Psychologist*, vol. 21, no. 1, pp. 39–49.

Marlowe, J. (2010a) 'Beyond the discourse of trauma: Shifting the focus on Sudanese refugees', *Journal of Refugee Studies*, vol. 23, no. 2, pp. 183–198.

Marlowe, J. (2010b) 'Using a narrative approach of double listening in research contexts', *International Journal of Narrative Therapy and Community Work*, vol. 3, pp. 43–53.

Marlowe, J. (2012) '"Walking the line": Southern Sudanese masculinities and reconciling one's past with the present', *Ethnicities*, vol. 12, no. 1, pp. 50–66.

Marlowe, J. & Adamson, C. (2011) 'Teaching trauma: Critically engaging with a troublesome term. *Social Work Education*, vol. 30, no. 6, pp. 623–634.

Miller, K., Kulkarni, M. & Kushner, H. (2006) 'Beyond trauma focused psychiatric epidemiology: Bridging research and practice with war affected populations. *American Journal of Orthopsychiatry*, vol. 76, no. 4, pp. 409–422.

Mills, C. W. (1959) *The Sociological Imagination*, Oxford University Press, London.

Milos, D. (2011) 'South Sudanese communities and Australian family law: A clash of systems', *Australasian Review of African Studies*, vol. 32, no. 2, pp. 143–159.

Mowbray, M. (2005). 'Community capacity building or state opportunism?', *Community Development Journal*, vol. 40, no. 3, pp. 255–264.

Murray, K., Davidson, G. & Schweitzer, R. (2008) *Psychological Wellbeing of Refugees Resettling in Australia*, The Australian Psychological Society Ltd, Melbourne.

Pupavac, V. (2008) 'Refugee advocacy, traumatic representations and political disenchantment', *Government and Opposition*, vol. 43, no. 2, pp. 270–292.

Reid, A. & Schofield, H. (2011) *Goodbye Sarajevo: A True Story of Courage, Love and Survival*, Bloomsbury, London.

Robinson, J. (2011) 'Sudanese heritage and living in Australia: Implications of demography for individual and community resilience', *Australasian Review of African Studies*, vol. 32, no. 2, pp. 25–56.

Schwandt, T. (2003) 'Three epistemological stances for qualitative inquiry', in *The Landscape of Qualitative Research*, 2nd edn. N. Denzin & Y. Lincoln (eds), Sage Publications, London.

Schwartz, W. (1969) 'Private troubles and public issues: One social work job or two', in *Perspectives on Social Welfare: An Introductory Anthology*, P. Weinberger (ed), Macmillan, New York.

Summerfield, D.A.H.S.L. (2005) 'Coping with the aftermath of trauma: NICE guidelines on post-traumatic stress disorder have fundamental flaw', *British Medical Journal*, vol. 331, no. 50. doi:10.1136/bmj.331.7507.50-a

Turton, D. (2003) 'Conceptualising forced migration', *Refugee Studies Centre, Working Paper Series No. 12*, Queen Elizabeth House, International Development Centre, University of Oxford, Oxford.

United Nations High Commissioner for Refugees (UNHCR) (2012) *UNHCR Global Appeal 2012–2013*, Author, Geneva, Switzerland.

Valtonen, K. (2008) *Social Work and Migration: Immigrant and Refugee Settlement and Integration*, Ashgate, Farnham, UK.

Westoby, P. & Ingamells, A. (2010). 'A critically informed perspective of working with resettling refugee groups in Australia', *British Journal of Social Work*, vol. 40, no. 6, pp. 1759–1776.

White, M. (2006) 'Working with people who are suffering the consequences of multiple trauma: A narrative perspective', in *Trauma: Narrative Responses to Traumatic Experience*, Denborough, D. (ed), Dulwich Centre Publication, Adelaide Australia, pp. 25–85.

Zetter, R. (2007) 'More labels, fewer refugees: Remaking the refugee label in an era of globalization', *Journal of Refugee Studies*, vol. 20, no. 2, pp. 172–192.

18

MENTAL HEALTH, SOCIAL WORK AND PROFESSIONALISM

Selma Macfarlane

CHAPTER OBJECTIVES

1. To present alternative constructions of professionalism from voices that are not always heard;
2. To invite consideration of the assumptions underpinning our understanding of mental (ill) health and our role as professionals;
3. To consider the potential value of alternative constructions of social work practice and professionalism in mental health.

Introduction

Critical social work perspectives in relation to mental health encompass a rich and thought-provoking expanse of ideas and practice possibilities. When considering the underpinnings of a 'critical' approach to social work, there are some key concepts. These include: openness to questioning assumptions; valuing diverse forms and sources of knowledge; concern with how our everyday actions contribute to personal and social change; and an acknowledgement of how social structures, language and discourse create power relations. There is an emphasis on respectful, dialogical relationships, acknowledgment of the fluid nature of identity and the significance of context. Such an approach draws on traditional critical theory with its focus on structural inequality and social change, as well as more recent thinking associated with postmodernism and poststructuralism. Walsh observes 'the postmodern call to multiple perspectives, to the critique of master narratives, to multiple truths and diverse voices is indeed familiar territory for social workers' (2011, p. 354). Critical approaches underpin social work's unique contribution to mental health practice in a field which is still strongly dominated by biomedical models of understanding health and illness.

Exploring these conceptual underpinnings and their relevance to mental health draws us into an ongoing and wide-reaching journey of critical reflection. For the purposes of this chapter, positioned in the research section of this book, my theoretical discussion is placed alongside the voices of individuals who shared their stories with me for my PhD research project. These voices provide insights from the experiences of workers and clients that challenge us to think about the nature of professional practice. I draw particularly on the writings of Amy Rossiter who suggests that social workers embrace 'unsettled practice', an approach that requires we 'suspend assumptions, place what we think we know at risk and leave ourselves open to revelation from the Other' (2011, pp. 12–13). She observes that, by 'privileging the question over answers . . . we can guard ourselves from the seductive belief that the acquisition of knowledge, and therefore answers about people, makes us professional' (2011, p. 13).

An example from research

Working in a residential psychiatric disability support service, based – at the time – on therapeutic community principles, drew my attention to the diverse ways people experienced such a programme in the context of their life journey. Residents were voluntary, had a psychiatric diagnosis, and were aged between 20 and 35; the average length of stay was around 12 months, with a structured exiting process. The weekly programme involved therapeutic and task-oriented group work, one to one counselling and support, body work, community meetings, outings and household responsibilities. The support staff was multi-disciplinary, including social workers, occupational therapists and psychologists. I was struck by how significantly everyone – staff and residents – was involved and affected by the 'culture of inquiry' fostered within the programme setting, which aimed at people having an opportunity to get back on track after psychiatric upheaval.

My research question was simple: how does living in a residential support service impact on an individual's life? Six hundred pages of interview transcripts later, I was swimming (or sinking) in wonderful and daunting complexity. I described my research approach as naturalistic: after receiving the approval of the community I engaged in approximately 50 loosely structured (taped) interviews with residents, former residents, staff and former staff. Transcribing each interview I was immersed in worlds of meaning-making and reflection; my thematic analysis grew and deepened as hunches I had started with expanded into new areas of consideration. One of these areas, and the focus for this chapter, is the nature of professionalism, within the specific context of the programme.

At the same time as I was involved with this research project, I was teaching in a university setting and deepening my understanding of how critical approaches based on structural analysis might be enriched by postmodern and poststructural thinking. These concepts began to inform my thinking around the narratives I was gathering.

I acknowledge my use of limiting language by referring to some people as residents and others as staff; while those roles were relevant at the time, they do not capture the complexity and dynamism of individuals who may occupy very different roles today.

Professionalism in social work

Professions are often defined through features such as possession of a distinctive body of knowledge and expertise, gained via legitimated pathways, incorporating a value dimension or mission of service, often expressed in a professional code of ethics (Healy, 2000; Ife, 2002). These features of professionalism are considered important in protecting persons from harm and creating accountability and guidance for practitioners.

Despite these beneficent characteristics, social work's relationship to professionalism has been debated. Critical/radical and community development approaches and more recently postmodern thinking have problematised the meaning of professionalism in social work, suggesting that some aspects of professionalism may be oppressive. In particular, reductionist and objectifying potentials of the professional gaze, the notion of professional certainty and exclusive possession of expert knowledge, and the mandate to fit individuals into preordained categories have been subject to questioning from a critical perspective (Adams *et al.*, 2002; Burkett and McDonald, 2005; Fook, 2002; Rossiter, 2001, 2011).

The professional gaze

Referring to the work of Foucault, Mullaly (1997, p. 143) suggests the professional gaze engenders 'observations [that] are not mere passing looks' but normalising gazes with the power to construct others as objects of professional knowledge. The 'gazer' (the professional) is positioned as the expert, and the 'gazed upon' (the client, patient or service user) constructed and positioned as relatively passive recipients to be fitted into the categorisations made available by the knowledge system of the gazer.

In relation to mental health, while psychiatric diagnosis and treatment can be a source of relief, there is also potential for the diagnosed individual to become 'a resource, but not an agent in the making of accounts of her behaviour' (Smith, 1990, p. 91). These ideas resonate with what some participants said about the disempowering nature of the mental health system:

> I had such a horrible experience in hospital. . . . the way you're treated . . . it's like you've done something wrong because you're unwell. . . . you don't get any insight into your illness and you definitely don't feel cared for.

. . . a lot of the issues for people with mental illness is that they've become isolated and disconnected, and DONE TO. . . . they're given medication by their
doctor, . . . counselling by somebody. . . . and they are put into a rec program
. . . Their sense of agency is diminished, of being able to DO on the world.

Producing order out of the chaos and complexity of individual experience, in
accordance with disciplinary or organisational meaning systems, is a key task of any
professional (Smith, 1990). The practice of assessment, central to the social work
process, is aimed at reducing uncertainty and providing explanations for problems
which can then be addressed (Potter, 1996, p. 236). We need to make sense of
people's experiences, in order to provide a focus for intervention. From a critical perspective, however, we need to be mindful of the limitations of our 'factual'
descriptions and the way in which they erase the identity of the knowledge producer through a process Potter (1996, pp. 150) calls constructing 'out-thereness'.
The social worker as expert becomes an 'external validator of meaning and identity'
and 'the more constraints in terms of externally defined meanings . . . the more
limited are the range of possibilities for self-narration' (Butler *et al.,* 2007, p. 292).
The mental health system, with its heavy biomedical overlay, is particularly rife with
possibilities for the restriction of self-narration to occur and for the client/service
user to 'become' their 'illness'.

The term 'expertosis' was coined by Rosemary Smart, a New Zealand social
worker whose daughter committed suicide after many experiences in the psychiatric system, to describe 'the deadly gap between professional expertise and lived
reality' that develops when professionals believe their knowledge is the only knowledge (1994, p. 2). Rossiter (2011) suggests a 'deliberate "suspicion" of professional
knowledge' may prevent the 'loss of the human' to our systems of knowledge, as our
representations of the client are always partial (2011, p. 9). Assessment, then involves
the construction of professional narratives, which are complex, partial, open to
change and dialogically created (Fook, 2002, p. 124). One staff member expressed
his reservations about the increasing expectation for PDS services to frame their
workers as experts who can fix things:

> What that makes us . . . is that we become experts who have the knowledge
> of a way to live . . . which is one of the great illusions of what we do. . . .
> My hope is that someone can get into contact what THEY want. . . . Not as
> objects of study, or objects of my knowledge, or objects of the state saying
> 'these are the outcomes for rehabilitation programs' . . . to be able to be a
> speaking subject not one that just has a number of terms about their malady
> from others.

While the professional gaze can limit and objectify, critical workers may also
harness it in ways that are experienced by others as empowering (Healy, 2000).
Podvoll (1983, p. 183) suggests the helping role can be one of uncovering a person's
'history of sanity' – to use one's professional gaze as a form of alertness to 'islands of

clarity' when a person's intrinsic health emerges. Barham and Hayward (1991) refer to the notion of 'personhood' that draws practitioners to share in the process of bringing into 'the light aspects that are obscured in a framework that focuses more narrowly on the disorder' (1991, p. 3); what Estroff in her seminal text *Making It Crazy* (1981) called the 'persistence of person' that calls out to be recognised under the 'crazy' identity. Comments from research participants affirmed the professional gaze was useful to them at times.

> It's important for workers to be "all eyes and ears" . . . noticing the person, what they're going through . . . when to approach them and when not to.
> One thing I've discovered . . . is that you can't see yourself going down . . . I've been helping a few people out, with their illness, and it's like they don't see it. I didn't see it. . . . I would like somebody out there to be able to tell me, not so much 'you're going off the rails' – that's the last thing you want to hear, but . . . to remind me of my coping mechanisms.

Professional power can be exercised repressively or productively through our interactions with others; the key to understanding power in any one context is 'to appreciate how it is expressed, experienced and created by different people' (Fook, 2002, p. 53). This requires that we critically reflect on our own practice and the discourses in which we are positioned as helpers.

Professional power

> This omnipotent fantasy. . . . I can't think of any staff who I've worked with [as a manager] . . . who didn't have a struggle with this fantasy, including myself. . . everyone who works in an organisation like this is impacted by [that desire to help] . . . the clients are so desperately wanting improvement in their life. . . . consequently [workers]can become quite unrealistic in inter- preting their role . . . to actually feel that you can impact on people's lives in a substantial way – that is very dangerous – you have to look at all of your assumptions in doing that.

Writing in the 1970s, Sanford observed that 'the humbling admission' that the real healing power comes from individuals themselves 'saves the humanity of the therapist [sic] . . . and also rescues the integrity and dignity of the client' (1977, p. 84). The pro- cess of 'dethroning' oneself does not imply abandoning professional knowledge and skill, but positioning oneself somewhat differently (Duncan, 1998). Saleeby (1994, p. 355) describes a 'helper myth' that underlies typical worker–client interactions, as the worker 'clumsily or deftly imposes his or her version of the situation' while clients 'surrender' or 'repress' their own story. As critical social workers, this is the opposite of what we intend to do. Two former residents described their experience:

> I always felt I was not as worthy as the professionals in the place. And this idea also, that it didn't end when you left [the programme] . . . it carried on

through your whole life . . . this feeling that I've done something, or something's happened to me in my life, which for the rest of my life has cut me off, has separated me from everybody else. And that's just not the idea that you want to give to people who have a mental illness . . . that's precisely the thing that should be prevented. . . . It's just another form of stigma.

One of my biggest problems was the staff resident dichotomy. It's very hard to set up structures like that [the programme] where there aren't power differentials . . . the [line between] the professional and you . . . you are actually spending a lot of time [being exposed to]. . . . You can say that whole process of delineating and dealing with boundaries is useful, but . . . I found it more frustrating.

Social workers are inevitably involved in power relationships; Rossiter suggests the crucial question is: 'How can we best handle our position at sites where power and help are interwoven?' (1996, p. 29) The non-egalitarian nature of worker-client relationships is to some extent unavoidable in terms of accountability, as the professional's role carries special moral and ethical responsibilities (White, 1995, p. 70). Given this inherent inequality, White suggests that workers must do whatever they can 'to make it very difficult for that power differential to have a toxic or negative effect' (White, 1995, p. 70); this was encapsulated by a staff member who commented:

It's how we work with it [the power differential] that's important, and the resident's experience of that difference as a supportive, non-threatening help, rather than being violated. Which is, I imagine, since they've all been in the psych system, their predominant experience of power. . . . Support, by its very nature is in some ways tied with the fact that we're in a certain role – the residents might use different words – perhaps safety.

If, in a Foucauldian sense, knowledge is power, being the holder of 'legitimate' knowledge is itself a powerful position. Monopolising knowledge and skills, and hence maintaining the position of powerful knower may be experienced as disempowering by service users, and, as Ife (2002) suggests, can reproduce relationships in which structural inequality is reinforced. Knowledge sharing, on the other hand, can potentially be an antidote to the negative effects of expert status and power (Hugman, 1998; Leonard, 1997; Rossiter, 1996). It can be difficult at times – and even feel risky – for workers to consider how to share knowledge. Several former residents commented on the notion of knowledge sharing, in ways that might be challenging for workers:

The idea that we have to be protected from [what a theorist has suggested] because it might not work – like 'I have to protect them [residents] from this information somehow,' is quite ridiculous. . . . What use are the articles in the library, if as a consumer none of it filters down to you?

I always got the feeling that the wool was being pulled over your eyes . . . because things weren't put openly in front of you. . . . For some people this wouldn't have been an issue ... but for me, I would have appreciated [being told by staff] 'this is a psychodynamic approach, these are the values behind it, which are not the values everybody believes in. This is such and such's view and he thinks you get this from this'. . . . Not 'this is life, this is just as it is'.

Positioning oneself professionally

It was not just the sharing of knowledge that residents and former residents reflected on, it was the sharing of human companionship and reciprocity, and at times, discomfort with professionals retaining the 'power not to be known' (Podvoll, 1990, p. 265).

> [I]n some cases, with professionalism, the roles were so defined, that it was just almost an excuse sometimes, I found, to not have to input personally into a situation. . . . staff would go back to saying 'oh, that's interesting that you feel like that.' And the old I'm-not-answering-anything-because-I'm-not-interested-in-your-ideas psychiatry chat that you get form some mental health professionals.

The non-reciprocal nature of worker–client relationships has been a long-standing feature of professional practice, challenged from time to time by feminist, community development and other social work theorists and practitioners. Almond (1974) discusses the impacts of what he refers to as a one-way flow of nurturance, which 'fixes a difference in role definition of staff and patient. . . . one is well and caring, the other is sick and needy:' such a polarised relationship, he suggests restricts possibilities for change (1974, p. 350). This was an issue a number of participants commented upon:

> It was awful . . . and I never got used to someone being your friend one minute and then clocking off work at five o'clock.
> [professionals] have always helped me, but they won't take my help back . . . so it's hurtful to both.

These are quite challenging and evocative comments. Are we 'allowed' to be changed by our interactions with clients, and if so, what sort of change might this be? Deegan comments that it is particularly unhelpful for staff to assume an attitude of assisting people in the 'abnormal world' to fit into the 'normal world,' creating an us/them dichotomy, where clients are expected to 'do all the changing and growing' (1988, p. 18). As we attempt to fit clients' experiences and problems into a 'circumscribed knowledge frame' we create subject positions for both worker and client in which the client is 'expected to learn, change or be healed' (Leung, 2010, p. 476). What might it mean to share the power of being the well ones; sharing a responsibility to learn, grow and change as a result of our interactions?

While 'real' professionals 'are generally seen as impervious to the effects' of interactions with service users, we are undoubtedly changed through our relationships and interactions; we 'need to stay open to this change and to the constant recon-struction that comes with it, in our understanding of who we are as social workers' (Butler *et al.*, 2007, pp. 294–295). Deegan suggests that ethical relationships between professionals and clients are empowering when both are available to 'be moved by the thoughts, perceptions and feelings of the other' (1990, p. 309). An experienced person then – a 'professional' – is someone 'who, because of the many experiences he [sic] has had and the knowledge he has drawn from them, is particularly well equipped to have new experiences and to learn from them' (Rossiter, 1996, p. 149, referring to the work of Hans-Georg Gadamer, 1992).

In this construction, professional expertise shifts from 'something acquired by an expert' to something held by an 'experienced person; who exercises responsibility by remaining open to new experiences and new understanding' (Rossiter, 1996, p. 33). Smart (1994, p. 9) says she has become 'less and less an expert and more and more a learner, having 'moved from *owning knowledge to owning my own knowl-edge.*' This learner stance can feel unsettling, as it seems to contradict professional and socio-political imperatives. However, it is precisely an 'unsettled' social work practice that Rossiter calls for: rather than seeking to apply the certainty of expert knowledge, the worker adopts a stance of not knowing, being open to the 'unset-tling of one's world by the call of the Other' (2011, p. 6).

After many years' experience as a counsellor, Watkins observes that 'what we are as a person, and the quality of our human presence with our clients may be a more powerful healing influence than we know . . . simple human companionship may indeed be the most potent healing factor of all' (1996, p. 41). Participants in the research project made the following comments in the course of our interviews:

> . . . when I often found the staff most useful is when you'd maybe be relaxed, and just in a relaxed setting, and you'd share some moments or just have a friendly conversation or something.
>
> I remember a few times I went shopping with a worker and it was really enjoyable. . . . just that half hour – I felt like a totally different person. It's important for your confidence . . . just going for coffee and maybe talking about something else, besides your problems.

Rather than something to fear, 'mutual vulnerability' between client and worker 'seems to be a crucial factor in how two people can affect each other . . . we could say that vulnerable means able to connect' (Welwood, 1983 p. 60). When asked what she thought was the most important role for staff, one resident commented:

> I know that I really appreciate it when [name] comes up and just sits in the smokers' room and has a cigarette and just chats. . . . She talks about things that are real . . . like person to person . . . and she'll admit . . . sometimes that she has vulnerabilities. . . . And I really appreciate it. I feel really safe with people when they do that. . . . I reckon that the best counsellors are those that acknowledge their own struggles . . . within reason.

At the same time, workers and services need, and are expected, to provide containment, structure and safety: worker authority, if critically enacted, can be used to create and sustain an empowering environment (Healy, 2000; Fook, 2002). In a residential programme this is particularly highlighted: the staff are primarily responsible for creating an atmosphere of 'tolerance, respect and caring', which everyone involved contributes to, but which the staff are primarily responsible for (Schimmel, 1997, p. 124). The following observations came from a resident and staff member, respectively:

> The staff play a really important role in making this house feel, for me, safe ... emotionally safe and supported. ... this is really important because I am [able to] feel pleasure in my physical environment.
>
> The boundaries are like an amoeba – if you poke at the amoeba's boundary, it moves away, but it doesn't mean the boundary is gone – the boundaries in the program are clear but flexible.

Boundaries can be rigid walls that 'block our hearts' (Podvoll, 1990, p. 269) or something more permeable; depending on the context, varying degrees of rigidity or permeability may be more or less empowering for worker and client. Is it possible to maintain a clear sense of one's role as a worker, insofar as that contributes to the wellbeing of clients, in ways that do not deny a sense of commonality, sharing of wisdom and mutual growth? Campling suggests that managing boundaries is about more than limit setting – 'managing boundaries well is about taking time' to reflect, hear different views, to struggle actively with confusion and fear (1995, p. 95) even if it goes against 'traditional' notions of professionalism and authority.

Conclusion

As social workers, we will always be making sense of people's experience; however, as critical practitioners, part of our professionalism may be to ask how the things we notice – the 'cues we extract' from a myriad of possibilities (Weick, 1995) – construct those we work with and our interactions with them. How does the selectivity of our professional gaze enable or oppress the other? Our openness to diverse forms and sources of knowledge – the client's, the community's, those of marginalised or alternative discourses – can be at the heart of our unique professional contribution to individual and social change. By allowing our 'theoretical and procedural frameworks to act as a resource for reflection and understanding rather than to restrict the ways we listen' (Schön, 1983, cited in Butler *et al.* 2007, p. 292) we may open ourselves as professionals to new ways of being, knowing and doing.

According to Rossiter, social workers need to be capable of being in uncertainties, to privilege doubt over certainty, and to understand that 'our professional stories of helping are partial and fallible ... as persons exceed representation' (Rossiter, 2001, pp. 4–5). One staff member made this powerful observation:

> One can never assume that you know. ... the danger is to assume too quickly, to give answers too soon. And so here [at the programme] what we offer is

a time to allow things to unfold . . . the place we occupy [as workers] is one which allows the possibility of some doubt around knowledge, and hopefully then, a space for someone to come into their own experience, and their history, and hopefully their own future . . . and I don't know what that place is.

According to Saleeby, 'the theories we arm ourselves with are really just stories, not facts' (1994, p. 355) – empowering fictions (Baker, 1993, cited in Rossiter, 1996, p. 33) that hold power to guide our understanding and actions. We rely on representations to think and conceptualise in social work; our sensemaking is unavoidable and indeed it underpins our unique contribution to individual and social change. However, critical social work must practise on the 'unsettled razor's edge of representation and injury' (Rossiter, 2011, p. 11). In this sense, the most important question to ask ourselves is what conduct do the discourses that guide us warrant (Curt, 1994, p. 190), and how does that conduct 'fit' with our critical intent?

Unsettled practice results in a 'much more humble version of social work knowledge and a much more fallible version of ourselves as social workers because we understand that there is no professional story that adequately represents the singularity of a person' (Rossiter, 2011, pp. 14–15). This view of ourselves, far from diminishing our professionalism, expands possibilities for practice and for valuing, understanding and responding to the needs and experiences of those we work with. As critical social workers, our capacity to challenge assumptions, to be open to diverse truths, to acknowledge the partiality of our expert knowledge, and to consider how power is played out in our daily interactions can be the hallmark of our profession.

QUESTIONS FOR REFLECTION

1. What are your responses to the views presented in this chapter? What theories, discourses, assumptions or experiences might underpin these responses?
2. Where do our notions of professionalism come from and what is their impact on critical practice?
3. How might placing what we think we know at risk (being willing to embrace uncertainty) lead to improved practice?
4. How can our research in relation to mental health reflect a critical approach, and why would we want to do this?

References

Adams, R., Dominelli, L., & Payne, M. (eds) (2002) *Critical Practice in Social Work*, Palgrave, Basingstoke, UK.

Almond, R. (1974) *The Healing Community: Dynamics of the Therapeutic Milieu*, Jason Aronson, New York.

Barham, P. & Hayward, R. (1991) *From the Mental Patient to the Person*, Tavistock/Routledge, London.

Burkett, I. & McDonald, C. (2005) 'Working in a different space: Linking social work and social development', in *Globalisation, Global Justice and Social Work*, I. Ferguson, M. Lavalette & E. Whitmore (eds), Taylor & Francis, Abingdon, UK, pp. 169–203.

Butler, A., Ford, D. & Tregaskis, C. (2007) 'Who do we think we are?: Self and reflexivity in social work practice', *Qualitative Social Work*, vol. 6, no. 3, pp. 281–299.

Campling, P. (1995) 'Managing boundaries in a therapeutic community', *Therapeutic Communities*, vol. 16, no. 2, pp. 83–96.

Curt, B. (1994) *Textuality and Tectonics: Troubling Social and Psychological Science*, Open University Press, Buckingham, UK.

Deegan, P. (1988) 'Recovery: The lived experience of rehabilitation', *Psychosocial Rehabilitation Journal*, vol. 11, no. 4, pp. 11–19.

Deegan, P. (1990) 'Spirit breaking: When the helping professions hurt', *The Humanist Psychologist*, vol. 18, no. 3, pp. 301–313.

Duncan, B.L. (1998) 'Stepping off the throne', *RFV Newsletter*, August, Melbourne, Australia.

Estroff, S. (1981) *Making it Crazy: An Ethnography of Psychiatric Clients in an American Community*, University of California Press, Berkeley.

Fook, J. (2002) *Social Work: Critical Theory and Practice*, Sage Publications, London.

Healy, K. (2000) *Social Work Practices: Contemporary Perspectives on Change*, Sage Publications, London.

Hugman, R. (1998) *Social Welfare and Social Values: The Role of Caring Professions*, MacMillan, Basingstoke, UK.

Ife, J. (2002) *Community Development: Community-based Alternatives in an age of Globalisation*, 2nd edn. Longman, Melbourne, Australia.

Leonard, P. (1997) *Postmodern Welfare: Reconstructing an Emancipatory Project*, Sage Publications, London.

Leung, T. (2010) 'Social work professionalism in self-help organisations', *International Social Work*, vol. 533, no. 4, pp. 474–488.

Mullaly, B. (1997) *Structural Social Work: Ideology, Theory and Practice*, 2nd edn. Oxford University Press, Toronto, Canada.

Podvoll, E. (1983) 'Uncovering a patient's history of sanity', in *Awakening the Heart: East/West Approaches to Psychotherapy*, J. Welwood (ed), NewScience Library/Shambhala Press, Boulder, CO, pp. 183–191.

Podvoll, E. (1990) *The Seduction of Madness*, Harper Collins, New York.

Potter, J. (1996) *Representing Reality: Discourse, Rhetoric and Social Construction*, Sage Publications, London.

Rossiter, A. (1996) 'A perspective on critical social work', *Journal of Progressive Human Services*, vol. 7, no. 2, pp. 23–41.

Rossiter, A. (2001) 'Innocence lost and suspicion found – do we educate for or against social work?' *Critical Social Work*, vol. 2, no. 1. Available at: http://criticalsocialwork.com/01_1_innocence_rossiter.html

Rossiter, A. (2011) 'Unsettled social work: The challenge of Levinas's ethics', *British Journal of Social Work*, vol. 41, no. 5, pp. 980–995.

Saleeby, D. (1994) 'Culture, theory and narrative: The intersection of meanings in practice', *Social Work*, vol. 39, no. 4, pp. 351–359.

Sanford, J.A. (1977) *Healing and Wholeness*, Paulist Press, New York.

Schimmel, P. (1997) 'Swimming against the tide? A review of the therapeutic community', *ANZ Journal of Psychiatry*, vol. 31, no. 1, pp. 120–127.

Smart, R. (1994) 'Expertosis: Is it catching?' *Australia & New Zealand Journal of Family Therapy*, vol. 15, no. 1, pp. 1–9.

Smith, D. (1990) *The Conceptual Practices of Power: A Feminist Sociology of Knowledge*, Northeastern University Press, Boston, MA.

Walsh, A. (2011) 'Jean Vanier: An alternative voice for the social work profession', *Journal of Religion & Spirituality in Social Work*, vol. 30, no. 4, pp. 340–357.

Watkins, J. (1996) '*The journey of recovery: What workers need to know, do and be*', *Recovery: Rethinking the community response to people who experience a psychiatric disability*, VICSERV 1996 cross-sector conference July 25th and 26th, ed. S. Rowland, VICSERV, Fitzroy, pp. 37–41.

Weick, K. (1995) *Sensemaking in Organizations*, Sage Publications, Thousand Oaks, CA.

Welwood, J. (ed) (1983) *Awakening the Heart: East/West Approaches to Psychotherapy and the Healing Relationship*, New Science Library/Shambhala Publishers, Boulder, CO.

White, M. (1995) *Re-authoring Lives*, Dulwich Centre Publications, Adelaide, Australia.

19

PARTNERING IN THE FIELD OF CHRONIC CARE SERVICE PROVISION

Christa Fouché

CHAPTER OBJECTIVES

1. *Provide an overview of the global challenge of sustaining resilience in the growing context of chronic illness;*
2. *Discuss partnering as a core competency to address this challenge;*
3. *Report on a descriptive study to investigate health professionals' views of core competencies in the context of chronic care.*

Introduction

Economic, social and political changes over the past century have meant many people – particularly those in developed nations – have enjoyed improved standards of living. Advances in medicine and technology have also meant people are now more likely to survive episodes of acute illness or injury than in the past (May *et al.*, 2005). These factors together have increased life expectancy rates and average population ages around the world. While longer lives and better standards of living are undoubtedly positive outcomes, these changes have also contributed significantly to an increase in chronic conditions. As more people are surviving acute illnesses and injury, or just generally living naturally longer lives, the likelihood that they live long enough to develop a chronic condition has also risen (Dowrick, *et al.*, 2005). The World Health Organization (WHO, 2006) has called chronic conditions the 'health challenge of the century' with chronic disease currently responsible for 60% of the global health burden. Chronic conditions can be defined as 'health problems that require ongoing management over a period of years or decades' and which 'typically affect the social, psychological and economic dimensions of a person's life' (WHO, 2005b, p. 13).

The word 'chronic' is used in contrast to 'acute', and indicates the longer duration of a condition (Dowrick *et al.*, 2005). Historically, acute illnesses have been the major cause of death and illness around the world. The provision of health care and the training of health professionals have also therefore been largely orientated towards the diagnosis and treatment of acute illnesses (Pruitt and Epping-Jordan, 2005), implying a reliance on 'expertise' and individualised care management. Last century however, chronic conditions began to overtake acute illnesses as the largest contributor to death, illness and burden on health resources (May *et al.*, 2005). Chronic conditions are currently the largest cause of death in almost every country (WHO, 2005b).

Substantial financial costs for both providers and consumers of health care services are also involved in the treatment of chronic conditions (WHO, 2003). Emphasising the magnitude of these costs and the role of lifestyle factors, WHO (2003, p. 137) states that 'The cost to the world of the current and projected epidemic of chronic disease related to diet and physical inactivity dwarfs all other health costs'. As populations globally continue to age and the prevalence of chronic conditions grows, so too will health care costs. Aside from deaths, there are also large numbers of people around the world who experience or are even disabled by the pain, loss of mobility, embarrassment or stigma that may be associated with their illness (Department of Health, 2001) and it is evident that social workers have a huge role in addressing these challenges.

Addressing the challenges

A common theme on addressing the challenges of chronic care is the necessity of shifting the focus of health care provision from hospital-based care to primary or outpatient care (May *et al.*, 2005; Pols *et al.*, 2009). In this environment, greater emphasis is being placed in policy on developing preventative and primary care, while inpatient care will always remain a necessity.

Alongside this shift in emphasis, the involvement of communities, families and individuals affected by chronic conditions is also seen as crucial (Wagner *et al.*, 2001; Whitehead, 2009; WHO, 2005a). At an individual level, there is a growing body of literature highlighting the importance of the chronically ill becoming active participants in their care, rather than passive consumers of health services (Department of Health, 2001; Pols *et al.*, 2009; Wilkinson and Whitehead, 2009). Communities and families are also seen as instrumental in the prevention and management of chronic conditions (Wagner *et al.*, 2001; Whitehead, 2009). Another important development is the emergence of approaches in health care which focus on 'management over cure' (WHO, 2005a, p. 51), where attention shifts from the elimination of disease towards the management of illness. These aspects of chronic conditions mean that, from preventative stages through to palliative care, those directly affected by these conditions are likely to come into contact with numerous professionals from a range of health and social services. Those with coexisting chronic conditions will experience this even more distinctly. In order to ensure safe and effective practice, improved continuity and communication between previously compartmentalised health services or professions is essential (WHO, 2005a).

Various efforts have been made internationally to improve health care for those with chronic conditions and to reduce the impact of these conditions (National Health Committee (NHC), 2007). In addition to the emergence of government policy documents, numerous initiatives for specific chronic conditions have also emerged locally and internationally. Models designed to improve the care of people with chronic conditions have been developed, with some (Wagner *et al.*, 2001) suggesting transformations in the relationships between health care systems, communities and patients, in order to improve health care. However, while the implementation of policy at the level of government and health organisations is instrumental to change, a purely 'top-down' approach to meeting the challenge of chronic conditions seems unlikely to succeed (Martin *et al.*, 2009). It has been suggested that the lag between the introduction of policy and models of practice, and the successful adaption to chronic conditions in practice, points to the need for education reform (Martin *et al.*, 2009; Pruitt and Epping-Jordan, 2005). Within this context, discussions emerge on the nature of 'core competencies' for future health practitioners. The WHO (2005a) defines competencies as 'the skills, abilities, knowledge, behaviours and attitudes that are instrumental in the delivery of desired results and, consequently, of job performance' (p. 14), and the intended aim of core competencies is to improve chronic health care by better equipping all health professionals, including social workers, to support those with chronic conditions. It is often indicated that specific core competencies for chronic conditions are needed in addition to existing discipline-specific skills. However, the nature of these core competencies across the different health disciplines remains unclear and prompted a research project reported in this chapter aimed at exploring the perceptions of health care professionals in the field of chronic care on core competencies.

A central document discussing the role of core competencies in reforming the education of health care professionals is the WHO's *Preparing a Health Care Workforce for the 21st Century* (2005a) which highlights five core competencies. The first entails a shift from 'provider-centred' health care to care which is organised around individual patients. *Patient-centred care* allows health care to be directed by an individual's needs, values and preferences, as well as acknowledges the expertise that they have, based on their own experience of illness. This requires social workers to acknowledge the existence of multiple layers of expertise. *Quality improvement* involves the measuring of care delivery and outcomes and encourages the translation of evidence into practice. This competency essentially requires social work practitioners to have the ability to reflect on the outcomes they are working towards, evaluate interventions and use available evidence to guide their practice. *Information and communication technologies* improve continuity between health providers and the communication of patient information by providing accurate and organised monitoring of patients over time and may also support increased management of patients in outpatient settings. It encourages the expertise of specialists to be solicited and shared. A *Public health perspective* encourages awareness of all health professionals beyond the care of individual patients, to the care of communities and whole populations, albeit difficult due to the daily pressures of individual patients' immediate needs.

The final core competency involves partnering and is the focus of this chapter. *Partnering* improves health care for those with chronic conditions by improving communication and continuity with patients, with other providers and with communities (WHO, 2005a). As mentioned earlier, chronic health care often involves numerous health professionals interacting not only with patients, but ideally their families and communities too. Partnering therefore plays a crucial role in improving health care for those with chronic conditions, by improving communication and continuity between all parties. This core competency contains three aspects: partnering with patients; partnering with other providers; and partnering with communities (WHO, 2005a), but for the purposes of this discussion, the focus will mainly be on partnering with other health providers.

Partnering

The common meaning of interdisciplinary collaboration (or multi-disciplinary working) relates to the fact that individuals from different professions are working together to achieve a common goal (Berg-Weger and Schneider, 1998). Historically and to this day, there have been widespread expectations of collaboration amongst health professionals (Bronstein, 2003; Workforce Taskforce, 2008; Xyrichis, 2008). Interdisciplinary teams have been identified as having an important role to play, particularly in relation to care for the elderly (Leipzig *et al.*, 2002), and in light of increasing numbers of patients with chronic conditions. Given the pooling of skills and knowledge of different members, this approach is being linked to improved patient outcomes (Sommers *et al.*, 2000) and quality of care (Oaandasan *et al.*, 2006). Other benefits include improved efficiency in terms of resources required (Xyrichis, 2008) and the potential to increase the level and quality of available services (Wagner, 2000).

As many social work practitioners in the health sector can attest, a multi-disciplinary approach is not without its challenges. Its success is dependent to some extent on how well team members can collaborate and this approach may well be viewed with scepticism by some social workers (Wagner, 2000). There is indeed a plethora of data on the obstacles to interdisciplinary collaboration (Dey *et al.*, 2011; Hughes and McCann, 2003; Xyrichis, 2008). There is evidence to suggest that there may be differences across disciplines in terms of the perceived value of collaboration (Leipzig *et al.*, 2002) with some practitioners more open to collaborating than others (Cooper and Fishman, 2003). Hierarchical barriers between different professions have also been widely discussed, with the dominance of general practitioners within health teams raised as an issue across a range of professions (Lymbery and Millward, 2002; Miers, 2010). Tension in relationships between health professionals may also be due to an unclear definition of each health professional's role and responsibility and a lack of understanding of the boundaries of individual roles (Soklaridis *et al.*, 2007).

Professional stereotypes would appear to have a role to play in the development of hierarchical barriers and may influence the level and nature of collaboration between different health professionals (Hean *et al.*, 2006). Differences in underlying philosophies may create difficulties for health professionals collaborating (Pollard, 2010). Cooper and Fishman (2003) highlight that, whilst social work education emphasises the value of joint work across professions, medical training takes more of an individualistic approach, and is traditionally concerned with addressing physical health without examining factors beyond this. Similarly, with medical knowledge often privileged over other forms of knowledge, a psychosocial approach may be considered inferior within a multidisciplinary team (Pollard, 2010) thus creating difficulties for social workers. Whilst there has been much written about the benefits of collaboration in the health sector, with health professionals being encouraged to work in an interdisciplinary manner, there is growing recognition that they do not always have the skills and experience to enable this to happen (Howe *et al.*, 2001; Leipzig *et al.*, 2002; McCallin, 2005; Soklaridis *et al.*, 2007). Other potential difficulties include a lack of time to collaborate (Dey *et al.*, 2011; Keefe *et al.*, 2009; Lymbery and Millward, 2002) and a lack of appreciation for what other professions do (Hughes and McCann, 2003).

Research methodology

A research project was undertaken in 2010–2011 aimed at exploring the perceptions of New Zealand health care professionals in the field of chronic care on the nature of the WHO (2005b) identified five core competencies. The research team comprised 12 health professional educators from medicine (1), pharmacy (1), social work (1), physiotherapy (2), occupational therapy (1), speech language therapy (2), nursing (3) and psychology (1). The research was undertaken in two parts, utilising an exploratory–descriptive design. Phase 1 comprised focus groups with membership derived through convenience sampling of Auckland-based recognised expert clinicians in the field of chronic care with representation from each of the health professional groups listed above, across both physical health and mental health. Twenty-one expert clinicians in the field of chronic care have participated in 4 focus group interviews. The average age of participants was 47.1 with the majority ($N = 17$) being females. They had a total of 423.5 years' practice experience – on average 21.17 years per person in their respective disciplines.

Data were collected by asking the focus group participants to share their views as expert health professionals in the field of chronic care on: a) what ideally needs to happen regarding meeting the needs and expectations expressed by chronic care consumers in relation to health and social services in New Zealand; and b) what they regard as barriers to achieve this. The transcripts from the focus groups were read and re-read by two people and coded separately to ensure accuracy of coding. Initially the five categories of core competencies of health care professionals as listed by the World Health Organization (2005a) were used to organise information. Once this was done, a general inductive analysis (Thomas, 2006) was used to develop themes under each of the competencies. Themes were developed drawing together similar recurring codes, which together formed and described the theme.

In phase 2, data from phase 1 were used to help develop a telephone-based semi-structured interview implemented with 25 novice and experienced practitioners representing the above range of health-related disciplines in the field of chronic care. Purposeful sampling was utilised by research team members to identify potentially eligible participants for this phase. We solicited their views on how health professionals in their discipline implement the core competencies with respect to the provision of care to people with chronic care needs in New Zealand and asked them what could be done in their view (assuming time, resources and training) in this regard? In the analysis of the individual interview data, the themes from the focus groups were further explored as a grid was developed to plot the responses per discipline per theme across the various competencies. As such, a clear indication of priority themes emerged within and across disciplines. As the scope of this chapter does not allow for the discussion of all these results, the next discussion reflects only some of the results from the one main theme that emerged from both the focus groups and individual interview data across all the disciplines, namely partnering.

Findings

The results from the research comprised insights across the five competencies, but partnering – both prompted and unprompted – surfaced as a key issue; often interwoven with the other competencies. Across each of the five competencies multidisciplinary work was seen to have a role to play. For example, one focus group participant (#9) noted that, in terms of a public health model, a collaborative approach within primary care teams was more effective. In relation to the delivery of 'patient-centred care', health professionals discussed sharing information with colleagues regarding the care of particular individuals; with 'information and communication' the need for integrated systems across disciplines was viewed as a key issue. Partnering in particular, related to relationships between the patient and their communities, between the family and carer, as well as between health care teams. The main coded responses, however, related to the latter – the relationships between health care team members.

Participating health professionals described different scenarios where partnering had, or was taking place, within their work environment. This sometimes entailed several health professionals working together as a team; in other cases practitioners were partnering with just one other colleague to meet the needs of their patients. Different configurations of health professionals working together were identified, and included familiar combinations such as general practitioners and nurses, or general practitioners and community pharmacists, as well as pairings of occupational therapists or speech language therapists and social workers. It should be noted that, while there were reports of some collaborative work going on, this was not widespread, and there was a strong sense that far more needed to be done in terms of facilitating this practice in managing patients with chronic conditions.

A number of advantages of working collaboratively were discussed by participants, including a streamlining of systems and processes, improved patient care (e.g. via the sharing of information and combination of different skills and knowledge), and ultimately better health outcomes for patients suffering from chronic conditions:

> We often do home visits together with nurses/OTs – really useful, get to know the questions they ask, and also learn more about their knowledge base – means that when you go out to do an assessment you have a much wider knowledge base to draw on, and the assessment is much better. (Interview participant 11)

The importance of collegial relationships with regard to effective collaboration within primary care has been widely reported in the literature (Bradley *et al.*, 2008, Sommers *et al.*, 2000). This was a recurring theme in this study, with participants highlighting the value of individual relationships formed with key colleagues. Indeed, a number of research participants spoke about the fact that these – rather than formal structures facilitating multidisciplinary working – played an important part in accessing information and/or facilitating additional assistance for a patient:

> It seems to me, an important part of your work is to actually know who the people are that you're going to be linking with. Or even just having contact with one person who then can lead you onto other people. It does take time but it pays dividends in the end and often people see it is important. (Focus group participant 4)

However, regarding an understanding of each other's roles, participants highlighted a lack of inter-professional learning, a lack of training in multidisciplinary working and a lack of understanding of different professional roles. This seems to affirm the view by Soklaridis *et al.* (2007), that tension in relationships between health professionals may be due to an unclear definition of each health professional's role and responsibility.

> Work in a multi-disciplinary team . . . is not taught at Uni, but [we have] learnt it through placement and on-the-job experience. [We need to] know the importance of knowing what other members of the team do, and they know your role. [This] could be taught more. (Focus group participant 17)
>
> Would be good to have more expert people from other disciplines coming in to talk to us in Uni about what they do and how it fits in. (Interview participant 16)

Amongst pharmacists in the study it was reported that most joint working takes place with general practitioners, although one pharmacist acknowledged that they sometimes partnered with social workers. Similarly, for social workers, it was reported that partnering mostly took place with nurses and occupational therapists (e.g. during home visits) or general practitioners. Pharmacists spoke about potential collaboration with 'new partners', including becoming involved with public health campaigns, having a presence in schools, and linking with other organisations in the community.

In relation to information sharing with other professionals the lack of integration of services and physical separation was a frequent comment.

> Interfaces between primary and secondary care are difficult. We tend to treat disorders rather than the whole person, and get caught up in our own professional goals rather than talking to the patient. We can do better working inter-professionally rather than in our own silos. (Focus group participant 1)

This participant added 'Often point scoring and egos get in the way', indicating that, as mentioned by Leipzig *et al.* (2002) and Sommers *et al.* (2000), patient outcomes are often determined by the ability (and willingness) of team members to collaborate.

Being in the same physical location or working in a multidisciplinary team, especially in the community, was suggested as a solution along with the use of a key worker or case manager. An alternative to this would be electronic links between teams. It was felt that it was really important that all professionals seeing an individual should be on the one page and that sharing information between services would alleviate much unnecessary duplication:

> [We] need a key worker for people with chronic health problems. It's often difficult for people to manage multiple appointments and they get muddled and then [do not attend appointments]. (Interview participant 5)
>
> Information systems are getting better but still need to improve. Also [we] partner with gerontology nurses and hospice [but] Social work, OT and NASC is a one way referral system. These need to be in primary care not secondary care. (Focus group participant 7)

Whilst information-sharing was emphasised as important, the need to keep client information confidential is sometimes seen as a barrier to a more collaborative practice that will benefit the client:

> There is rampant paranoia round confidentiality, especially Mental Health. Need more shared care with expectation of sharing taking place. (Focus group participant 11)

Accessing community groups was seen by participants as a valuable way of reaching a large number of people at one time rather than trying to deal with one person at a time. However, a number of professionals felt ill prepared to do group work and/or networking amongst community resources.

there are many, many forms of groups . . . so I think those skills are really important at the outset as a training component. (Interview participant 1)

Pragmatism seems to get in the way of real collaboration:

GPs are funded to see patients not to be part of team meetings. GPs do understand [the need for] other members of the team but also find them difficult to access – either no one there or they are too expensive. We need to put all community services as part of primary care – e.g. social workers and OTs etc., so that we have a good information flow between these services. Other professionals like SLTs and dieticians are too hard to find and too expensive to locate and use. (Focus group participant 8)

On the whole, the findings indicated a support for and belief in the value of partnering, but highlighted that this mostly happened where individuals deemed it important enough to make and maintain the connections. Within this context, the implications for collaborative practice in the field of chronic care should be considered.

Conclusion

The growing prevalence of chronic conditions is a cause for concern globally, both in terms of its impact on the health of populations and also the strain it is predicted to place on health resources. Various efforts are under way to meet this challenge and the core competencies proposed by WHO provide a strong basis for equipping health professionals, including social workers, to support people with chronic conditions to live better and live longer. However, as became clear from the findings, health professionals may acknowledge the importance of these competencies (and in particular the competency of partnering as described here), but the practice thereof still seems idealistic. There is a push to value skills of relationship-building and to adopt more holistic and collaborative approaches to care, but it is clear that the education of health care professionals must also be reformed if these efforts are to be successful. This is very true also for social work. It is evident that, in addition to technical skills and knowledge, changes in various attitudes and behaviours are also required.

Successful partnering in the context of chronic care service provision seems to depend, in the first instance, on other partnering relationships: between educators in different health disciplines, in understanding and appreciating other professions; between health professionals-in-training in ensuring pre-existing perceptions positively influence future likelihood and/or willingness to collaborate; and between education providers and health organisations, to ensure that the work environment is consistent with, and supportive of, the principles and attitudes contained within the core competency of partnering. This may enable chronic care service provision to attain goals that may not be possible when individual professionals work independently.

QUESTIONS FOR REFLECTION

1. Do you regard yourself as adequately informed about the potential contribution of other health professionals as partners in delivery of services to people with chronic care needs?
2. If not, why not, and what do you think can be done to better promote social work and learn more about other disciplines?
3. If yes, where and how did you obtain those insights, and how can those strategies be implemented more widely in the partnering of health professionals?

Acknowledgement

The project reported in this chapter has been completed in collaboration with an interdisciplinary and inter-university research team. I acknowledge with gratitude the involvement of the following team members: Professors John Shaw, Glynn Owens, Matthew Parsons, Associate Professors Tim Kenealy, Brian McKenna, Drs John Parsons, Diane Jorgensen, Ms Lisa Stewart (University of Auckland); Drs Sally Clendon, Annabel Grant (Massey University); and Ms Jennifer Mace (Auckland University of Technology). I also acknowledge the valuable contribution of Rowan Magill as the most competent research assistant.

References

Berg-Weger, M. & Schneider, F. (1998) 'Interdisciplinary collaboration in social work education', *Journal of Social Work Education*, vol. 34, no. 1, pp. 97–107.

Bradley, F., Elvey, R., Ashcroft, D., Hassell, K., Kendall, J., Sibbald, B. & Noyce, P. (2008) 'The challenge of integrating community pharmacists into the primary health care team: A case study of local pharmaceutical services (LPS) pilots and interprofessional collaboration', *Journal of Interprofessional Care*, vol. 22, no. 4, 387–398.

Bronstein, L.R. (2003) 'A model for interdisciplinary collaboration', *Social Work*, vol. 48, no. 3, pp. 297–306.

Cooper, B.S. & Fishman, E. (2003) *The Interdisciplinary Team in the Management of Conditions: Has Its Time Come?*, Partnership for Solutions, Baltimore, MD.

Department of Health (2001) *The Expert Patient: A New Approach to Chronic Disease Management for the 21st Century*, Department of Health, London.

Dey, R.M., De Vries, M.J.W. & Bosnic-Anticevich, S. (2011) 'Collaboration in chronic care: Unpacking the relationship of pharmacists and general medical practitioners in primary care', *International Journal of Pharmacy Practice*, vol. 19, no. 1, pp. 21–29.

Dowrick, C., Dixon-Woods, M., Holman, H. & Weinman, J. (2005) 'What is chronic illness?', *Chronic Illness*, vol. 1, no. 1, pp. 1–6.

Hean, S., Clark, J.M., Adams, K. & Humphris, D. (2006) 'Will opposites attract? Similarities and differences in students' perceptions of the stereotype profiles of other health and social care professional groups', *Journal of Interprofessional Care*, vol. 20, no. 2, pp. 162–181.

Howe, J.L., Hyer, K., Mellor, J., Lindeman, D. & Luptak, M. (2001) 'Educational approaches for preparing social work students for interdisciplinary teamwork on geriatric health care teams', *Social Work in Health Care*, vol. 32, no. 4, pp. 19–42.

Hughes, C. & McCann, S. (2003) 'Perceived interprofessional barriers between community pharmacists and general practitioners: A qualitative assessment', *British Journal of General Practice*, vol. 53. no. 493, pp. 600–606.

Keefe, B., Geron, S.M. & Enguidanos, S. (2009) 'Integrating social workers into primary care: Physician and nurse perceptions of roles, benefits and challenges', *Social Work in Health Care*, vol. 48, no. 6, pp. 579–596.

Leipzig, R.M., Hyer, K., Ek, K., Wallenstein, S., Vezina, M.L., Fairchild, S., Cassel, C.K. & Howe, J.L. (2002) 'Attitudes toward working in interdisciplinary healthcare teams: A comparison by discipline', *Journal of the American Geriatrics Society*, vol. 50, no. 6, pp. 1141–1148.

Lymbery, M. & Millward, A. (2002) 'Community care in practice', *Social Work in Health Care*, vol. 34, nos. 3–4, 241–259.

Martin, C.M., Peterson, C., Robinson, R. & Sturmberg, J.P. (2009) 'Care for chronic illness in Australian general practice – focus groups of chronic disease self-help groups over 10 years: Implications for chronic care systems reforms', *Asia Pacific Family Medicine*, vol. 8, no. 1. doi:10.1186/1447–056X-8–1

May, C., Finch, T., Mair, F. & Mort, M. (2005) 'Towards a wireless patient: Chronic illness, scarce care and technological innovation in the United Kingdom', *Social Science & Medicine*, vol. 61, no. 7, pp. 1485–1494.

McCallin, A. (2005) 'Interprofessional practice: Learning how to collaborate', *Contemporary Nurse*, vol. 20, no. 1, pp. 28–37.

Miers, M. (2010) 'Learning for new ways of working', in *Understanding Interprofessional Working in Health and Social Care*, K.C. Pollard, J. Thomas, & M. Miers (eds), Palgrave MacMillan, Basingstoke, UK.

National Health Committee (2007) *Meeting the Needs of People with Chronic Conditions*, National Health Committee, Wellington, New Zealand.

Oaandasan, I., Baker, G., Barker, K., Bosco, C., D'amour, D., Jones, L., Kimpton, S., Lemieux-Charles, L., Nasmith, L., San Martin Rodriguez, L., Tepper, J. & Way, D. (2006) *Teamwork in Healthcare: Promoting Effective Teamwork in Healthcare in Canada*, Canadian Health Services Research Foundation, Ottawa, Canada.

Pollard, K.C. (2010) 'The medicalization thesis', in *Understanding Interprofessional Working in Health and Social Care. Theory and Practice*, K.C. Pollard, J. Thomas, & M. Miers, (eds), Palgrave Macmillan, Basingstoke, UK.

Pols, R.G., Battersby, M.W., Regan-Smith, M., Markwick, M.J., Lawrence, J., Auret, K., Carter, J., Cole, A., Disler, P., Hassed, C., McGuiness, C. & Nguyen, H. (2009) 'Chronic condition self-management support: Proposed competencies for medical students', *Chronic Illness*, vol. 5, no. 7, pp. 7–14.

Pruitt, S.D. & Epping-Jordan, J.E. (2005) 'Preparing the 21st century global healthcare workforce', *British Medical Journal*, vol. 330, no. 7492, pp. 637–639.

Soklaridis, S., Oandasan, I. & Kimpton, S. (2007) 'Family health teams', *Canadian Family Physician*, vol. 53, no. 7, pp. 1198–1199.

Sommers, L.S., Marton, K.I., Barbaccia, J.C. & Randolph, J. (2000) 'Physician, nurse, and social worker collaboration in primary care for chronically ill seniors', *Archives of Internal Medicine*, vol. 160, no. 12, pp. 1825–1833.

Thomas, D.R. (2006) A general inductive approach for analyzing qualitative evaluation data, *American Journal of Evaluation*, vol. 27, no. 2, pp. 237–246.

Wagner, E. (2000) 'The role of patient care teams in chronic disease management', *British Medical Journal*, vol. 320, no. 7324, pp. 569–572.

Wagner, E.H., Austin, B.T., Davis, C., Hindmarsh, M., Schaefer, J. & Bonomi, A. (2001) 'Improving chronic illness care: Translating evidence into action', *Health Affairs*, vol. 20, no. 6, pp. 64–78.

Whitehead, L. (2009) *Living with Chronic Illness: Support for Family Members who Live with Heart Failure*, Families Commission, Wellington, New Zealand.

Wilkinson, A. & Whitehead, L. (2009) 'Evolution of the concept of self-care and implications for nurses: A literature review', *International Journal of Nursing Studies*, vol. 46, no. 8, pp. 1143–1147.

Workforce Taskforce (2008) *Working Together for Better Primary Health Care. Overcoming Barriers to Workforce Change and Innovation*, Report to the Minister of Health from the Workforce Taskforce, Ministry of Health, Wellington, New Zealand.

World Health Organization (2003) *Diet, Nutrition and the Prevention of Chronic Diseases*, World Health Organization, Geneva.

World Health Organization (2005a) *Preparing a Workforce for the 21st Century: The Challenge of Chronic Conditions*, World Health Organization, Geneva.

World Health Organization (2005b) *Preventing Chronic Diseases: A Vital Investment*, World Health Organization, Geneva.

World Health Organization (2006) *An Estimation of the Economic Impact of Chronic Non-communicable Diseases in Selected Countries*, World Health Organization, Geneva.

Xyrichis, A.L.K. (2008) 'What fosters or prevents interprofessional teamworking in primary and community care? A literature review', *International Journal of Nursing Studies*, vol. 45, no. 1, pp. 140–153.

20

CRAFTING SOCIAL CONNECTEDNESS

A community development model

Jane Maidment, Uschi Bay and Michelle Courtney

It's a wide world out there when you've got a needle in your hand.

Nola

CHAPTER OBJECTIVES

1. *To examine the relationship between craft group participation, personal health and wellbeing;*
2. *To demonstrate the association between principles of community development and Country Women's Association (CWA) craft group activities and processes;*
3. *To argue the case for increasing practitioner use of community development practice strategies to address issues of health and structural inequality.*

Introduction

Older people loneliness and social isolation

Multiple studies have measured and determined the impact of both loneliness and isolation on the health status of older people. This material has provided substantive recognition of the deleterious effect of both conditions on quality of life (Hawton *et al.*, 2010). Specifically, social isolation amongst older people is associated with increased mortality (Seeman, 1996), greater susceptibility to dementia (Fratiglioni *et al.*, 2000) and poor self-rated health (Cornwell and Waite, 2009). These findings provide a strong public health argument for developing robust practice and social policy responses to tackle isolation and loneliness amongst older people. Even so there 'remains considerable uncertainty regarding the characteristics of interventions that are successful and cost-effective in achieving these goals' (Dickens *et al.*, 2011).

Recent research in New Zealand indicates that 8% of older people rate themselves as being severely lonely. This figure equates to 48,000 older people, based on the March 2012 population statistics (Statistics New Zealand, 2013). A further 44% of those surveyed rated themselves as being moderately lonely (Age Concern, 2012). Across the Tasman a similar story is evident with a survey of social attitudes showing loneliness is a significant issue for many Australians, with 35% of men and 29% of women experiencing loneliness as a serious problem (Australian National University, 2009). The existence or absence of connections with community is not necessarily the key to ageing well, with research indicating instead that it is the strength of community ties and a qualitative sense of belonging that prompts well-being (Griffiths *et al.*, 2007). This finding signals the need for policy and practice development that helps create relationships that matter, providing a sense of meaningfulness and belonging especially for those potentially on the margins of society.

In this chapter we will draw on findings from a qualitative study to argue that community-building processes as seen naturally occurring amongst Country Women's Association (CWA) craft group participants, can actively address issues of social isolation and loneliness. Community building aims 'to bring people together, to strengthen the bonds between community members, and to emphasize the idea of interdependence rather than independence' (Ife and Tesoriero, 2006, p. 279). Community building helps to create social capital and strengthen community ties. From our research it is evident that these craft groups cultivate a milieu of social inclusion, providing opportunities for meaningful community participation, peer support, friendship, continuing learning and development in later life. Data from our research clearly illustrate how the activities and processes used by the craft groups strongly reflect community-building principles, giving rise to enhanced health and wellbeing outcomes for participants. As such, we argue that craft group participation provides a potential approach and way ahead for addressing the important public health concerns of isolation and loneliness amongst some older people. For the purposes of examining the role of craft in fostering wellbeing, in this chapter we draw from Velde's description of craft as 'things that use materials for decorative, useful, or manipulative purposes and are made from a variety of substances . . . linked to manual dexterity, attention to detail and skill' (1999, p. 95).

Relationship between craft and health

Research located mainly within the disciplines of cultural studies, textile design and occupational therapy have highlighted the close association between engaging in crafting activities and fostering a sense of wellbeing and identity. In particular the activity of handcrafting enables women to have ongoing opportunities for meaningful social interaction with others; instils a sense of autonomy and self-esteem; and provides the means for self-directed lifelong knowledge and skill development (Schofield-Tomschin and Littrell, 2001). Further, participation in crafting has also been found to strengthen women's sense of identity and place in the world, and facilitate meaning-making through the process of creating, using or gifting the finished product (Starr Johnson and Wilson, 2005).

The therapeutic value of crafting has been well recognised in diverse community, health and social care settings, demonstrating the utility of its application to a broad age range of participants (Futterman-Collier, 2012; Gandolfo and Grace, 2009; Maidment and Macfarlane, 2008). Specifically, the therapeutic value of crafting has been identified as relating to the development of new skills and enhancing creativity; improved problem solving, increased self-esteem and community participation; and fostering intrinsic and extrinsic reward gained through recognition from others (Truong, 2011). A further significant benefit of crafting identified through the work of psychologist Csikszentmihalyi (1990) is experiencing 'the flow'; that is, the complete absorption in the present moment characterised by an energised and positive focus on the intrinsically motivating activity at hand. This emotional state, sometimes colloquially referred to as being 'in the zone' has been proven to address stress and agitation through creating a strong sense of calm (Carr, 2013).

Research method

During 2010 we interviewed 20 women who belonged to CWA craft groups throughout Victoria, Australia. The aim of the research was to explore the relationship between engagement with crafting activities and participant reports of health and wellbeing. Participants were recruited through volunteering their involvement at the St Arnaud CWA state craft exhibition, by making contact via a magazine article published after the exhibition, and through researcher contact with group leaders. Audio-recorded interviews with the women lasted from between 30 minutes to an hour-and-a-half. Most interviews occurred face to face but some were conducted over the telephone due to distance. Participants were spread throughout Victoria with 15 of the women living in rural areas. Once completed, transcriptions from the interviews were sent back to participants for member checking.

Analysis of the text data occurred using first-and second-order coding. First-order coding yielded 40 categories and these were later refined down to a set of four main themes including *Accomplishment, Learning, Health and Wellbeing* and *Sustainability*. Nvivo 8 was used to organise the coding process. All three authors conducted the research and completed data coding. As such it was possible to use peer debriefing of coding decisions to increase the rigor of analysis (Padgett *et al.*, 2004). A summary of results was prepared and delivered back to CWA Victoria in July 2011. This research was conducted after approval from Deakin University Ethics Committee in conjunction with agreement from CWA Victoria. Names associated with each of the participant quotations have been changed to preserve confidentiality.

The following discussion outlines some key elements associated with community-building work. Using the findings from our research we demonstrate how the CWA craft group activities reflect these community-building principles.

Generating social capital

Understanding the role of social capital, including the way it is generated and maintained, is key for working within both informal and intentional community settings. The notion of social capital

> refers to resources accessed by individuals and groups within a social structure that facilitate co-operation, collective action and the maintenance of norms. In health research, social capital has been measured by indicators such as levels of interpersonal trust, the presence of reciprocal exchanges between citizens, and membership of civic organizations. (Fujiwara and Kawachai, 2008, p. 139)

As such, the impact of social networks on individual and community wellbeing can be examined. Characteristics such as the existence of trusting relationships, meaningful friendships and reciprocity are increasingly being associated with determinants of health and the existence of social capital for both individuals and communities (Ziersch *et al.*, 2005).

A distinction can be made between different forms of social capital, with *cognitive* social capital referring to norms of trust, solidarity and reciprocity and *structural* social capital relating to the composition, extent and activities of local level institutions and networks (Krishna and Shrader, 2000, cited in Eriksson, 2011, p. 5).

> The influence of social capital on health status has been demonstrated through increased levels of self-esteem, better access to resources and the provision of social support during stressful life events (Campbell and Wood, 1999). On an individual level, having a strong sense of connection to, and belonging within, an enduring wider community instils personal security and feelings of worth. Recent research with older Australians has borne out the importance of maintaining social contacts and community connections for addressing loneliness and fostering a sense of belonging (Stanley, 2010). These conditions were certainly evident within the CWA craft groups with most women we spoke to:

> But it's a comradeship, you know. They've all got sick husbands and they've all got aches and pains and dramas with their kids, but being together really you know helps you. . . .You talk about, say 'Oh yes, I can relate to that,' and 'I know a good doctor,' or 'I know a good pill' or something like that. So it's the networking and that, and it's not actually doing the craft work – there's a lot more besides the craft work. (Eva)

> Ah, we were dairy farmers. We're now living in a town, and periodically times would get tough but I always made sure I went to my CWA meetings, because I got the friendship and support of other members there. (Hetti)

Participants identified how crafting and group participation impacted on health and esteem:

> I'm a panicker, but I think if you've got to get up and actually do something, it means you've gotta get up and shower and you've gotta get your breakfast and do the dishes and that and then you've gotta get yourself dressed and gather all your clutter and your sewing notions and you've gotta go out, going out and to meet other people, see what they do and appreciate, I think just getting out of the house takes your mind off your aches and pains. I think it's great therapy. (Inez)

> But I do get a lot of satisfaction. I'm very proud of the pictures that I've got here at home. I've also sent one to my husband's relatives, or a cousin of my husband's that was over in England. We'd never met them 'til a couple of years ago, and one of my bark – it was nearly all bark that one – . . . I get a lot of satisfaction . . . well, I have done about every type of craftwork. . . . And I'm very proud of the fact that they can walk into my lounge room and see pictures on the wall. (Emily)

The contribution the CWA craftswomen made to strengthening social capital at local, state, national and international community levels was also evident. Local craft groups supported schools, hospitals, sporting clubs, emergency services and businesses. These efforts took many forms: teaching children in schools to knit and crochet; fundraising for charities and clubs by selling and raffling craftwork; staging state craft exhibitions in small drought-ridden rural communities to bring visitors and money into local economies; and collecting and sending sewing machines to Pacific Island communities to support micro-business ventures. These efforts were achieved through the collective action of the women, and in this way benefited the individuals involved through engagement in meaningful, purposeful activity. At the same time these initiatives very much speak to the notion of demonstrating reciprocity and support towards local institutions using crafting as the medium to generate social capital. These examples demonstrate craftswomen contributing to the health and wellbeing of whole communities (structural social capital) by strengthening the economics and infrastructure of essential services and institutions.

> We've just been asked to think of some projects for the elderly at (name of residential care facility) to occupy these people. We're thinking of beading and making pom-poms and things like that. So everybody's still participating. (Eva)

To help support small rural communities . . .

> And then they do a state exhibition, . . . we try and have them in the country towns like – we had the one in Cronulla . . . last year. We've got that in Longwarry this year. Next year we're hoping to have it up towards Mildura. It's to help the people in need to get the people in and get people in to the town. (Lily)

And you did that in St Arnaud? (Interviewer)

Oh we did. We had a lovely lot of people up there helping. They were so pleased. Because of the drought they needed people there. All the motels were full. All the businesses were busy. Yes. It was good. (Lily)

Capacity building in small communities

While there is increasing rhetoric about the importance of personal and community resilience and capacity building within health policy, precise definitions of this concept remain elusive. A recent systematic review of literature on measuring community capacity building defined the concept as

> a function of capabilities (aggregates of individual and community level endowments) and socio-environmental conditions (facilitating conditions minus barriers). Community capacity is not an inherent property of a particular locality, or of the individuals or groups within it, but of the interactions between both. (Jackson *et al.*, 1999, cited in Labonte and Laverack, 2001, p. 114)

Out of this review key attributes associated with capacity building were identified including accessing learning opportunities and skill development; enabling partnership, linkages and networking to occur; facilitating leadership and participatory decision making; providing a sense of community; using an assets-based approach (Liberato *et al.*, 2011, pp. 5–6). In our research we were readily able to identify how each of these attributes was demonstrated within the CWA craft groups, providing evidence of how these older women contributed to local capacity building. This important work occurred quietly behind the scenes, without reference to contemporary ideas on health promotion, engagement with civil society or feminist ideology, yet the principles underpinning these concepts were evident in the day-to-day functioning of the groups.

In relation to knowledge and skills development:

> We teach each other. And you know how to do something, so you'll show someone else. And that's how the classes operate. We rarely pay anyone to teach us. We learn from one another. (Nola)

In terms of promoting partnerships, networks and linkages the CWA groups use their extensive infrastructure, locally, nationally and internationally to strengthen diverse communities:

> Just a huge amount of goods, we distribute it and financial assistance given in the times of the bush fires on Black Saturday. We will be assisting financially with the flood relief when things settle down a little. That's a different type of need than the bush fires, which you had to act straight away. We do a lot with our hospitals and homeless people, and supporting people that help homeless

people. And of course we're part of the AC – Associated Country Women of the World, who have nine million members. And in our area, we support the Island ladies, New Guinea and Tonga and those areas. (Nola)

Facilitating leadership skills amongst older women:

I was the homebody. And when I got into state council for two years, I never said a thing for two years and as it's developed, yeah certainly ... and it's made me think. . . . So now I'm quite au fait to talk in public and speak in front of a conference for 1500 ladies and things like that where once. . . . So that's another side of CWA that's been great for me. (Eva)

These particular findings illustrate significant transformative opportunities that emerge out of craft group participation that strongly align with the principles associated with critical social work practice.

Social inclusion

Those responsible for formulating health policy recognise that active participation in cultural and creative activities results in better physical and mental wellbeing among older people (NSW Government, 2012, p. 19). The craft groups provide a ready forum for promoting this type of inclusion:

It [craft group] means a lot certainly. It's like this: see I've been on my own a long time. I've been on my own 35 years and I'm the sort of person, I can sit here day after day after day, and do my little bit of this, little bit of that, read a book and be quite content. But with going to CWA . . . that makes me get up and go. Whereas other than that, I would be more or less – well I can say, cut off. (Brenda)

Even so, in order to actively participate older women need to be able to access the crafts groups. In this regard the organisational infrastructure of the CWA is critical in enabling access. Currently the Victoria branch of CWA has 40 groups with 33 of those situated in rural communities, some in very sparsely populated areas enabling older women to readily join a local group.

And now I've finished work and I'm sort of feeling a little bit lonely and then I contacted a lady that I used to know and she said, 'Oh why don't you come to our group?' And that was actually the nearest place to where I lived. (Malva, who lives in a rural area)

The CWA craft groups are just one example of how an everyday inexpensive activity such as crafting can be used as a vehicle for promoting social inclusion and enhancing wellbeing. Other arguably better known initiatives of a similar ilk include the 'Men's Shed' movement, a 'health by stealth' initiative gaining popularity in both Australia and New Zealand (Wakelin *et al.*, 2011). This initiative involves groups of men gathering together to fix things, learn mechanical and carpentry skills, overcome boredom and develop friendship and resource networks. Some have argued for the sheds movement to become a recognised integrated strategy in primary health care planning in Australia (Sergeant, 2009). The 'Choir of Hard Knocks', made popular in the 2007 Australian television series and auspiced by Reclink Australia is another example of promoting inclusion, this time with the hard-to-reach homeless population in Melbourne and using music as the vehicle for social connectedness.

Implications for social work practice

Where is social work in creating and supporting similar low-key, low-cost community-embedded ventures? The focus of almost all statutory social work practice in Australia and New Zealand occurs at the micro-end of the intervention continuum using individual case management models characterised by the elements outlined by Moore and MacDonald (2009). Using case management, practitioners are engaged in a form of social care that incorporates:

> (i) *Caring about*, in the sense of developing an awareness of the needs of others; (ii) *Taking care of*, by assuming responsibility and planning a response; (iii) *Care giving*, or doing the work to meet the care needs; and (iv) *Care receiving*, in which the recipient responds, at the end of which process changes in the situated are noted and new needs identified. (Moore and MacDonald, 2009, p. 3)

There is no doubt this form of practice is both appropriate and required to address the needs of some vulnerable populations. Case management, however, has become the dominant modus operandi for almost all social work intervention at the expense of supporting more sustainable community-oriented initiatives.

Difficulties associated with measuring 'outcomes' and 'effectiveness' of community capacity building and social inclusion are additional obstacles to social work engagement with these activities. In the current environment where evidence-based practice has been described as the 'gold standard' for practice (Morgenshtern *et al.*, 2011, p. 554) it is a real professional challenge to argue for staff time to be put into intervention where the impact is usually not immediately evident or measurable.

The neoliberal agenda of targeting scarce resources towards 'at risk' individuals who potentially drain the welfare economy, is undoubtedly a driver towards case management practice, and away from emancipatory community-based modalities. At the same time, government discourse aimed at promoting community participation and strengthening social connectedness is no substitute for substantive policy measures that address material disadvantage amongst marginalised populations (Baum *et al.*, 2010).

In this research we found plenty of evidence that the strong social connections experienced by participation in the CWA enhanced in many ways the lives of the women we spoke to. These findings demonstrate 'that *community* can be a rich resource to support people's capacity to make and maintain social connections as they age' (Baum *et al.*, 2010, p. 56). As social workers committed to social justice and promotion of wellbeing we have a role to play in helping communities to flourish; and creating opportunities for increased agency and participation.

The secretary general of the International Federation of Social Work (IFSW) used the opportunity of World Social Work Day (2013) to remind practitioners and the public in general that:

> people thrive when they live in secure communities and environments; societies where a person's dignity is honoured and they are able to contribute to their own and others' wellbeing. Our experience also tells us that unreliable, unequal, fluctuating societies and weak communities undermine health and wellbeing and erode potential positive futures. (Truell, 2013)

Individually focused micro-intervention is ineffective for strengthening whole communities, and masks systemic social issues that cause isolation, exclusion, while compromising wellbeing. The practitioner mandate to actively pursue community-oriented interventions comes from the highest level of our discipline with IFSW stating: 'Social work facilitates social development and social cohesion. Core to social work is supporting people to influence their social environments to achieve sustainable wellbeing' (IFSW, 2013). To act on this mandate, practitioners need to shift their gaze away from the immediate demand created by the individual referral, towards identifying the link between the 'problems' experienced by the individual and a more public agenda. Clearly this message is not new to social work. Making the link between 'personal troubles and public issues' (Mills, 1959), has been a mantra within the discipline for decades (Bailey and Brake, 1975; Beddoe and Maidment, 2009; Silverstein and Parrott, 2001). Even so, an obvious commitment towards pursuing community development practice is not evident within Australian and New Zealand social work.

Although community development, with its emphasis on a grassroots social justice agenda is very aligned with social work as a discipline, there remains an ambivalence about where this activity is rightly positioned. Proponents of community development being a discipline in its own right argue that social work is an inherently conservative discipline with strong elements of social control, and as such does not provide a rightful 'home' for community development knowledge and practice (Kenny, 2006). This assertion is challenged in the work of social workers such as Weeks *et al.* (2003) with a proven track record in doing 'hands on' community development in ways that have inspired and strengthened diverse populations. The persistence of ambivalence about social work engagement in community development and approaches to support or initiative community building potentially weakens support for this model within social work education, relegating its position to the margins of the curriculum, being increasingly taught by more inexperienced or sessional staff (Mendes, 2009, p. 250).

Conclusion

In social work we are all looking to make the lives of others better in some way. Often we struggle in our attempts to meet the needs of all the referrals that cross our desks, and in many cases we simply cannot. Through doing this research we found that the simple activity of crafting with others significantly enhanced, on many different levels, the lives of the women we spoke to.

We know from this research and many other similar studies that community-embedded interventions create health-supporting environments and health-enhancing networks; where the benefits of intervention have the potential to be felt and enjoyed by greater numbers of individuals and institutions. We encourage practitioners to think about how they might re-engage with the skills and work with communities to develop socially relevant interventions. Church halls, community centres, libraries and cafes are all potential sites for informal social group gatherings that may welcome strangers and provide a place and space for people who want to learn new skills, and meet others. We encourage you to think about ways in which you can use these spaces and engage others in your practice to build strong, sustainable, life-enhancing networks. We leave the last words to Emily who told us about introducing a new person to a CWA craft group:

> You can take a person along to that and they'd say, 'Yeah I enjoyed that.' They'd be with company, they would have made something, they would have learnt something. (Emily)

QUESTIONS FOR REFLECTION

1. How might you use and help contribute to strengthening informal community group oriented activities in your practice?
2. Identify informal community groups that your clients might be interested in connecting with. What can you do to foster these connections?
3. How can you or your organisation seek greater funding opportunities for developing community oriented initiatives?

Acknowledgement

We wish to sincerely acknowledge and thank the Victoria Branch of the Country Women's Association of Australia for enabling us to undertake this research into the crafting activities undertaken by members and learn more about the work of the whole Association.

References

Age Concern (2012) *Action on Social Isolation and Loneliness* [online]. Available at: http://www.ageconcern.org.nz/keeping-connected/action-social-isolation-and-loneliness

Australian National University (2009) *Australian Survey of Social Attitudes* [online]. Available at: http://aussa.anu.edu.au/data.php

Bailey, R. & Brake, M. (eds) (1975) *Radical Social Work*, E. Arnold, London.

Baum, F., Newman, L., Biedrzycki, K. & Patterson, J. (2010) 'Can a regional government's social inclusion initiative contribute to the quest for health equity?', *Health Promotion International*, vol. 25, no. 4, pp. 474–482.

Beddoe, E. & Maidment, J. (2009) *Mapping Knowledge for Social Work Practice: Critical Interactions*, Cengage Publishing, Melbourne.

Campbell, C., & Wood, R. & Kelly, M. (1999) *Social Capital and Health*, Health Education Authority, London [online]. Available at: http://www.hda-online.org.uk/downloads/pdfs/socialcapital_health.pdf

Carr, A. (2013) *Positive Psychology*, 2nd edn. Taylor and Francis, Hoboken, NJ.

Cornwell, E. & Waite, L. (2009) 'Social disconnectedness, perceived isolation, and health among older adults', *Journal of Health and Social Behavior*, vol. 50, no. 1, pp. 31–48.

Csikszentmihalyi, M. (1990) *Flow: The Psychology of Optimal Experience*, Harper and Row, New York.

Dickens, A., Richards, S., Greaves, C. & Campbell, J.L. (2011) 'Interventions targeting social isolation in older people: A systematic review', *BMC Public Health*, vol. 11, no. 1, p. 647.

Eriksson, M. (2011) 'Social capital and health – implications for health promotion', *Global Health Action*, vol. 4, no. 5611, pp. 1–21.

Fratiglioni, L., Wang, H., Ericsson, K., Maytan, M. & Winblad, B. (2000) 'Social capital and health-implications for health promotion', *The Lancet*, vol. 355, no. 9212, pp. 1315–1319.

Fujiwara, T. & Kawachi, I. (2008) 'Social capital and health: A study of adult twins in the US', *American Journal of Preventive Medicine*, vol. 35, no. 2, pp. 139–144.

Futterman-Collier, A. (2012) *Using Textile Arts and Handcrafts in Therapy with Women: Weaving Lives Back Together*, Jessica Kingsley, London.

Gandolfo, E. & Grace, M. (2009) *. . . It Keeps Me Sane . . . Women Craft Wellbeing*, Vulgar Press, Spotlight, Victoria University, Melbourne, Australia.

Griffiths, R., Horsfall, J., Lane, D., Kroon, V. & Langdon, R. (2007) 'Assessment of health, well-being and social connections: A survey of women living in Western Sydney', *International Journal of Nursing Practice*, vol. 13, no. 1, pp. 3–13.

Hawton, A. Green, C, Dickens, A., Richards, S., Taylor, R., Edwards, R., Greaves, C. & Campbell, J. (2010) 'The impact of social isolation on the health status and health-related quality of life of older people', *Quality of Life Research*, vol. 20, no. 1, pp. 57–67.

Ife, J. & Tesoriero, F. (2006) *Community Development: Community Based Alternatives in an Age of Globalisation*, Pearson Education Australia, Frenchs Forest.

International Federation of Social Work (2013) *The Future of Social Work* [online]. Available at: http://ifsw.org/get-involved/the-future-of-social-work/#_edn3

Jaworski, K. & Moyle, W. (2008) *Alone in a Crowd: Supporting Older Australians Managing Loneliness*. Stage One Discussion Paper. Australian Research Council, Canberra, Australia.

Kenny, S. (2006) *Developing Communities for the Future*, 3rd edn. Cengage Learning, Melbourne, Australia.

Labonte, R. & Laverack, G. (2001) 'Capacity building in health promotion, Part 1: For whom? And for what purpose?' *Critical Public Health*, vol. 11, no. 2, pp. 111–127.

Liberato, S., Brimblecombe, J., Ritchie, J., Ferguson, M. & Coveney, J. (2011) Measuring capacity building in communities: A review of the literature. *BMC Public Health*, vol. 11, no. 850, doi:10.1186/1471-2458-11-850

Maidment, J. & Macfarlane, S. (2008) 'Craft groups: Sites of friendship, empowerment, belonging and learning for older women', *Groupwork*, vol. 19, no. 1, pp. 10–25.

Mendes, P. (2009) 'Teaching community development to social work students: A critical reflection', *Community Development Journal*, vol. 44, no. 2, pp. 248–262.

Mills, C. W. (1959) *The Sociological Imagination*, Oxford University Press, New York.

Moore, E. & McDonald, C. (2009) 'Origins, influences and challenges of contemporary case management', in *Case Management for Community Practice*, E. Moore (ed), Oxford University Press, Melbourne, Australia, pp. 1–23.

Morgenshtern, M., Freymond, N., Agyapong, S. & Greeson, C. (2011) 'Graduate social work students' attitudes toward research: Problems and prospects', *Journal of Teaching in Social Work*, vol. 31, no. 5, pp. 552–568.

New South Wales Government (2012) *Ageing Strategy* [online]. Available at: http://www.artsandhealth.org/public/pdf/2012/NSW%20Government%20Ageing%20Strategy%202012.pdf

Padgett, D., Mathew, R. & Conte, S. (2004) 'Peer debriefing and support groups: Formation, care and maintenance', in *The Qualitative Research Experience*, D.K. Padgett (ed), Wadsworth/Thomas Learning, Belmont, CA, pp. 229–239.

Schofield-Tomschin, S. & Littrell, M. (2001) 'Textile handcraft guild participation: A conduit to successful aging,' *Clothing and Textiles Research Journal*, vol. 19, no. 2, pp. 41–51.

Seeman, T. (1996) 'Social ties and health: The benefits of social integration', *Annals of Epidemiology*, vol. 6, no. 5, pp. 442–451.

Sergeant P. (2009) *Men's Sheds – A Catalyst for Indigenous Men's Health,* 10th National Rural Health Conference (Australia) [online]. Available at: http://10thnrhc.ruralhealth.org.au/papers/docs/Sergeant_Peter_A1.pdf

Silverstein, M. & Parrott, T. (2001) 'Attitudes toward government policies that assist informal caregivers', *Research on Aging*, vol. 23, no. 3, pp. 349–374.

Stanley, M. (2010) '"Nowadays you don't even see your neighbours": Loneliness in everyday lives of older Australians', *Health and Social Care*, vol. 18, no. 4, pp. 407–414.

Starr Johnson, J. & Wilson, L. (2005) '"It says you really care": Motivational factors of contemporary female handcrafters', *Clothing and Textile Research Journal*, vol. 23, no. 2, pp. 115–130.

Statistics New Zealand (2013) *New Zealand in Profile: 2013* [online]. Available at: http://www.stats.govt.nz/browse_for_stats/snapshots-of-nz/nz-in-profile-2013/interntl-comparisons-top-five-countries.aspx

Truell, R. (2013) 'World Social Work Day: Calling for a fair and just global economy', *The Guardian*. Available at: http://www.guardian.co.uk/social-care-network/2013/mar/19/world-social-work-day-fair-global-economy1

Truong, H. (2011) *The meaning of craft in the personal and professional lives of occupational therapists in South-Western Australia*, Unpublished BOT (Honours) Thesis, Deakin University, Geelong.

Velde, B. (1999) 'The language of craft', in *Activities: Reality and Symbol*, G. Fidler & B.Velde (eds), SLACK Incorporated, Thorofare, NJ, pp. 95–106.

Wakelin, R., Thoms, A., Bradley, V., Rice, S. & Fallon, B. (2011) *Evaluating health and wellbeing: Outcomes of men's sheds – Koo Wee Rup men's shed*. Paper presented at 4th National Men's Shed Conference. Brisbane, Australia, August 2011.

Weeks, W., Hoatson, L. & Dixon, J. (2003) *Community Practices in Australia*, Pearson Education, Frenchs Forest, Australia.

Ziersch, A., Baum, F., MacDougall, C. & Putland, C. (2005) 'Neighbourhood life and social capital: The implications for health', *Social Science and Medicine*, vol. 60, no. 1, pp. 71–86.

21

PREGNANCY IN AN AGE OF MEDICAL TECHNOLOGY

Decisions, loss and research with a vulnerable population

Judith L. M. McCoyd

CHAPTER OBJECTIVES

The health of societies is predicated on the health and wellbeing of the children and families who live in that society. Family creation (pregnancy and childbirth in most cases) is both a culturally defined time and a medically mediated one. Decisions about when and how to have children, what is 'appropriate' medical care, and what control the pregnant woman has in her medical care, are all culturally bound and socially mediated. In countries with high technology use, many of these decisions are made in conjunction with technological interventions. This creates an intersection of health, gender, socio-political context, risk interpretation and stigma that is complex, and yet rich for identifying the challenges and rewards of undertaking research with women regarding reproductive health care. This chapter has three primary objectives:

1. *Discuss the challenges of sampling, recruitment, data interpretation and dissemination in a study of women who have experienced termination of a desired pregnancy due to the finding of a fetal anomaly;*
2. *Provide an overview of the socio-political, family and medical context women experience as they traverse the medical trajectory from identification of risk for fetal anomalies through the aftermath of a pregnancy termination for anomaly;*
3. *Consider the implications for a grieving process when it occurs within a medicalised context and is viewed both as a decision of one's own volition and a stigmatised 'choice'.*

Introduction

Women enter pregnancy with varied levels of preparedness. Certainly, many pregnant women had not planned to become pregnant; indeed fewer than 50 per cent of all pregnancies are planned in the United States (Guttmacher Institute, 2012). Yet, the majority of women come to embrace the pregnancy and do all they can to assure the health of the pregnancy – by caring for themselves and making efforts to care for the fetus they carry. In this chapter, we will consider the way that a healthy condition, pregnancy, becomes monitored and surveilled, and what happens when a fetal anomaly is detected. We will consider how health care providers tend to respond to this situation. We will analyse how the socio-political context frames the decision to terminate a pregnancy within the context of the abortion debate (a contentious debate in many countries), and how this is in tension with views from those who are concerned about various disabilities and disability rights (Goodley and Tregaskis, 2006). We will also consider the micro-level impacts of women's decisions and grief on the way they move forward into their futures.

This chapter will report on research conducted with women with a desired pregnancy who have received diagnosis of and termination for fetal anomaly (TFA). Although the results of the research will be shared, my focus is to contextualise problematised pregnancies within the medical care system, within the socio-political context of today, and also to discuss some of the challenges of sampling, recruitment, data interpretation and results dissemination that come about when working with women (an already marginalised group) who experience stigma as a result of making a decision to terminate a pregnancy due to the finding of a fetal anomaly.

The evolving context of pregnancy

Medical technology has evolved dramatically over the last decades and is deployed extensively in the monitoring of pregnancy. Early ultrasound is used routinely to measure minute aspects of the growing embryo and fetus for purposes of screening and diagnosis of fetal anomalies (Ivry, 2009). Ultrasound technology enables women and their medical caregivers to see within the uterus and indeed within the body of the fetus to ascertain the health status of an entity previously unseen and unknown until its birth. This impacts the way women conceive their babies, literally, figuratively, and emotionally (Zechmeister, 2001). Technology allows intervention possibilities such as treatment of a fetus for Rh incompatibility, termination of pregnancies affected by anomalies and fetal surgery as a treatment for neural tube defects and other surgically amenable conditions (Casper, 1999).

The technologies described both enable and force women to make decisions about whether to terminate pregnancies that often were lovingly planned and nearly always sincerely desired at the point where a diagnosis occurs. Although nuchal translucency screening and sequential blood tests now enable earlier identification of heightened risk for anomalies, fetal diagnosis still often occurs after the point where a woman begins to feel the fetus move and has become attached to 'the baby' she has conceived in her body and in her mind and imagination.

My research thus far

I was a perinatal social worker working in hospitals for the early part of my career, and I still identify as a perinatal social worker. My second year internship of my MSSW programme allowed me to work with women experiencing medically high-risk pregnancies and in the Intensive Care Nursery. Prenatal diagnosis via amniocentesis was just starting to be more broadly utilised and I worked with women who were struggling to decide what to do when a fetal anomaly like Down syndrome or spina bifida was diagnosed. I was also of an age to remember when abortion had been illegal, and I recognised the intense dilemma of wanting to continue a pregnancy, yet not wanting to have a baby with ill health as those wishes intersected with the stigma of utilising abortion (Major and Gramzow, 1999). I still see women and couples struggling with these issues in my private practice. I pursued doctoral education in social work from 1998 to 2003 and explored the bereavement process of women who had terminated a desired pregnancy after the discovery of a fetal anomaly.

I eagerly approached my doctoral research, certain that my clinical background and extensive connections with obstetrician offices and perinatal specialists would lead to quickly recruiting, interviewing and analyzing the experiences of 20 to 30 women. There was little written about the topic from the women's point of view other than the seminal work of Barbara Katz Rothman in sociology (1988, 1993/1989) and Rayna Rapp (1999) in anthropology. I was certain that my insider knowledge as both part of the health system, but also a critical observer of it, would mean that I would have much to contribute. Because the area was not well researched, qualitative methods were most appropriate for exploration and theory building. Specifically, I conducted intensive interviews that explored the domains of the diagnosis, the woman's social, familial, spiritual and medical networks and their responses, her decision-making process and her views on technology. I explored the bereavement process in relationship to each of these domains and triangulated the data with the Perinatal Grief Scale (Toedter et al., 1988). I also did interviews with two physicians who perform surgical terminations after fetal diagnosis and did a focus group with social workers who work with prenatal diagnosis decision making to explore their beliefs about the process of diagnosis, decision making, implementation and aftermath.

I had some difficulty getting Internal Review Board (IRB) ethical approval because IRB committee members were rightly concerned that this population of women was vulnerable and hurting and they wanted assurance that I could refer for psychiatric follow-up if my questions stirred too much grief or emotion (we must set aside the fact that physicians and psychiatrists typically referred grieving women to me for such counseling). Once the IRB approval was finally granted (two full applications, three months), I was sure the responses would pour in. I could not have been more wrong. Although recruitment and response rates are often difficult, the reality was that most physicians, even those who were highly supportive and who knew and trusted me, were reluctant to encourage women to be in touch due to physician fears of exposing the women, or in some other way adding to their discomfort. After months of virtually no response, I requested IRB approval to post my recruitment letter on a website that provided support for women after termination for anomaly. At that point, responses did come rolling in as the women were anxious to share their stories, their pain and their rationales about the experiences they had been through and the decisions that they had made. The implication here is that the health providers may 'over-protect' women from research, even when the women themselves are grateful for the chance to participate in the research (McCoyd and Shdaimah, 2007). One must wonder if the ongoing perceptions of women as fragile or weak lead to this sense of needing to protect them from research participation.

An interesting serendipitous finding as a result of the recruitment changes was related to the modality for interviewing. Most of the women on the website were well beyond the 300-mile radius I had established for in-person interviews. As a result (after yet another amendment for IRB approval), I conducted interviews in person where I could and offered the option of email interviews or phone interviews. The majority elected email interviews (a method that was relatively new in 2001 and 2002), and they took place over the course of several weeks as back-and-forth communications got deeper and deeper into the participants' experiences and they shared their reflexive thinking as it evolved over the course of their participation. I transcribed the in-person and telephone interviews verbatim, and cleaned the emails of identifying information, yielding over 700 pages of single-spaced narrative data to code. The email interviews were by far the more detailed, nuanced and rich as they occurred over time and allowed for many follow-up probes and clarifications (McCoyd and Kerson, 2006). Another notable finding was that procedures for terminating the pregnancy (surgical vs. induction) varied by geographical area (and ultimately appeared attributable to the availability of physician training). The findings related to the women's experiences were the most compelling.

When fetal anomalies are diagnosed, women describe it as 'a two-by-four to the face' and they describe an agony of decision-making under tight timeframes and often tremendous yearning pain after they terminate a pregnancy. In the first publication of my dissertation research with 30 women who had terminated for fetal anomaly, I describe the 'Mythic Expectations' with which women arrive at pregnancy (McCoyd, 2003, 2007). The first involved an expectation that 'our baby would be fine,' a belief held by even the most educated women, despite the fact that they were utilising technology for the express purpose of identifying fetal anomalies. They often were past the 12th week of pregnancy and believed 'I was home free – no miscarriage in the first trimester.' These early expectations mean that findings are even more upsetting due to the level of surprise. Additionally, many women assume the abortion debate will never touch them – their pregnancy is deeply desired and they carry the mythic expectation that 'I wouldn't terminate anyway'; yet, when faced with the likelihood or certainty that the baby will not be healthy, they elect to end the pregnancy in order avoid the baby's suffering. In a later analysis of the TFA decision-making, additional nuance to the avoidance of suffering was seen; women also assessed their own ability, or the ability of their family, to support a child born with disabilities both in terms of concrete resources and emotional resilience. They based their decision to terminate the pregnancy on the assessment that they and/or their families would not be able to support such a child (McCoyd, 2008).

Another mythic expectation was that 'testing is nothing to worry about,' a finding frequently repeated in the anthropological literature where the expectation of a bonding experience is the primary goal women identify for diagnostic ultrasound (Zechmeister, 2001). The women's sense that the testing should not raise anxiety not only left them surprised, but distrustful of medical providers who originally reassured them at various stages that everything would be fine. Later analysis of these findings also yielded a more nuanced understanding of how women felt betrayed by the medical establishment, as well as by their bodies and 'Mother Nature', when they felt they had done all the things required of a good mother and yet had a bad outcome (McCoyd, 2010b). Another mythic expectation was that 'Down syndrome was the worst that it could get'. If women worried about tests revealing anything, it was Down syndrome. Yet other trisomies, missing organs, significant morphological or other chromosomal problems are diagnosed, as are deletions of chromosomes and other anomalies for which prognosis is uncertain. Decision making when the outcomes may vary added to the frustration women experienced and a sense that the promise of medicine was unfulfilled.

After the termination for anomaly, women were surprised by the level of grief they experienced, asserting 'the right decision couldn't possibly hurt this much' and they carried the expectation that by the time of the post-operative doctor visit that 'the healing would be all done by then,' an expectation that tended to be true physically but not emotionally. These become clinical issues as both women and their medical providers need to be aware that they have already attached to the imagined child and grieve that loss. They need to be validated and prepared that the occurrence of grief does not mean the decision itself was the problem. An area of future research interest for me is to further explicate how these chosen losses, in the face of what have been called 'choiceless choices' (personal communication, Myra Bluebond-Langner, July 2004), complicate the grieving trajectory and may lead to the absence of the very support that grievers need to move through their grief most effectively.

This lack of support has multiple sources, not the least of which is the social prohibition against abortion and the high level of stigma attached to women who abort for any reason. Women reported being 'very afraid of running into someone who would pass judgment' so frequently that the theme of abortion became a lens for re-analysing the data related to the topic and the way it is framed in the United States (McCoyd, 2010c).

Women's mythic expectations (the themes that emerged from the original grounded theory coding of data) led to an understanding of several conceptual dilemmas experienced by them. The first related to the dilemma of conception and bonding. If one follows typical US norms, one begins to bond with a desired pregnancy even before the actual conception and confirmation of the pregnancy. The first early pregnancy test, early ultrasound and heart tone monitoring only further this process. Yet, the very technologies that enable more knowledge and attachment to the growing embryo and fetus lead to even more emotional pain if an anomaly is diagnosed and TFA is elected. This is related to the dilemma of testing. Testing is viewed as the way a good mother takes care of herself and her baby; it reveals the entity within and promotes further creation of the imagined child. Yet, the only real options women have if the testing reveals an anomaly are to continue the pregnancy and expect an ill child, or to terminate the pregnancy. Testing implies an ability to respond with medical options for cure and treatment, yet the options are few and unwanted as Borovoy (2011) has recently considered from a bioethical perspective; she concludes that prenatal screening and testing are not 'choices' when women are uninformed about the consequences of findings, and when there is little by way of treatment to offer them.

A further dilemma comes with framing the diagnosis as a reason for women to make a choice. As above, there is little choice about using prenatal screening, and there is also little by way of choice once a fetal anomaly is diagnosed. Notably, most physicians view this as the mother's decision (Heuser *et al.*, 2012). It makes sense that only the pregnant woman can decide what should happen within the confines of her own body boundaries (despite many political attempts to restrict women's body integrity and question her decision-making capacity), yet it is one of the few places where physicians are clear that they avoid influencing women in most situations. Women need to choose, and yet what can women make of a 'choice' when there is no good option? The choice they had made to hopefully have a healthy child has been taken from them and they are left only with a 'choice between bad and awful'.

Women also identify the dilemma of identity on multiple levels. They wonder if they have the right to claim their status as a mother (especially when the affected pregnancy is a first pregnancy), yet they also believe that they have had to make difficult parental decisions to protect the fetus from a birth to a torturous life. They wonder if they have fulfilled the role of a 'good mother' who has protected their child from suffering, or a 'bad mother' who has rejected the imagined baby for whom most already feel love. They feel the stigma of abortion, but also note that they and their child would experience the stigma of disability if they were to bring the pregnancy to fruition. There are no clear answers about their identity.

The additional dilemma is related to the disability itself. Many women expressed ambivalent feelings about terminating a pregnancy due to a disability. They wonder if the child might have had happiness in her or his life, and they worry about the social justice implications of not giving birth and preventing people with disabilities from being more common in society. They wonder if the type of disability diagnosed in their fetus would lead to a child who could have some quality of life or to one who would live forever institutionalised and less connected to human love and experience; they also worry about the extent and type of pain and suffering their child might experience, if born, and their (in)ability to prevent or alleviate this. With no way to diagnose the severity of most anomalies, these questions cannot be answered and the related dilemmas persist.

A pervasive dilemma is whether to tell the whole story and to whom. The fears of judgment or retribution for having an abortion are strong, yet women also are bereft of friendships and support when they elect not to tell the whole story to intimates from whom they might reasonably expect support. The fear of rejection is often so strong that women 'are as fragile as glass' and they avoid sharing the story to protect themselves. This secrecy and stigma are directly related to the abortion debate and cut women off from support at the very time when they are in most need of it. Likewise, the male partners in this sample had a hard time expressing support because they were busy trying to get their wives to feel better (often with efforts that provoked precisely the opposite reaction). This need for support was the very thing that had sparked my interest in this research topic back in my days of hospital work. It was clear to me even then that the nature of stigma was making the experience of grief tremendously more difficult for women who TFA, and yet they really had no good option once the conception of a fetus with an anomaly was under way. Clinically, we would often come to the realisation that the woman truly had no choice; once the conception had occurred, there was no good 'choice' because there was no way of getting the healthy child she had planned and fallen in love with in her mind (Ginsburg and Rapp, 1999).

Perspectives on pregnancy health care

What would happen if prenatal diagnosis was not a normalised part of pregnancy care? In the early days of the feminist movement's impact on health care, the movement toward 'natural child birth' and efforts to reduce the impact of medicalisation were prevalent. Feminists regularly questioned the patriarchal and interventionist approaches of reproductive health care from prenatal testing and infertility work through labour and delivery care (Arditti et al., 1984/1989; Ginsburg and Rapp, 1995). Concerns about the ways male physicians colonised women's bodies during pregnancy were articulated (Rowland, 1989) and feminists questioned the expertise of physicians more generally (Ehrenreich and English, 1978/2005). These concerns led many women to adopt very polarised views about reproductive technology, despite efforts on the part of most feminists to recognise that technology had also added more safety to childbearing and that some technologies such as infertility work added more options for women in regards to childbearing.

Some of the early research and theory by Barbara Katz Rothman was steeped in concerns that use of amniocentesis would change the nature of the mother–baby bond (creating distance) (1986/1993) and commercialise child-bearing (wanting the perfect child) (1988), all concerns that seem to have validity, though not to the extent that was feared. As Ginsburg and Rapp (1999) observed, women using prenatal screening do not insist on 'a perfect child' so much as work diligently to avoid giving birth to a baby with known disabilities. Yet this too problematises prenatal diagnosis and TFA decisions. What does it mean to routinely abort fetuses with diagnosed disability? What does this mean for the self-valuing of individuals (and sometimes living siblings) who have the same condition? What does it mean for the ability of people with that disability to have enough critical mass politically to fight for access to services and to be recognised as citizens of worth in a society that values typicality and productivity? There are no easy answers to the issues that arise when prenatal assessment technologies are broadly disseminated, yet minimally understood for the implications in women's lives. Although nation-states have regulated these issues differently (Lichtentritt, 2011; McCoyd, 2010b), feminist, social work and legal scholars come to the same conclusion: that only women themselves can make these life-altering choices and that they must have as much information and knowledge as possible to make these decisions and live with the consequences of them.

Lazarus (1997) found that women have developed a much more nuanced approach to technologies utilised in pregnancy and childbirth; some women with less education agree to 'natural childbirth' with little awareness of what that even means while quite educated women (her examples come from women who are anesthesiologists and obstetricians) may opt for some of the highest levels of technology consumption available. There are no 'average' or 'normal' women in this regard. Yet, prenatal diagnostic screening and testing has become normalised (Browner and Press, 1995) and the vast majority of women in developed countries experience screening in some form. Although the experience of prenatal testing has become normalised, women have varied understandings about the meaning of problematic test results. They are often unprepared to manage the decision-making and emotional maelstrom into which positive test results thrusts them. Women often grant authoritative knowledge (Jordan, 1997) to their health care providers and technology, and only more critical approaches to this knowledge building (fully informing women about the implications of prenatal screening for instance) are likely to bring changes (McCoyd, 2010a). Even so, once prenatal screening is deployed, any out-of-the-norm result draws the pregnant woman into increasing use of technology. Explicit debate around whether and how to use technologies is muted, if not absent altogether (Bernhardt *et al.*, 1998; Gottfredsdottir *et al.*, 2009). Psychosocial implications and impacts have been ignored in the focus on the biomedical model.

Implications for social work practice

It is clear that women experience the diagnosis and termination of a desired pregnancy due to fetal anomaly as a confusing, challenging and even traumatic time (McCoyd, 2003; Rapp, 1999) that leads to a period of grief. Although medical providers seldom speak with women about the psychosocial aspects of the decision and its aftermath (Leithner *et al.*, 2006), women seem quite clear that they need (McCoyd, 2009a) and want (McCoyd, 2009b) full information and someone trustworthy with whom to process the information. Societal silencing (Kluger-Bell, 2000) and stigmatisation (Major and Gramzow, 1999; McCoyd, 2010b) leave women isolated with medical providers who often limit their communications to asserting that the woman must make her own decision (Bernhardt *et al.*, 1998). It is not socially just to have pregnant women only semi-informed about the decisions they may face; it is also unfair to stigmatise them for either aborting or giving birth to a baby with disabilities. It is the role of the social worker to help the medical team recognise these binds and dilemmas, and to help women process the consequences.

It is only by continuing to explore the lived experience of reproductive contexts that we learn some of the unintended consequences of technology, observe the impacts of social forces on women in these circumstances, and identify the health care practices that pregnant women and their supporters desire. When we remain constrained within biomedical views of reproductive medicine, we lose sight of the major impacts of social norms (and their continuing evolution (McCoyd, 2009a)) on women's lives.

QUESTIONS FOR REFLECTION

1. If you wanted to research the experiences of a marginalised group (such as women undergoing in-vitro fertilisation, TFA, or the birth of a baby with congenital anomalies), how might you approach heath care providers to help recruit participants? How would you address their intent to protect their patients (from you)?
2. What social norms do you see impacting the health populations with whom you work and how do these norms help or hurt your population?
3. Assess your own values-position on the decision to TFA. Consider what an opponent of your values position would believe and try to argue that position.

References

Arditti, R., Klein, R.D. & Minden, S. (eds) (1984/1989) *Test Tube Women: What Future for Motherhood?*, Pandora Press, London.
Bernhardt, B.A., Geller, G., Doksum, T., Larson, S., Roter, D. & Holtzman, N.A. (1998) 'Prenatal genetic testing: Content of discussions between obstetric providers and pregnant women', *Obstetrics and Gynecology*, vol. 91, no. 5, pp. 648–655.
Bluebond-Langner, M. (2004) Personal communication.
Borovoy, A. (2011) 'Beyond choice: A new framework for abortion?', *Dissent*, vol. 58, no. 4, pp. 73–79.
Browner, C.H. & Press, N.A. (1995) 'The normalization of prenatal diagnostic testing', in *Conceiving the New World Order: The Global Politics of Reproduction*, F.D. Ginsberg & R. Rapp (eds), University of California Press, Berkeley, pp. 307–322.
Casper, M. (1999) 'Operation to the rescue: Feminist encounters with fetal surgery', in *Fetal Subjects, Feminist Positions*, L.M. Morgan & M.W. Michaels (eds), University of Pennsylvania Press, Philadelphia, pp. 101–112.
Ehrenreich, B. & English, D. (1978/2005) *For Her Own Good: Two Centuries of Experts' Advice to Women* (rev. edn), Anchor Books, New York.

Ginsberg, F.D. & Rapp, R. (eds) (1995) *Conceiving the New World Order*, University of California Press, Berkeley.

Ginsberg, F.D. & Rapp, R. (1999) 'Fetal reflections: Confessions of two feminist anthropologists as mutual informants', in *Fetal Subjects, Feminist Positions*, L.M. Morgan & M.W. Michaels (eds), University of Pennsylvania Press, Philadelphia, pp. 279–295.

Goodley, D. & Tragaskis, C. (2006) 'Storying disability and impairment: Retrospective accounts of family life', *Qualitative Health Research*, vol. 16, no. 5, pp. 630–646. doi: 10.1177/1049732305285840

Gottfredsdottir, H., Bjoyrnsdottir, J. & Sandall, J. (2009) 'How do prospective parents who decline prenatal screening account for their decision? A qualitative study', *Social Science and Medicine*, vol. 69, no. 2, pp. 274–277. doi: 10.1016/j.socsimed.2009.05.004

Guttmacher Institute (2012) *National Reproductive Health Profile* [online]. Available at: http://www.guttmacher.org/datacenter/profiles/US.jsp

Heuser, C.C., Eller, A.G. & Byrne, J.L. (2012) 'Survey of physicians' approach to severe fetal anomalies'[on-line abstract], *Journal of Medical Ethics* [Epub ahead of print]. Available at: http://jme.bmj.com/content/early/2012/01/19/medethics-2011–100340.abstract

Ivry, T. (2009) 'The ultrasonic picture show and the politics of threatened life', *Medical Anthropology Quarterly*, vol. 23, no. 3, pp. 189–211.

Jordan, B. (1997) 'Authoritative knowledge and its construction', in *Childbirth and Authoritative Knowledge: Cross-cultural Perspectives*, R.E. Davis-Floyd & C. Sargent (eds) University of California Press, Berkeley, pp. 55–79.

Kluger-Bell, K. (2000) *Unspeakable Losses*, Quill, New York.

Lazarus, E. (1997) 'What do women want? Issues of choice, control, and class in American pregnancy and childbirth', in *Childbirth and Authoritative Knowledge: Cross-cultural Perspectives*, R.E. Davis-Floyd & C.F. Sargent (eds), University of California Press, Berkeley, pp. 132–158.

Leichtentritt, R.D. (2011) 'Silenced voices: Israeli mothers' experience of feticide', *Social Science & Medicine*, vol. 72, no. 5, pp. 747–754.

Leithner, K., Assem-Hilger, E., Fischer-Kern, M., Loffler-Stastka, H., Thien, R. & Ponocny-Seliger, E. (2006) 'Prenatal care: The patient's perspective: A qualitative study', *Prenatal Diagnosis*, vol. 26, no. 10, pp. 931–937.

Major, B. & Gramzow, R.H. (1999) 'Abortion as stigma: Cognitive and emotional implications of concealment', *Journal of Personality and Social Psychology*, vol. 77, no. 4, pp. 735–745.

McCoyd, J.L.M. (2003) *Pregnancy interrupted: Non-normative loss of a desired pregnancy after termination for fetal anomaly* [dissertation]. Bryn Mawr College, Bryn Mawr, Pennsylvania. Available at: Proquest, Ann Arbor, MI; 3088602.

McCoyd, J.L.M. (2007) 'Pregnancy interrupted: Loss of a desired pregnancy after diagnosis of fetal anomaly', *Journal of Psychosomatic Obstetrics and Gynecology*, vol. 28, no. 1, pp. 37–48.

McCoyd, J.L.M. (2008) '"I'm not a saint": Burden assessment as an unrecognized factor in prenatal decision making', *Qualitative Health Research*, vol. 18, no. 11, pp. 1489–1500.

McCoyd, J.L.M. (2009a) 'Discrepant feeling rules and unscripted emotion work: Women terminating desired pregnancies due to fetal anomaly', *American Journal of Orthopsychiatry*, vol. 79, no. 4, pp. 441–451.

McCoyd, J.L.M. (2009b) 'What do women want? Experiences and reflections of women after prenatal diagnosis and termination for anomaly', *Health Care for Women International*, vol. 30, no. 6, pp. 507–535.

McCoyd, J.L.M. (2010a) 'Authoritative knowledge, the technological imperative and women's responses to prenatal diagnostic technologies', *Culture, Medicine and Psychiatry*, vol. 34, no. 4, pp. 590–614.

McCoyd, J.L.M. (2010b) 'The implicit contract: Implications for health social work', *Health & Social Work*, vol. 35, no. 2, pp. 99–106.

McCoyd, J.L.M. (2010c) 'Women in no man's land: The US abortion debate and women terminating desired pregnancies due to fetal anomaly', *British Journal of Social Work*, vol. 40, no. 1, pp. 133–153.

McCoyd, J.L.M. & Kerson, T.S. (2006) 'Conducting intensive interviews using e-mail: A serendipitous comparative opportunity', *Qualitative Social Work: Research and Practice*, vol. 5, no. 3, pp. 389–406.

McCoyd, J.L.M. & Shdaimah, C.S. (2007) 'Revisiting the benefits debate: Salubrious effects of social work research', *Social Work*, vol. 52, no. 4, pp. 340–349.

Rapp, R. (1999) *Testing Women, Testing the Fetus*, Routledge, New York.

Rothman, B.K. (1986/1993) *The Tentative Pregnancy: How Amniocentesis Changes the Experience of Motherhood*, W.W. Norton, New York.

Rothman, B.K. (1988) 'Reproductive technology and the commodification of life', *Women and Health*, vol. 13, nos. 1–2, pp. 95–100.

Rowland, R. (1989) 'Reproductive technologies: The final solution to the woman question?' in *Test Tube Women: What Future for Motherhood?*, R. Arditti, R.D. Klein & S. Minden (eds), Pandora Press, London, pp. 356–369.

Toedter, L., Lasker, J. & Alhadeff, J. (1988) 'The perinatal grief scale: Development and initial validation', *American Journal of Orthopsychiatry*, vol. 58, no. 3, pp. 435–449.

Zechmeister, I. (2001) 'Foetal images: The power of visual technology in antenatal care and the implications for women's reproductive freedom', *Health Care Analysis*, vol. 9, no. 4, pp. 387–400.

INDEX

Page numbers in *italics* indicate figures or tables. Page numbers followed by 'n' indicate notes.